Readings in
MARRIAGE
AND FAMILY 79/80

ANNUAL EDITIONS
the dushkin publishing group, inc.
Sluice Dock, Guilford, Ct. 06437

Volumes in the Annual Editions Series

Abnormal Psychology
- Aging
- American Government
- American History Pre-Civil War
- American History Post-Civil War
- Anthropology
Astronomy
- Biology
- Business
Comparative Government
- Criminal Justice
Death and Dying
- Deviance
- Early Childhood Education
Earth Science
- Economics
- Educating Exceptional Children
- Education
Educational Psychology
Energy
- Environment
Ethnic Studies
Foreign Policy

Geography
Geology
- Health
- Human Development
- Human Sexuality
- Macroeconomics
- Management
- Marketing
- Marriage and Family
- Microeconomics
- Personality and Adjustment
Philosophy
Political Science
- Psychology
Religion
- Social Problems
- Social Psychology
- Sociology
- Urban Society
Western Civilization
Women's Studies
World History

● *Indicates currently available*

Library of Congress Cataloging in Publication Data
Main entry under title:
Annual editions: Readings in marriage and family.
   1. Family—United States—Periodicals. 2. Marriage—United States—Periodicals. I. Title: Readings in marriage and family.
HQ536.A57   301.42'0973   74-84596
ISBN 0-87967-260-9
5 4 3 2 1

CONTENTS

1

Formation of Interpersonal Relationships

2

Maintenance of Relationships

3

Change as a Function of Relationships

4

Termination of Relationships

5

Alternative and Future Relationships

TOPIC GUIDE

This topic guide can be used to correlate each of the articles in *Readings in Marriage and Family 79/80* to one or more of the topics normally covered by textbooks in Marriage and Family. Each article corresponds to a given topic area according to whether it deals with the subject matter of the topic in a primary or secondary manner. These correlations are intended for use as a general study guide and do not necessarily define the total coverage of any given article.

TOPIC AREA	TREATED AS A PRIMARY ISSUE IN:	TREATED AS A SECONDARY ISSUE IN:
Aging, Dying and Death	39. "Old" Is Not a Four-Letter Word 41. Coping with Death in the Family	31. Family as Cradle of Violence 38. When Fathers Have to Raise Families Alone
Courtship	8. Measure Your Marriage Potential 43. The Sexual Bond 48. How to Write Your Own Marriage Contract	7. Coupling, Marriage and Growth 12. The Fragmented Family 15. The Three Stages of Marriage 21. The Eight Myths of Marriage 24. Going It Alone
Divorce	19. Marriage Counseling 34. Personality and Divorce 35. Is Divorce Contagious? 36. Divorce: The First Two Years Are the Worst 37. The Case for Joint Custody	8. Measure Your Marriage Potential 12. The Fragmented Family 18. Banking on Women 22. Whatever Happened to Ma, Pa, and the Kids 27. Who Takes Care of the Children 31. The Family as Cradle of Violence 32. Battered Women 38. When Fathers Have to Raise Families Alone 46. What Happens When a Homemaker Loses Her Job
Family Interaction	12. The Fragmented Family 13. The Siege of the Family 15. The Three Stages of Marriage 31. The Family as Cradle of Violence 32. Battered Women 33. The Battered Husbands 40. Marital Adjustment in the Post-Retirement Years	1. The Family vs. the Individual 7. Coupling, Marriage and Growth 14. Marriage as a Wretched Institution 19. Marriage Counseling
Family Planning	23. Looking to the ZPGeneration 25. Are Children Going out of Style 26. The Coming Baby Boom	27. Who Takes Care of the Children 28. Adoption 29. Fathering: It's a Major Role
Honesty and Openness in Marriage	7. Coupling, Marriage and Growth 21. The Eight Myths of Marriage	1. The Family vs. the Individual 2. Why Some People Can't Love 6. Interpersonal Heroin 12. The Fragmented Family 19. Marriage Counseling
Human Sexuality	20. Sex Therapy 31. The Family as Cradle of Violence 43. The Sexual Bond	12. The Fragmented Family 14. Marriage as a Wretched Institution 21. The Eight Myths of Marriage
Institution of Marriage	8. Measure Your Marriage Potential 10. The Family's Not "Dying" 11. The Family: Is It Obsolete 12. The Fragmented Family 13. The Siege of the Family 14. Marriage as a Wretched Institution 21. The Eight Myths of Marriage 27. Who Takes Care of the Children	7. Coupling, Marriage and Growth 18. Banking on Women 24. Going It Alone 28. Adoption 29. Fathering: It's a Major Role 38. When Fathers Have to Raise Families Alone 45. Living Together
Living Together	8. Measure Your Marriage Potential 44. Cohabitation: Does It Make for a Better Marriage 45. Living Together	43. The Sexual Bond
Love	2. Why Some People Can't Love 5. The Love Research 6. Interpersonal Heroin 21. The Eight Myths of Marriage	3. The Self-Inflicted Pain of Jealousy 15. The Three Stages of Marriage 36. Divorce 43. The Sexual Bond
Marital Adjustment	7. Coupling, Marriage and Growth 8. Measure Your Marriage Potential 14. Marriage as a Wretched Institution 15. The Three Stages of Marriage 16. The Inexpressive Male 18. Banking on Women 21. The Eight Myths of Marriage 40. Marital Adjustment in the Post-Retirement Years	1. The Family vs. the Individual 11. The Family: Is It Obsolete 12. The Fragmented Family 19. Marriage Counseling 20. Sex Therapy 31. The Family as Cradle of Violence

TOPIC AREA	TREATED AS A PRIMARY ISSUE IN:	TREATED AS A SECONDARY ISSUE IN:
Marriage in the Future	7. Coupling, Marriage and Growth 12. The Fragmented Family 13. The Siege of the Family 27. Who Takes Care of the Children	17. The Confused American Housewife 18. Banking on Women 22. Whatever Happened to Ma, Pa, and the Kids 25. Are Children Going out of Style 26. The Coming Baby Boom
Relationship Contracts	7. Coupling, Marriage and Growth 21. The Eight Myths of Marriage 45. Living Together 48. How to Write Your Own Marriage Contract	8. Measure Your Marriage Potential 10. The Family's Not "Dying" 15. The Three Stages of Marriage 18. Banking on Women
Relationship Development	1. The Family vs. the Individual 2. Why Some People Can't Love 12. The Fragmented Family 15. The Three Stages of Marriage 21. The Eight Myths of Marriage 47. It's My Turn Now	3. The Self-Inflicted Pain of Jealousy 4. Making It to Maturity 6. Interpersonal Heroin 7. Coupling, Marriage and Growth 18. Banking on Women
Role Relationships	1. The Family vs. the Individual 12. The Fragmented Family 14. Marriage as a Wretched Institution 15. The Three Stages of Marriage 16. The Inexpressive Male 21. The Eight Myths of Marriage 27. Who Takes Care of the Children 40. Marital Adjustment in Post-Retirement Years 42. Alternative Life-Styles	2. Why Some People Can't Love 4. Making It to Maturity 8. Measure Your Marriage Potential 13. The Siege of the Family 17. The Confused American Housewife 18. Banking on Women 43. The Sexual Bond 47. It's My Turn Now

TOPIC AREA	TREATED AS A PRIMARY ISSUE IN:	TREATED AS A SECONDARY ISSUE IN:
Self-Identity in Relationships	2. Why Some People Can't Love 7. Coupling, Marriage and Growth 12. The Fragmented Family 16. The Inexpressive Male 17. The Confused American Housewife 18. Banking on Women 47. It's My Turn Now	3. The Self-Inflicted Pain of Jealousy 4. Making It to Maturity 6. Interpersonal Heroin
Sexual Therapy	20. Sex Therapy	43. The Sexual Bond
Single Life	24. Going It Alone 28. Adoption 38. When Fathers Have to Raise Families Alone 42. Alternative Life-Styles 45. Living Together	43. The Sexual Bond 44. Cohabitation: Does It Make for a Better Marriage
Starting Over	42. Alternative Life-Styles 46. What Happens When a Homemaker Loses Her Job? 47. It's My Turn Now	19. Marriage Counseling 24. Going It Alone 30. When Mommy Goes to Work 38. When Fathers Have to Raise Families Alone
Women's Issues	17. The Confused American Housewife 18. Banking on Women 27. Who Takes Care of the Children? 30. When Mommy Goes to Work 32. Battered Women 46. What Happens When a Homemaker Loses Her Job 47. It's My Turn Now	19. Marriage Counseling 21. The Eight Myths of Marriage 25. Are Children Going Out of Style 26. The Coming Baby Boom 28. Adoption 33. The Battered Husbands 37. The Case for Joint Custody 43. The Sexual Bond

Preface

Although we may choose different kinds of lifestyles, it seems that we share certain concerns no matter if we are unattached, living together, married, remarried, or divorced. We care whether we are loved, and we care about the quality of our relationships with the important people in our lives. In more traditional societies in which the bonds of family and friendship are often more rigidly prescribed than they are in our industrialized and impersonalized society, people do not find themselves paying the kind of attention that we do to the quality of love between spouses, or the adequacy of self-love, or the problems of certain fragmented social roles, to mention just a few modern preoccupations.

One of the most pervasive of our preoccupations has been the nuclear family, its state of health and chances for survival. The experts disagree quite dramatically on this issue. What is certain, however, is that the nuclear family, like any social institution, changes over time. It is estimated that no more than 30 percent of Americans live within the nuclear family structure at any one time.

An examination of the statistics on marriage would lead us to the following conclusions: 1) most people—over 90 percent—choose marriage; 2) of this group, about one-third divorces. Our high divorce rate may indicate problems within the institution of life-long, monogamous relationships or with the way that we socialize people for marriage. Perhaps it is in areas in which people have most trouble that they can most benefit from some kind of training in interpersonal competence.

In this fifth edition of *Annual Editions: Readings in Marriage and Family 79/80,* we will be examining relationships in four stages of development: formation, maintenance, change, and termination. In addition, we will also consider alternative and future relationships. We will use the word "relationships" in this volume most often as it applies to relationships that are leading toward or away from marriage or that are in fact a marriage. Of course, other forms of relationships do exist: homosexual relationships, the single life, living together without marriage, and marriages without children. But whatever type of relationship one prefers, satisfaction in that relationship requires a true commitment. The strength of the interpersonal bond is what determines its quality. Thus *Readings in Marriage and Family 79/80* focuses on a broad range of guiding principles and ideas for all interpersonal relationships.

We secure satisfying relationships through the active processes of study, thought, and verbal communication. And we hope that this reader can provide the stimulation for you to communicate your feelings, thoughts, and values to those people who are important to you.

We think that *Annual Editions: Readings in Marriage and Family 79/80* is one of the most useful, up-to-date books available, but we would like to know what you think. Please fill out the reader response card on the last page of this book and let us know your opinions. Any anthology can be improved. This one will continue to be—annually.

Robert Walsh,
Editor

1 Formation of Interpersonal Relationships

The need to form relationships is not confined to human beings. The courtship and mating behavior of other species—the gorgeous plumage, the intricate dance, the battles of dominance and rejection—are true parallels to human courtship rituals, geared to provide for the continuation of the species. Nor are humans the only animals to form bonds for companionship and protection. Yet humans are, apparently, alone with their exquisite burden of sophisticated thought, their drive to question, to experiment, to perfect, and to examine. Life might be simpler for other animals, but only humans have ideals. Most important, only humans have cultures which affect, and are affected by, the values of their members.

At various times and places in history, marriages have been arranged with very little regard for the participants' personal feelings. Considered an economic transaction between two families, a marriage was intended to protect such assets as land, cash, or wealth, and to produce certain assets, such as children and sufficient food. Your ancestors may have had their marriage arranged—meeting for the first time at their wedding, having sex and bearing children, and living their lives together without ever conceiving of forming more than an efficiently functioning unit. So long as the unit ensured survival, the relationship was a success.

With the development of romantic love, young people of marrying age began rebelling, insisting that they needed to form and fashion a relationship out of love and knowledge rather than trusting to luck and necessity. Scandalous as this valuing of romantic love might first have seemed to our ancestors, to us their proposition sounds quite reasonable and traditional— one falls in love and marries, one has sex with one's spouse, and one remains faithful.

The articles in this section of *Annual Editions: Readings in Marriage and Family 79/80* explore some basic issues in the formation of interpersonal relationships. These issues are examined under the general topics of developing yourself for relationships, and love and partnership relationships. The articles deal with such topics as: self growth vs. relationship growth, the importance of caring, and determining potential for marriage. Problem areas in relationships —jealousy, narcissism, and immature types of love— are also explored in this section.

Looking Ahead: Challenge Questions

Is it possible for any relationship to meet all of one's physical, emotional, and social needs?

Might such an expectation of a love relationship be so unrealistic as to destroy it?

Is love different from self-love?

Must jealousy always be destructive to a relationship?

How can an intense couple relationship be developed while still maintaining a sense of self and personal growth?

How does one develop real intimacy in relationships without developing overdependence?

THE FAMILY
VS. THE INDIVIDUAL

Photo by Ray Borges

James L. McCary

The institution of marriage, as it exists in our Western culture and in most advanced societies of the world, is coming under increasing attack as an anachronism. Its critics decry its hypocrisy and its frequent disappointments and maintain that it has become merely a consumer unit exploited by society and business and that it degrades and hampers the freedom of both women and men.

The greatest source of concern is the disparity between the goals and values of our traditional form of marriage and the goals and values that human beings are beginning to have for themselves as individuals. Humanity has collectively explored and conquered the world and has even extended this exploration into extraterrestrial territory. The individual modern man and woman, however, find themselves small, isolated beings in an increasingly complex society. Automation and technology have removed the need for physical conquests, so people are now turning to the most exciting and mysterious challenge of all—themselves. To become acquainted with oneself, to *know* and *be* oneself, fully and completely, to experience life in all its joy and pain and conflict, to utilize all of one's senses as well as one's intellect—these are the goals of modern men and women.

To realize these goals, or even to strive toward these goals, requires freedom of thought and action unrestricted by religious, societal, or marital conformity. To develop one's full potential as a human being means to expose oneself to the uncertainties and the perils that exist in any exploration into the unknown. To become one's own person requires faith in oneself and the courage to experience failure as well as success.

The very nature of our traditional form of marriage precludes the possibility of such risks and of such human development. The **yoked** nature of most marital relationships provides a buffer against the terror of loneliness, but at the same time it binds two people into a compromise of Golden Mediocrity. If one partner feels inclined to go in one direction to add a new dimension to awareness and selfhood, and the other is inclined in another direction, the bound couple must compromise and take a middle path—or move in one direction at the expense of the other partner. As they plod forward, yoked together in a rigid marital harness that allows no personal deviation, each may very well feel a gnawing sense of dissatisfaction and a secret regret that the adventure and experience of becoming the person each knows he or she could be is forever denied by the need to conform to the marital expectations of society.

An example of compromise conformity is the couple who never go anywhere together because he likes opera and she hates it; she likes movies and he hates them; he likes the symphony and she likes rock concerts. They compromise by staying home and watching TV reruns and feeling resentful and disappointed. Yet their yoked ties are so inflexible that neither could countenance the other's going alone—or worse, with a same-sex friend, and intolerable, with a friend of the opposite sex—to the kind of entertainment that is preferred. To the yoked pair, doing *anything* without the other, except for reasons of employment, is tantamount to disloyalty and is threatening to the marriage.

The basis for the fear of independent or autonomous activity is, of course, the fear of loss of the other. "He might meet somebody else who enjoys the same things he enjoys, and decide he doesn't love me anymore!" Better that the other partner be doomed to a life of doing none of the things he enjoys than the possibility that he will meet and enjoy the company of somebody else, or that he will meet and be attracted to somebody else.

A particular threat to the couple who have a togetherness compulsion is the possibility of extramarital sexual interest or activity. Our culture is so steeped in the romantic notion that sexual attraction is the equivalent to "falling in love" that the yoked couple will frequently subject themselves to a marriage deadened by suspicion, accusation, and fear of abandonment because of sexual jealousy. The sexual act has been so romanticized and idealized that yoked couples are willing to terminate their marriages if the act is performed by one partner with someone other than the spouse. And if one partner does have a sexual relationship outside the marriage and is discovered or feels obliged to "confess" to the other and is subsequently "forgiven," the marriage henceforth may be based on the guilt of the one and the generosity of the other.

Wives and husbands are frequently exhorted by newspaper advice columnists and by ministers and marriage counselors to **forgive** a sexually errant spouse and to give him or her a second chance. All parties involved overlook the fact that forgiveness is an emotion that exists solely in connection with judgment and condemnation. To say "I forgive you" means "I have judged you and found you lacking in qualities that are worthy of respect. *I* have these qualities, but you do not. I recognize my superior moral strength and your weakness. We will henceforth have a relationship based on that recognition." The forgiven is unconsciously aware of a morally subordinate position, but to express resentment or anger would make this partner look even more unworthy of the other's magnanimous "love."

Each member of a yoked union is therefore in the position of being both a potential sinner and a judge. The fear of being judged by the other while simultaneously judging the other creates a relationship that is not likely to foster trust, self-confidence, or total acceptance between the partners. And it is definitely not one that will foster the independent growth of human beings who have the urge to become completely self-actualized individuals. The traditional marriage, then, seems counter to the emotional growth needs of individuals.

The paradox is that individuals reach their greatest potential and experience their fullest humanity when they are involved in a close relationship with another person with whom they can share their triumphs and failures, to whom they can open themselves and be unconditionally accepted, with whom they can experience honest conflict that is either resolved satisfactorily or accepted as unresolvable, and toward whom they can fearlessly express the tenderness, eroticism, dependency, nurturance, admiration, and anger that all who live intimately together feel toward one another.

Without such relationships, human beings would be closed in upon themselves, living solitary emotional lives, always peripherally involved with others, and never deeply involved. We would become a society that relied on sensory experiences alone to define ourselves. Our emotional responses of compassion, love, desire, and empathy would be denied full expression. Rather than becoming more fully human, we would become less human and less aware of ourselves and of others. For most human beings, the closeness of a rewarding relationship is best realized in a union of a man and a woman who live together with the sanction of society, and this is a **marriage.**

Furthermore, there is the inescapable fact that some form of marriage *must* form the basis of our social structure. For civilization to continue, new generations must be born and nurtured, educated and socialized. The ability to love, to relate to others, and to have the desire and the courage to strive for self-actualization comes about through interaction with other human beings. An infant, helpless and dependent, must have an atmosphere that provides not only physical needs, but affectional needs as well. He must, if he is to grow into adulthood as a complete individual, experience acceptance and the freedom to be himself. These needs can best be met within the framework of an ongoing family. The elimination of the institutions of marriage and family would therefore not only be chaotic for society, but could also be a pathogenic factor in the lives of many individuals.

It is for these reasons that the family will probably endure, in one form or another, as long as humanity exists. However, our present form of marriage must be reevaluated in light of the individual partners' needs for human growth. That our present form is not satisfactory to society or to individuals requires no elucidation. Its deficiencies are all too apparent to even the most disinterested observer. That changes must come about in our marriage form is also apparent. We must, for the sake of the individual and of society, develop a form of marriage that allows the partners to freely realize their own human potential, to experience the close sharing of each other's adventure in human growth, and to foster the development of emotionally secure children who can also form close personal involvements as adults. This, then, is the challenge that faces us today: to retain the function of the family while restructuring the institution of marriage.

WHY SOME PEOPLE CAN'T LOVE

Incapable of loving themselves, they cannot give to
their partners in a relationship—nor can they ever
be really satisfied by what they receive. The causes are
in childhood, says a leading authority on narcissism;
and the cures are in middle age.

Otto Kernberg
interviewed by Linda Wolfe

"EVERY AGE DEVELOPS its own peculiar forms of pathology, which express in exaggerated form its underlying character structure," writes social critic Christopher Lasch. He and others have said that ours is an age of narcissism, recalling the beautiful youth of Greek legend who fell in love with his reflection in a pool and pined away in rapture over it.

Some observers see the preoccupation with self and the decline of interest in public life and social goals as evidence of a growing narcissism in the national character. Others see narcissism in the proliferation of therapies that declare we should be our own best friends, devote ourselves to self-growth and self-actualization, and look out, above all, for "No. 1." Others see it in the tendency of young Americans to eschew marriage and child-rearing in favor of remaining single, "living together," or living alone.

In recent years, psychiatrists have grown increasingly interested in narcissism as a clinical syndrome. They claim to see patients every day who display a constellation of traits indicating problems in their capacity to love others—or even to really love themselves. Freud theorized that what he called primary narcissism was a necessary stage in the infant's development: before he could love others, the child first learned self-love, which required a phase of total self-absorption. Freud's successors have modified his analysis of how the child learns to love others.

Several psychiatrists who assembled recently for a conference called "Narcissism in Modern Society" at the University of Michigan argued that there are so far no solid clinical data proving that the incidence of narcissism has increased in recent times. Nevertheless, a task force of the American Psychiatric Association that is preparing a new edition of the APA's diagnostic manual has included in its draft a new syndrome called "narcissistic personality disorder" (see box on page 9), which it defines as combining an "exaggerated sense of self-importance" with "a lack of sustained positive regard" for others.

One of the chief theorists of narcissism is psychoanalyst Otto Kernberg, medical director of the Westchester Division of the New York Hospital–Cornell Medical Center. Dr. Kernberg makes a careful distinction between normal and pathological narcissism. We are all in love with ourselves to some extent, and seek validation through the approval of others. But the pathological narcissist, according to Kernberg, differs from the rest of us in the extreme intensity of his self-absorption; he can, indeed, be said to suffer from a psychological ailment that requires and deserves treatment. Curiously, the pathological narcissist, says Kernberg, does not really love himself at all; he actually holds himself in low esteem. In Kernberg's books, *Borderline Conditions and Pathological Narcissism* (1975) and *Object Relations Theory and Clinical Psychoanalysis* (1976), he argues that it is self-hatred, rather than self-love, that lies at the root of pathological narcissism.

What are the other differences between the normal and pathological narcissist? How can we distinguish between the two in the people we know? How are extreme forms of narcissism manifest in our relationships to others and our sexual lives? And to what degree are social forces in our society responsible for the clinical symptoms of narcissism? To explore these and other questions, *Psychology Today* sent behavior writer Linda Wolfe to discuss this phenomenon with Kernberg at his office in New York's Westchester County.

Linda Wolfe: Aren't we all narcissists? Don't we all, secretly or not so secretly, love ourselves, take our own lives more seriously than the lives of those around us, enjoy feeding and grooming ourselves, and spend a great deal of effort at soliciting the admiration and approval of others?

Otto Kernberg: Yes, but if our self-esteem is totally dependent on the manifestations of admiration by others, then something is wrong with us. The pathological narcissist cannot sustain his or her self-regard without having it fed constantly by the attentions of others.

Wolfe: Is the extreme narcissist, then, a dependent individual?

Kernberg: Yes, but he usually resents other people because of his dependency on them. Or he envies them. He experiences little empathy for them and doesn't really like them. Other people count only as admirers. The applauding crowd is welcome, but not people in and of themselves.

Wolfe: How does this show itself?

Kernberg: The pathological narcissist will anticipate receiving tribute from others and may for a time be very charming to them. But once the tribute is given, he quickly becomes restless and bored. Often, then, he treats even his former admirers with contempt. In general, his relationships with other people are exploitative or parasitic, although this may be masked behind a surface which is very often engaging and attractive.

Wolfe: That's a very interesting point. I gather you are saying that the pathological narcissist often appears to be a quite likable individual.

Kernberg: Yes, very often he is a person with great capacities for attracting others. He may have talent, or the ability to do active consistent work in areas which permit him at least partially to fulfill his ambition of being admired and applauded by others. I have had a number of highly intelligent patients with narcissistic personality structures who appear to be quite creative in their fields. And, of course, narcissistic personalities can often be found as leaders in political life, or in industry or academia, or as outstanding performers in the theater or other arts.

Wolfe: It sounds to me as if the narcissistic personality might be a particularly productive one.

Kernberg: No, and there's the catch, because careful observation of their productivity over a long period of time will give evidence of superficiality and flightiness in their work, of a lack of depth which reveals emptiness behind the glitter. Quite frequently, narcissists are the "promising" geniuses who then surprise other people by never fulfilling the promise of their talents, whose development ultimately proves to be banal.

Wolfe: Are there other ways in which the narcissist is banal or shallow?

Kernberg: Yes. Narcissists lack emotional depth. Their feelings tend to be undifferentiated, and they have quick flare-ups of emotion followed by sudden dispersal of feeling. They are especially deficient in genuine feelings of sadness and mournful longing; their incapacity for experiencing depressive reactions is a basic feature of their personalities. When abandoned or disappointed by other people, they may show what on the surface looks like depression, but on further examination this emerges as anger and resentment, loaded with revengeful wishes, rather than real sadness at the loss of a person they appreciated. And many of them have never fallen or been in love.

Wolfe: I suppose this is because the narcissist is too much in love with himself.

Kernberg: No, the abnormal or pathological narcissist does not, as it turns out, really love himself or herself at all. He may give the surface impression of doing so, but on psychoanalytic exploration, it turns out that self-hatred is more dominant in the narcissist than is self-love. Narcissists have very low opinions of themselves and this is why they constantly seek approbation. They consider themselves unworthy and unlovable, and seek constantly to hide this fact from themselves by trying to get the outside world to proclaim them unique, extraordinary, great. But beyond that, they suffer from intense, unconscious envy that makes them want to spoil, depreciate, and degrade what others have and they lack, particularly others' capacity to give and to love. So the pathological narcissist cannot be really satisfied by what he receives from others, and always ends up frustrated and feeling empty.

Wolfe: What causes pathological narcissism?

Kernberg: It is a condition that stems from the first few years of life. Chronically cold parental figures with covert or intense aggression toward their children are a very frequent feature in the background of narcissistic personalities. A composite picture of a number of cases that I have been able to treat shows that narcissistic patients have consistently had a parental figure, usually a mother or a mother-surrogate, who functions well on the surface and runs a superficially well-organized home, but who nevertheless is extremely callous, indifferent, or spitefully aggressive toward the child. This figure begins by frustrating the child orally, and thus sets up the greed and envy of others that later become so characteristic of the narcissist. Also, many narcissistic patients possess some inherent quality that can objectively arouse admiration. They may, for example, possess unusual physical attractiveness, or some special talent. These qualities then become a refuge for the narcissist. By gaining attention for his qualities, he can temporarily offset the underlying feeling of being unloved or of being the object of revengeful hatred on the part of the parent. Sometimes, of course, it is the cold, hostile parent's own narcissistic use of the child which sets him off on the search for compensatory admiration and greatness. For example, I have had two patients who were used by their mothers to gain the attentions of others. They were dressed up and exposed to public admiration in an almost grotesque way, and eventually they began to link exhibitionism with the notion that it could bring them power and greatness. They did this in a compensatory effort against oral rage and envy. In addition, narcissistic patients often occupy a pivotal point in their family structure, such as being the only child, or the only brilliant child, or the one who is supposed to fulfill the family's aspirations. A good number of them have a history of having played the role of genius in their families during childhood.

Wolfe: You said earlier that the narcissist, typically, is incapable of falling in love. What is it that happens when we fall in love, and why is the narcissist precluded from the experience?

Kernberg: The capacity to fall in love implies the ability to idealize another person. In a sense, all love begins as infatuation. We see the loved one as extraordinary, remarkable, even perfect. Inevitably, disappointment sets in; things look different in the light of an ongoing relationship. But when one is in love, one can regenerate the feeling of idealization of the other person again and again throughout a long-term commitment. I have often observed this clinically with good couples. But the narcissist cannot idealize any individual for very long. As soon as an idealized person responds to the narcissist, that person loses his or her value. The narcissist is thus purely exploitative in his relationships with other people. It is as if he were squeezing a lemon and then dropping the remains. For example, I had one narcissistic patient who thought he was in love for a time with a woman he considered very gifted, beautiful, warm—in short, completely satisfying. For a while she didn't respond to him, and he wanted her to do so, and even wanted to marry her. Finally she did respond, and then accepted his offer of marriage. But after their marriage, he quickly became bored with her and soon he was altogether indifferent to her.

Wolfe: Does the pathological narcissist, then, tend to move from one person to the next more often and more rapidly than the normal narcissist?

Kernberg: Yes, again typically, the pathological narcissist tends to be sexually promiscuous. Pathological narcissists feel sexual excitement for people considered valuable or attractive by others, or for those who seem unattainable and withhold their bodies. Their unconscious envy and greed is stirred up by such people, and they long to take possession of them, thus proving their own greatness. They even

DIAGNOSING THE NARCISSIST

The narcissistic personality disorder will achieve official clinical status in 1980 if the American Psychiatric Association approves the present draft of its new *Diagnostic and Statistical Manual of Mental Disorders*. The manual is the ultimate diagnostic authority in the psychiatric profession, and an APA task force has been revising the second (current) edition since 1973. Dr. Robert L. Spitzer, chairman of the task force, gives the rationale for the proposed category 301.81, Narcissistic Personality Disorder:

"Although not yet fully described or studied, the disorder as a clinical concept has in recent years become the subject of enough interest to merit inclusion in the diagnostic handbook, whose aim it is to help clinicians concerned to identify and deal with such disorders. We hope that future studies will determine the extent to which it is a valid [useful] category."

The draft contains almost three pages of description of the syndrome. The diagnostic criteria listed are:

A. Grandiose sense of self-importance or uniqueness, *e.g.*, exaggerates achievements and talents, focuses on how special one's problems are.

B. Preoccupation with fantasies of unlimited success, power, brilliance, beauty, or ideal love.

C. Exhibitionistic: requires constant attention and admiration.

D. Responds to criticism, indifference of others, or defeat with either cool indifference or with marked feelings of rage, inferiority, shame, humiliation, or emptiness.

E. At least two of the following are characteristic of disturbances in interpersonal relationships:

1. Lack of empathy: inability to recognize how others feel, *e.g.*, unable to appreciate the distress of someone who is seriously ill.
2. Entitlement: expectation of special favors without assuming reciprocal responsibilities, *e.g.*, surprise and anger that people won't do what he wants.
3. Interpersonal exploitiveness: takes advantage of others to indulge his own desires or for self-aggrandizement, with disregard for the personal integrity and rights of others.
4. Relationships characteristically vacillate between the extremes of overidealization and devaluation.

---

long, although this is usually unconscious, to devaluate and spoil that which is envied. For a short while, insofar as sexual excitement heightens the illusion of beauty or value, the narcissist may feel himself to be in love. Soon, however, sexual fulfillment gratifies the narcissist's need for conquest, and the narcissist then moves on to the next person.

Wolfe: Does this trouble the narcissist, or does he feel powerful and important as a result of placing himself repeatedly in the role of the rejecting party?

Kernberg: He may feel pleased early in life, but over the years, there is a change. Moving on becomes a losing proposition for the narcissist because he begins to lose his ability to idealize an unavailable sex object and thus his interest in pursuing one. With experience, the narcissist begins to understand that all encounters will be just the same, regardless of how attractive the partner. This produces a general deterioration of the capacity for getting excited with potential sexual partners. Very often we find a general impoverishment of sexual life in narcis-

sistic personalities, even in those who were very active sexually in their youth. We see them in their late 40s or 50s, and they are sexually inactive and suffering from feelings of frustration, disappointment, and emptiness.

Wolfe: Can you change—treat—the narcissist?

Kernberg: Yes, but, interestingly, the best time to work with some narcissists is when they are in their 40s or 50s. Prior to that time, although the narcissist may have some feelings of emptiness and dissatisfaction, he is usually so busy seeking admiration and imagining that its receipt will solve all his problems that he is not a good candidate for therapy. But later in life, when he has begun fully to perceive the emptiness of his existence and the fact that his self-esteem remains recalcitrantly low, he is more interested in making efforts to change. Thus change is more likely.

Wolfe: Are there other sexual patterns besides promiscuity that distinguish the pathological narcissist?

Kernberg: Yes, frequently the narcissist seems to value and talk about a sex partner's body parts more than the partner himself or herself. Typically, a narcissistic male might be interested in a woman's breasts, buttocks, vagina, skin, and, when he focuses on those, one gets the impression that in effect he is dismembering the woman. He does this because deep down he knows that he cannot reach, cannot fully possess, the other person. By dismembering that person into body parts, he gratifies a need to deny the importance of that unattainable object. Let me give you an example. Years ago, I had a patient who felt a very intense unconscious envy toward his wife. It became worse over the years because the wife, who originally was a very sexually inhibited and socially awkward person, blossomed into a full and attractive human being. This was very frustrating to my patient, and their sexual life became of less and less interest to him. But he reawakened his interest in her by requiring her to travel with him to other cities and engage in sex with other men in his presence. He felt when other men had her that all they had were her breasts and genitals, and since all this really belonged to him, there was nothing of hers that they really had. And at the same time, he was degrading his wife. She became a walking sex organ and nothing else. And this somehow reassured him that there was nothing else to her except bodily parts. He wasn't giving up anything of value, for she *had* nothing of value.

Wolfe: What about the female narcissist? Does she also think of the male body in dismembered terms? Does she also tend to be promiscuous?

Kernberg: There are different social and cultural factors operating for women. Some female narcissists are like the males, but one is more likely to find with narcissistic women that they exploit men and use their sexuality to obtain admiration or financial support. Let me give you two examples. I had one narcissistic woman patient who divorced three husbands because after a time each rebelled against being a slave to her.

Another woman had a husband and a lover. She felt superior to her husband, whom she didn't love, because she had a lover and because her lover was an extremely wealthy man who gave her gifts she was able to keep secret from her husband. The woman was satisfied with the arrangement, but the lover was not. Eventually, he arranged to divorce his wife and he asked my patient to leave her husband and marry him. She refused to do so. She was afraid that in marrying her lover, she would no longer hold the reins of the relationship. Once rejected, the lover stopped seeing her, and she was left with the husband she did not love and became depressed. Narcissism takes a different form in women, but the dynamic is the same. Like men, the female narcissist can't find love or hold on to it.

Wolfe: Do you believe there's any validity to the notion that our society is fostering narcissism? Are we, as a people, becoming more and more self-involved and less capable of feeling for others?

Kernberg: I'm not sure. I'm troubled by this. The question is raised constantly, and of course since I am not a sociologist I must go somewhat beyond the limits of my own knowledge to answer it. But let me say this: I am aware that our society stimulates narcissistic needs in our social interactions. Our society does this by fostering superficial ways of being accepted and admired, namely, through emphasizing the accumulation of material goods.

Obtaining material proof of personal value is very similar to the narcissist's obtaining praise in order to feel worthwhile. A society that fosters competition, with its concomitants of envy and greed, may be fostering pathological narcissistic traits. And, theoretically at least, there are other societies in the world which, by eliminating competition and insisting on people's mutual responsibilities toward one another, may foster the altruistic traits that are part of normal narcissism.

However, I find it hard to believe that this could do more than just smoke out the pathological narcissists who are already among us in our own society, and, in the more altruistic society, force the pathological narcissists to go underground. I don't think society can produce normal or pathological narcissism since I believe that such traits are formed during earliest childhood and not, as some sociologists imply, by receiving a social go-ahead later in life. So the most I would be willing to say is that society can make serious psychological abnormalities, which already exist in some percentage of the population, seem to be at least superficially appropriate.

Wolfe: But isn't it society that determines what is or isn't abnormal? What I'm getting at is this: if, as sometimes seems to be happening, our society begins to place greater value on an individual's ability to have a great quantity of love affairs rather than on his ability to sustain a single one throughout life, then won't the promiscuous pathological narcissist begin to seem less pathological?

Kernberg: Only in one regard. Society could, to some extent, protect some pathological narcissists for some period of time from feeling the emptiness and meaninglessness of their lives by providing them with a cultural rationalization. But I don't think those individuals would feel comfortable indefinitely, and I also don't think that society would favor the pattern for very long. It's an interesting fact about society that it keeps changing its attitudes. It experiments. There are some things that cannot be resolved in theory, and so we get social experiments. Take sex. We experiment for a period of history with sexual suppression. But we notice that it ends up with the deterioration of

human relationships, and we move on to a different pattern. Or we experiment with sexual freedom. But we notice that it ends up in the boredom and trivialization of sex. Human nature, seeking its own fulfillment, asserts itself, and the experiments change. To put it slightly differently, individual maturity may demand a personal road for improvement that goes on no matter what current social policies are.

Wolfe: It sounds to me as if you are saying that while society may change, neither human nature nor the concept of what is most likely to satisfy human longings changes—no matter what society decrees. You are suggesting that it is a given that in order to feel fulfilled as human beings, we must feel deeply for others, whether our society promotes attachment or urges us away from it.

Kernberg: Yes, I think so. All other things being equal, there is something that happens to one in a deep relationship with someone else which brings great satisfaction to the individual. It has been called transcendence, the sense of extending beyond oneself and feeling a sense of unity with all others who have lived and loved and suffered before—whether it is one's parents or people throughout history. And when this can't be attained, one feels emptiness and chronic dissatisfaction.

Wolfe: Then you think there's no real danger of narcissism becoming the prevailing trait of our society because the individual psyche will rebel against it?

Kernberg: Yes. Individuals will simply continue to choose the patterns that fulfill them, despite what society promulgates.

Linda Wolfe, formerly a senior editor of *Psychology Today*, writes frequently on behavior. She is the author of *Playing Around*, a study of extramarital relationships (Morrow, 1975) and is currently at work on a novel.

For further information, read:

Jacobson, Edith. *The Self and the Object World*, International Universities Press, 1964, $11.50.

Kohut, Heinz. *The Analysis of the Self*, International Universities Press, 1971, $18.50.

Mahler, Margaret S. *The Psychological Birth of the Human Infant*, Basic Books, 1975, $15.

Rosenfeld, Herbert A. *Psychotic States*, International Universities Press, 1966, $12.50.

THE SELF-INFLICTED PAIN OF
Jealousy

Gordon Clanton and Lynn G. Smith

Gordon Clanton is a graduate of Louisiana State University and received his Ph.D. in sociology from the University of California at Berkeley. He taught at Rutgers University and Trenton State College in New Jersey, and is now an assistant professor of sociology at San Diego State University. He also lectures and leads workshops on personal and family relationships.

Lynn Smith also earned her Ph.D. from U.C., Berkeley, in social psychology. She wrote her doctoral dissertation on new sexual lifestyles, and is co-editor of Beyond Monogamy: Recent Studies of Sexual Alternatives in Marriage. She and Clanton are co-editors of *Jealousy*, a collection of articles on the subject published by Prentice-Hall, from which this article is excerpted.

WHEN A MAN FIRST NOTICES that his wife is interested in another man, he has at least two possible responses:

1. "His interest in her confirms my suspicion that he is on the make. I never did trust him. Her interest in him shows she is dissatisfied with me. He's quite attractive. I guess she's grown tired of me. And he's so attentive to her, so appreciative. I guess I've come to take her for granted. No wonder she's so turned on by his little courtesies. They want to go to the opera together, and I feel left out. I wonder what other excuses they'll find to spend time together. Maybe she'll take time away from me to be with him. Maybe I'll have to cook dinner and take care of the kids while she's off at the 'opera.' If I can't count on my own wife, what the hell can I count on?"

2. "His interest in her confirms her at-tractiveness. I'm proud of her. Her interest in him shows she is alert and alive. I'm glad for that. An inert partner, no matter how secure the relationship, is a bad deal. He's like me in some ways, so I am affirmed by her choice of him. He's different from me in some ways, which suggests she has some needs that I don't meet. I must consider these needs carefully and try to find out if I could do a better job of meeting them. But I realize I cannot meet all of her needs without violating my own autonomy, so I must work to become glad she has other friends who can fulfill her in ways I do not, and would rather not. Thank God, she's found someone who wants to go to the opera with her. I want to be reassured that our relationship means as much to her as it does to me, but I won't demand that she renounce all others in order to demonstrate that to me."

As these two responses to the same situation show, there can be considerable latitude with regard to how you interpret and react to experiences that trigger the jealous flash. Your own experience and social learning will determine which of these reactions seems more natural to you. Most of us have been programed with some version of the first response. Perhaps we can change ourselves so that the second response becomes more likely.

The experience of jealousy varies enormously from age to age, from culture to culture, from couple to couple, from person to person, and within the same person from time to time. In the United States, particularly among young adults, there has been a change of attitude toward jealousy in recent years. "Normal" jealousy, which had been seen as an inevitable accompani-ment of love and supportive of marriage, has come to be seen by some as evidence of personal insecurity and weakness in the relationship, and therefore as a threat to intimate partnership.

The types of jealousy. To sort out the various types of jealousy, one might ask if a particular experience of jealousy comes from feeling excluded, or from a fear of loss. The distinction is important, for it signifies the difference between a small problem and a big one, between the benign and the malignant.

Most jealous flashes come from feeling left out of an activity involving your partner and another person or other people. When your partner pays attention to another, your first reaction is to note that they are "in" and you are "out." They are not noticing you, or at least not giving you as much attention as they are giving each other. You feel excluded, ignored, unappreciated.

This kind of experience is common in our society, and dealing with it gracefully is part of the etiquette of our time—especially as women become more involved in occupational and social activities outside the home. The boss wants to dance with your wife; a woman spends most of the evening at a party in conversation with your husband; your partner and a friend both discover they adore Bergman's films, which you never particularly enjoyed. Such experiences trigger the jealous flash, but typically they do not fan it into a flame. The jealous feelings usually fade when the precipitating event is over, although one might still say on the way home, "I cannot imagine what

From *Psychology Today*, March 1977. Adapted from JEALOUSY, Gordon Clanton, Lynn G. Smith, °1977. Reprinted by permission of Prentice-Hall, Inc., Englewood Cliffs, New Jersey.

you and Pat could have found interesting enough to discuss for so long."

If you find yourself troubled or upset by having to share your partner in ways normally considered appropriate among your circle of friends, your feeling of exclusion may be a symptom of an underlying fear of loss, the more serious type of jealousy. If you literally cannot stand to let your partner out of your sight, your jealousy is probably rooted in a persistent fear rather than a temporary irritation. This is more serious, but it need not be fatal to your self-esteem or to your relationship with your partner.

To treat this problem, you must diagnose it more precisely. Exactly what is it you are afraid of losing? Perhaps it is loss of "face" that frightens you. If your wife is vivacious in company, perhaps the guys you drink with will think you "can't keep her in line." If your husband is appreciative of attractive women, perhaps your friends will suspect he's dissatisfied with you. If your mate is too friendly with a person of the opposite sex, perhaps others will assume they are sexually involved. If you don't like the third party, if he or she seems unworthy of your mate's attention, the fear of loss of reputation can be especially powerful.

Losing control. But perhaps you fear more than loss of face. Perhaps you fear you are losing control; control of your spouse, control of the relationship, control of the future, control of yourself. You cannot predict your partner's behavior. You are reluctant to voice complaints because you don't know how your partner will react. You don't trust the third party. Your anxiety breeds tension, which corrodes your relationship.

This fear of loss of control, rooted in insecurity, is a specific form of neurosis quite common today. As we lose control of other sectors of our lives, or discover we never really had control, we wish all the more to be secure in our intimate relationships and our family life. If things are chaotic at work, if the crime rate is going up, if the country's government seems to be corrupt or incompetent, the security and stability of the home become all the more important.

The most serious form of jealousy is the fear of loss of the partner, and of the love, affection, and support he or she provides. This can be terrifying, and not surprisingly you become anxious and defensive. You assume, on questionable

grounds, that if you lose your mate it will be to someone else, so you view others with suspicion and fear. Such behavior makes you less attractive to your partner. Thus jealousy begets the very aloofness one suspects, and thereby deepens the basic fear of loss that leads to increased jealousy.

The jealousy you feel—regardless of what type—is shaped in part by elements such as your mood. When you feel good about yourself, you are less likely to feel jealous. When you are depressed and dissatisfied with yourself, you are more susceptible. When you feel secure in your relationship, jealousy is less apt to be a problem. When you are unhappy or unsure about the relationship, you will be more fearful. Your feelings about the third party are also important. If you like and consider him or her a worthy friend for your partner, their occasional affectionate hugs may not bother you. If you don't, the same gestures may be unsettling and even threatening.

At its root, jealousy is an instinctive reaction to certain types of threats. In human beings, as in other animals, self-protection appears to be instinctive. In the physical sense this is obvious; if we fall, we grab for support; if we are punched, we hit back or run away or cover our heads. We are programed to do something other than stand there and absorb a beating.

Our readiness to protect the psychological self seems similarly instinctive, although our self-perception and social definitions tell us when to feel threatened, and how to respond. The conditions under which one feels the jealous flash and the ways in which it is expressed are profoundly influenced by personal experiences and by the norms and values of society.

Our natural biological propensity toward jealousy is reinforced by certain childhood experiences common to us all. As infants, each of us had to learn to let go of the mother, to share her with the father and usually with siblings. We learned that we would not have full control over and total access to those on whom we depend. These experiences were more traumatic for some than for others, but we all learned certain basic lessons about jealousy in the first few months of our lives.

This developmental element of jealousy is literally part of our nurture, and not inborn. But it is necessary because

of the nature of the human organism. Each of us was born very dependent upon the mother. Each of us learned to modify that dependency, to adjust to the loss of oneness with and apparent control over the most significant other person. From infancy onward, each of us learned about jealousy from what we heard and saw, and from our own experiences. Most of this learning was informal, unstructured, and quite subtle.

Learning to be jealous. The process by which we learn when to be jealous, how to express jealousy, and how to react to jealousy is lifelong and continuous, but certain steps are particularly important. The way your parents handled your infant reaction to the "loss" of your mother gave you your first gauge for measuring future jealousies. If you felt loved and approved of despite your abandonment, you may have developed a relatively low propensity for jealousy. If you were punished for your clutching and crying out, you may have learned to repress a great deal of jealousy. If your parents truly rejected you, beyond the necessary separation, you may have become anxious, insecure, and more susceptible to jealousy.

The parents' handling of sibling rivalry also contributes to a person's understanding of jealousy. If you always felt that Mom liked your brother best, you may be prone to jealousy. If your parents and others commented often on your sister's beauty and kidded you about your freckles, you may worry about your attractiveness, and fear that your partner will leave you because of it. Even small put-downs and jests can have a devastating effect on a child or adolescent growing up in a society with so much competition, comparison, and ranking.

In adolescence, the first experiences with sexual interest, competition, love, loss, and recovery contribute to one's sense of jealousy and how to deal with it. As adolescents begin to read more widely, and to view television shows and films with adult themes, they learn more about sex, violence, and attendant jealousy.

For the increasing number of persons who do not marry early, young adulthood may be a time of several important love affairs. Each one, whether or not it leads to marriage, introduces a new concern. Now you must learn about your lover's experiences, feelings, and values with regard to sexuality, fidelity, and jealousy. Candor and trust at this point can help the partners construct a shared understanding of jealousy. However, if one partner imposes a set of definitions on the other, or if the partners simply assume they see eye-to-eye on such matters, disruptive experiences of jealousy are more likely to occur.

Experiences of romantic love in adolescence and young adulthood recreate the near-total dependency upon the other person that infants feel for their mothers. Once again, we must learn to share a highly significant other person with his or her own friends and interests.

In a changing society with high mobility and elaborate, overlapping communication systems, adulthood is no longer a distinct stage in the lifecycle. It is a sequence of stages and phases through which understandings of sex, love, fidelity, and jealousy may vary considerably. You and your partner are constantly being influenced by the people around you as well as those you encounter on television, and in movies, books, magazines, and newspapers.

The demands of society are powerful. A man may wish to forgive his wife's adultery, but he knows his friends will not respect him unless he reacts strongly. A woman may be tolerant of her husband's flirtations, and then have to endure the pity of friends who would be scandalized if their husbands behaved the same way. A person may wish to express jealous anger, but be inhibited by the expectation of disapproval from a circle of "liberated" friends. These societal values and demands are not only "out there," they are also inside us. We have internalized the beliefs and values of the persons and institutions around us—some consciously, some unconsciously.

Jealousy, then, is a complex mixture of physiological (or instinctive), developmental and social experience. Your jealousy, to put it simply, is a part of you. To reject it, to repress, deny, or condemn it, is to reject part of yourself. You cannot detach your jealousy from yourself and observe it objectively any more than you can do so with your arm or your brain. To understand your jealousy is to know yourself. To seek to manage your jealousy is to gain a measure of self-control or self-mastery.

The uses of jealousy. One basic and legitimate function of jealousy is to alert us to threats to our personal security and to the well-being of an important relationship. The jealous flash is the psychological equivalent of the physiological system of skin receptors and nerves which protects us from bodily harm. Physical pain warns us that the security of the organism is being threatened by some physical object or force. Psychological pain, such as jealousy, warns us that our psychic security is being threatened, that a relationship upon which we depend requires attention.

The experience of jealousy can also lead to catharsis, the cleansing, purifying release that reduces anxiety. To freely admit that one feels jealous may reduce distress and make destructive expressions of jealousy unnecessary.

The language and gestures of jealousy can be employed in a variety of ways. A jealous outburst may simply be a cry for attention, a way of saying, "I am hurting! Notice me!" If no constructive use is made of such a declaration, the expressions of jealousy may become part of a masochistic pattern. The jealous person broods over the partner's real or imagined infidelities, demands detailed accounts of the partner's experiences with others, wallows in self-pity and depression, and seeks the sympathy of anyone who will listen. This pattern may pay off. It can generate feelings of self-righteousness and justify the decision to avoid the hard work that might reduce the jealousy. The jealous outburst can also serve as a vehicle for sadism. Jealousy gives one the right to be cruel by making retaliation an acceptable option. It can be used to justify withdrawal from the partner or to drive him or her away.

Jealousy can also be used to control the behavior of the partner and the third party. The expression of jealousy carries the implicit message: "Stop what you are doing or I shall be even more miserable." This may be accompanied by threats or retaliation or flight. This strategy typically fails outright, or if successful, produces resentment in the manipulated partner.

The attempt to control a partner through jealousy is often accompanied by an appeal to duty: "You owe it to me to stop seeing her." But this ploy has limited usefulness. As Bertrand Russell has written: "In former days parents ruined their relations with their children by preaching love as a duty; husbands and wives still too often ruin their relations to each other by the same mistake. Love cannot be a duty, because it is not subject to the will."

Jealousy can also mark the beginning of constructive dialogue. It can trigger communication that leads to clarification of needs, meanings, beliefs, and values. Such discussion may lead to negotiations that reduce the pain of jealousy and strengthen the relationship.

But the same discussion can also be the occasion for unconstructive conflict, and another means by which the partners attempt to manipulate and blame each other. For example: "Melissa, we won't be able to get anywhere with our jealousy problems until you do something about your low self-esteem and your fear of true intimacy and ..." When negotiations deteriorate into this type of name-calling, it's time to either draw back or to look for outside help.

Working with jealousy. The steps you take to manage your jealousy depend upon the type of jealousy you are feeling, and upon the kind of work you want to do on your relationship. Some couples wish to enrich their marriages without questioning traditional sex-role expectations and definitions of fidelity. Others seek to remodel their marriage. They may renegotiate roles and expectations in response to the women's movement, the human-potential movement, or the popular self-help literature.

Certain nondefensive strategies for dealing with jealousy are useful in all types of intimate partnerships. Others may be suitable only for remodeling relationships. You should employ only those strategies congenial with your own history, your present relationship, and your realistic hopes for the future.

If you are interested in enriching your relationship, in preserving its structure but improving its quality, begin with a close look at yourself. How do you feel when you feel jealous? How would you like to feel? Why are you choosing to deal with these feelings now? If you see yourself as incomplete without your mate, and cannot imagine living without him or her, you will be more susceptible to jealousy. Successful management of your jealousy, however, will make you feel more autonomous, less dependent.

A child moves beyond his dependency on the mother, and learns to manage his jealousy of her by developing a sense of himself and his own value. The same process must be repeated in the intimate partnerships of adulthood. The best antidote against recurrent jealousy is growth toward autonomy and self-direction. This kind of personal strength can make a person more attractive to the partner, and less susceptible to feelings of insecurity, thereby reducing the likelihood of jealousy.

You may wish to go beyond self-analysis and self-improvement, to open discussion with your mate on issues having to do with jealousy. At least talking is a form of contact, and better than being silent and out of touch. Talking is also less disruptive than flight or violence. You might begin by talking about past experiences of jealousy. Sometimes we can learn a great deal from a replay of an event that no longer carries high emotional significance. Discuss your expectations and hopes for the future. Be specific about what you expect from one another. What kinds of behavior are OK, and what kinds are out of bounds? Remember that your fantasies or your mate's innocent flirtations are not always subject to the will. It is unrealistic to demand of one's mate the complete suppression of affection for others.

One warning: in talking over your jealousy problem with your partner, you may discover it is part of a larger pattern of distrust, deception, and manipulation in your life together. In talking it through you may learn things you were unaware of, and that may disrupt a relationship which, despite its flaws, you do not want to lose. Talking it through can heighten awareness and diffuse existing power relationships. You may learn things you did not know, and learn to express yourself more effectively.

Be ready to revise your plans if it appears that discussing your jealousy together will disrupt the relationship profoundly by reopening old wounds or by renewing bad habits. If this happens, it may be time to try working with a marriage counselor or in some form of group setting. Counseling or therapy may help smooth and speed constructive interaction between partners. Whatever the method, it will only work if both of you want to do it; if both of you will listen as well as talk; and if both of you are willing to confront thorny issues rather than retreat into wounded silence.

Remodeling marriage. Candid communication in an atmosphere of trust is useful in marriage enrichment, but absolutely essential for those who seek to remodel marriage in accord with the revolutions of morals and manners of the last two decades. The accelerating integration of women into all sectors of society, the new candor with which people express their sexuality and sensuality, and the various let-it-all-hang-out schools of interpersonal relations have inspired and facilitated reappraisal of certain previously taken-for-granted aspects of marital life for millions of people, particularly young adults.

Implicit and explicit renegotiations of sex-role expectations are underway throughout the land. Many women are demanding more freedom to control their own lives. They are becoming more assertive in their relationship with men. Standards of appropriate sexual behavior are changing, leaving many married persons confused about their own needs and values. Some marriages have undergone small revolts against the ideology of togetherness.

If you are in the process of remodeling your marriage or partnership, and jealousy becomes an issue, it's time for some straight talk. Tell your partner what kinds of behavior and what kind of people are most likely to trigger your jealousy, and get your partner to tell you the same. Talk about what you would both do in various hypothetical situations. Find out what your partner expects of you, and make sure he or she knows what your expectations are. Be willing to negotiate new limits. Discuss particular persons and situations, but don't limit yourself to that. Discuss your needs and limits, your beliefs and values. Seek congruence, but don't be upset if you discover discrepancies.

As long as human beings need affection, there will be some jealousy. It probably cannot be completely eradicated. Even if you are relatively successful in working with your jealousy it will most likely recur in some form at some time. Don't be surprised when this happens. The jealous flash is a perfectly natural response. You'll feel it every time an important relationship appears to be threatened. Your jealousy is neither proof of love nor evidence of personal failure. It is merely a signal which tells you to attend to your relationship, and to yourself.

For more information, please read:

Clanton, Gordon and Chris Downing. Face to Face: An Experiment in Intimacy; Dutton, 1975, $7.95; Ballantine, 1976, paper, $1.95.

Smith, Lynn G. "Jealousy and Its Alternatives" in *Getting Clear*, Anne Kent Rush, ed. Random, 1973, paper, $5.95.

Watson, Jane, Robert E. Switzer and J. Cotter Hirschberg. Sometimes I'm Jealous; Golden Press, 1972, $1.95.

MAKING IT TO MATURITY

David C. McClelland, Carol A.
Constantian, David Regalado,
and Carolyn Stone

A Harvard team sought to measure the maturity levels achieved by some young adults who had been raised by various methods. They found that what mattered was not technique but a few intangibles. Like love, and whether the home had been adult-centered.

ABOUT 25 YEARS AGO, three psychologists at Harvard carried out one of the most thorough studies of child-rearing ever done in the United States. Believing that the future of a society was more or less unconsciously shaped by the way it brought up its children, Robert Sears, Eleanor Maccoby, and Harry Levin felt it was vital to learn more about the impact of different parenting techniques on personality development. They were particularly interested in how a mother handled a range of developmental problems: Was she permissive or severe in dealing with sex play? Did she control the child by spanking? By withdrawing her love? By depriving him or her of privileges?

The Sears group interviewed 379 mothers of kindergartners in two towns near Boston in the early 50s. They rated each mother on about 150 different child-rearing practices. They compiled a complete record of the parenting methods typical of American mothers at that time and place, including variations of social class and sex and birth order of the child.

But they were less successful in demonstrating that one method or another had a significant effect on the child's personality, possibly because they did not study the children themselves but relied on the mothers' descriptions of them. Most important, they could not touch at all the key question that was the reason for much of the fuss over child-rearing in the first place: Did the way the mother treated the child really make a difference in adulthood? Did it really matter, years later, whether she had breast-fed the child, punished it, rejected it, or smothered it with love? Were the Freudians right in assuming that, for better or worse, what the parents did in the first five years was crucial?

Most of these questions remain unanswered today, despite all the attention given them in recent years. It is difficult to draw any clearly supported generalizations from the different kinds of studies that have been done, and this has led some psychologists—for example, Arlene Skolnick of the Institute of Human Development in Berkeley—to argue that parents have very little control over the formation of their child's personality and character (*Psychology Today*, February 1978).

We had an opportunity to seek some answers of our own last summer when we contacted many of the children of the mothers who had been interviewed by the Sears group 25 years ago. They were now 31 years old, and most of them were married and had children of their own. We were especially interested in determining how the different ways they had been brought up had helped or hindered them in achieving social and moral maturity. We based our measurements on Erikson's theory

of stages of psychosocial development and the Piagetian theory of cognitive development. Under both theories, early stages are characterized by dependence on external authority, intermediate stages by greater self-reliance, and the highest stage by genuine concern for how others feel.

Through interviews and psychological tests, we concluded that most of what people do and think and believe as adults is not determined by specific techniques of child-rearing in the first five years. With Arlene Skolnick, we believe that parents should rest assured that what they *do* is not all that important in how their children turn out; many other influences in later life serve to shape what adults think and do.

But this hardly means that the way parents *feel* about their children cannot have a substantial impact. We found that when parents—particularly mothers—really loved their children, the sons and daughters were likely to achieve the highest levels of social and moral maturity. The only other dimension that had major importance for later maturity was how strictly the parents controlled their children's expressive behavior. A child was less apt to become socially and morally mature when his parents tolerated no noise, mess, or roughhousing in the home, when they reacted unkindly to the child's aggressiveness toward them, sex play, or expressions of dependency needs. In other words, when parents were concerned with using their power to maintain an adult-centered home, the child was not as likely to become a mature adult.

The Interviews and Tests

When we approached the young men and women whose mothers had been part of the Sears study, we informed them that we wanted to compare their

> "Most of what people do and think as adults is not determined by how they were reared in the first five years."

views on child-rearing with those held by their mothers in the 1950s. It was thus easy to talk about moral values with them in the interviews, which were conducted by three graduate students in psychology who were about the same age as they.

Because of limits on time and money, we concentrated on the children of mothers who had been considered middle class by the Sears team. We succeeded in interviewing 78 of them. Of these, 49 had children of their own. About 35 percent were Jewish, 25 percent Catholic, and 18 percent Protestant. The sample was fairly representative of the original group of middle-class mothers. But we were able to persuade only 47 of the 78 children to come in after the interviews for psychological tests—and this smaller group was probably less representative.

For the most part, the informants were allowed to tell their stories freely. However, the interviewers made certain to elicit information from them on such things as friendships, work experiences, illnesses, what organizations they belonged to, whether they had ever been in trouble with the law.

When we asked them what things they thought were most important to teach children, they usually mentioned some general virtues, such as respect for the rights of others, confidence in themselves, knowing how to make their own decisions. The interviewer would then probe for concrete examples and explore them fully: what were the circumstances of the incident, what were the people involved thinking, what did they eventually do? Finally, each person was also asked what kinds of problems they thought their children were likely to run into when they grew up. Many of them mentioned such things as the pressures to experiment with drugs, the problems of getting a job, the difficulties of getting along with people.

Later on, the interviewer rated each individual on 37 outcome variables, including the number of children, occupational achievement, participation in voluntary organizations. They also judged each on how important he or she considered a number of values, from 1 ("not very important") to 3 ("very important"). Among the things the interviewers tried to evaluate was how important the subjects considered other influences on their lives besides their parents. Most important, from all their material, the interviewers attempted to evaluate (on the 1 to 3 scale) how important each young adult considered the values in Erikson's stages of psychosocial development:*

Stage I (Receptivity). Showing respect for authority or tradition. Behaving properly, decently, or obediently.

Stage II (Autonomy). Self-reliance, ability to make up one's own mind about things, not always being dependent on others. Showing willpower, determination, or courage.

Stage III (Assertion). Doing well in school or on the job, developing skills, learning to appreciate music, nature, or art, speaking well, getting along with or influencing others.

Stage IV (Mutuality). Understanding other points of view, serving others or the common good (but not just following decent behavior, which is Stage I). We will refer to these characteristics as the "valuing" measure of maturity.

Those subjects who were willing to come in for further testing were first given a version of the Thematic Apperception Test (TAT). They were asked to write stories to go with six pictures, among them one showing two women scientists in a laboratory, another with a couple sitting on a bench by a river, and a third with a man and woman swinging on a trapeze. From their

---

* Two judges read all the interview summaries and independently rated each subject on the values in Erikson's stages. They agreed with the ratings made by the interviewers 80 percent of the time.

stories, we obtained further data on whether their thought patterns clustered around one or another of Erikson's stages by using an objective coding system empirically derived by Abigail Stewart of Boston University. We refer to this as the "thinking" measure of maturity.

Next, they took a multiple-choice version of Lawrence Kohlberg's well-known moral-dilemmas interview. James Rest of the University of Minnesota has developed a Defining Issues Test, which gives scores for each of the six stages of moral development spelled out by the Harvard psychologist. We evaluated our respondents on a summary score for the highest stages (5A, 5B, and 6), which Rest calls "principled thinking" (for example, "I will act morally because there are certain basic, universal principles that should govern my behavior"). There is considerable evidence that they represent a higher level of moral reasoning than Stage 4 reasoning ("I will be good because that's the law") or Stage 3 reasoning ("I will be good to please others"). We will call this measure of maturity "principled judging," to avoid confusion with our thinking measure of maturity, which derives from the TAT.

Of course, many psychologists would argue that there is no good evidence for a stage sequence of psychosocial maturity, but we have every reason to believe our three measures do represent actual stages in development (see box on page 50). We do not mean to imply, however, that maturity is the ultimate value that people must strive for at all costs. Moral maturity can conflict with survival needs, as Jesus and Socrates found out, and it may not be very functional for people who live under conditions of poverty and oppression. There is some truth in the old saw that only the rich can afford to be virtuous.

The Hypotheses

When we had finished testing, we had generated more than 4,000 correlations among a set of 35 child-rearing variables, 37 adult-outcome variables obtained in the interviews, and 85 other characteristics from the psychological test results. When we stripped down the list of variables to a few key ones, we found that the number of statistically significant relationships between child-rearing practices and adult outcomes only slightly exceeded what one would expect from chance.

The only conclusions to come from this first stage of analysis were that mother's affection relates to more adult outcomes than one would expect by chance, while physical punishment did not seem to be significantly related to any of the outcomes. Thus, how the parents had reared the children was not associated in any meaningful way with the number of children our subjects

> "The parental policy we call strictness inhibited maturity later in life —unless there was also love in the home."

had, their occupational success, whether they married, how they felt about their parents, the importance they attached to such things as friends, sports, religion, or work.

To look at it another way, wide variations in the way parents reared their children didn't seem to matter much in the long run. Adult interests and beliefs were by and large not determined by the duration of breast-feeding, the age and severity of toilet-training, strictness about bedtimes, or indeed any of these things. Even the mother's anxiety about whether she was doing a good job didn't hurt (or help) her children.

We went on to check out specific hypotheses on how parenting practices might influence moral and social maturity. As already noted, we had developed three measures of maturity based on the Eriksonian and Kohlberg models. From the Erikson stages, we had a measure of the level of the subject's thinking maturity (stage stories from the TAT) and of his valuing maturity (based on values they said in the interviews they would teach their children). And from James Rest's multiple-choice version of the Kohlberg moral-dilemmas interview, we had a measure of the subject's capacity for principled judging.

Other researchers had studied the influence of child-rearing practices on so-

cial and moral maturity, and several years ago Martin Hoffman of the University of Michigan attempted to state a few propositions that appeared to be best supported by the findings from all sources. Hoffman concluded, in brief, that (1) power assertion by parents, as in heavy use of physical punishment, retards the development of both moral and social maturity; (2) "induction," or the use of reasoning to explain what the parents are doing and why, promotes it; and (3) parental affection also promotes it.

We tested each of Hoffman's three hypotheses. To measure the first, we made an index of punitiveness based on the average ratings of the Sears interviewers in 1951 on how often the children had been spanked by their fathers, how much they had been punished for aggressiveness toward their parents, how often they had been deprived of privileges as a punishment.

We found a slightly negative, insignificant correlation between punitiveness in childhood and adult functioning at the most mature level, by any of our three measures.

More inhibiting to adult maturity was the related parental practice called "strictness," because it defined the extent to which the parents suppress any tendency for the child to act out, be aggressive or noisy, or demand attention. Our data show that this type of parental policy strongly inhibits Stage IV maturity in thinking and judging in adulthood, as well as Stage III maturity in valuing—which may encompass the values most Americans associate with true maturity. (Further analyses showed that the impact of strictness depended very much on whether there was love in the home. If the mother really loved the child, how strict the parents were didn't seem to make much difference later on.)

Americans are strongly oriented toward self-reliance and doing well, which in the Eriksonian scheme are coded as Stage II and Stage III respectively. Thus, it is not surprising that in describing the values they want to teach their children, our sample scored higher in the average ratings in these two stages than for Stages I and IV.

But, theoretically, the highest stage of maturity—Stage IV—requires some loss of self-orientation in the interest of a higher good, as in parenting, mutual love, serving God and country. Our

data for Stage IV show an interesting difference between the thinking and valuing measures. Our sample was, on the average, strong on Stage IV for thinking and weak on Stage IV for valuing, meaning that people thought in terms of mutual give-and-take, but did not consciously stress service to others, tolerance, and understanding as the most important virtues to teach children. Instead, they valued self-reliance and self-actualization more. This strongly suggests that the two measures are getting at different aspects of maturity. It may be that the thinking measure reflects more how a person is actually functioning, while the valuing measure reflects cultural norms, which in America emphasize self-actualization. If we assume the thinking measure is less influenced by cultural values, this may indicate that our sample of adults is more mature—functions more at a Stage IV level—than their conscious stress on Stage II and III self-reliance and self-assertiveness suggests.

Our second hypothesis, much less strongly supported by previous research, is that reasoning with children or withdrawing love (Hoffman's "induction") promotes maturity. That is, parents who explain why they are doing things to their children develop an understanding that contributes to the child's maturation. We found no evidence of it in our sample. Those who were reasoned with more as children do not show signs of greater maturity as adults. Similarly, withdrawal of love has been associated with early development of conscience (if there is any love to begin with, according to Sears and his colleagues) and, consequently, adult maturity. Again, such is not the case in our sample.

Mother Love and Maturity

What is important for developing maturity is the amount of affection the mother shows for the child in the first place, just as our third hypothesis, based on previous research, predicts. Does a mother like her child and enjoy playing with him or her? Or does she consider the child a nuisance, with a lot of disagreeable characteristics? In the Sears study, the researchers rated mothers on the variable they called "mother's affectionate demonstrativeness toward the child." We called it "mother's warmth," and found that it is a key determinant of adult maturity,

and the father??

as measured by any of our three ways.

Father's affection for the child is also important for thinking maturity (based on the TAT), to a lesser extent for judging maturity (based on moral reasoning), but not at all for the Stage IV virtues of tolerance and service to others (based on the interviews). We are not sure why this is so, but can only speculate that the affectionate father provides a role model that is more associated with assertiveness (since he is the breadwinner) than with understanding and mutual love. Nevertheless, it is important to realize that children of affectionate fathers, whatever they may say they value, are, in fact, more apt to think and reason in ways that show tolerance and understanding. Perhaps it helps a child move beyond relying entirely on the self by providing an attractive authority figure, but does not promote valuing development to Erikson's Stages III and IV.

Many theorists, especially Urie Bronfenbrenner and Edward Devereux of Cornell, have argued that it is moderation in love and discipline that most promotes maturity. The clinical literature is full of examples of children who are crippled by too much love or too little discipline. As far as our measures of the conscious value placed on tolerance and service to others are concerned, the more mother love the better. But the seven mothers who were rated at the top of the mother's-warmth scale had children whose thinking showed fewer aspects of the kind of mutual give-and-take associated with Erikson's Stage IV maturity.

In other words, it looks as if strong mother love had given these children the conscious values of tolerance, sharing, and understanding, but had inhibited the development of actually thinking at this level. If the thought measure is tapping a deeper level, as it seems to be, one can infer that "smother love" can inhibit the development of the highest level of functioning. The same is not true of father love, which, even when it may seem excessive, promotes thinking or functioning at level IV—perhaps because fathers are home less often and therefore can't "smother" their children the way mothers might.

Was moderate strictness better than too easy or too strict discipline? We sorted parents into easy, moderate, and strict groups on the two disciplinary dimensions—punitiveness and strict-

ness—to see if moderate control fostered greater Stage IV thinking, valuing, or judging. The results do not conform to expectations. Moderately strict control by itself does not appear to favor the development of social and moral maturity by any of the three measures.

Only one other parental practice, not covered in our three hypotheses, came close to satisfying our criterion of being substantially related to at least two out of the three maturity measures. It was the habit some parents have of threatening punishment and not carrying out the threat. Not surprisingly, this kind of inconsistency inhibited the development of maturity, particularly as measured by the way people think about human relationships (the Stage IV scores from the TAT).

A Test of Moral Behavior

When psychologists first started studying morality, they concentrated on moral behavior, in line with the American belief that actions speak louder than words. One may now ask whether the measures of maturity included in this study are related to *acting* morally.

We estimated the deceitfulness of our subjects with a simple test. All were given a list of names of public figures, many of them very obscure, and asked if they knew who they were and the fields in which they were prominent. We measured the extent to which a subject misrepresented his knowledge by counting the number of times he said he knew the obscure figures but wrongly identified their fields. In addition, the subjects were asked to check how frequently they had performed a number of impulsive, aggressive, often antisocial acts, such as yelling at someone in traffic, not paying a bill because they were mad at someone, throwing things around a room, deliberately slamming a door, or taking a sign from a public place. The combined standard score on these two items represented a person's penchant for engaging in antisocial behavior.

At the same time, we tried to get a sense of their inclination to behave in a prosocial way. In one questionnaire item, we asked them to list several things they might do if they unexpectedly received $10,000: if they thought about giving some of it away, that was considered prosocial, as was willing-

ness to cooperate in our study. We found considerable variation in the extent to which they were willing to help us out—and contribute to science. The single most important measure was whether they came in to be tested when given several opportunities and offered pay for their time. But there were also differences in whether they refused at the outset, said they would

> "Parents can buy conformity in moral behavior from their children, but at the cost of true maturity."

come and didn't, or agreed willingly and came the first time—all of which were scaled on a dimension that might be called cooperativeness.

The results of these combined measures of moral behavior are a little surprising but also illuminating: people with high Stage I and Stage IV scores on the thinking measure (from the TAT) behave more morally than those with high Stage II and III scores, although none of the relationships is very strong (underlining the importance of situational factors in shaping moral actions).

Moral acts, as here defined, involve primarily relations with others, either helping them or at least not hurting them. Moral-maturity theory suggests that people may act morally for two different reasons—out of a relatively immature conformity to authoritative codes (Stage I) or out of a genuinely mature concern for others (Stage IV). People primarily concerned about the self (Stages II and III) will be more apt to behave antisocially because they are pursuing their own ends. For example, they exaggerate how many people they know in order to look good in the eyes of the experimenter or their own eyes. From the moral or social point of view, this is dishonesty.

The results obtained for the valuing and judging estimates of moral maturity fit in fairly well with this interpretation. They agree in showing that people at lower levels of maturity are more apt

WHAT ARE THE QUALITIES OF MATURITY?

Why do we believe that the measures in our study were really assessing maturity? One reason is that all ethical systems describe a similar hierarchal order of social and moral values: an unselfish person is better than a selfish one; one who freely chooses a moral act is better than one who is moral by compulsion. In our three measures of moral reasoning, the lowest stages reflect moral conformity based on external pressures; intermediate stages imply the capacity to incorporate the standards of one's teachers and make the free choices necessary for a moral act; and the highest stage represents some unselfish concern for others.

Another reason is that children go through the stages in this order as they mature cognitively. At the earliest stage, children act morally because they don't know any better; external forces shape their behavior. At the next stage of cognitive growth, they are able to think for themselves and make choices. Finally, at a still later stage, they are capable of taking the view of another, of seeing things through others' eyes; once they do that, they begin to act in ways that take others into account.

Still a third reason is empirical. Those who are more mature by our measures show other characteristics that ought to be related to maturity. For instance, education was significantly related to scoring higher on all three of our measures of maturity. Mothers with more education had children who as adults thought more maturely and chose more mature values to teach their children, according to the Eriksonian stages, and reasoned or judged more maturely about ethi-

cal dilemmas, according to the Kohlberg scheme. And if the children themselves had had more education, they also thought, valued, and judged more maturely. Since education should promote maturity, the fact that it correlates so consistently with our measures gives us more confidence in our method.

The same inference can be drawn from the fact that maturity was significantly correlated, by all three estimates, with a high score on a scale of "psychological mindedness." The scale measures the importance people give to dreams, fantasies, emotions, and self-knowledge, and whether they are inclined to interpret their dreams and try to understand why they do things. In short, these are individuals who observe their own psychological processes. They are more aware of what they are thinking, doing, and feeling. Thus, they believe in Socrates' motto, which has always been associated with maturity: "Know thyself."

Other characteristics of more mature individuals also give us confidence in our scales. By any measure, more mature people tended to report that they had remained closer to their parents after growing up. But this did not mean that they were not making their own decisions. The most mature individuals tended to report that they had grown away from their parents' views, and they were inclined to downplay the importance of tradition and authority.

The interviewers also tended to like them more. We had asked the graduate-student interviewers to state how much they enjoyed talking with each person. Plainly, they liked those indi-

viduals most who turned out to be more mature by later measures. Of course, this might mean the interviewers were biased, that they were giving higher maturity ratings to people they liked. But we emphasized to the interviewers the distinction between their report on their emotional reactions and their rational judgment of a person's stage of social maturity. The interviewers' subjective reaction was a potentially important datum, moreover, since Stage IV people, who are more service-oriented, were expected to be more interested in other people, easier to communicate with, and more likable.

We expected a Stage IV concern for other people to be linked with participation in voluntary organizations, in which people come together for the purpose of service. Indeed, we found that the higher the level of psychosocial maturity, either by the thinking or valuing measure, the more the individual took part in such organizations.

We also predicted from the theory of stages that occupational success or status would be most closely associated with Stage III, since a person at this level is most concerned with developing skills and impressing the world. If our measures reflected a true stage sequence, then occupational success would progress regularly up through Stage III and then fall off for those oriented toward Stage IV. Such was the case for both the thinking and valuing measures. And it was true for both men and women. On the whole, our measures of maturity corresponded with other things in a person's life that are related to maturity.

—D. McC. et al.

to be moral, or at least to avoid antisocial behavior. Those who stress the Stage I virtue of decency, or who reason at the level of law and order (Stage 4 in the Kohlberg scheme), lie less and are less aggressive. However, as we move up these scales of maturity, there is a tendency to engage in less moral behavior. How can we account for that?

Can we seriously contend that our measures reflect levels of maturity if people at the higher levels of maturity *behave* less morally?

The dilemma can be resolved, at least in part, if we assume that the conscious valuing and judging (or reasoning) measures are more influenced by cultural values and do not tap as high a

level of individual maturity as the thinking measure. In other words, the highest levels for valuing and judging still reflect a focus on the self, on self-actualization in line with American norms, rather than on the concerns and feelings of others. And focus on self-development, on being sure the individual knows his own mind and stands up for his rights and principles, does not particularly promote helping or not hurting others. Instead it may lead a person to violate codes of decent interpersonal behavior when he thinks a higher principle is involved.

Thus, as Kohlberg has insisted all along, moral maturity does not guarantee decent social behavior. Moral immaturity may be more effective for that—at least in preventing antisocial behavior. After all, Socrates, who scores high in moral reasoning by Kohlberg's theory, was notorious for neglecting his wife and children.

The Paradox of Maturity

How can parents do right by their children? If they are interested in promoting moral and social maturity in later life, the answer is simple: they should love them, enjoy them, want them around. They should not use their power to maintain a home that is only designed for the self-expression and pleasure of adults. They should not regard their children as disturbances to be controlled at all costs.

It was the easygoing, loving parents whose children turned out to be most mature. Is that a remarkable finding? Isn't it just common sense? The trouble with comon sense is that it is so uncommon.

But suppose the parents are interested, like most Americans, in moral *behavior*, in discouraging antisocial acts and encouraging social contributions. Herein lies a paradox. The mother who doesn't love her child much and insists on traditional Stage I decent behavior may produce an adult who conforms—but at the cost of his or her fuller development. To make the

point more dramatically, mothers who didn't love their children much turned out adults who acted more morally: they did not misrepresent their knowledge as much on our tests. But strict parents also produced adults who were less inclined to engage in prosocial behavior. So parents can buy Stage I conformity in moral behavior, but at the cost of true maturity.

The paradox is that *promoting maturity leads first to a decrease in moral behavior*, as the person moves out of a Stage I reliance on external authority and becomes more oriented to making choices on his or her own. Only at the highest stage, when people become genuinely and emotionally aware of the feelings and viewpoints of others, do they again begin to behave less antisocially and more prosocially. This is not a new idea at all to moralists, who have always insisted there is a world of difference between being good out of custom or fear, and real goodness that comes from the heart. Jesus talked about "whited sepulchres"—those who slavishly followed Jewish law to the letter, but had no real charity in their hearts.

So parents also need faith—faith that loving and believing in their children will promote maturity in the long run, even though some of their offsprings' behavior seems outrageous in the short run as they learn to make their own decisions. There are no shortcuts to perfection. Children have to explore some detours if they are to reach the heights. The best we parents can do to help is to love them, and not stand in the way of their groping attempts to grow up or force them at all times to conform to adult-centered codes of moral behavior.

David McClelland, professor of psychology at Harvard University, is the author of both *The Achieving Society* (Halsted/Wiley, 1976) and also *Power: The Inner Experience* (Halsted /Wiley, 1975). He has had a lifelong interest in the study of human motivation and is now preparing a report by several contributors for The Cleveland Foundation on what behavioral scientists know about educating children for values. This article is based on research carried out for that report.

Carol A. Constantian is a doctoral candidate in the Department of Psychology and Social Relations at Harvard University. After receiving her B.A. in psychology in 1972 from Wellesley College, she worked in Los Angeles for four years, primarily in publishing. Her main interests in psychology include small-group behavior, human motivation, nonverbal sensitivity, and applications of social psychology within organizations.

David Regalado is a second-year graduate student in the Department of Psychology and Social Relations at Harvard University. After serving three years in the military, he received his B.A. *summa cum laude* from California State University, Long Beach, in 1976.

Carolyn Stone received her B.A. in psychology from Wellesley College in 1972. Currently she is a doctoral candidate at the Laboratory of Human Development of the Harvard Graduate School of Education. Her research interests include social cognitive development, peer relations in children, and the family's influence on development.

For further information, read:

Erikson, Erik H. *Childhood and Society*, 2nd ed., W. W. Norton, 1963, $10; paper, $3.45.

Kohlberg, Lawrence. "Stage and Sequence: The Cognitive-Developmental Approach to Socialization," in *Handbook of Socialization, Theory and Research*, David A. Goslin, ed., Rand McNally, 1969, $40.

McClelland, David C. *Power: The Inner Experience*, Halsted/Wiley, 1975, $16.95.

Rest, James R. "New Approaches in the Assessment of Moral Judgement," in *Moral Development and Behavior: Theory, Research, and Social Issues*, Thomas Lickona, ed., Holt, Rinehart and Winston, 1976, $15.95.

Sears, Robert, Eleanor Maccoby, and Harry Levin. *Patterns of Child Rearing*, Stanford University Press, 1957, $17.50; paper, $7.50.

The Love Research

ZICK RUBIN

For centuries, poets have been trying to capture the essence of whatever it is that makes the world go around. Now behavioral scientists are having their turn.

Zick Rubin, PhD, is professor of social psychology at Brandeis University and the author of *Liking and Loving: An Invitation to Social Psychology.*

Love has always been one thing, maybe the only thing, that seemed safely beyond the research scientist's ever-extending grasp. With an assist from Masters and Johnson, behavioral scientists have, to be sure, dug rather heavily into the topic of human sexual behavior. But whereas sex might now be explored scientifically, love remained sacrosanct.

Or so we thought.

Love was a taboo topic for researchers as recently as 1958, when the president of the American Psychological Association, Dr. Harry F. Harlow, declared in faintly mournful tones, "So far as love or affection is concerned, psychologists have failed in their mission. The little we know about love does not transcend simple observation, and the little we write about it has been written better by poets and novelists." Since the poets and novelists had always been notoriously contradictory about love, defining it as everything from "a spirit all compact of fire" to "a state of perceptual anesthesia," this was a pretty severe indictment.

But the psychologists did not take this charge lying down. Instead, they rallied to the call and started a quiet revolution. Over the past dozen years, and at a positively accelerating pace, behavioral scientists have begun to study love. They have done so on their own terms, with the help of such tools of the trade as laboratory experiments, questionnaires, interviews and systematic behavioral observation. And although the new love research is still in its early stages, it has already made substantial progress. The research has proceeded on several fronts, including explorations of the psychological origins of love, its links to social and cultural factors and the ways in which it deepens—or dies—over time.

Recent studies of falling in love have indicated that there is a sense in which love is like a Brooks Brothers suit or a Bonwit dress. For one person's feelings toward another to be experenced as "love," they must not only feel good and fit well, they must also have the appropriate label. Sometimes a sexual experience contributes to such labeling. One college student told an interviewer that she was surprised to discover that she enjoyed having sex with her boyfriend, because until that time she had not been sure that she loved him. The pleasant surprise helped to convince her that she was actually "in love."

Paradoxically, however, people sometimes label as "love" experiences that seem to be negative rather than positive. Consider the rather interesting case of fear. Ovid noted in *The Art of Love*, written in first-century Rome, that an excellent time for a man to arouse passion in a woman is while watching gladiators disembowel one another in the arena. Presumably the emotions of fear and repulsion stirred up by the grisly scene would somehow be converted into romantic interest.

Ovid himself did not conduct any controlled experiments to check the validity of the fear-breeds-love principle, but two psychologists at the University of British Columbia, Drs. Donald L. Dutton and Arthur P. Aron, recently did so. They conducted their experiment on two footbridges that cross the Capilano river in North Vancouver. One of the bridges is a narrow, rickety structure that sways in the wind 230 feet above the rocky canyon; the other is a solid structure upriver, only 10 feet above a shallow stream. An attractive female experimenter approached men who were crossing one or the other bridge and asked if they would take part in her study of "the effects of exposure to scenic attractions on creative expression." All they had to do was to write down their associations to a picture she showed them. The researchers found that the men accosted on the fear-arousing bridge were more sexually aroused than the men on the solid bridge, as measured by the amount of sexual imagery in the stories they wrote. The men on the high-fear bridge were also much more likely to telephone the young woman afterward, ostensibly to get more information about the study.

The best available explanation for these results comes from a general theory of emotion put forth by Dr. Stanley Schachter of Columbia University.

1. FORMATION OF INTERPERSONAL RELATIONSHIPS

Schachter's experiments suggested that the experience of emotion has two necessary elements. The first is physiological arousal—a racing heart, heightened breathing, sweating and the like. These symptoms tend to be more or less identical for any intense emotion, whether it be anger, fear or love. The second necessary element, therefore, is the person's subjective labeling of his or her arousal. In order to determine which emotion he or she is experiencing, the person must look around and determine what external stimulus is causing the inner upheaval.

This labeling is a complicated process, and (as Ovid apparently knew some 2,000 years ago) mistakes can happen. In the Capilano Canyon study, subjects apparently relabeled their inner stirrings of fear, at least in part, as sexual arousal and romantic attraction. This sort of relabeling is undoubtedly encouraged by the fact that the popular stereotype of falling in love—a pounding heart, shortness of breath, trembling hands—all bear an uncanny resemblance to the physical symptoms of fear. With such traumatic expectations of what love should feel like, it is no wonder that it is sometimes confused with other emotions. As the Supremes put it in a song of the 1960s, "Love is like an itching in my heart."

In the case of the Capilano Canyon study, of course, one cannot say that the subjects actually "fell in love" with the woman on the bridge. But the same sort of labeling process takes place in more enduring romantic attachments. In the process, social pressures also come crashing into the picture. Young men and women are taught repeatedly that love and marriage inevitably go together, and in the large majority of cases they proceed to act accordingly on this assumption.

Americans are more likely than ever to get married (well over 90 percent do so at least once), and all but a minuscule proportion of people applying for marriage licenses will tell you that they are in love. It is not simply that people who are in love decide to follow their hearts' dictates and get married. It also works the other way around. People who are planning to get married, perhaps for economic reasons or in order to raise a family, invariably follow their culture's dictates and decide that they are "in love."

The pressure to label a promising relationship as "love" seems especially strong for women. Sociologist William Kephart of the University of Pennsylvania asked over a thousand Philadelphia college students the following question: "If a boy (girl) had all the other qualities you desired, would you marry this person even if you were not in love with him (her)?" Very few of the respondents (4 percent of the women and 12 percent of the men) were so unromantic as to say yes. But fully 72 percent of the women (compared with only 24 percent of the men) were too practical to answer with a flat no and, instead, pleaded uncertainty.

One of Dr. Kephart's female respondents put her finger on the dilemma, and also on the resolution of it. She wrote in on her questionnaire, "If a boy had all the other qualities I desired, and I was not in love with him—well, I think I could talk myself into falling in love."

Whereas women may be more highly motivated than men to fall in love with a potential spouse, men tend to fall in love more quickly and less deliberately than women.

In a study of couples who had been computer-matched for a dance at Iowa State University, men were more satisfied than women with their dates, reported feeling more "romantic attraction" toward them and even were more optimistic about the possibility of a happy marriage with their machine-matched partners. In a study of dating couples at the University of Michigan, I found that among couples who had been dating briefly—up to three months—boyfriends scored significantly higher than their girlfriends did on a self-report "love scale." These men were more likely than their partners to agree with such statements as "It would be hard for me to get along without———," "One of my primary concerns is———'s welfare" and "I would do almost anything for———." Among couples who had been together for longer periods of time the male-female difference disappeared.

The idea of measuring love on a paper-and-pencil scale is, incidentally, not an entirely new one. When Elizabeth Barrett Browning wrote, "How do I love thee? Let me count the ways," she was, as any mathematician can tell you, referring to the most basic form of measurement. Six years ago, when I was searching for an unspoiled topic for my doctoral dissertation, I decided to take Browning's advice. ("Why do you want to measure *that*?" my dissertation committee asked me. "Why not measure something more conventional like cognitive dissonance or identity diffusion?" I looked down at the rocky canyon 230 feet below and answered, voice trembling, "Because it's there.") The items on the scale that emerged refer to elements of attachment (the desire to be near the other), caring (the concern for the other's well-being) and intimacy (the desire for close and confidential communication with the other). The ancient Greeks had a similar conception of love. Where they went wrong was in never asking the masses to put their *eros* and *agape* for one another on nine-point scales.

Skeptics may point out, of course, that a paper-and-pencil love scale does not really measure how much people love each other, but simply how much they *say* they love each other. But there is some corroborating behavioral evidence for the scale's validity. For example, scores on the scale checked out with the well-known folk wisdom that lovers spend a great deal of their time gazing into each other's eyes. Surreptitious laboratory observation through a one-way mirror confirmed that "strong lovers" (couples whose members received above-average scores on the love scale) made significantly more eye contact than "weak lovers" (couples whose scores on the love scale were below average). Or, as the popular song puts it, "I only have eyes for you."

Whereas men seem to fall in love more quickly and easily than women, women seem to fall out of love more quickly and with less difficulty than men, at least in the premarital stages. For the past several years, my coworkers and I have been conducting an extensive study of student dating couples in the Boston area. We found, to our initial surprise, that women were somewhat more likely to be "breaker-uppers" than men were, that they saw more problems in the relationship and that they were better able to disengage themselves emotionally when a breakup was coming. Men, on the other hand, tended to react to breakups with greater grief and despair.

These tendencies run counter to the popular stereotypes of women as star-struck romantics and men as aloof exploiters. In fact, women may learn to be more practical and discriminating about love than men for simple economic reasons. In most marriages, the wife's status, income and life chances are far more dependent on the husband's than vice versa. As a result, the woman must be discriminating. She cannot allow herself to fall in love too quickly, nor can she afford to stay in love too long with "the wrong person." The fact that a woman's years of marriageability tend to be more limited than a man's may also contribute to her need to be selective. Men, on the other hand, can better afford the luxury of being "romantic."

Sociologist Willard Waller put the matter most bluntly when he wrote, some 40 years ago, "There is this difference between the man and the woman in the pattern of bourgeois family life: a man, when he marries, chooses a companion and perhaps a helpmate, but a woman chooses a companion and at the same time a standard of living. It is necessary for a woman to be mercenary." As more women enter business and professional careers, and as more men make major commitments to homemaking and childrearing, it is likely that this difference will diminish.

In spite of these culturally based sex differences, the usual course of love is probably pretty much the same for human beings of both sexes. A key task for love researchers is to explore the stages and sequences through which love develops. To this end, Drs. L. Rowell Huesmann of the University of Illinois at Chicago Circle and George Levinger of the University of Massachusetts recently developed a unique computer program, called RELATE, that simulates the development of close relationships. Given information about the personalities of the two partners and following a built-in set of rules and assumptions, RELATE is able to generate a "scenario" of the likely course of their relationship. In its maiden effort along these lines, RELATE simulated the relationship of two hypothetical sweethearts, John (who was described to RELATE in the computer-language equivalent of "attractive, but shy") and Susan (introduced to RELATE as "outgoing and popular").

After a few minutes of whirring and clicking, RELATE came up with its prediction. It hypothesized that after a period of time during which they interacted at a superficial level, "John learns that Susan is willing to disclose intimacies in response to his disclosures, and he confides in her completely. This leads the pair into active striving for a deep romantic involvement." By the end of RELATE's love story, John and Susan were both oriented toward a permanent relationship, although neither had yet proposed marriage. Erich Segal, eat your heart out!

Since John and Susan are only hypothetical, it is impossible to know how accurate RELATE's scenario really is. Moreover, Drs. Huesmann and Levinger freely acknowledge that at present the simulations are greatly oversimplified, providing at best pale reflections of the events of real-life relationships. But the computer-matchmaker has already proved to be of value to researchers in refining their models of the development of love in real life.

Note, for example, that John and Susan's romance did not get very far until John learned that Susan would reciprocate his disclosures. My study of Boston couples, conducted in collaboration with Drs. Letitia Anne Peplau (now at UCLA) and Charles T. Hill (now at the University of Washington) has confirmed RELATE's working assumption along these lines, to wit: love is most likely to flourish when the two partners are *equally involved* in their relationship. In our study of 231 dating couples, 77 percent of the couples in which both partners reported that they were equally involved in 1972 were still going together (or, in some cases married) in 1974, as compared with only 45 percent of unequally involved couples.

The importance of equal degrees of involvement makes it clear that love, like water, seeks its own level. As Columbia University sociologist Peter M. Blau explains, "If one lover is considerably more involved than the other, his greater commitment invites exploitation and provokes feelings of entrapment, both of which obliterate love. . . . Only when two lovers' affection for and commitment to one another expand at roughly the same pace do they mutually tend to reinforce their love."

Because of this mutual reinforcement, love will sometimes beget love—provided that the first person's love is communicated to the second. To help make the point, Dr. Paul Rosenblatt of the University of Minnesota sifted through anthropologists' reports of "love magic" in 23 primitive societies, from the Chaga of East Africa to the Kwoma of New Guinea. He came to the conclusion that although love magic often works, it isn't really magic. Instead, such exotic practices as giving one's "victim" a charmed coconut, flashing a mirror at her or blowing ashes in her face all serve to heighten the woman's love by indirectly communicating the man's love for her. When love magic is practiced without the victim's knowledge, it is not nearly so effective. (Other studies have made it clear, however, that expressions of love must also be well-timed. If too much affection is expressed too soon, equity is undermined and the tactic will backfire.)

Dr. Rosenblatt's study illustrates quite directly what some observers fear most about the new love research— that it will rob love of its magic and mystery. Sen. William Proxmire is one of those who takes this point of view. In a much-publicized statement last year, Sen. Proxmire identified a study of romantic love sponsored by the National Science Foundation as "my choice for the biggest waste of the taxpayer's money for the month of March. I believe that 200 million Americans want to leave some things in life a mystery, and right at the top of the things we don't want to know is why a man falls in love with a woman and vice versa."

Dr. Ellen Berscheid, the University of Minnesota researcher whose work was singled out by the senator, responded vigorously to the attack: "I assume the senator has some knowledge of the divorce rate in this country and understands that the absence of love is the basis on which many divorces are instigated. I believe he has been divorced and recently was reconciled with his second wife [in February, 1975]. He ought to realize better than most people why we should know all we can about the determinants of affection."

Writing in the *New York Times*, columnist James Reston also defended the love researchers. "Mr. Proxmire is a modern man," Reston wrote, "who believes that government should help people with their problems. He is a land-grant college man and will vote any amount of money for basic research on the dangers of natural selection in animals, and on how to get the best bulls and cows together on the farms of Wisconsin, but he is against basic research on the alarming divorce rate or breakup of the human family in America. You have to assume he was kidding."

But, of course, the senator was not kidding, and his sentiments are undoubtedly shared by a large number of Americans, even if not by the entire 200 million claimed in his statement. Even some psychologists themselves share his viewpoint. At a symposium sponsored by the American Psychological Association Convention several years ago, one panelist declared that "the scientist in even attempting to interject love into a laboratory situation is by the very nature of the proposition dehumanizing the state we call love."

My view of the matter, and that of other love researchers, is rather different. We are quite aware of the difficulties inherent in the attempt to study love, and we have no illusion that we will ever unlock all of love's mysteries. But we also believe that especially at a time when many people are terribly confused about what love is or should be, the scientific study of love can make a positive contribution to the quality of life. To shun this task is no more justified than the taboo until several centuries ago against scientific study of the human body, on the grounds that such research would somehow defile it. In the words of one of the most humane of modern psychologists, the late Dr. Abraham H. Maslow, "We *must* study love; we must be able to teach it, to understand it, to predict it, or else the world is lost to hostility and to suspicion."

Interpersonal Heroin
Love Can Be An Addiction

Stanton Peele and Archie Brodsky

Peele received his Ph.D. in social psychology at the University of Michigan, and now is an assistant professor of organizational behavior at the Harvard Business School. He is President of Fred's Firm, Inc., where coauthor Brodsky is Creative Director. Fred's Firm is designed to help people achieve control over their lives in an institutionalized environment. The firm consults with nonprofit organizations and small businesses, as well as individuals interested in communicating their political and artistic ideas to others.

PEOPLE CAN BECOME ADDICTED to other people in the same way they become addicted to drugs. We are not using the term addiction in a metaphorical sense; we mean it literally. The interpersonal dependencies in the cases that follow are not *like* addictions. They *are* addictions.

Richard and Joan became lovers and isolated themselves from their friends while he was a sophomore in college and she was still in high school. Neither had ever had another lover. Whenever possible, they spent their time together and passed the evenings when they were apart on the phone. They supported each other in conflicts with family and friends. In this way, individually and as a pair, they ignored criticism from the outside. After a few years, they married and moved to a different university. There a more active social and political life beckoned them. They found they no longer needed each other as much. On the new campus Richard felt free from old male rivalries, and Joan grew more self-confident. She had no further use for a dominant man to direct her actions and her feelings about herself. The marriage ended immediately upon Joan's revelation that she had been having a clandestine affair.

Guy, a capable, young physician, lives in constant need of a woman's devotion.

An attractive, desirable man, Guy approaches every eligible partner with a sense of weakness and desperation, which he masks with bravado. When he finds a lover and begins to feel secure with her, he becomes manipulative, demanding that the woman show her loyalty by catering to him. His demands increase until the relationship is destroyed. Then he experiences withdrawal—sleepless nights, rapid heartbeat, muscle tightness and alternating periods of lethargy and frenetic movement. Until he finds another lover, his professional life suffers and he is listless and detached with friends. These symptoms show that Guy is addicted.

Something Is Missing. By addiction, we mean the classic, quasi-physiological syndrome identified by tolerance and by withdrawal. When a person requires larger and larger doses of a substance in order to obtain the desired effect, he has built up a tolerance to it. Withdrawal is the body's traumatic readjustment to a drugless state. Severe withdrawal looks like an attack of the flu—fever, sweating and shivering, nausea, rhinitis, alternating sleeplessness and drowsiness. Most agonizing to the addict, however, is an intangible feeling that something central is missing from his body and his existence.

Since tolerance and withdrawal are known through subjective reports and observations of behavior, there is no reason to think of them, and addiction, as primarily physiological phenomena.

Over the past few years, drug researchers have realized that the pattern of addiction can be generalized. Alcohol users, barbiturate users, tranquilizer users, tobacco smokers, and coffee drinkers, as well as narcotics users, may build up a tolerance and go through withdrawal, even though each of the drugs in question is chemically distinct from the other.

Although each drug acts differently on the body, the manifestations of tolerance

1. FORMATION OF INTERPERSONAL RELATIONSHIPS

It is natural that potential addictive objects are not limited to drugs alone. Anything that is safe, repetitive, predictable, and sufficiently consuming will do.

and withdrawal remain the same. In trying to explain why this is so, researchers have moved from the old concept of addiction as a physical dependence to a concept of addiction as a psychic dependence. The new orientation emphasizes the experience a person has with a drug. It asks, "What does the fixation do for the addict?" It suggests that drugs do not victimize a person, but that a person uses drugs to give his life a structure and to secure him against novelty and challenge.

People, including addicts, react to drugs according to their mental set and social setting. Both of these are cultural factors. Stanley Schachter's classic studies of emotional arousal demonstrated that the way a person behaves after a shot of adrenalin depends on his expectations and the social setting of the shot. Through field observations of marijuana smokers in the 1950s, Howard Becker found that learning to be a drug user involves more than mastering techniques and implements. It means learning what sensations the user is supposed to feel and why he is supposed to enjoy them. Louis Lasagna showed that the effects of morphine can be simulated by a placebo. Andrew Weil's marijuana research at Harvard [see "The Natural Mind," PT, October 1972] wiped out any serious doubt about the central role of set and setting. These data suggest that the biochemical aspects of addiction are only half the story. Addiction is partially self-induced. It is a function of the way a person interprets his experience. To understand this other half of the story, we need to look at the general pattern of addiction—the pattern revealed in the case histories of Richard and Joan and Guy.

Safe, Repetitive, Predictable. As a person becomes progressively more involved with a drug, he becomes more dependent on the reassurance it offers. He becomes less able to deal with the problems and uncertainties that made the drug desirable in the first place. Eventually, that person reaches a point where he cannot be deprived of this source of reassurance without considerable trauma. This is addiction. What has happened has little to do with physical dependence. By now, the addict not only feels more helpless facing the world at large, he also feels helpless facing the drug he needs. He believes that he can neither live without it nor free himself from

its grasp.

If addiction is something that happens inside a person's consciousness, if it is largely a matter of how someone responds to and organizes his experience, then it is natural that potential addictive objects are not limited to drugs alone. Anything that is safe, repetitive, predictable, and sufficiently consuming will do. It may be a job (as in Wayne Oates's *Confessions of a Workaholic*), or a socially or institutionally defined role.

The Jesus freak movement provides a striking contemporary example of the way religion can serve as the opiate of the people. Young people who join religious communes get an integrating concept for their lives. They abide by a set of rules and rituals, and in return bypass the chaotic flow of direct personal experience. They resolve any uncertainty by a cure-all faith in a higher power. Fundamentalist religion is a common form of addiction today, but not the most common. The most prevalent form, which to some degree probably touches all our lives, is interpersonal addiction, or addiction to someone we think we love.

Few Are Free. The susceptibility to addiction, interpersonal or otherwise, is not an all-or-none proposition. Very few of us are free from the impulse to retreat to safe ground. The shadings that separate interpersonal addiction from real love are as imperceptible as the changing color of the sky at twilight. But so are the shadings separating a drug addict from a drug user. Addiction is not only a quasi-physiological syndrome. It is a state of being. It is a word we often use to describe persons with a set of specific, interrelated personality traits.

In *The Road to H*, Isidor Chein lists some of the traits that go into the making of heroin addicts in the ghetto: passivity, low self-esteem, excessive consciousness of life's dangers, distrust of other people, high need for predictable oral gratification, defensively constricted personality structure, lack of creative motivation except when pushed, and an exploitative orientation toward others. Among the GI heroin users in Vietnam these characteristics were often absent. It was only the perils and constraints of their immediate situation that turned them into drug users. Thus, when the GIs returned to U.S. civilian life, most of them quit heroin, even though according to all the clichés about "drug fiends" they

were physically hooked on heroin [see "A Conversation with Jerome Jaffe," PT, August 1973].

Most of us come from the middle class. Passivity, low self-esteem and other interrelated personality traits curse the suburbs as they do the ghettos. But drug addiction, with its disruption of stable living habits, does not fit into the middle-class lifestyle. Interpersonal addiction, which accentuates possessive love and family privatism, fits only too well. Lee Rainwater has shown that lower-class persons are likely to form dependency relationships with concrete objects (e.g. alcohol, drugs), while middle-class persons are inclined to seek self-gratification through emotional attachment to other people.

The middle class prepares its offspring for an exclusive, one-to-one relationship in adulthood. Not finding many sure sources of interpersonal gratification in the open community, the middle-class adolescent comes instead to expect a single relationship to provide compensatory comfort. "The rest of the world may be cold and forbidding, but my spouse will still be with me."

Just as ghetto residents are constantly exposed to drugs, we in the middle class are constantly tempted by the false security of interpersonal addiction. Which of us succumb? It is possible to have a close relationship, or a marriage, without becoming addicts. An addictive relationship, like drug addiction, is a single overwhelming involvement that cuts off a person from life.

Addicted lovers become less able to cope with anyone or anything else. The relationship itself becomes paramount. It becomes the only point of certainty in a bewildering and dangerous world. The addicted lovers gradually let go of all other interests and activities.

Using a Lover. In contrast, a mature conception of love involves a desire to grow and expand oneself through the relationship, a desire for one's lover to do the same. If you love someone, you welcome anything that adds to the richness of your partner's experience, partly because it makes him or her more stimulating. If you are self-completed, you can welcome even the kind of experience that draws your lover away from you. Only if you are using your lover to fill up the emptiness within yourself do you begrudge him or her personal growth. This begrudging

As an addictive relationship unfolds, the lovers may seem to be seeing each other for the pleasure and excitement of it, but this doesn't last.

leads to jealousy and possessiveness.

An addictive relationship shows through when it ends in an abrupt, total and vindictive breakup—as traumatic as heroin withdrawal. When two people who have been extremely intimate suddenly turn around and hate each other, it is usually because they have been thinking more of themselves than of each other. When Richard and Joan broke up, their acquaintances were shocked that two people who had seemed so much in love could walk away from each other with such callous disregard for each other's feelings. But their love had been merely a temporary solution for their individual problems. *It was no love at all!!*

"Addiction" and "mature love" are words, black and white words. Some persons are "interpersonal addicts"; others are "mature lovers"; but most relationships only tend toward one extreme or the other. Most relationships are a combination of the two.

Addictive Vs. Mature Love. Are the lovers improved by the relationship? By some measure outside the relationship are they better, stronger, more attractive, more accomplished, or more sensitive individuals? Do they value the relationship for this very reason?

Do the lovers maintain serious interests outside the relationship, including other meaningful personal relationships?

Is the relationship integrated into, rather than set off from, the totality of the lovers' lives?

Are the lovers also friends? Would they seek each other out if they should cease to be primary partners?

Does each lover have a secure belief in his or her own value?

Answers to questions such as these only begin to untangle the subtleties differentiating addictive from mature love.

As an addictive relationship unfolds, the lovers may seem to be seeing each other for the pleasure and excitement of it, but this doesn't last. After awhile, the lovers are just there for each other, not for mutual growth or self-expression, but for comfort and familiarity. They reach a tolerance for each other. As for withdrawal, we have all seen the emotional and physical havoc that follows in the wake of some breakups, and the desperate ploys a jilted lover will try in order to get another "shot" of his or her beloved.

Trajectory of Self-Destruction. An addictive relationship is ultimately self-destructive, for the pair and for the individuals involved. The case history of Larry and Sheena traces the trajectory of this self-destruction.

When Larry arrived in New York to start his first job after taking a graduate degree in mechanical engineering, he contacted Sheena. On a previous visit to the city he and Sheena had enjoyed a brief fling together. Actually Larry had another woman in mind with whom he wanted to live, but that would take some working out, and in the meantime he needed a place to stay.

Larry told Sheena that he did not plan on staying with her long. He told her about the other woman. Sheena was a practicing clinical psychologist, and Larry thought of her as an independent professional woman who might enjoy a casual affair. He misjudged her. Sheena had married while still in her teens. She had become a mother when she was 19. Ever since her husband had drowned in a boating accident she had moved from one intense clinging relationship to another.

In the big city, Larry eagerly went ahead with his plans. At the same time he took advantage of the domestic comforts Sheena was only too happy to provide. One evening he went out to see the other woman. He returned to find Sheena hysterical. She had badly injured herself in a fall from a ladder, though whether accidentally or deliberately was uncertain. By the time Larry realized that his other, more passionately conceived affair was not going to get off the ground, he began to feel that he had stumbled into a horrible bind. He moved out of Sheena's apartment and in with a male friend. But when he returned to Sheena's to pack up his belongings, she implored him to stay, and he changed his mind again. He stayed on for several months more.

Next, Larry announced that he was moving out because he was not prepared to live with Sheena's child. He said he did not want the child getting too accustomed to him. He thought this would force a separation from Sheena, but Sheena sent her child to live with her former in-laws.

Larry stayed on in the apartment for two more years. Whenever he told Sheena that she was little more than a roommate to him, she would tell him he was crazy, that he was out of touch with his feelings. He, by not making good on his threats to move out, made her interpretation of the relationship as plausible as his own. In a sense, they had two relationships going on simultaneously, both of them self-serving and self-deluding. Nonetheless, neither partner had the self-respect to walk out.

The pair frequently fought, but no changes in behavior ever resulted. Finally, Larry found an engineering job in the north of England. He justified the move to Sheena as a step forward in his career. He told friends that by going to Europe he would be able to get away from her. But Sheena found an opening in a psychiatric program in London, and the couple flew to Europe together.

Larry settled in the north of England and Sheena settled in London. In her letters and phone calls to him, Sheena sounded sane and reasonable. Like a heroin addict feigning a cure to gain some ulterior end, she spoke of a new lover—not to make Larry jealous, but to reassure him that she would no longer cling to him.

Intimacy Begrudged. Larry invited Sheena to come for a visit. He knew he was in trouble when he got a call from her at the local railroad station the night before she was supposed to arrive. The visit was a running battle reminiscent of their days in New York. Sheena demanded, and Larry begrudged her, promises of future intimacy. Sheena's London lover either did not exist or did not matter. But Larry still did matter to her, above all else, and he apparently could not do without her.

Today, the relationship goes on in this manner. It takes a heavy toll. For one thing, it seriously retards Sheena's growth because it cushions her from reality. Instead of developing a broader, more open outlook in the aftermath of her husband's death, she has continued to live by the same limited conception of choices that led to her early marriage. "If we break up now," Sheena has said to Larry, "then all the time we've spent together will have been wasted." She is like a heroin addict obsessed with the next fix. She does not value the relationship for any meaning it has for her, or for what it contributes to her experience. She is interested only in Larry's continuing presence.

As for Larry, outwardly more adventurous and self-contained, his behavior is no more rational than Sheena's and just as

1. FORMATION OF INTERPERSONAL RELATIONSHIPS

Dependency on drugs is akin to middle-class dependency on spouses. It just so happens that society finds drug addiction unredeeming and so outlaws the syndrome.

self-destructive. Despite his efficient, expeditious air, Larry does not seem sure about what he wants from life. He is powerfully moved by someone who looks after him in small, domestic ways. Perhaps this makes him think he is being taken care of in larger ways. Incapable of dealing with his emotions, he needs a person like Sheena who bestows her affection indiscriminately. Larry is not only an ideal foil for an addict. He is an addict himself.

Larry and Sheena, as well as other interpersonal addicts, are not afflicted by an act of fate. Parents transmit their tendency toward interpersonal addiction to their children. Usually parents simply pass on to children their own need for external supports, their own need for an outside organizing principle for their lives. Sometimes, however, parents are directly dependent on their children, and in turn get their children addicted to them. This may lead to a situation where a child remains dependent on his or her

parents long after becoming an adult, as when a young divorcée moves back in with her parents and accepts their management of her personal and sexual affairs. Or it may lead to the kind of complicated mutual dependency depicted in *Portnoy's Complaint*—mutual, because Portnoy's obsessive preoccupation with his parents prevents him from acting autonomously.

Take the case of Alice, a clerk working in a large downtown office. Every day precisely at 4:00 p.m., Alice's telephone rings. Her 10-year-old son is calling to say that he is home safely from school. If the boy does not call, Alice frantically dials dozens of numbers all over her neighborhood. She will leave the office early if she cannot locate her son. But more often it is the boy himself who makes the extra calls, consulting his mother for detailed advice about some minor problem.

The broader outlines of this case history are more familiar. Alice is bright. She

is a single parent. She wants to go back to school. She says she can't because of her boy. In this way she avoids confronting her predicament. In return, Alice is teaching her son dependency instead of how to deal with life.

Love Vs. Exploitation. We believe that our concept of addictive love sheds light on the nature of middle-class family life as well as on the nature of addiction. Juxtaposing "love" and "addiction" gives us another way of looking at the world. By generalizing the pattern of addiction we can see that heroin users, for instance, are not a race apart. Dependency on drugs is akin to middle-class dependency on spouses. It just so happens that society finds drug addiction unredeeming and so outlaws the syndrome.

The concept of addictive love can provide us with another means of self-examination. Like Erich Fromm in *The Art of Loving*, we believe that if persons are to work toward mutual understanding and actualized love, we must learn to distinguish between love and the destructive exploitation of self and others that takes the name of love. *which is not love!*

COUPLING, MARRIAGE, AND GROWTH

What are the secret contracts and hidden conspiracies
that prevent us from being happy with a mate?
Why do we often cling to singleness out of the fear
that we will be somehow swamped by a love
union? Here, from an important new book, thoughtful
answers to these and other vital questions . . .

Roger Gould, M.D.

☐ Whether heterosexual, gay, or bisexual, we all feel an
increasing desire to have someone special and to be special
to someone else. By our late twenties, as our friends couple
off and spend time with other couples, if we *don't* have
someone special we feel left out.

Those of us who couple early sometimes feel superior to
our single friends. We have demonstrated our ability to be
intimate, yet in the back of our minds we wonder if we
would have the guts to bear the loneliness and rejection of
life without a partner. And that is why we stay married.

Those of us who remain single sometimes feel superior to
couples because we feel more self-reliant and independent,
but in the back of our minds we wonder whether we are just
too frightened of intimacy and dependency to find a
partner.

What's the right formula? Twenty-five years ago, the only
right way to live was as a heterosexual married couple planning to have children. All other life styles were deviant;
bachelorhood was a disease to be cured; most people cured
themselves by marrying in their early twenties. In 1978, our
society not only has a great deal of tolerance for bachelorhood but also tolerates homosexual bachelorhood and
nonpermanent couplings. Some even say marriage is bad for
human growth.

In this heyday of life-style variations and experimentation, a successful couple knows that when love is good, it is
addictive. The world looks and feels different. A walk in the
park with someone special is no longer just a walk in the
park. Our shared secrets become love-bonds, and we feel
confirmed as loving, lovable, worthwhile, and wanted.

As a couple, we *strive* for the ideal of two healthy, self-
reliant, clear-thinking people sharing a life enriched by each
person's contribution. We want to believe we are two independent people forming an interdependent unit. But alongside this hope is a fear—the fear that the other person will
siphon off our life energies and crowd out our sunlight. The
challenge of coupling, then, is how to have an intense relationship without losing our *self* in the other person.

But the truth is that we can lose our self only if that self
is already confined by our *own* rigid internal prohibitions—
as we all are to some degree—and if we go on to *confuse*
the location of that internal constraint. This can be formulated as a rule: *The only way a mutual relationship can
cause us to lose our self is when we blame our partner for
our own internal prohibitions*—that is, when we begin to
believe that he or she *could* make us feel more confident as
lovers, parents, men, women, social beings but, instead, *will-
fully* and *stubbornly* refuses to give us that confidence.

Once that mistake has been made—attributing to loved

ones the authority we should keep for ourselves—we feel
trapped and *controlled* by our partner; we must then
persuade, manipulate, or cajole him/her to gain permission
to grow.

Let's put this yet another way. The fears underlying our
particular lack of confidence—fears that we do not want to
face—tempt us to believe in an old false assumption left
over from childhood: *My loved ones are able to do for me
what I haven't been able to do for myself.*

The Cure of Love and the Conspiracy of Coupling

How does it happen that we tell ourselves that we lack the
capacity to remedy our inadequacies and that only a special
loved one can do this?

All of us occasionally feel inadequate in some area of our
life. "I have no talent" or, "I'm not strong enough, loving
enough, smart enough, masculine enough, or feminine
enough" are typical feelings we all share. Mostly, these feelings of self-doubt are what I have called "internal prohibitions." We are divided against ourselves and are afraid to
acknowledge our capacities and talents. They are not realistic
feelings, but feelings that express internal subjective fears.
Thus, we feel inadequate in the midst of success, or inconsistently attach obscure feelings of inadequacy to our body,
thinking it is ugly at one time and beautiful the next.

The loved one enters into these dynamics when we try to
get rid of the feelings of inadequacy by the "cure" of love
and the devotion of a loved one. It is quite true that being
told we are respected and important and cared for can wash
away our feelings of inadequacy—temporarily. The problem
is, it prevents us from confronting the feelings that we must
learn to outgrow—the fears that underlie our feeling of
inadequacy. And this is the danger: that too great a reliance
on the "cure" of love arrests our growth too much.

Now, this "cure" is in fact an unhealthy conspiracy with
those who have a special relationship to us. And the more
special the relationship, the more likely we are to depend on
the other person to help us. In this conspiracy—to avoid the
sources of our inadequacy—we don't have to do anything;
they, our loved ones, will do all that we can't do for
ourselves.

The problem is that such a relationship must eventually
become hostile because of its built-in dependency. Although
I no longer feel as inadequate, I still feel inferior to my
partner because he or she is able to do for me what I can't
do for myself.

The conspiracy is a no-win situation. Eventually, I feel
either hostile or dependent, and often both. In any case, my
simple pact with my loved one becomes a destructive
conspiracy that prevents my developing a fuller, more independent adult consciousness.

It is in this way, then, that we can "lose our self" when we
couple with another person. For the most part, only a small
portion of each relationship is based on the cure-by-love
conspiracy, though that part is where the problems are.

Conspiracy as an Interference With Coupling

There are many good practical reasons to remain uncou-
pled during one's twenties. There's complete freedom to

come and go as one pleases. It's so much easier to keep our own self-image in mind when it's not being blurred by someone else's constant presence. Being involved with many different people highlights different parts of us. We can make commitments to low-paying public-service or political jobs more easily if only our own living standard is being sacrificed. Jobs requiring extensive traveling and frequent dislocations can be taken. There's no reason to restrict whom we meet for lunch and no reason not to strike up a friendship when there's no potentially jealous partner waiting for a report. Love affairs, which are usually profound learning experiences, can be entered into fully without guilt or a makeshift schedule or a premature ending.

Single life clearly has advantages. Still, there are many in their twenties who don't want to remain single, yet are unable to couple. The problem is the conspiratorial relationships they stimulate. If we cannot let new relationships evolve naturally, but immediately insist that a new partner become a coconspirator with us in a script meant to cover up our inadequacies and fears, this demand interferes with intimacy and prevents coupling.

Joan, a beautician, was always abandoned early in a new relationship because she unilaterally decided the man was hers for the asking; she became petulant when the man continued to date other women.

Robin, a tall, slim beauty constantly wearing Daisy Mae shorts and revealing a bare midriff, couldn't understand why men didn't want to be just friends. Why did they always make a pass at her? It always ended her interest in them.

The common imperative buried in these patterns of behavior is: "Those who want me, I don't want. Those who don't want me, I do want, but only until it seems I can have them." The patterns are all organized by the old false assumption: "My loved ones can do for me what I can't do for myself."

Like the people in the examples above, we are all waiting for our special demands to be met. We demand a partner with traits that complement our special configuration of traits like a lock and a key. We run prospective partners through an obstacle course; we withdraw love for missteps. Partners looking to be loved by us end up feeling controlled, criticized, and guilty for not being what we decided they should be. Then they leave; or, if they stay, they come to resent us.

Though many people live out their love lives confined to these neurotic patterns, most of us learn not to place unrealistic expectations and dependence on our loved ones. We begin to have open, evolving relationships that can grow deeper because we are living in the present, not the past.

Marilyn. We all have patterns that continue to interfere with our intimacy, and living with someone brings them out more clearly than just dating. *When we believe that our loved ones can do for us what we are unable to do for ourselves, even a temporary partner has the power to hurt or help our self-image temporarily.*

Marilyn's relationships with the many men she lived with were all characterized by her proclamation: "I am a crushed little girl who can't bear pain and must be protected from the world by a big strong man." Her soft voice and kittenish ways softened her demanding look: "I am hurt; what are you doing just standing there?" But she was determined enough to leave each man after a year or so because he didn't take good enough care of her.

What's more, by the time she left, each man had her up on a pedestal, which made her feel quite powerful and superior. At one and the same time, she felt contemptuous of the men for letting her get away with her childish demands and felt resentful of anyone who didn't let her get away with it. After many such episodes, she knew she

couldn't grow up unless she learned to relate in a new way, but she couldn't bring herself to give up the indulgences she won by being a "crushed little girl."

Marilyn feels that someone special has to come along and forcibly take away her privileges. So far, no such man has appeared, so she moves from one man to the next when it's convenient for her, and despite the impact on the man she is leaving. She always considers marriage, then leaves just as the next affair begins. It's while making the decision about marrying Alan that Marilyn finally conquers the assumption that someone special will do for her what she can't do for herself. Marilyn knows she isn't going to marry Alan. However, she prefers to stay with him until a new man comes along. But she also knows that Alan couldn't stand to lose her to another man.

It's a conflict she has managed to avoid with all the previous men in her life—her need for a painless, free-floating life versus a friend's right not to be hurt needlessly by her. Her wish to be the powerful baby who is spared pain through the sacrifices made by indulgent parents (Alan is just a substitute) must be reconciled with the fact that she's a twenty-seven-year-old adult who is consciously choosing to badly hurt a trusting human being.

Is she going to wait for someone to discipline her, or is she going to discipline herself? "I know I should, but I don't want to" is her first response. She can't convince herself that her intuition is wrong about not marrying him, nor can she pretend that he won't be hurt unnecessarily if she leaves for another man. She can't ignore the contradiction. She must decide whether she will remain a spoiled, indulged child or whether she will become an adult who accepts her own mind, whether it causes her pain or not.

Marilyn chose to leave Alan as her conscience dictated, and after a year of living alone and enjoying her independence, she met a man who cared for her deeply but wouldn't respond to her demands. "I'm a real danger to you," he said, "because you can't control me; you're going to hate me for being strong, but then you'll love me." And so it was.

For many singles who begin to couple, power and control are the issues. No matter how we disguise it, when we're relating with the assumption that someone special owes us a special feat of magic, we're exercising our childhood desire for omnipotence. We are treating our partner as an actor in our personal drama. Anyone who won't play out the assigned script, we stay away from. Anyone who goes along with us, we feel in control of, even while we're bitterly complaining about being controlled or misused. These dramas are multilayered sadistic-masochistic games reflecting a basic fear of and anger toward the opposite sex.

We escape these self-imposed traps through the same sequence Marilyn went through in her decision to leave Alan: We must first recognize the pattern, then remain scrupulously honest at a critical decision-point, and then have the good fortune or good sense to choose someone who is not vulnerable to our controlling ways.

Laura. There's more to learn from living together than just the important lessons of how we interfere with intimacy. When we live with someone, our defenses are penetrated every day and our deepest personality secrets are exposed. Our lack of confidence comes out through our bravado; our timidity shows through our intimidating postures; our ignorance shows despite our know-it-all attitude; and our dependence pokes through our self-reliance.

If we're lucky, our nakedness will not hurt us badly but will teach us a beautiful lesson. Laura was such a person— lucky, and willing to accept it and learn from it.

After John returned to his wife, Laura reviewed what living with him had taught her during their six months together. Laura learned that pretending to know all of the answers didn't work and wasn't necessary. John could see when she was bluffing and called her on it and convinced her he didn't think she was stupid if she didn't have an encyclopedic knowledge or a well-thought-out opinion on every subject. When she shared her personal feelings, he listened and understood instead of telling her she was "crazy" for not being more conventional.

But it could also have turned out badly. John could have made Laura feel she was odd for having her own views, or crazy and stupid for pretending to know it all. She was quite vulnerable and instead of promoting her self-confidence, he could have worked her over viciously.

Had that happened, Laura would have learned a bitter lesson in life—that people can work you over for their own purposes and that people have blind spots that don't allow them to understand you or tolerate your individuality. Laura could have left that six-month relationship wondering for years what was wrong with her before she finally came to see clearly that it was not her, but him. By allowing John into her special space, Laura gives him some of the same enormous power that our parents had—to determine what's "real" about us. That John did not misuse that power is Laura's great fortune.

From Coupling to Marriage

As stated earlier, the more special the relationship, the more we expect from the other person. Also, the more intimate the form of the relationship, the greater our fear of it. For example, we are less afraid to date than we are to live together, and less afraid to marry than to have children.

Each form of relationship carries its own advantages and disadvantages, its own degree of intimacy or specialness. From single life up to marriage with children, the more intimate or special the form of the relationship, the greater the threat—and the greater our opportunity for happiness.

What are the threats associated with marriage? When a relationship deepens and marriage is considered, we're afraid of being trapped by greater commitment, and the latent fears about our partner's long-run potential reach center stage. Is he or she a loser, someone who will be too dependent or too overpowering; or someone who will falter under the pressures of family responsibility?

Having lived together is not a reliable guide to future behavior because that kind of impermanence has differing effects on people. It makes some of us miserable. We can't enjoy the relationship even when it's good because we're worrying about when it's going to end. We're afraid to put too much into it, for fear we'll end up with nothing. On the other hand, that same impermanence is what allows others of us to join the relationship more fully, for we have an easy escape to allay our fears of being trapped. The partner who is most pained by the impermanence is more likely to flourish in the marriage; the one who feels most relieved by the impermanence is most likely to feel trapped in marriage.

"I don't understand it; we lived together for two years, but after we married he turned into a stranger. He's become bossy and picky." "Before, she was industrious and optimistic; since we've been married, she's become morose and lazy; the only time she became her old self again was when I hurt my back and she had to work and take care of things."

So marriage is quite different from living together. But many of us don't have negative reactions to marrying; we luxuriate in the advantages. There is a great release of energy from the worries of impermanence. Competition is markedly reduced. We're not on the make, looking for a better fit. Fidelity becomes a background concern. There is a calm sense of direction; we can invest in the future by working out our problems in a new way—with the door to escape closed. We face our more intense problems with the understanding that they have to be resolved. With this commitment, we feel more solid in our everyday life.

Now, whether we can work out our problems—escape the trap of conspiracy and grow—depends in part on our conception of marriage.

If we see marriage as a static arrangement between two unchanging people, any substantial change in either of those people must initially be perceived as a violation of the unspoken contract on which the marriage is based. Change sets off guilt in one partner and envy in the other because it's not "supposed" to happen.

In a really happy, really adult marriage, change in one partner is met gladly by the other partner, who is not afraid of the growth, but welcomes it, intellectually, at least, as an interesting improvement in the relationship—and also sees it as the beginning of his or her next induced growth step. Then, when envy occurs—and it is bound to—it is not cause for righteous indignation; instead, it is the sign that a personal inadequacy has been exposed; it is a source of information to the individual who feels envious.

The static concept of marriage fosters the conspiracies of marriage that warehouse and slow down growth; the growth concept of marriage encourages empathic separateness and a continuous, flowing rhythm of change. In a growth marriage, we are married and divorced many times in the sense that we are continually divorced from old arrangements and married to new ones. We negotiate from the present only. "But you were that way before" is irrelevant. No guilt about our new self surfacing. No responsibility to remain as we were. Only a responsibility to handle change with integrity and sensitivity to our partner.

What are our chances of forming a growth marriage? If we look at this question sociologically, we can see that our chances are good. The static and growth concepts of marriage co-exist right now in our society. If one partner embraces the ideology of growth while the other tries to stop the change because of the belief that marriage should be static, then divorce is inevitable. But as society creates more partners who believe in the growth concept of marriage, we may see not only a new stabilization of marriage, but also a new form of the institution. Living through the rhythms of one's own growth against the pushes and pulls of the changes of a beloved partner over a lifetime creates a dynamic relationship. Society may come to view marriage not so much as a fixed economic unit, but as potentially the best route to the highest level of personal unfolding.

On the other hand, we may be witnessing the beginning of a new form of married family-life where we exchange partners whenever a new part of ourselves requires confirmation. All children will be members of extended families; everyone will have half brothers, half sisters, half mothers, half fathers, and dozens of grandparents.

The cement of static marriages was loosened forever when we became a sexually permissive society. Once children have grown up believing in their right to be sensuous and sexually free, they're never going to buy the same principle of fidelity that all of us bought when we were young. Once any of us discovers our mate does not have to be our only sexual resource, the power of the sex-drive will no longer serve as the cement it used to be during the rough times.

Perhaps as a society we're conducting a grand experiment by forcing this next generation of adults to do battle with sexual jealousy directly. On the one hand, if each partner sees his or her own sexual freedom as an inalienable right, battles over jealousy/possessiveness issues are inevitable. On the other hand, if they succeed in resolving these issues constructively, the present painful aspects of living within a growth ideology will be greatly diminished. If monogamy and fidelity prevail, it could be at a higher level of maturity: "I choose this because it's the best way, not because I'm told it's the only way."

(1) that is, a relation based mostly on sex, is no relation

Measure Your Marriage Potential: A Simple Test That Tells Couples Where They Are

A very simple test is described that has proved highly effective when used by married couples. It is a subjective instrument, so it need not be administered or scored by a professional. Yet couples who use it consistently can learn a great deal about their relationship and do so in terms of positive insights which they can then use to promote mutual growth. It can be an effective tool when used with married couples in an educational setting, in an enrichment or therapy group, or in counseling.

David R. and Vera C. Mace

David R. Mace and Vera C. Mace, are Founders and Presidents of the Association of Couples for Marriage Enrichment (ACME), P. O. Box 10596, Winston-Salem, N.C. 21708.

On a recent assignment in South Africa, our program included a public meeting in Kempton Park. It was to be held in the town hall, with the mayor in attendance. In order to create public interest, the local newspaper ran a competition open to all its readers, for which a prize was offered. Each entry had to list ten items considered important for the achievement of a successful marriage.

A week or so before we were due to arrive, we were requested to submit in a sealed envelope our own list, with the items in order of importance. The prize, we were informed, was to go to the entry or entries that most nearly corresponded to our list.

We dutifully made our list, and found it a challenging exercise. At a later public meeting in another South African town, we decided to take the list as our theme. Sitting together on the platform, we dialogued about our own marriage, reporting what progress we felt we had made in some of the listed areas, and inviting the couples in the audience to go home and do likewise. The meeting went very well, and the audience response was enthusiastic.

Reflecting on this experience, we realized that we had made an exciting discovery. We had stumbled on something we had always felt we needed—a simple way of enabling married couples to measure their appropriated marriage potential. We revised our list, jumbled the order, and turned it into a test. We then tried it out on groups of couples with whom we worked while we were still in South Africa. Back in North America, we continued to use it with couple groups, large and small, in programs from coast to coast. It worked like a charm every time. In program evaluation sheets turned in by participating couples, again and again the marriage potential test was mentioned as having been unusually helpful.

Before describing the test, let us try to put the issue in perspective.

The marriage enrichment movement represents a new approach to a field that has been largely dominated by pathology-oriented and static concepts. The "medical model" sees certain couples as having "sick" marriages—they are afflicted by some infection, crippled by some injury, and must be healed or restored by applying an appropriate remedy. The "rehabilitation model" thinks in similar terms—the marriage is "in trouble," the couple have "problems," and the resulting disorder must be "tidied up" or "straightened out" by making appropriate repairs. The "rescue model" sees the couple being swept away by some destructive force, threatened by some awful catastrophe, and the marriage must be saved," the couple "reconciled" or "restored." Beneath all this language there lies a conceptual framework that sees marriage as *static*. The operation to be performed is viewed as picking up something that has fallen out of place and been damaged, repairing it and putting it back where it was before, or where the "normal" marriage ought to be. The literature of marriage counseling is replete with this kind of thinking.

Much of our research has been based on similar concepts. Marriages have been studied to find out how "successful" they are, whether they have brought "happiness," or "satisfaction," whether they are "stable" or "harmonious," "cohesive" or "adjusted." While these terms are not wholly static, they imply that there is some kind of fixed reference point that is typified by the "good" marriage, the couple who have "made it" or "arrived."

By way of contrast, we offer for consideration a dynamic concept of marriage as a fluid, flexible interaction process which can never be stable, never established or completed; a process of ongoing growth, adaptation, and change that never ends, moves toward objectives but never completely arrives because the objectives themselves change. The word "enrichment" is perhaps not the best term to express this, but it does suggest a continuing process of getting better. "Marital growth" is a more apt term. Reuben Hill has suggested "development," and this also conveys the right idea. Even "marital potential" suggests an end or goal. However, it serves well in getting the idea across; because where it is demonstrated, as in the test we are describing, couples grasp it clearly.

In promoting marriage enrichment, our greatest difficulty is in communicating this new way of looking at the dyadic relationship. Talk to the average couple about "marital growth" and their minds seem to go blank. They have no frame of reference into which to fit such an idea. The momentary mental paralysis is then followed, for many, with vague feelings of alarm, revealed by such defensive responses as, "Oh, we don't need any help. Our marriage is all right." The idea that there might be room for improvement in their relationship is frightening to them because it carries the subtle implication that they might have "problems," which would mean that they were inadequate or incompetent.

Since most couples appear to be in this unfortunate situation, we must conclude that they are not open to the concept of marital growth, and that they are, therefore, living far below their potential. This is a disturbing thought, but it seems to be valid. Every marriage counselor knows how skillfully couples in serious trouble can put up a brave show in public. Today's high divorce rates, however, are bringing out into the open the grim facts about the low levels at which married couples have been living. The estimate of Lederer and Jackson (1968) that couples in their highest marital category represent no more than 5-10 per cent of all married couples, is probably pretty near the truth. The difficulty, until now, has been to find some way to bring home this fact to the average couple, to convince them that with appropriate help they can greatly improve their relationship, and to assure them that this can be very rewarding to them both. This is exactly what the marriage potential test now makes possible.

The test is extremely simple, and it is self-administered and self-scored. The procedure is to have husband and wife take it separately and *without collaboration of any kind*. Then they sit down together, compare their scores, and discuss the implications.

All they need are paper and pencil. We ask the partners—it can be done in a counseling interview, a couples group, or a public meeting—to write down the list of ten areas of the marriage relationship. Our current list is as follows:

1. Common Goals and Values
2. Commitment to Growth
3. Communication Skills
4. Creative Use of Conflict
5. Appreciation and Affection
6. Agreement on Gender Roles
7. Cooperation and Teamwork
8. Sexual Fulfillment
9. Money Management
10. Parent Effectiveness

We now explain that we want each partner to enter a score, on a scale of 0 to 10, to the right of each item. The score represents where the marriage now stands, in relation to what it could be if every possible resource were put to work in bringing it up to its full potential, as perceived by the individual. We take a couple of items and comment on what a perfect score might represent—under "appreciation and affection," for example, it would mean that neither partner ever missed an opportunity to give the other warm support and praise, or to communicate feelings of love and tenderness. We add—"If that's where your marriage is now, give yourself 10." We suggest, however, that just as few couples would rate their marriage 0 in any area, so few would feel able to rate it 10. However, we say, "Give your marriage an honest score, but don't underrate it, either."

As a method of scoring, we suggest first running quickly down the list and making quick, spontaneous judgments, and entering the figures in pencil. Then go back over the items, make a more careful evaluation of each, and if necessary change the figures to represent your considered verdict. All this may take about ten minutes.

When all scores are complete, they should be added up. The resulting figure represents the percentage of your marriage potential which you have already appropriated, the difference between that and 100 indicating your unappropriated potential.

The next step is for husband and wife to set a time when they can be alone together, uninterrupted, for at least an hour—two hours if possible. They then share the scores they have given the marriage and compare them—first the total percentage, then the scores for the separate items.

Nearly all couples who have taken this test have found it a significant experience. Some find their percentage scores identical or nearly so, which usually means that their separate perceptions of the marriage as a whole are closely congruent. We have worked with couples, however, with percentages widely separated—in one extreme case the difference was 50 per cent, which led to a crisis that motivated the couple to seek the counseling they desperately needed. When a significant disparity in total scores exists, this obviously calls for careful and thorough examination, and confronts the couple with the necessity of finding out why they place such different values on their relationship.

Next, the couple will go through the various items. Again, some scores may be identical or very close. In these areas, they are obviously in agreement. But if the scores agree and are low, they clearly have some work to do. "Don't be discouraged about those low scores," we tell them. "What they mean is that you have money in the bank that you've never used. There are some good things waiting to be claimed."

For many couples, the discussion of the test has been very challenging. "We've been avoiding the realities of our marriage for years," some have said. "But this really confronted us with what we have always known, but never faced. Now we mean to do something about it." Also couples, faced with a disparity in a particular area, have said, "We couldn't at first figure out why we disagreed about this. But as we talked it over, we discovered something about our relationship that we never knew before. This has put us on the track of some exciting new possibilities."

One couple who had joined a group, as they put it, "to see for ourselves some of the techniques you use—we don't need any help for our own marriage", came back after doing the test and said, "We've been kidding ourselves and other people that we have a very good marriage. Our relationship is certainly on a plateau—but now we know that it isn't a very high plateau. We've been shaken out of our complacency, and now we've got a lot of growing to do."

When we realized how powerfully this test can give couples motivation to start working on their marriage, we began suggesting that, following the private session in which they share their scores, they should go on to make a "growth plan" together. We give them no specific instruction about this—we simply suggest that they agree on the steps they want to take to improve their relationship in their deficient areas, put this in the form of a written statement, and both sign it. This constitutes a commitment they have made to each other, and to which they can refer back later. We are careful to warn them against the danger of attempting too much too quickly. "Do it in easy, manageable steps," we caution. "If you try to jump over a 4-foot wall, and you're only able to clear a 3-foot wall, you're going to hurt yourselves." Ideally, we recommend that they share their commitment with another couple or couples to whom they can report progress, or with a counsellor who can guide them through the growth process.

One interesting feature of the test is that it can be taken again and again. Since the measure of marriage potential used is subjective, and not objective, your score can change over time. Obviously this can rise as growth takes place. Also, as you gain clearer understanding of yourselves and each other, you may alter your evaluation of what is possible for the marriage, either downward or upward. The test scores change as you progressively move toward a more realistic perception of what you are capable of achieving together.

Why did we select only ten areas, and why those particular ten? We made it ten because we wanted the test to be very simple and easy to take. Of course the list could be expanded to 20, 30 or more items. But then it would take longer to do and interest might lag. Also, calculating the percentage of achieved potential would be more complicated. The couple's discussion together would also have to cover many more items. Experience has confirmed our judgment that ten items is a convenient number to use. But there's nothing to prevent anyone else from using any number of items.

The items we first selected have been changed a little and they now represent areas of marriage that are brought up for discussion again and again in couple groups. Some that could well be added are Decision Making, Use of Time Together, Balancing Separateness and Togetherness. We do in fact suggest one of these as an alternative to Parent Effectiveness for couples who are childless or have grown-up children. Again, if you don't like the ten on our list, you can substitute your own.

We have asked ourselves why this test, upon which we stumbled almost by accident, has been so effective. Here, by way of summing up, are some of our answers—

1. *It is Simple*, both to explain and to take. No elaborate explanations are required. People easily understand it. All they need is a pen or pencil, and a very small piece of paper. Less than thirty words have to be written down, which takes a matter of minutes. It can be administered, without any preparation, in a public meeting. If necessary, you can explain it briefly, and ask people to do it privately at home later.

2. *It is Self-Administered and Self-Scored*. No printed materials are handed out, then collected up. We have thought of using printed sheets to save time, but decided that the act of writing down the items one by one, and having them in your own handwriting, makes it more personal. No technical or professional processes are involved that might arouse suspicion or put you on your guard. All you have in your hand is what you have yourself written down, and it remains in your possession. This is really a do-it-yourself project.

3. *It is Specific*. It brings what might otherwise be vague theoretical concepts right down to earth. A person could listen to endless talk about marital growth and marriage enrichment and never really apply it to his or her own relationship. But take this test, and it immediately comes alive. "Now I see exactly what you mean, and now we know exactly where we are," people will say. This is the complete answer for the defensive couple who say, "Our marriage is all right." Once they have done the test, they know just how "all right" they are.

4. *It is Private*. No third person is involved. No one else works out your score—you do it yourself. You don't have to report it to anyone—you can tear it up if you like, and no one will ever know what your score was. You don't even have to share it with your partner—but in that event it doesn't get you very far. In fact, sharing the scores with someone else proves to be very helpful; but the point is that you are not *required* to do so—the decision is your own.

5. *It Fosters Cooperation*. Though an individual can do the test alone, in order to be effective it must bring husband and wife together in a realistic encounter such as they have often not experienced for years, sometimes never before. For some it opens up creative and constructive communication that gets them off to a new beginning. It is impossible to be indifferent to the facts which the test reveals. They cannot be evaded or denied. Whatever they do or refuse to do about it, the partners know that—"This is our marriage."

6. *It Activates to Positive Action*. Once the couple know where they stand, they are strongly impelled to do something about it. If the test results are encouraging, they feel affirmed; if challenging, they now know on the basis of their own judgment that things can be better, and this is a powerful stimulus to act together. It they evade the challenge, it is hard to forget, hard to blame anyone or anything else for their failure to take responsibility. What the test says is—"Now you know that your relationship can be better than it is. It's up to you."

7. *It Can be Repeated*. We would, in fact, recommend that couples take the test once a year, or more often. This will give them an opportunity to check on their growth, and be aware of their changing perceptions of their relationship. It would be interesting and helpful to compare your test scores over a period of years, and to try to interpret what the changes mean.

We might add, in conclusion, that the test is entirely at your disposal, free of charge! There are no materials to buy, no royalties to pay. You don't need to have a franchise, you don't need to undergo training to be a qualified instructor, you don't have to complete any forms to indicate to whom you gave the test, and where, and when. We offer it to anyone who can make use of it—unconditionally, free, gratis, and for nothing!

REFERENCE

Lederer, W. I., & Jackson, D. D. *The mirages of marriage.* New York: W. W. Norton, 1968.

2 Maintenance of Relationships

Once two individuals have formed a relationship, their foremost task is to maintain it. Historically, where the family functioned as a relatively complete economic unit, its maintenance tasks were straightforward tasks of necessity. The adults and their children all worked toward a common goal—economic and physical survival, via the production of goods, services and new family members.

Your great-grandmother perhaps married at eighteen, bore many children, and died at fifty. Today's woman will probably marry later, choose to have one or two children, and will live some thirty or forty years past child-bearing age. She is likely to work outside the home, and only slightly less likely to be divorced.

Today we have the luxury and the burden of choice. We choose whether or not to marry, to have children, and to conform to the old moral, sexual, and social standards. The more alternatives a culture allows, the greater the burden on individuals to fashion a relationship that will work for them personally. And once this relationship is formed, the process of sustaining it becomes the foremost task of the participants. Keeping a living unit functioning satisfactorily involves at least three elements—communication, compromise, and consideration.

Communication involves identifying our feelings and sharing them with others. Good communication is extremely important to the success of a relationship. Compromise helps to maintain a relationship and is often experienced during problem solving. Compromise blends communication and consideration. Consideration, also important to maintaining relationships, entails taking into account another's feelings along with your own.

This section of *Annual Editions: Readings in Marriage and Family 79/80* is divided into three subsections. The first presents various perspectives on marriage and family, the second examines the current transition in sex roles, and the last subsection explores means of enriching the marital relationship. The critical questions asked by social scientists and others who want to know if the family is dying, obsolete, fragmented, or under siege is examined in the first subsection. Both positive and negative views are presented. These views vary from viewing marriage as a "wretched institution" to the suggestion that there is "no better invention than the family." The second subsection evaluates sex roles and the constraints they put on people. On the other hand, the problems and confusion of working through the changing roles and goals for both men and women are discussed. The final subsection explores marriage counseling, sex therapy, and several myths in the areas of love, sex, children, and marital happiness.

Looking Ahead: Challenge Questions

What factors have brought the American family to the point that some say it is dying? Have the onslaughts come from within or outside the family?

Does the American marriage contribute to interpersonal growth?

Have women made significant advances in their roles within the family? Have men?

What changes, if any, can we expect to find in the structure and function of marriage and the family in the year 2,000?

Changing sex roles requires adjustment by many people. Do the benefits of such adjustments outweigh the disadvantages?

What is the role of "love" in maintenance of a marriage?

The Future of the American Family

Kenneth Keniston

Over the last century parents have had dwindling control over the resources they need, the people with whom they share the job of raising children. In colonial days, the American family worked together on the farm. The parents had a very large say in the kind of work their children did. Most schooling was done inside the home and not in schools outside the home. Health care was a family matter except in extreme or unusual cases.

Although parents weren't really self-sufficient, at least they didn't have to go to professionals, experts or outside institutions for the normal job of raising children. Today, that's changed very drastically—now it's impossible for any two people to raise children without extensive help.

On the good side, that means that children get a quality of health care that was unimaginable one or two centuries ago. Many people feel, in fact, that education is better, particularly in dealing with kids who have some difficulty in learning. And there is education for everyone today; there wasn't a century or two ago.

On the other hand, it means that parents have to deal with a whole array of professionals and often faceless institutions over which they have very little control. They don't have any say over the way the local schools run, very little say over the kind of advertising on television, of what is on television at all. They confront the pediatrician or the health care person from a position of, often, confusion. They don't really know how to talk to this person.

It's not that families are collapsing, but in the last quarter of a century, there's no question that there have been very large changes going on in families, the way they organize themselves and do their business. You can measure, for example, the increase of women in the paid labor force and that is very dramatic. It's not just an American phenomenon, it happens all over the world. A majority of mothers with school-aged children are out working. A very high percentage, over a third of mothers with preschool children, are working outside the home. So that overall, the typical American woman today is a mother who works—part-time, full-time or a combination of both.

Another crucial factor is the rising divorce rate. It's not that those children live forever in single-parent families, because many people who divorce remarry. But there are two phenomena: the children who spend significant portions of their childhood in the single-parent home, which people estimate is up to 42 percent for children born now. Obviously, some people never remarry, some people do, but there's a period of separation that's going to affect between one-third and one-half of all American children being born today. About one out of six children in America lives in a single-parent family at the moment, and up to half will spend some time in a single-parent family. And then there is the new phenomenon of a reconstituted family in which one of the parents, usually the father, is a stepfather, so that approximately the same percentage of children are now living in families where they have one biological parent and one by marriage.

But other factors make much more difference to a child's life than marital status of the parents—a lot of those things are immeasurable. Other things being equal, though, it looks like the best arrangement for a child is to be raised by two grownups, a man and a woman who want a child and will care for him. That's a good arrangement, even if one is not a biological parent.

There are strains with stepparents, but they are felt more by the parents than the kids. The stepparent often questions his or her goodness as a parent, but the kids seem to do fine. The worst thing for children is a mother and a father who don't get along well at all, particularly if their not-getting-along involves the child in their conflict.

Many other things are so much more important than a divorce. It is still true in this country that if you want to predict which children are going to have measurably successful adulthoods—do well, say they're relatively happy, have reasonable incomes, not end up in mental hospitals, and so on—the best way of predicting this is the economic and social status of the family in which they're born. The best prediction is that kids who were born well-off and under good circumstances will end up better off than kids who are born in the bottom 30 percent of the population. The richer you are at birth, the better your chances of being rich as an adult: The poorer you are, the smaller your chances.

The other things that matter are very hard to measure. They're not all luck, though luck does play a role. They have to do with the things we've always talked about—the consistency and fidelity of parents toward their children, responsiveness, and the child's ability and resourcefulness, which are inborn. A lot of the research on child development suggests that the most determining things as far as the children's liveliness and interaction with the world has to do with the capacity of the parents to respond to those children as unique individuals. To play with them. To affect and be affected by the children's behavior in some unique way. There are all sorts of technical words—contingency, interaction and so on. It comes down to spending time with and respecting the child. Those things really matter as far as developing a child's sense of the world.

One of the reasons why poverty and being on the bottom of the heap affect people so much is that it takes away energy and attention. The struggle to survive—whether there's going to be enough to pay the fuel bill, how you get food for the kids, how you deal with the welfare agency, find a job—takes so much of a person's spirit and morale that the kind of playful attentiveness that we know is a good thing for parents to develop just isn't there.

Mothers who work have a particularly difficult problem finding enough time to do everything they want to do. The notion that women are working because they're fed up with their families or they're doing it just for spending money or they want luxuries—it's just an enormous fallacy. She works because she needs the money, because the income is important for her family, not against her family. Women are working for reasons similar to men's and that involves income.

There are very few working mothers who don't worry about neglecting their children. "What's happening to the children? I should be with them." And there's no question that breaking the role sort of stereotype—the tradition of the stay-at-home mother who has all the cookies ready when the kids come home from school and is always available, always on tap, is very difficult.

The evidence about working mothers and their effects on children doesn't support that. If the mother is forced to stay home against her wishes, against her better judgment and what would be good for the family, herself, and is bored and restless and feels she's giving up too much, then the kids are going to suffer. And they visibly do. They don't do quite as well at school and they're more upset and they have more problems.

There are other mothers, particularly mothers who either don't have husbands or do have husbands but feel compelled to work in order to keep the family finances going at all, who, in their best judgment would be better off at home. They really want to be at home with their kids. That's what is meaningful to them, and if they have to go to work for economic reasons or whatever reasons, their children also seem to suffer. The people who stay home because they want to be at home or are working because they want to be working—their kids seem to do the best.

If you ask, "What makes the working mother feel okay about working?," then you get into some of the more traditional things. Can she find good, adequate care for her children when she's not working? Does her job allow her enough flexibility so that she can still spend time with her husband, so that she can still get to the school conference, take the kids to the dentist, whatever? It's almost always been true, until recently, that when the job and the family conflict, the family has to go.

The job has to be flexible and somehow the mother and father have to juggle the kids. That's one of the things that makes many people unhappy about working—and rightly so. A mother has to be able to respond to what the kids need, when they need it. If they get sick or need her at a school conference, she has to be able to go. This applies to the father, too, if he is raising the children.

Families face many other pressures too, including the pressures of high technology. I think there's a feeling among parents at all levels that living in this very ambiguous man-made universe, where there are all these good things we want, presents great problems. We need appliances, automobiles; electricity comes from atomic reactors somewhere; we put things into foods to prevent spoilage. And at the same time, they're saying all this may be destroying us, poisoning us, wasting our minds.

We don't know how to deal with it. It's too complicated for the average person and above all, we don't have any say. In tangible forms, the thing that every parent faces is what to do about television. What do you allow kids to see? How do you monitor it? What about advertising? The programs are violent. They deal with adult sex—a whole lot of things you may not want your child to see. Or they're just idiotic and mindless. But how does a parent exercise any influence over this? It contributes to a general feeling of hopelessness. Everybody talks about it, but how can you do anything about it, short of just turning off the television set?

I'm not being optimistic or pessimistic, but I think it's possible for parents to get together and to have some influence on their local television shows, for example. It is possible for parents to say, "Look, we think that standards of radiation activity or chemical safety really ought to be set with the most vulnerable person, say a pregnant woman, in mind." It wouldn't happen automatically, but in the long run it would have an effect.

The parents' roles have been redefined so that the parent is not the coordinator, like an orchestra conductor, who really did have a responsibility for coordinating all these outside forces: for monitoring television, for reviewing teachers, for health care, day care, for periodic checks of this or that, for dealing with special consultants on the other. This was sort of the new parental role. It's caricatured in the picture of the suburban housewife in the sixties who ran around with a station wagon going from one place to another, and spending all of her time—it's always a her—arranging things for the kids, taking them from one lesson to another. The parent as chauffeur. The level of living in a high technology society that has costs and benefits is not going to go away. There's no magic solution for it.

What's terrifically important is the whole so-called changing of sex roles and family goals. It's clear there are more and more women outside the home. Also, there are fewer men working. In fact, the women's labor force is basically going up; men's is dropping slightly. The two lines are coming closer and closer together.

The reality is that not only are women doing things that have been traditionally defined as male, like working outside the home. But men have to take more care of the house. They have to do the shopping. There's more child care shared. There's split-shift marriages, for better or worse. There's a whole kind of personal level at which these big economic changes are affecting people very drastically and painfully.

A lot of people are deciding, "Gee, now that I don't have to be economically dependent, that also raises the question of whether I have to be psychologically dependent. And maybe I don't like this marriage at all." The man who says, "Gee, now that my wife is earning so much, I won't have to support her."

I don't think there will ever be a time when everybody is

doing the same thing. There is a biological difference between the sexes, and I think it will be a long time before men spend as much time with small children as women do.

On the other hand, more and more families are deciding who is going to do what. They are achieving some sort of parity, in terms of sharing the household tasks, of sharing the homework, the jobs that women have done in the past. This is coming increasingly without a sense of political consciousness in a lot of cases. There are a lot of people who don't like all this women's liberation stuff necessarily, but they end up changing their roles really because the facts of their lives have changed.

I'm often struck that among professional and highly-educated families there is a lot of talk about sharing. And there are some cases where it really happens. But so often a man has a very high level job when his wife goes back to work that somehow when push comes to shove, it's the wife and the wife's job that gives way. They revert to the old roles again.

If there's a question in the family of who stays home—well, obviously, the man says, he's got a very important job, he has to go to a conference, a crucial meeting—then it's the wife again who is in charge of the family.

There is going to be a lot more parity as the wife's work becomes more important financially. It will be no less important than the man's in terms of prestige. As this happens the roles will come more in balance with each other, and both the wife and husband will have to decide together how the demands of both of their jobs will affect their homelife.

If you really were deciding what you want a child to have, you'd start with caring parents who want a child. You'd want people who were responsive and loving, who would set limits, yet were flexible. You'd want some sort of great parent-person. You'd certainly want to start with human qualities in the parent-child relationship and in other people surrounding the child.

But those are things which there's no way for a government to guarantee or prescribe. In fact, all the younger parent can do is try to make those things more likely to be there. Conditions that make it more likely to grow or prosper.

And so that means that the government has a rather limited role as far as families are concerned. The role should be to try to provide diffuse support for families. The right way to go about it is to try to provide a kind of general support, particularly for those who need it the most.

Specifically what that means, in terms of the things we can measure that are bad for children, is that the greatest harm to kids occurs in those kids who fall in the bottom quarter of the income levels. Our estimate was that about 25 percent of all American children grow up today in conditions of economic hardship that are really damaging to them and their families, where it is terribly hard to survive. We included a realistic line, which for a family of four is $8500 now. That's an awfully low income for four people to live on, and anybody who does it knows that they can just barely make it, if that. Also, there are those families where the family is barely

above some minimal level because the mother works. The family can't hack it, economically, unless she does work.

There are a lot of things this country should do about that. None of them is going to happen next year. All of them are going to be expensive. But the first priority would be a full employment policy which is not easy to implement, but if there were jobs for everybody who wanted one, then that would really take care of millions of children who live below the poverty line.

There are lots of ways of redesigning the tax system to give people with below-middle, particularly low-middle income, a break. Just because you're below the poverty level doesn't mean you're not pushing.

The fact is that people of below-average incomes often pay as much or more in taxes than high-income people do. So one way of easing the financial burden a little on families who are earning $12,000 or $13,000 is through tax reforms of various kinds, just to make the taxes a little more progressive.

Another thing that affects families is the problem of corporate mobility. The traditional reaction to this was acquiescence. You didn't think of raising questions. You were just moved every three years and the company explicitly said, "We do this because we don't want you to get too attached to any one place." The wife may have had a nervous breakdown but nobody paid any attention.

I'm struck that many people—some women's groups, men's groups, everybody—are beginning to say, "Hey, look at what you're doing to our families." The corporate or public leaders are much more responsive to that now. People are getting up their courage to say, "Really, I've got my kids to the point where I don't want to move them."

We also can do a lot about becoming far more flexible in the demands that jobs place on people. Businesses and other offices can adjust their hours or work out part-time and shared-time opportunities for people. Husbands and wives can share jobs in some cases.

Employers can be flexible in their demands so that a mother can leave the office, for example, when her child is sick or needs her—if she is then permitted to make up for the work she missed at some other time.

There are some costs. If you get into, say, upgraded part-time work, then the company has to provide prorated benefits and that can be more expensive. Once you start providing job security you're getting into something that a lot of firms don't want to do, particularly in a time of economic shakiness. These things are not going to happen overnight, but they will come bit by bit—and they'll make it increasingly possible for mothers to work without feeling they're neglecting their children.

The traditional view of a woman, the stereotype at least, was that she was a helper to her husband and she stayed home and followed him wherever he went and tried to make an attractive home for him. He came home and she had whatever was appropriate on the table. And the children were all clean and ready. And the children and the family were sort of attached to the breadwinner and what went along with it. I think as that concept changes, then the entire society—all of us—will be much better off.

The Family's Not 'Dying'

August Gribbin

If Prof. Mary Jo Bane of Wellesley College is correct, we Americans for years have been singing a dirge over an institution that is neither dead nor dying but is in fact as healthy as it has ever been.

The institution is the American family, and the requiem goes like this:

There was a time when the extended family—two or three generations living under the same roof—was the norm. This gave nurture to children and care to the aged, who otherwise might have been packed off to an old folks' home. But the extended family is almost extinct nowadays, and the family itself—indeed, even the institution of marriage—is in peril because of a soaring divorce rate, one-parent households, the increasing number of working mothers, and a mobile, rootless population. Result: Children don't get the kind of nurturing they once did, family bonds have weakened, and old folks' homes are filled with people whose children don't want the bother of caring for them.

That's cause for lamentation, all right, except for one thing: Bane says it isn't true. A 34-year-old assistant professor and associate director of Wellesley's Center for Research on Women, Bane refutes what she terms the romanticized, mythical view of the American family in her recent book, *Here to Stay: American Families in the Twentieth Century* (Basic Books. 195 pages. $11.50).

Bane's book—it's her third—is a statistical analysis of past and current data on U.S. population characteristics. Using the same data they do, she reaches conclusions diametrically opposite those of such well-known behaviorists as Urie Bronfenbrenner and popular authors such as Vance Packard (*A Nation of Strangers* and *The Naked Society*).

Her thesis, advanced in her book and in interviews with The Observer, is the American family is still strong because:

✓ The extended family never really existed on a wide scale. Data from colonial America show that only 6 per cent of U.S. households contained children, parents, and grandparents. The latest figures, for 1970, show it's still 6 per cent.

✓ More families have two parents now (84.3 per cent) than in colonial days (70 per cent).

✓ What divorce is doing to disrupt families today, death did in earlier times. As the death rate has dropped, the divorce rate has increased—but most divorced people remarry to stay.

✓ It's doubtful that Americans move more often now than they did in the Nineteenth Century. So if mobility is fraying America's family and social fabric, it has been doing so for a long time.

✓ There's no evidence that yesterday's mothers, laboring from dawn to dusk to do housework without labor-saving devices, devoted more time to their children than today's working mothers do.

Some other demographers think Bane may be correct. "Bane's book successfully shows the enduring commitment Americans have to traditional marital and family relationships," says Yale's Richard Fox. Peter Glick, senior demographer in the Census Bureau's Population Division, calls her book an objective, "serious study." And Mary Ellen Reilly, a University of Rhode Island sociologist, independently reached the same conclusion as Bane in a study she did for the nonprofit Center for Information on America. "The American family is not an imperiled institution," says Reilly, adding that it's only changing, not dying.

Richard Fox does criticize Bane for failing to raise the "prior question" of whether such a thing as "the American family" even exists. He says she doesn't consider the differences in families of various classes and ethnic backgrounds. And even if she is right about the enduring commitment to traditional family life, Fox says, Bane doesn't explore whether the "quality of the relationships" between family members has deteriorated.

Bane says her goal was to separate "myth from reality." That's vital, she adds, because public officials create policies regarding the family, abortion, divorce, and welfare on the basis of accepted general assumptions. "Assuming that the family is dead or dying may lead to policies that, in their desperate attempt to keep the patient alive, infringe unnecessarily on other cherished values . . . [or] bring about its untimely death.

"There's a general tendency to romanticize the past; it's persistent through history. In the Seventeenth Century, people were talking about how bad the family was, saying it was falling apart. Even scholars fail to take a long view of statistical data, thus they don't see the longer-term trends nor perceive the longer perspective. You really have to look at the family in a large context."

In doing that, Bane finds yesterday's family was much like today's. "The nuclear family, consisting of parents living with their own children and no other adults, has been the predominant family form in America since the earliest period on which historians have data. . . . Relationships among relatives appear to have been historically what they are now: complex patterns of companionship that only occasionally involve sharing bed and board."

2. MAINTENANCE OF RELATIONSHIPS

Bane says of extended families: "Three-generational households can exist only where one generation lives long enough to see its grandchildren. . . . People may have wanted three-generational families but lacked the three genrations." Death, of course, saw to that.

So whether in frontier forests, on farms, or in cities, yesterday's fathers commonly left homes to work, and mothers stayed behind, tending the brood—mostly without help—until at about the age of 10 the youngsters could contribute their labor at home or elsewhere. Young people usually left home to live with other families for disciplining, apprenticeship, or lodging as they began their working careers.

Working Mothers Compensate

Bane refuses to beatify those hard-laboring mothers of yore, saying they frequently ignored their children during a long day's work. They probably gave less attention to their offspring than working mothers do today, she says. "There is no evidence as to how much time mothers a century ago spent with their children. Undoubtedly it was less than contemporary nonworking mothers, since mothers of a century ago had more children and probably also had more time-consuming . . . tasks."

But Bane points out that modern mothers don't spend all that much time solely on caring for the kids either. Recent studies show that the average stay-at-home mom invests 1.4 hours a day specifically on child care.

"There is no evidence that having a working mother *per se* has harmful effects on children," adds Bane. Middle-class working mothers try to compensate by reading more to their youngsters and otherwise spending more time with them than nonworking moms.

Women work now, as in the past, to improve the family's economic position, and time hasn't yielded a way to avoid it. Bane tries to. She suggests a broadly outlined "social insurance" program that in effect would give certain young families the kind of income support during child-rearing years that Social Security now provides retirees. Bane wants children to have "economic decency," and in a way her book boils down to a plea for that.

Bane says that throughout the Nineteenth Century, families "may have taken in relatives when the arrangement provided economic benefits to both parties." Pay was so low it was "quite popular" for relatives to board needy kin. When financial pressures eased, however, "coresidence became less attractive."

Americans liked living on their own then, and they still do, Bane says. Yet today they still expand their families temporarily to help single or married youths get a start in life and to help divorced, widowed, or elderly relatives.

Criticism that Americans dump their aged kin in institutions seems overstated, Bane continues. In 1970,

for instance, old folks' homes housed just 2 per cent of all Americans aged 65 to 74 and only 7 per cent of the males and 11 per cent of the females 75 and over, census data show.

Bane reflects that the proportions of the aged who live with families may be high, yet still smaller than in the past. That fact could support the view that many American families abandon the old. Bane writes:

Change, Not Decay

"Taking in relatives has . . . declined somewhat over the last three decades. What this means depends. . . . One plausible interpretation [is] that people prefer to live in their own households when they can afford to and when they are relatively healthy and active. . . . The increasing proportion of old people living on their own might [then] reflect better health and better economic conditions. An alternative assuption is that people dislike living alone because they have no children or relatives willing to take them in. . . . The increased proportion of old people living on their own might result from the increasing wickedness of American children or decreasing family sizes.

"It is hard to know whether wickedness is increasing or decreasing. But it is true that people who were over 65 in 1970 were members of the generation . . . that had low marriage rates and high rates of childlessness. Since about 10 per cent never married, and since 15 to 20 per cent of those who did marry had no children, almost a quarter of the old of the 1970s have no children—wicked or not—to take them in."

Families *have* changed, Bane goes on, but the evidence of caring is too great to allow the conclusion that the American family is in peril. "Children are still raised in families, and families have a lot of strength today." The institution of marriage is healthy, too, she adds.

Mobility's Nothing New

Most marital breakups today occur because of divorce. Yet Bane contends that the proportion of youngsters deprived of a parent rose only recently after dropping earlier in this century. The reason: Death rates plummeted and divorce rates have not climbed rapidly enough to offset the drop. Consequently, "The total number of marital disruptions affecting children did not increase," Bane reports.

So why fret over the divorce rate? It's worrisome "in and of itself only if staying together at all costs is considered an indicator of healthy marriages or healthy societies," answers Bane.

Most marriages stay intact, "the vast majority" of divorced persons remarry, and few wed more than twice, Bane points out. "In general, the remarriage rate has kept pace with the divorce rate. . . . We are thus a long way from a society in which marriage is rejected or replaced by a series of short-term liaisons."

But what of Americans' mobility and its supposed deleterious effect on family and community? It's doubtful that "modern America is peculiarly transient," answers Bane. She says Americans were on the move in the Nineteenth Century too. The transients then were mostly young people making short-distance moves away from their parents to set up housekeeping alone or as newlyweds.

And that's also the way it is now, Bane adds. In the 1970s about 20 per cent of the population moved annually, with just 4 per cent going out-of-state. The transients tended to be young and to stay within the same metropolitan areas. In fact, half of all Americans live in the same states all their lives. "The historical studies suggested that Twentieth Century Americans are about as mobile as Nineteenth Century Americans. If mobility is destroying community and social life in America it has been doing so for a long time, Bane concludes.

We want your advice.

Any anthology can be improved. This one will be—annually. But we need your help.

Annual Editions revisions depend on two major opinion sources: one is the academic advisers who work with us in scanning the thousands of articles published in the public press each year; the other is you—the person actually using the book.

Please help us and the users of the next edition by completing the prepaid reader response form on the last page of this book and returning it to us. Thank you.

THE FAMILY: IS IT OBSOLETE?

WHAT ROLE FOR THE FAMILY NOW?

Amitai Etzioni

Mr. Etzioni is Professor of Sociology at Columbia University and Director of the Center for Policy Research, New York City. From "The Family: Is It Obsolete?" by Amitai Etzioni, Journal of Current Social Issues, *Winter 1977, pages 4-9:*

The American middle-class family, already stripped of most non-essential duties, now faces an attack on its remaining last bastions. Sex is available premaritally, extra-maritally and non-maritally to more and more Americans. Thus, Morton Hunt reports that to the present generation of young Americans, age 18 to 25, premarital sex runs as high as 81 percent for females and 95 percent for males. Extra-marital sex is reported by about half of the males, and one out of five women. Education has long ago been taken from the family and invested in special institutions, the schools. While in the old days the members of one family often worked one farm, very few families today are also a "work" unit. The rapid rise in women who work (more than 60 percent of all married), or are on welfare, breaks economic dependence as a source of a family bond. Meals can be readily obtained at the mushrooming fast-food franchises, at the supermarket and at "Take-Homes."

Thus, as this short history of the modern family suggests, there is a continued, expanding divesture of missions from the family to other institutions. Now, even the upbringing of *young* children, once considered by social scientists *the* family duty (indeed, in many societies the marriage is not considered fully consummated until there are offspring), is being downgraded by an increase in the number of persons who decide not to have children at all, and those who decide that they do not need a family to bring up infants. They either delegate this duty to day care centers, as available to singles as to couples, or do the job on their own. Nine million children under the age of 18 are being raised by one parent only, mostly by women. Thirty percent are under the age of six. There are about 2.4 million one-parent families as compared to 29 million nuclear families. The growth rate of single-parent families has increased by 31.4 percent, almost three times the growth of two-parent families. According to my calculations, if the present rate of increase in divorce and single households continues to accelerate as it did for the last ten years, by mid-1990 not one American family will be left.

The historical trends which propel the decline of the family are now accelerated by an additive, a slew of arguments which justify, legitimate and, indeed, even welcome these developments. They characterize the progressive decline of the nuclear family as "progress" and provide people with additional incentive to take to the exit, to dismantle the often shaky marital bond, instead of providing for a cooling-off mechanism to cope with the occasional centrifugal forces every marriage knows. While we have not reached the stage where breaking up one's family to enjoy "all that life has to offer" has become *the* thing to do, in many and growing circles the stigma attached to divorce—even when young infants are involved—has paled, the laws' cooling mechanisms have weakened, and reasons which "justify" divorce have grown in acceptance. Indeed "no-fault" divorces, which require no grounds at all, are now available in most states.

Until quite recently these trends were viewed as pathological. In the fifties, for example, the rising divorce rate was defined as a social problem, and marriage counseling was on the rise. The attitude of marriage counselors and that of society-at-large was typified by Dr. Paul Popanoe, marriage counselor and *Ladies Home Journal* columnist, who asked "Can this Marriage be Saved?" and month after month related case histories to prove that "yes," it almost invariably could be.

During the sixties, however, an intellectual and to a lesser extent, a public opinion turn around began to take place. The idea that spouses were morally obligated to hold their marriage together and that nine times out of ten they could succeed in doing so if they were willing to work at it moved increasingly to the right of mainstream thinking. Today's popular experts on marriage and the family seldom ask first, "Can this marriage be saved" but instead, "should it be?" And more and more often the answer given is not only "no" but an optimistic and affirmative "no." This is due to a new popular wisdom which says that people might be better off dissolving an unsatisfactory marriage, and either live single or try again, than to go through great contortions to fix their present marriage. While the many marriage and family experts of the fifties saw their task as shoring up the family's defenses so that it could better withstand attack, a significant contingent among today's experts is ready to view the invading social forces as potential liberators.

ONE: DIVORCE IS AOK

Several related lines of argument are currently being used to identify and explain what are seen as positive aspects in the rising divorce rate. The most novel one is the idea that *second marriages are better than first marriages*. Thus, Leslie Aldridge Westoff, a Princeton demographer, writes about "blended" or "reconstituted families" rather than second marriages, in an article entitled "Second-time *Winners*." (The labels are important; blended or reconstituted sounds more approving than "second time around.") Westoff reports that for the couples she interviewed the first marriage was a dry-run. In the second marriage they applied the lessons learned, did not repeat the same mistakes, and chose mates more wisely. "In retrospect many of the couples saw their first marriage as a kind of training school; . . . divorce was their diploma. All agreed that the second marriage was the real thing at last. With both partners older, more mature, somewhat expert at marriage, everything moves more smoothly, more meaningfully."

While Westoff may feel she is just reporting the results of some interviews with some couples, the implication to the reader, the music her writing vibrates, is that the first marriage is to the second one what premarital sex is to marital sex: evidence shows one improves the other. And indeed *if* there were sufficient data to support a view of the first marriage as a dry-run, there would be less reason for concern. But Westoff herself laments the lack of systematic research on second marriages; her insights are based on a few interviews. She also concedes that second marriages are less stable than first ones. Statistically, 59 percent of second marriages as opposed to 37 percent of first marriages, will end in a divorce, according to Dr. Paul Glick of the U.S. Census Bureau. Nor does she show that such re-marriages, even if they do last, have no detrimental effects on the children. Do the children also consider their parents as a dry-run and their step-parents as an improvement?

TWO: DISPOSABLE MARRIAGES

The "if-at-first-you-don't succeed, try, try again" optimism about divorce is at least not down on marriage as an institution. Another increasingly common viewpoint, however, is one which interprets the rising divorce rate as a symptom that something is radically wrong with marriage and/or the family. This school of thought rejects the view that marriage can work once you know yourself well enough and choose the "right" partner; it sees it as *healthy* that individuals in great numbers want to get out of what it views as a decaying social bond. It tends to look upon the rising divorce rate with much the same hopefulness with which a Marxist approaches a new recession: as a condition which cannot be tolerated for long, and hence will force revolutionary changes in social structures. Those who subscribe to this view tend to see new family forms waiting in the wings, from contractual marriages to group-marriages.

Significantly, a common feature of most of these new marital styles is that they seek to take some of the strain off the nuclear family by de-intensifying the husband-wife relationship. One way is by limiting the duration of the relationship a priori to an agreed period of time and defining the terms of the dissolution of the relationship from its very inception. Thus, by this school's terms, divorce has become no more of a crisis than completing a stint in the army or delivering the goods as agreed to a supermarket. Another alternative is to diversify one's emotions by investing them in a large number of intimate relationships, making each one less intense and hence less all-important. Thus, it is often said that sexual fidelity puts too much of a strain on many marriages—acceptance of one or both partners' adultery may well save some relationships, since the couple can stay together while getting the sexual variety, affection or whatever from outside persons. Better yet, it is said, group-marriage secures that you'll always have a mate, even if you divorce one, two, or three. Such deemotionalization and de-emphasis is however a two-edged sword. On the one hand, spouses who do not depend exclusively on each other and who obtain satisfactions from other persons may be able to continue living together for long periods without having to resolve their conflicts, at the risk of bringing them to a destructive head. On the other hand, such relationships may be too shallow to provide the needed emotional anchoring and security many people seek and need.

The contractual marriage or contractual cohabitation mentioned above has been widely advocated and has aroused a fair degree of popular interest. Those who favor contractual marriages tend to look upon all social life as a series of exchanges. Conflict and tension arise when one or both parties fail to live up to their parts of the bargain. Conflict is seen as more likely to arise in a relationship, such as that characterized in the traditional marriage, where the reciprocal "rights and

why?

45

duties" of each partner are not clearly spelled out and agreed to in advance. Thus, the male swinger who marries may do so with the implicit understanding that this change in legal status will not cramp his lifestyle while his bride may be marrying under the illusion that her husband-to-be will transform his lifestyle once they are wed. Those who propose contractual marriage suggest that a great deal of subsequent conflict between spouses (and disappointment with marriage) could be avoided by bringing such unspoken expectations into the open, to be discussed and agreed upon and then formalized in a marital contract akin to the contracts that govern relations between parties in a business transaction.

For example, the prospective marital partners might agree to write monogamy into the contract or, alternatively, include a clause permitting sexual side-trips or bi-sexual relations. But once each party had signed the agreement each would have to abide by the stated rules. Violation of such contractual terms could be declared in writing and signed by both parties to be grounds for immediate unilateral termination of the contractual marriage. In addition, unlike the traditional marriage bond which was supposed to be entered into as a lifelong commitment, contractual marriage typically provides for periodic review and renewal (or non-renewal) of the contract, say every three to five years.

The problem, however, is that contracts work in the business world primarily because the relationships involved are highly limited and specific, and calculative motivations are enough to sustain them. But for two people to live together, to share wealth and ill fortune and the slings and arrows of life, required a deep, encompassing, positive relationship of the kind implied in marital vows but antithetical to any contract. Contracts put people continuously on their guard: did I get my share, did he (or she) do his job? Marriage requires more altruism, less accounting, and above all a greater sense of commitment to a *shared* life.

THREE: GRANNY—YES, HUSBAND—NO

Another viewpoint which has become intellectually chic recently is the celebration of the extended family. Like contractual marriage it claims to reduce the pressure on the nuclear family by de-intensifying the emotional bonds between husband and wife, parent and child. The idea is that if family members had a multiplicity of sources of satisfaction for their various needs they would not become overly dependent on one single source or parent. Some of the theorists of the extended family favor a revival of older family forms in which several generations of blood relatives lived under the same roof or within close geographic proximity. Others favor the formation of "extended families of choice," e.g., communes. Thus, it is said that our typical middle class suburban "nuclear" family is emotionally unwholesome. Segregated from grandparents and other kin, it provides the child with only two warm caring adults, both of whom are increasingly absent or harried, instead of the abundance provided by the grandparents, uncles, aunts, and nieces and nephews of the extended family.,

In India, where extended families often run to hundreds of members, a baby "is never put down," there is always an uncle, cousin, or someone, to comfort a crying child. Among immigrant families extended family members provided many of the support services offered by welfare agencies, day care centers and other institutions, at great cost to the tax-payers, and often with highly impersonal if not bureaucratic paternalism. A number of Unitarian congregations, concerned with the "too many stresses which are being placed on the small nuclear family," are forming hundreds of artificially-extended families whose members vacation together or help each other with problems such as babysitting or care of elderly infirm relatives.

What does this have to do with the survival of the nuclear family? Ostensibly, by easing the burden on parents to be constantly responsive to one another and to their children, the extended family makes it less likely that break-up will result from spouses continually over-burdening one another. However, several of the extended family advocates take the next step and say that with family security provided by a circle of grandparents, cousins and uncles, a permanent husband's presence loses its importance. Look, they say, at how well impoverished families have managed, despite the comings and goings of common-law husbands. The mother, because she has the support of her mother and kin, is able to manage quite well.

The rub is that although it would be useful to have an extended family, most middle-class couples could not necessarily be induced to belong to or maintain one. The forces which in the past undermined the extended family pattern in the middle class—from the need to be mobile for economic success, to the desire for individualism and privacy—are powerful ones and difficult to reverse. Thus, while a middle class granny might be available to baby-sit here and there, if she lives nearby, and brothers and sisters may be good for a loan now and again, it is a long way from such occasional aid to surrogate parenthood. Indeed, in most societies, even those looked upon so enviously because of exotic extended family arrangements, the kernel of child raising is not the mother but a couple, the husband-wife, the nuclear family. The artificial extended families do provide a nice *supplement* to the nuclear family, but are much too thin and frail *to replace* its vital core.

FOUR: BROKEN IS BETTER

Perhaps the most sophisticated argument against the notion that husband-wife families are needed for the character formation and psychological well-being of young children emerges from studies of children from *broken* homes. In the public mind, and that of most officials, it is widely assumed that broken homes breed juvenile delinquents, truant or runaway kids, young drug addicts and most recently teen and pre-teen alcoholics. Statistical correlations are frequently uncovered. For instance, Dr. Gordon H. Barker found a high correlation (r=.79) between broken homes and delinquency. However, the commonsense interpretation of such results has been seriously challenged on the elementary ground that when broken homes are compared to non-broken ones, the fact that broken homes occur so frequently among the poor and minorities while non-broken ones are generally middle-class, is ignored. Or to put it differently, lower-class families produce more delinquent kids, whether they are children from broken homes *or not.* Indeed, if families of the same class background are compared, *most of the difference* in juvenile delinquency rates between the children from broken vs. unbroken homes *disappears.* Those familiar with these findings thus tend to conclude that having both a father and a mother is not vital to character formation.

Looking at the same data, I suggest that proper economic conditions, housing and employment may well be more important for the proper upbringing of a child than a lasting positive relation between the parents, and between parents and child. At the same time, I am not convinced it has been shown that family stability is irrelevant; it may just be a less important factor than social class. Less important is not the same as unimportant.

Moreover, Dr. Urie Bronfenbrenner of Cornell University suggests that one way poverty damages kids is by disintegrating their families. Both suicide and lower scholastic achievement are particularly high among children whose families earn less than $4,000 a year and as many as 80 percent of such families in central cities are single-parent ones.

Finally, another finding has been widely disseminated, and even many people not familiar with the evidence cite it on their way to the marital exit: rotten marriages are worse than broken homes. In his research on adolescents in boys' training schools and high schools, Dr. F. Ivan Nye found that less delinquent behavior was evidence in broken but happy homes (35 percent) than in unbroken but unhappy homes (48 percent). These data led Nye to conclude: "The *happiness* of the marriage was found to be more closely related to delinquent behavior in children than whether the marriage was an original marriage or to a remarriage or one in which the child was living with one parent

only." According to Professor William J. Boode, "Psychiatric studies emphasize the difficulties experienced by people who as children lived in 'empty shell' families, in which people carry out their formal duties toward one another, but give no understanding, affection or support, and have little interest in communicating with one another. . . .It seems likely that role failure within the home has a more destructive impact on children than the withdrawal of one's spouse."

On the other hand, to the extent that families are needlessly undone by rationalizations, beliefs and arguments, probably the most widely held and destructive myth is the quest for the *perfect* relationship. The incessant search for "more" is a direct descendant of American optimism and romanticism which looks for a marriage which will be harmonious and loving, full of communication, understanding, mutual respect, joy and fulfillment through children. When all this is found out to be as close to the reality of most families as Marcus Welby is to your M.D., a million Americans a year take to the exits, not because they are anti-family but anti-*their* family. Thus, 80 percent of divorced persons will try again, and many of these will risk a third time, restlessly looking for that Hollywood made-in-heaven marriage. Even after they grow more accomodating, they still believe that they have missed out. Others, dating at 40, 50 and older, living together, breaking up, trying again, are still looking for that "happily ever after" promise that keeps eluding them.

Encouraging such utopian quests are several psychotherapists and psychiatrists, many of whom are trained to deal with individuals, not couples. Thus, sometimes deliberately, often unwittingly, by trying to help each individual client achieve a full life, they encourage their patients to break up their marriages (although many do ask people not to make major life changes while in therapy). The trouble is that if any person seeks to maximize his or her own happiness and freedom without considering the consequences to others and to a relationship, the result can be highly detrimental to all those involved and to the family as an institution. People must learn to balance the personal rewards of "doing one's own thing" against the hurt it might entail to others. No relationship, no institution, family or society can survive otherwise. In many instances, however, the effect of therapy is to encourage people to focus on their psycho-dynamics, feelings and needs, to the neglect of their spouses and even children. It does encourage divorce.

WHAT COULD BE DONE?

Faced with the progressive dismemberment of the American family, there is surprisingly little public action for two reasons: first, the arguments that the

2. MAINTENANCE OF RELATIONSHIPS

current rate of family break-up may be a blessing in disguise raise doubts concerning the nature and extent of the crisis; and second, public officials feel that there is little the government could or should do in this intimate matter. To my mind, we need a thoroughgoing review of evidence concerning the consequences of family break-up to determine whether or not we have a national social problem on our hands. A Presidential or Congressional Commission could be given the task of investigating the harmful consequences of family dissolution bringing together and examining existing data and, where reliable data are not available, by carrying out studies of its own. Should the Commission find that single-parent families, contractual families and reblended families are doing as well as the declining traditional two-parent families, we can relax and enjoy the marital merry-go-round. Should it establish that the slew of "new" family rationalizations are ill-founded and we have a serious and growing problem on our hands, the very fact that a highly visible study has reached such conclusions, presenting evidence and airing pro and con arguments in public hearings, should help puncture these arguments.

Moreover, the recent fashion of "the less-the-better-Presidency" should not be allowed to obscure the great agenda-setting power the White House has in many areas outsde the administrative scope of government. Hence, without at all suggesting that the federal government should take on the job of fixing a million dissolving families a year, or even one, by launching a National Institute of Marital Health or any other such agency, we do believe that a few well-presented speeches by the President or a White House Conference on the future of the family could go a long way to call public attention to the problem.

Second, as Walter Mondale keeps reiterating, the "family impact" of various government programs should be assessed and taken into account as old programs are revised and new ones formulated. Thus, day-care centers are a blessing for working women and certainly a better place for a young child than roaming the streets. But they are also costly institutional substitutes for family, and by de-emphasizing the importance of parents in children's lives, they may well further contribute to the erosion of family bonds. More opportunities for *half* time jobs, without loss of privileges (such as benefits and promotion) both for women and men, may provide some parents with an alternative preferable to day-care centers, one which is less costly to the public, less bureaucratic and more compatible with a viable family.

Also, laws which work against the family should be altered, both because the government should not encourage the dissolution of families *and* because laws symbolize public attitudes. As has often been pointed out, it is still true in about half of the states that the only way an unemployed male wage earner can get his children on welfare is to divorce his wife. There is no AFDC for unemployed fathers. Thus, to the extent that welfare laws and regulations still penalize marriage, they should be altered.

Furthermore, the regulations governing Social Security benefits for retired persons favor individuals who are single by reducing the total monetary awards to couples. An unmarried woman is eligible to receive 100 percent of her Social Security benefits, whereas this amount is significantly reduced if she is married to a man who is also receiving benefits. This is said to be a significant factor for many retired couples living together rather than marrying. It might be asked—what ill effects result from old people living together unmarried? The answer is that (a) they should be free to choose to live together or marry, but not pushed into living together by government regulations, and (b) older people set models for younger people; "If granny does not marry the guy, why should I?"

In a similar vein, Martin M. Spencer, writing in the *CPA Journal,* cities a divorced couple who reconciled but decided not to remarry, because remarriage would have jacked up their income tax bite by $5,460. Generally, income tax rates for single persons are lower than for married persons filing separate returns. (Married persons benefit from filing joint returns only if one spouse earns much more than the other.) The recent provisions allowing people to deduct the cost of child-care under certain circumstances futher reward the single parent over two working partners in a marriage whose joint income tends to put them above the ceiling for allowable deductions.

Finally, it might well be advisable that a divorce cooling-off period and opportunities for counseling be reinstituted by those states that went somewhat overboard in making divorce easy and painless. While most divorce reforms are desirable, especially those that remove the necessity of declaring one party "guilty" and the other "innocent" and those which serve to avoid bitter wrangling between spouses which may be communicated to their children, divorce by mail and other reforms which have the effect of divesting divorce of its seriousness over-liberate divorce. The state should not imply that divorce is a trivial matter—something one can do on an impulse. Reinstituting—or beginning again to enforce—a 30-day minimum cooling-off period with opportunities for counseling, if the couple desires, would seem to be a reasonable compromise.

Other steps may well be devised. The main point is that preoccupied as we are with prices, jobs, shortages and energy—all related to the material aspects of our societal existence—we should not neglect what to many sociologists still seems to be the vital cell of our society. The disintegration of the family, one must reiterate these days, may do as much harm to a society as running out of its favorite source of energy.

THE FRAGMENTED FAMILY

Robert Thamm

The family may neither vanish nor enter upon a new
Golden Age. It may—and this is far more
likely—break up, shatter, only to come together
again in weird and novel ways.

—Alvin Toffler, *Future Shock*

Compared with our modern nuclear family, our traditional extended family was generally more supportive. The early American family, for example, was dominated and controlled by the father, and women were expected, primarily for economic reasons, to have several children. The early family as a group was composed of husband and wife, numerous children, children's children, and dependent relatives. Spinsters and widows were in great demand for their competence in household management, and adult male relatives were assets because of their ability to work the land and contribute to the family income. Many families, usually related, lived close to one another and shared the responsibilities for providing economic and psychological aid to other family members. Children typically had several adults of each sex with whom they could closely identify.

As the children developed strong emotional ties to relatives other than their biological parents, their dependencies for economic as well as psychological rewards became more dispersed. Because of this diffused involvement, children in the early American family could tap several sources of gratification. In the event that one or both of their parents left the family setting, were deceased, or even temporarily rejected them, the children had easy access to other adults who were willing to care for them and assume the roles of their parents. Because of the larger size of the family clan, a great deal of security for the children was built into the structure itself.

Although this kind of family provided for economic and psychological security in the rearing of children, in other respects it was quite restrictive. Occupational choices were extremely limited, roles were rigidly defined, and strong punishments were handed out to those who dared to innovate. Social mobility, both up and down in the class structure and from one position to another at the same social level, was curtailed in the former by an inflexible caste or status structure and in the latter by custom and tradition. Membership in a family was usually determined along blood lines and by marriages planned and controlled by family elders.

The authoritarian traditional family was usually headed by a strong patriarch. There was little respect for women and children who were relegated to lower status positions. The presence of a rigid hierarchy of family positions with privileged persons filling the top ranks was apparent in most traditional societies. An excessive demand on conformity, order, and obedience was reflected in the symbolism and the seriousness of the family rituals. Many people seemed to be property or possessions of someone else (for example, slaves, concubines, child labor, subservient wives) and people functioned according to highly restrictive roles and values. There was little or no opportunity for rebellion or change.

Our traditional family, then, had some characteristics which contributed to increasing need-satisfaction and some which did not. The extended structure provided the opportunity for children as well as adults to develop a larger number of deep and more meaningful relationships within the family itself. This could have led to a greater amount of economic and psychological security if it weren't for the many accompanying restrictions, taboos, and authoritarian impositions. There was little question of the identity of each member, for few if any alternatives were available and expected behavior was rigidly constructed. These limitations, because they were largely predetermined, failed to take individual differences into account. Individuals, for example, could not select their own mates nor the number of mates. They could not easily move from one community to another without greatly disrupting the course of family living. Rather than encouraging people to go into positions which corresponded to their own traits, capacities, and interests, these capacities and interests were made to fit roles dictated by age, sex, and social class of parents.

THE NUCLEAR FAMILY

Frustrations and discontent arising from the failure of our traditional family to adapt to individual needs laid the groundwork for its eventual breakdown. In addition, the Industrial Revolution, bringing the deterioration of an agrarian economy, gave impetus to a growing technology. Because of better forms of communication and transportation, family and individual mobility became more prominent and acceptable. The migration from a small, highly personal, and integrated family situation to a more impersonal, bureaucratic, and urban environment had the effect of fragmenting the relatively stable and secure extended structure.

Two conclusions can be drawn from examining these changes in family structure.

1. Children and adults in the *traditional structure* had a greater amount of psychological security due to the larger number of people who served as dependable sources of emotional and affective gratification, but they had a great deal of frustration due to the rigid system's failure to allow for the expression of individual differences.

2. Children and adults in the *nuclear structure* have much less psychological security and fewer emotional resources, due to the small size of the unit, but have increased mobility, flexibility, and freedom to make choices, due to increased structuring for individual differences.

Our nuclear family evolved favorably in all respects except in the area of providing increased security and emotional benefits for its members. Although the fragmentation of the extended form, because of its psychologically threatening implications,

2. MAINTENANCE OF RELATIONSHIPS

should be considered an undesirable trend, the breakdown of traditional authoritarian structures which occurs in the nuclear type can be seen as a more positive development.

> One could, for example, point to many liberating effects which this change has brought about. It has liberated creative activities from the bondage of familistic servitude and opened up the personality market for freer unfolding of talent, aptitude, and individualistic choice. In short, one must not lose sight of the general principle that any change brings about a host of reactions. Some may be judged functional and some dysfunctional.[1]

Today, the traditional extended family structure and norms have almost completely disappeared. Our primary socializing agency, the extended family, failed to adapt to a modern growing industrialized world. From the shattered extended family, a residual, smaller, and more mobile nuclear structure emerged. The general characteristics of this newer family contrast sharply with the traditional type. Blood relatives are located throughout a wider geographic area and children must rely more upon parents than other relatives for economic and psychological support. These conditions as well as the smaller size of the unit and the detached and depersonalized surroundings of urban life, result in a lesser sense of family security.

In other respects, the nuclear family offers us an increasing amount of flexibility, mobility, and emancipation from the traditional family's rigid and discriminatory practices. Choice of occupation is a function of interest and capacities, rather than being ascribed. Because of the breakdown of the rigid caste system, the possibility of upward social mobility increases, allowing for greater variation in the selection of roles. Younger members of the traditional family migrate to larger urban centers, breaking down the authority of the family elders and providing themselves with the opportunity to select their own mates and govern their own family units. A more recent trend emancipating women from narrow household and child-rearing duties, as well as from male domination, allows them wider choices in deciding occupation and general life style. The relaxing of the traditional structure thus enables family members who were most discriminated against to rebel and to search for new identities.

However, alternative institutions which center around more egalitarian values are not readily available. Because of this, an increasing number of single and divorced people who are in some way involved in a personal crisis are desperately searching for a new way of life but have no place to go, no institution to identify with, and no hope of enjoying any kind of family living. Their alienation and despair suggests the grave necessity for experimenting with and institutionalizing new life styles and family forms.

SIZE OF THE FAMILY

One of the major changes that has been taking place in our family is the gradual decrease in the number of members constituting a unit. The average size of the U.S. household decreased from 5.5 per unit in 1850 to 3.14 in 1971.[2] As a result of this decrease, our family seems to be moving toward more and more isolation residentially and economically; with this fragmentation it is becoming less able to meet the more generalized traditional functions. The family now focuses on socialization and the exchange of emotional support and affection. The small size of our nuclear family and its isolation thus have ramifications on the socialization process of children and their emotional security. Parent-child tensions are increased, leading to a greater possibility of dissolution. As the family unit becomes smaller, the chances for parental error increase. "Each child

becomes more crucial."[3]

Somewhat contrary to these notions are findings suggesting that smaller families are less authoritarian, and that there is more parental affection toward children and vice versa and thus less parental stress.[4] Perhaps the crucial factor is the ratio of children to parent figures in the family unit. Maybe larger families with larger numbers of adults than children will show the most favorable dispositions and gratifications on the part of the members. Such a family might be more representative of the general population in terms of age distribution. If there are about two or three adults for each child in society, perhaps this ratio could be maintained in larger families not based upon kinship. Our children would have several parental models to relate to in contrast to the situation in large middle-class families where many children in the unit are confined to one or two parent relationships. Tension and competition for affection could be lessened allowing for greater integration in the family.

Parents also use children to satisfy their own needs, sometimes more than they use themselves to satisfy the children's needs. They "hang on" their children their own unrealized potential and see not the child but the projected image of the person they themselves would like to be. The loving parents clothe their children with a great deal of themselves and cling to the children possessively. The fewer the number of children they have, the more intense the desire to retain their property. In a more extended family or in the family with a larger number of children, this need on the part of the parents to possess their children might be decreased or at least diffused.

Because of the possessive demands which many of us impose upon our children, there is an increased tension which occurs in the life cycle of the family as the children reach maturity and begin to break the parental ties. This tension is aggravated by the extreme dependence on the parents encouraged in the small nuclear family. The lack of continuity, as family members grow up and move into adult roles, is a weakness in the nuclear structure. The move involves breaking off old ties and creating a new family unit which is stable largely to the extent to which the new marriage is stable. The probability of this stability resulting is rather dismal as seen later in a review of the trends in divorce rates.

Children's emotional identification and dependency upon one adult male and one adult female are also limiting factors in our modern family. In our extended family, young boys and girls could choose models from among a number of visible adult relatives and could derive an image of what he or she wanted to be. But in the nuclear family such choice is limited, particularly if one parent is not easily observable. As a consequence, children of nuclear families seek models in their peer groups and adults outside of the family setting. Generally, these models lead to conflicts in loyalties, value systems, and time commitments.

I previously suggested that parents should have more than one child, so as to decentralize their possessiveness and dependency upon any one of them. Perhaps children should have more than one parent of each sex, so as to provide them with a larger number of consistent, available, and dependable role models. I am acquainted, for example, with an experimental extended family consisting of three adult males, three adult females, and two children. They have been together for several years, have pooled their resources, and have shared child-rearing responsibilities. When one of the father figures is not available, the children gain in the security that they can turn to one or both of the other adult males in the family. When one of the "mothers" is not particularly interested in the kind of activity desired by the children, the children can find an adult female more receptive to their needs. Each of the children has three adults of each sex to provide them with multiple role models and increased options in obtaining the kinds of gratifications that parents provide. The children seem to be quite content with their family life. Having more than two parents thus stabilizes socialization and allows for better solutions to problems related to family crisis.

If these criticisms of the size of the modern nuclear form are valid, perhaps we should reconsider some variation of an extended family model. This might be even more important when we are reminded that children of the divorced, because they generally only have one adult to identify with at any given time, suffer without the more generalized emotional support that was so common in traditional extended clans. With the development of working mothers and baby-sitting, security is absurdly minimized in that our children are subjected to an environment which provides for the least amount of genuine care and the maximum amount of superficial and temporary involvement.

SEX-ROLE DIFFERENCES

It is an understatement that the role of the adult male in the marriage and family institutions has been traditionally different from that of the adult female. Men were socially independent, complete individuals. Women, confined to reproductive and domestic roles, were never considered equal to men, those producers whose existence was justified by the work they did. The expectations of the husband-father in the nuclear structure are still highly differentiated from those of the wife-mother.

It is my contention that these role differences and inequalities contribute significantly to the breakdown of the modern family. In discussing this, I will not be concerned with the fact women are biologically and physiologically different from men, only that sex-role differences are systematically produced primarily through child-rearing practices. These practices are defined by the norms of society in general and by the role structure of the nuclear family in particular. The role definitions and the norms which support them will be the target for discussion. I will direct my remarks and evidence to the personality and behavioral effects of the roles in the nuclear family.

Self-Alienation

Expectations in the family generally require, among other things, that men be more rational, independent, aggressive, self-confident, innovative, realistic, and competitive than women. Women are expected to be more emotional, dependent, passive, self-conscious, conventional, idealistic, and compassionate than men. By not allowing each sex to display the characteristics attributed to the opposite sex, half of these personality traits are suppressed. Males, for example, may feel inadequate if they fail to control their emotions, become dependent upon females in some way, or are not interested in competitive activities. Females, on the other hand, may feel some negative social pressures if they become too intellectual, respond aggressively, or become economically independent. Thus, each sex must hold back half of its potentials so as to fit into the prevailing structure.

My concern is what happens to us when this sort of structure is imposed upon us. The Putneys' thesis concerning the "adjusted American" is again relevant. They suggest that those traits which are ascribed to the other sex are alienated from ourselves. Because we cannot accept these traits in ourselves (cannot admit that we have these potentials), we project them onto members of the other sex.

> Having alienated those aspects of himself which he has learned to regard as incompatible with his manhood, the male projects them onto the women around him. In his mother, his daughter, his wife, and particularly his sweetheart, he sees and loves his own desire to be dependent, vain, impractical, demonstrative, and all the other things he has learned to consider unsuitable in himself. Indeed, he often demands that his women display such characteristics.
>
> In a parallel but reverse manner, the little girl in America is encouraged to seek comfort when she scrapes a knee, to be openly affectionate, to be proud of her curls and ruffles—and is scolded for a dirty face or a bold manner. She learns to alienate her potential for being aggressive, self-assertive, proficient in sports and mechanics. She is likely to adore masterful men.[5]

As we project these alienated aspects of ourselves onto our mates, however, we also desire to reunite with them. When the projections become very strong, we become miserable without their constant presence. We are jealous of anyone else who is close to our spouse, for we want exclusive and constant possession of the potential we project.[6]

Sex-role differences thus restrict us from expressing half of our humanity. The sex-role structure in the family is ineffective in that it leads to self-alienation, projection, restrictions in expressing certain behaviors and emotions, mate idealizations, possessiveness, and jealousy.

Cross-Sex Empathy

Because males and females have been socialized into such different kinds of roles, they have become different kinds of people with different kinds of behaviors, attitudes, and feelings. A common complaint among husbands and wives is that their spouses do not understand them. This might be attributed to the differences in the way they were raised. These differences make it more difficult for them to put themselves symbolically in the place of their mates and to feel and think as their mates feel and think. If being able to empathize with one's spouse is an important part of understanding, and understanding and empathy between men and women are desirable, then perhaps the perpetuation of differences in the roles of males and females in the modern family should be halted.

Intimacy *(= in marriage!)*

Intimacy to some extent emerges with empathy and understanding. These qualities seem less apparent when couples are products of different role prescriptions. I would also expect that as two people become more intimate, their antagonisms would tend to be reduced. George Bach maintains in *The Intimate Enemy* that when partners don't fight they are not involved in an intimate relationship.[7] However, when hostility arises between partners, the blame should more properly be attributed to marital expectations. The institution places its demands and restrictions on the couple, producing aggressive and hostile feelings. These feelings are not inevitable, but are socially determined. The practice, which Bach advocates, of learning to "fight fair" in marriage is a poor substitute for discovering new forms which will bring aggression from inevitability to extinction. I agree that aggression and frustration are inevitable, given the prevailing marriage institution, but not inevitable or even common in other social contexts. Bach is obviously treating the hostile effects of marriage, not the causes. To make an analogy: cancer is an inevitable disease; let's live with it through radiation treatments rather than find its causes. Given marriage, I suppose we need the treatments, but let's not assume that we have to put up with a major cause of hostility—marriage itself.

In a study of male-female interaction, it was found that with more intimacy, the dominant sex in each pair became less

2. MAINTENANCE OF RELATIONSHIPS

dominant. Thus, there was a decline in traditional sex-role differences with increased intimacy.[8] If we are interested in bringing about more intimacy among people, then this result suggests that a de-emphasis of sex-role distinctions might be a move in the desired direction.

Sex-role differences are imposed upon us rather early in life. During adolescence the norms in dating groups emphasize sexual antagonism and exploitation, since males and females gain prestige in peer groups in directly opposite ways: the male by maximizing physical contact and minimizing expenses, the female by minimizing the former and maximizing the latter. Intimacy is minimized if each partner, even during physical contact, is keeping an account with regard to these dating norms.

These opposing norms then create social distance between males and females at an early age, and it is no surprise that this distance, antagonism, and exploitation later carry over into the family setting. Thus, the nuclear family is not functioning to the extent to which it curtails an early, more open and frank interchange between the sexes leading to the development of intimacy. Sex-role distinctions learned by the young do not contribute to that end.

Sexuality and Sex-Roles

If sex-role differences lead to antagonism and a lack of intimacy, it would seem to follow that in situations in which these differences are magnified, problems in heterosexuality would be more common. In a cross-cultural study of marital sexuality, Lee Rainwater concluded that in societies with separation in the roles of husbands and wives, the couple will not develop a close sexual relationship, and the wife will not find sexual relations with her husband sexually gratifying.[9] Although the evidence is limited, sex-role distinctions seem to detract from satisfying sexual relationships.

Personality Correlates

What kinds of personalities do people who believe in the virtues of maintaining role distinctions between the sexes have? In a recent study of 284 college sophomores, I found that those subjects who favored the traditional roles of males and females also tended to be significantly

1. More racially prejudiced.
2. More authoritarian.
3. More schizophrenic.
4. More dogmatic.
5. More marriage oriented.
6. Less self-autonomous.
7. Less self-esteemed.

It is interesting to note that they also tended to agree that "familiarity breeds contempt."[10] These finding seem to confirm some of the previous discussion and research reports.

In summary, it is my contention that the sex-role structure in the modern family is unfavorable in that it promotes prejudicial, dogmatic, and authoritarian attitudes; it promotes self-alienation, projection, and a lack of self-esteem and autonomy; it blocks effective communication, understanding, and intimacy; it destroys cross-sex empathy; it magnifies social distance, antagonism, and exploitation between the sexes; and it leads to dissatisfaction in sexual relationships.

ROLE OF THE FEMALE

The problems inherent in the role of the female are of no recent origin. It is a part of the long-standing Christian tradition.

Unto the women [God] said, I will greatly multiply thy sorrow and thy conception; in sorrow thou shalt bring forth children; and thy desire shall be to thy husband, and he shall rule over thee.
—Genesis 3:16

And, as ruling husbands, men have imposed the duties which they found less desirable upon their wives. And their wives, as good Christian wives, have learned their roles well and have even thought these duties were honorable and fulfilling. But only when women decided to question the role structure of the "sacred" family were they able to see, in an objective sense, the inequality, the oppression, and the exploitation built into the traditional female role.

In the traditional role, women are not given the opportunity to grow to their full capacities and to retain their human individuality. They have been bought off by men to be content with washing diapers, cleaning house, buying groceries, and the like. Their reward is economic security; the cost, in many cases, is sexual and emotional gratification for their husbands.

Perhaps it is not an exaggeration to call the state of the housewife a sickness. Betty Friedan asks if the house of the American suburban wife is in reality a comfortable concentration camp. She suggests that they have adjusted to their biological role and have become dependent, passive, childlike; they have given up their adult status to live at a lower human level. The work they do is simple, endless, monotonous, and unrewarding.[11]

The increasing isolation of the nuclear family is best exemplified in the housewife role, for the male is out of the house all day and therefore can be neither overlord nor companion.

> With the father absent, radio and television provide the mother with a watery substitute for adult companionship. A young colleague told me recently that his wife leaves the radio on all day merely to hear the sound of a grown-up voice. The continual chatter of little children can be profoundly irritating, even to a naturally affectionate person. The absence of servants from nearly all American middle class households brings the wife face to face with the brutalizing features of motherhood and housework. If she had the mentality of a peasant, she might be able to cope with them more easily.[12]

But this isolation, leading to emotional and intellectual poverty, is not universal. In societies in which the domestic role works, the housewife is part of a large extended family or a close-knit village community or both. Both the small size of the nuclear family and its isolated nature contribute to the restrictions imposed upon the average housewife. But what happens to her under these kinds of conditions?

Many women attempt to escape the monotony and boredom of their daily existence. Perhaps TV soap operas provide the greatest escape for the American housewife. The afternoon "soaps" foster an ideology based upon female passivity, ineptness, and subservience, even for women of the highest professional status. They are raped, divorced, abandoned, misunderstood, given drugs, attacked by mysterious diseases and go mad, and have more brain tumors and die more than the males do. The TV commercials follow the same pattern, showing women inside of the home involved in household tasks 43 percent of the time, as adjuncts to men 38 percent of the time, and 17 percent of the time as sex objects. The plots in these series may make the housewife feel safe and secure but may make these same viewers dissatisfied with their own dull lives. When she turns off the TV, looks into the mirror, and greets her husband, the comparison is not pleasant.[13] Thus, women use the mass media, the soap operas, the love magazines, and the gossip they can conjure up in coffee sessions with neighbors as mechanisms for creating fantasies. In these fantasies, they live as they would like to live, but they live vicariously, not in the real world. Their escape from reality only points out the possibility of a more severe problem: a total reliance upon fantasies for satisfying needs frustrated by the family system. The possibility of schizophrenia, or even worse, suicide, looms over them.

Others may try to recreate themselves through their children. They may project so much of themselves onto their daughter or son that they find the child's presence indispensable. The "adjusted" American mother, in this context, maintains the needs of her child leaving little time for other things. This she sees as evidence of her conscientiousness. She insists that a child needs her full attention and that she loves her baby so much she is glad to devote her life to her child. The latter is true enough. The result may well be a continuous destructive interference with the life of the child and an inevitable emptiness in her own.

If she cannot find fulfillment through her children, she may turn to material things. Since she *does* nothing, she seeks self-fulfillment in what she *has*. If these material possessions become her raison d'être, she could spend her days endlessly polishing and cleaning them, always being prepared to display them proudly to whoever might pass by. She eventually loses sight of *who she is*, for all of her rewards come as a result of *what she has*.

When fantasy, vicarious living, and materialism have failed, she still has two realistic alternatives, neither of which contributes to the maintenance of the old family. Either a job or an affair may serve as a release from domesticity.

Another problem which faces the woman in the family is her role in the completion of the child-rearing functions. Increasingly, child rearing is concentrated into a substantially shorter period of time than before. As of the most recent information, women are on the average likely to bear their last child at the age of 30 or 31. Thus, partly by living longer in a better state of health and partly by reducing the time span of their primary attention to motherhood, women are freed for other functions. There is a vacuum between the ages of 40 or 45 until death, an average of about 30 years. I already noted the increased suicide rate of women over 40. This would suggest a deterioration of their psychological well-being, to say the least. A study of Vassar graduates who were 20 or 25 years out of college showed that for the most part they were adjusted as suburban housewives, conscientious mothers, and were active in their communities. It was also found, however, that upon graduation they did not continue to grow mentally, emotionally, or personally, and after 20 years, those with the most psychological problems were the most traditionally feminine.[14]

The role of the housewife thus seems detrimental to the growth and development of middle-aged women. It defines their function as child rearing but fails to provide a meaningful alternative function once the children are reared. It is almost impossible for elderly women to participate in a child-rearing role later in life, given the present evolution of the family.

The housewife role, in summary, limits the aspirations which most women have of reaching their full potential. They are commonly exploited and forced to become parasites. In their traditional role, they fail to grow mentally, emotionally, and personally; in the more isolated family setting, they are left with fantasy, materialism, possessiveness of their children, and a feeling of emptiness in their later years. The fate of the married woman, as expressed by de Beauvoir, is one of becoming "a gilded mediocrity lacking ambition and passion, of aimless days indefinitely repeated, of living a life that slips away gently toward death without questioning its purpose."[15] The prognosis is more positive. Women's roles are beginning to become more optional and diversified. As the possibilities for new wife and mother roles increase, there might emerge a more egalitarian sex role structure in the family of the future.

ROLE OF THE MALE

The male's role in the family perhaps is more appealing than the female's. He initially marries to obtain anchorage which satisfies his sexual-emotional needs and provides him with a sense of belonging and of self-esteem. He desires to confine his wife and children to the home for ready access to his gratifications, but not to be himself confined. He is bored by repetition, and seeks novelty, opposition, risks, and friends outside the marriage unit.

But the absence of the father from the family setting in many situations places a good deal of stress on the stability of the marriage and upon the father-child relationship. The successful maintenance of the family unit is partially a function of the extent to which the father is present. When occupational and military obligations call him away for long periods of time, family continuity is disrupted. The children lose the one adult male model with whom they can identify and the wife is left without the one male companion the institution allows her. During this period, the wife has to assume some responsibility for the children that would normally belong to the husband. When the father returns, the roles must be redistributed and the lines of authority reestablished. In a research project during World War II, Reuben Hill discovered that it was not always easy for the couple to "pick up where they left off" when the father returned from the armed forces. An unpublished study was made of blue-collar construction workers who had to work out of town. Almost all of these men agreed such jobs posed real problems for them and their families.[16]

An additional problem is that the family is not designed for a mobile father. The needs which the family supplies to the father are also commonly frustrated during his departure. He is expected to remain faithful and lonely until the time he can be reunited with his family. If his commitment to his wife is exercised, he endures his frustration. When this happens, the family system can be seen as reinforcing sexual-emotional masochism on the part of the wife as well as the husband. If the commitment is not abided by, extramarital relationships may lead to deceit at least, or at most, to dissolution of the marriage.

The stability of the family is also contingent upon the sexual compatibility of the couple. Family stress is more likely to occur if the husband is not a satisfactory lover or becomes involved with another woman. Men are expected to be faithful to their wives or leave the home and marry "the other woman." What all of this means is that if anything happens to the marriage, the male may find himself separated from his children, in spite of his honest desires to be a good father.

The closeness between the father and his children is dependent upon a close relationship between the man and his wife. Family norms place strong emotional pressures upon the father as he is torn away from his children due to an incompatible marriage. The increased mobility of the father, due to occupational or military obligations, as well as the expectation that he leave the family setting in case of an incompatible marriage, both contribute to a weakening of the father-child relationship and the loss of the only adult male model for male children. Kingsley Davis argued that the weak link in the family group is this father-child bond. He maintained that there is no necessary association and no easy means of identification between the two as between the mother and child.[17] The weak bond between father and child may be attributed to the trend which gives the father more freedom and mobility and more access to additional sexual involvements.

2. MAINTENANCE OF RELATIONSHIPS

Our family has thus failed to evolve in a direction which would allow for this increased mobility and still provide a basis for family stability, strong bonds between adult males and children, and an adult male role model. It also fails to provide for continuous sexual-emotional gratification for separated parents whether the separation be one day or a divorce.

SEXUALITY NORMS

Our old nuclear family has a monogamous structure. The couple enact a contract wherein they explicitly agree that other intimate relationships with the same or the other sex shall cease and each partner shall be the sole source of comfort and gratification for the other. Within these norms exists an assumption that it is only possible to love one mate. We as spouses are expected to meet each of our partner's sexual and emotional demands and in effect come to accept the equation of our mate satisfying our needs with the needs themselves. So long as our spouse is ever-present to satisfy frustrated needs (which doesn't happen), there is no problem. Even if habitual behaviors are not effective, we have difficulty recognizing this fact or altering our behaviors. What I am suggesting is that norms which provide for only one source of gratification, as does monogamy, are not adequate. They provide no alternative means of sexual-emotional satisfaction. In specifying our mate as the sole means of meeting these needs, such norms prevent continuous gratification and frequently lead to neurosis.[18] Part of this neurosis can be attributed to the more or less total mutual dependency that the members of the couple develop for each other, which in turn may lead in monogamy to monotony, restrictiveness, the demise of romantic love, and other evils.

Perhaps one of these "evils" is the degeneration of sexual desire for the spouse and the increase in vicarious fantasy. An example of this is

> the case of a woman of twenty-five who could attain a slight orgasm with her husband if she imagined a powerful older man was taking her by force. Thus the wife imagines that she is being raped, that her husband is not himself but an *other*. The husband enjoys the same dream; in his wife he is possessing the legs of some dancer he has seen on the stage, the bosom of a pin-up girl whose picture he has looked at, a memory, an image. Or he may fancy his wife desired, possessed, violated, which is a way of restoring her lost alterity.[19]

If it were possible to get an open response from married couples of long standing, some vicarious sexual imagery as described above might be more the rule rather than the exception.

One manifestation of vicarious living is a structured over-dependency on our spouse, a need for his or her constant presence and acceptance. This need is often mistaken for love. The intense pleasures produced while being with that one person who is allowed to give such gratifications can be more objectively defined as a dependent attachment rather than a loving commitment. These attachments are possessive and lack the essential characteristics of genuine love—devotion, understanding, and extreme satisfaction in the individuality of the partner.

The effect of all of this is a mechanical, depersonalized interaction between the two people who seem to be controlling and threatening each other, or in the less extreme cases, compromising themselves to maintain the dependency contract. Sexual pleasure and exploration are degraded to a form of "joint masturbation." If they continue to make love to one another, it is in a sense of shame and guilt, for they are aware of their extramarital desires. For this reason the frequency of lovemaking may decrease over the duration of the marriage. For sexual release, each member of the couple may resort to increased independent masturbation in secret. A friend of mine, for example, told me that he masturbated more when he was married than at other times. During his marriage he hesitated to inform his wife of his self-gratification for fear of reprisal. Because of the mechanistic, routine and somewhat frustrating manner in which he related sexually to his wife, he preferred to fantasize, at his convenience and need, that he was having sexual intercourse with his wife's best friend, to whom he was very attracted, and thereby satisfy himself. Many couples, however, cannot admit this kind of repression to themselves, least of all to each other. So they live the vicarious life regarding each other only as a tool for the satisfaction of their needs.

Another problem arises because monogamous norms restrict sexual activity to our spouses. When gratification is not sufficient on the part of one of the couple, frustration results. If this need cannot be satisfied in some manner consistent with the conjugal norms, aggression directed to our mates or to others may develop. Restrictions on sexual expression, far from neutralizing aggression, tend to arouse it, just as the frustration-aggression hypothesis suggests. Sexuality norms function in the monogamous situation when both members are equally demanding of sexual gratification and when monotony and a lack of desire for variety prevail. Not very many couples are able to meet these conditions. Differences in demand for frequency of sexual intercourse and a real desire for a variety of sexual partners (repressed in most couples) places a heavy stress on the monogamous bond.

There is frequent resort to divorce, but within the pretension of monogamy, promiscuous petting outside of marriage, adultery, prostitution, and various other forms of non-monogamous sex relations are quite prevalent. Our monogamy is honored more often in theory than in practice. A. C. Kinsey found that by age 55, for example, one out of two American men engaged in extramarital sex. These figures are conservative because they are so outdated. In a recent study comparing the prevalence of extramarital relations to Kinsey's findings 25 years ago, it was found that young husbands are only a little more likely, but young wives are much more likely, to engage in extramarital sexual activity today. Twenty-four percent of wives and 32 percent of husbands under 25 had done so. Virginia Satir elaborates by pointing out that many people engage in either extramarital affairs or some kind of polygamy (mate-swapping or consecutive marriages).[20]

Monogamy is talk for friends and relatives; polygamy is the reality of our guarded behavior and our subjective feelings and desires. In maintaining the monogamy myth, we have perpetuated the sacredness of the marriage institution and have discouraged experimentation with possibly more rewarding family models. In maintaining the monogamy myth, we have also reinforced a norm that has partly led us to become jealous, possessive, guilt-ridden, self-repressive bundles of anxiety, full of fear and frustration. In confining our mates, we have helped destroy ourselves. The norms which govern this kind of activity surely must be ineffective in part, if not in their totality.

SOCIALIZATION

The process of socialization involves teaching children to become effective participating members of society. The patterns of child rearing have changed to some extent as the family has developed from the extended traditional type to a smaller fragmented form. The new patterns have made the child-adult transition more difficult. The gap between child and adult status is accentuated in the nuclear model and generates considerable difficulties for the adolescent. Among the structural properties of the nuclear family that contribute to these problems, Hans

Sebald lists:

1. The limited number of potential adult models.
2. Formation of adolescent subcultures outside the family system.
3. Adult responsibilities being largely invisible to youth.
4. Transfer of guidance and authority from the family to impersonal secondary institutions.
5. Limits of the modern family in meeting needs of belonging and security.
6. Status of the young being achieved by the individual in a solitary fashion.
7. Decline of both the "we" feeling among members of the nuclear family and value indoctrination by the family as a unit.[21]

Perhaps the most significant of these is the first point suggesting the limited number of adult models that children have to learn from. The small size of the nuclear family certainly has some effect upon children's personality and skills. Children being reared in the nuclear family quickly develop a high dependency upon their parents in general and their mothers in particular. This overdependent relationship is detrimental to children for a number of reasons.

It first allows for parental biases to be narrowly imposed upon children. Talcott Parsons, a leading sociological theorist, has pointed out that in an achievement-oriented society like the United States, parents tend to foster high-level achievement motivation. This is brought about by the increased leverage that the parents have as a result of the child's extreme dependence upon them. As a result of the conditional love of the parents —conditional upon achievement in school and peer situations—the child develops a strong motivational commitment to achievement.[22]

Thus, parents inject narrow biases upon children attempting to make them in many cases into something which they themselves have failed to realize. In the more extreme cases, parents relate to their own children in a somewhat "vampiresque" way.

> They feed on the child's accomplishments, sucking sustenance for their pale lives from vicarious enjoyment of his or her development. In a sense this sucking is appropriate since the parents give so much—lavish so much care, love, thoughtfulness, and self-sacrifice on their blood bank. But this is little comfort for the child, who at some point must rise above his guilt and live his own life—the culture demands it of him, and after all, a vampire is a vampire.[23]

Because of this restricted and exploitive manner by which parents impose motivation upon their children in the narrow confines of the nuclear family setting, it has been suggested that children be left with their parents for infinitely less time than at present. One alternative is for their studies and diversions to be carried on among other children, under the supervision of adults whose bonds would be more impersonal.

Another bias imposed upon children is their limited exposure to adults of different age groups. Parents are usually between 20 and 35 years of age during the child-raising period. When children are in their formative years, they tend to get little exposure to teenaged, middle-aged, and elderly people. Older siblings and grandparents may serve temporarily in this capacity but they are becoming less available with the increased fragmentation and mobility of the modern family.

As the size of the family decreases—a trend I already noted—children are raised in an environment which fails to prepare them for parenthood. Many parents feel that they themselves are not prepared to raise a family, since they grew up in relatively small families and had very little experience caring for younger brothers and sisters. The trend toward smaller families produces inadequate training grounds for effective parenthood.

Another trend relevant to effective child rearing is the steady increase in the percentage of working mothers. In 1940, for example, approximately 4 percent of married women with children of their own at home under the age of six were working; by 1963, this figure had risen to 22.5 percent.[24] With the increase in the percentage of working mothers, children are increasingly being turned over to baby-sitters and day-care facilities. The poor qualifications of most baby-sitters are rather obvious, and although studies have shown that existing child-care centers are adequate as perceived by mothers, the number of centers available is grossly inadequate. In 1958 only 2 percent of the children of working mothers in the United States were getting group care away from home, and 8 percent were getting no care whatsoever but were left to run the streets.[25] What this amounts to is the growing inadequacy of the nuclear family and society to provide healthy supervised socialization for its children.

Now, let's turn to the effects of the socialization process upon the mother. Most mothers still do not work. Motherhood in these cases is an 18-hours-a-day job, unless relieved by baby-sitters or nurseries. The total dependency of infants compels focusing upon their needs without regard to the mother's. The continuous demands of the small child can seem like a prison from which there is no escape but to wait out the years. As the years release the mother from her bondage, they also rob her of her youth. The rising curve of child neglect also may be related to the percentage of increase of early marriages, compounded by the total dependency of the child upon the young mother.

Another question to consider is whether or not mothers are happy with their children. In an extensive study of Detroit parents, it was concluded that more than one out of every ten mothers found the arrival of a new baby more depriving than rewarding. In another pioneer project of marital adjustment, couples with no children or one child rated their marriages significantly happier than couples with two or more children. These findings were confirmed in a later study. In another project, it was reported that the higher the ratio of children per years of marriage, the less satisfactory the marriage experience. Other research has shown that there seems to be increasing marital dissatisfaction as time passes through the child-rearing stages. After the child-rearing period, marital satisfaction increases slightly but never approaches the original level. Research by Gurin, Burr, Pineo, Paris, Luckey, and others as summarized by Mary Hicks and Marilyn Platt revealed a gradual decrease in marital satisfaction over time.[26] Thus, it seems that children fail to bring happiness into the nuclear family. The old myth is not supported by the evidence. Family life instead of providing a favorable setting for parenthood, provides for a gradual decrease in the contentment of parents.

In review, then, socialization in the nuclear family is inadequate in that it:

1. Makes the child–adult transition difficult.
2. Limits the number of adult models for children to follow.
3. Produces an overdependency of children on their parents.
4. Provides for the teaching of bias of parental values.
5. Allows for an exploitive and vicarious imposition of motivation of the parents upon their children.
6. Confines the exposure of children to people of narrow

age ranges.

7. Fails to adequately prepare children for parenthood.

8. Fails to provide adequate parent substitutes when

parents are not available.

9. Produces marital dissatisfaction especially in larger families.

NOTES

1. Hans Sebald, *Adolescence: A Sociological Analysis* (New York: Appleton-Century-Crofts, 1968), p. 51.

2. U.S. Bureau of the Census, *Statistical Abstract of the United States, 1972* (Washington, D.C.: Government Printing Office, 1972), p. 39.

3. E. E. LeMasters, *Parents in Modern America* (Homewood, Ill.: Dorsey Press, 1970), p. 4.

4. F. Ivan Nye, John Carlson, and Gerald Garrett, "Family Size, Interaction, Affect and Stress," *Journal of Marriage and the Family* 32, no. 2 (May 1970): 216–225.

5. Snell Putney and Gail Putney, *The Adjusted American* (New York: Harper & Row, 1964), p. 111.

6. Ibid., p. 114.

7. George Bach and Peter Wyden, *The Intimate Enemy* (New York: William Morrow, 1969), p. 6.

8. Jerold Heiss, "Degree of Intimacy and Male-Female Interaction," in *Family Roles and Interaction; An Anthology,* ed. Jerold Heiss (Chicago: Rand McNally, 1968), p. 91.

9. Lee Rainwater, "Marital Sexuality in Four Cultures of Poverty," *Journal of Marriage and the Family* 26, no. 4 (November 1964): 466.

10. These were some of the results of unpublished data collected by the author from a sample of 284 sophomores at Michigan State University in the winter of 1969. Each of the correlation coefficients calculated was significant at the .01 level or less.

11. Betty Friedan, *The Feminine Mystique* (New York: Dell Publishing, 1963), p. 296.

12. Barrington Moore Jr., "Thoughts on the Future of the Family," in *Identity and Anxiety,* eds. Maurice Stein et al. (New York: The Free Press, 1960), p. 395.

13. Nora Scott Kinzer, "Soapy Sin in the Afternoon," *Psychology Today,* August 1973, p. 48.

14. Mervin B. Freedman, "Studies of College Alumni," in *The American College,* ed. Sanford Nevitt (New York: Wiley, 1962), p. 878.

15. De Beauvoir, *Second Sex,* p. 422; also, F. Ivan Nye and Feliz Bernardo, *The Family, Its Structure and Interaction* (New York: Macmillan, 1973), pp. 255–260.

16. Reuben Hill, *Families Under Stress* (New York: Harper and Brothers, 1949). For unpublished study, see LeMasters, *Parents,* p. 143.

17. Kingley Davis, *Human Society* (New York: Macmillan, 1949), p. 400.

18. Putney and Putney, *Adjusted American,* p. 13.

19. De Beauvoir, *Second Sex,* p. 421.

20. A. C. Kinsey et al., *Sexual Behavior in the Human Male* (Philadelphia and London: W. B. Saunders Co., 1948), p. 259 and pp. 585–588; for the more recent study, see Morton Hunt, "Sexual Behavior in the 1970s," *Playboy,* October 1973, p. 88; Virginia Satir, "Marriage as a Human-Actualizing Contract," in *The Family in Search of a Future,* ed. H. A. Otto (New York: Appleton-Century-Crofts, 1970), pp. 62–63.

21. Sebald, *Adolescence,* p. 50.

22. Talcott Parsons, "Certain Primary Sources and Patterns of Aggression in the Social Structure of the Western World," *Psychiatry* 10 (1947): 11.

23. Philip Slater, *The Pursuit of Loneliness* (Boston: The Beacon Press, 1970), p. 59.

24. U.S. Bureau of the Census, *Statistical Abstract of the United States, 1964* (Washington, D.C.: Government Printing Office, 1964), p. 65.

25. Vance Packard, *The Sexual Wilderness* (New York: David McKay, 1968), p. 376.

26. For the study of Detroit parents see Daniel Miller and Guy Swanson, *The Changing American Parent* (New York: John Wiley, 1967), p. 215–233; for studies of marital adjustment, see W. Burgess and L. Cottrell Jr., *Predicting Success or Failure in Marriage* (New York: Prentice-Hall, 1939), p. 258–259; also, see Ernest W. Burgess and Paul Wallin, *Engagement and Marriage* (Philadelphia: J. B. Lippincott, 1953), pp. 712–713; for the project on the ratio of children per years of marriage, see John Hurley and Donna Palonen, "Marital Satisfaction and Child Density Among University Student Parents," *Journal of Marriage and the Family* 29, no. 3 (August 1967): 483–484; for marital satisfaction studies, see, for example, Robert O. Blood and Donald Wolfe, *Husbands and Wives: The Dynamics of Married Living* (Glencoe, Ill.: The Free Press, 1965), or Boyd Rollins and Harold Feldman, "Marital Satisfaction Over the Family Life Cycle," *Journal of Marriage and the Family* 31, no. 1 (January 1970): 20–27; also see Mary Hicks and Marilyn Platt, "Marital Happiness and Stability, A Review of the Research in the Sixties," *Journal of Marriage and the Family* 32, no. 4 (November 1970): 564–566.

The Siege of the Family

Christopher Lasch

The plight of the family, so long a professional preoccupation of social scientists and social pathologists, now commands anxious attention among legislators and government bureaucrats. Everyone talks about the need for a "family policy." President Carter has repeatedly stressed the importance of holding the family together, and a growing number of agencies—the Senate Subcommittee on Children and Youth, the Select Committee on Education of the House of Representatives, the HEW Office of Human Development, among others—devote at least part of their time to problems of the family.

According to a theory currently popular in Washington, the United States already has a de facto policy on families, since the income tax, social security, medicaid, and many other governmental programs impinge in one way or another on the family. Tax laws reward marriage and discriminate against single taxpayers. Welfare programs help to break up families by restricting aid, in half the states, to fatherless households. Military and foreign service transfers often contribute, inadvertently, to the same result. The $750 personal exemption in the income tax code, which amounts to a partial subsidy of child care, favors the rich, like all personal tax exemptions, and thus puts an additional burden on the poor. These and other programs, formulated with an eye to other objectives, influence the family in an unplanned and often contradictory fashion. What the country needs, according to this reasoning, is a policy designed to promote "family health" and to correct the "anti-family bias" that often results, unintentionally, from other programs.

Current concern about the family probably derives not so much from the crisis of the family itself as from two important policy studies of the Sixties, the Moynihan Report and the Coleman Report. Government officials respond more readily to events in Washington than to events in the rest of the country,

and both these documents have had great influence in official circles. The Moynihan Report, although widely criticized and denounced, reinforced a long-standing belief that poverty and broken homes go hand in hand. The Coleman Report, followed a few years later by Christopher Jencks's elaborate study of education and achievement,[1] seemed to show that schooling has little effect on academic achievement (or on jobs, income, or social mobility)—that achievement for the most part reflects the attitude toward schooling that children bring to school from their families.

According to Coleman, "it appears that variations in the facilities and curriculums of the schools account for relatively little variation in pupil achievement insofar as this is measured by standard tests." Even racial integration showed a "rather small" correlation with scholastic achievement. On the other hand, "a pupil's achievement is strongly related to the educational backgrounds and aspirations of the other students in the school." In other words, middle-class children in middle-class schools expect more from schooling and get it. Jencks insisted even more strongly that families, not schools, determine the course of a child's educational career and hence his access to good jobs and a good income. Because "family background explains nearly half the variation in educational attainment," he concluded that school reform "cannot make adults more equal."

The new interest in the family thus reflects a certain disillusionment with the school. It also reflects a growing disenchantment with the public institutions and welfare agencies that have taken over so many functions of the family—the hospital, the mental asylum, the juvenile court. The medical profession, after upholding the hospital as an indispensable alternative to the family, now begins to think that patients might

[1] *Inequality: A Reassessment of the Effect of Family and Schooling in America*, by Christopher Jencks and others (Basic Books, 1972).

be better off if they were allowed to die at home. Psychiatrists are having similar second thoughts, not only because existing facilities are overcrowded but because they have failed to attain the high rates of cures once predicted with such confidence. Lawyers have begun to criticize the courts for removing "neglected" children from their homes without evidence that such children suffer serious harm and without proof that institutionalization or transfer to foster parents provides any solution. Even the school's claim on the child has begun to give way to parental claims. In *Wisconsin* v. *Yoder* (1972), the Supreme Court ruled that Amish parents have a right to keep their children out of the public schools. "The child is not the mere creature of the State," the court said; "those who nurture him and direct his destiny have the right, coupled with the high duty, to recognize and prepare him for additional obligations."[2]

[2] Justice William O. Douglas, dissenting in *Yoder*, presented the argument for state intervention in its most attractive form. Suppose an Amish child wished to follow an occupation that required him to break from the cultural tradition of his parents. Suppose he wished to become "a pianist or an astronaut or an oceanographer." The Court's decision made this impossible, Douglas argued. Without consulting the preferences of the children themselves, the Court had delivered them into a narrow, backward, and parochial environment, barring them "forever" from the "new and amazing world of diversity."

Persuasive as it appears at first sight, this argument on examination proves to be a classic example of the sentimentality of liberal humanitarianism, which invokes "diversity" to support a system of uniform compulsory schooling and proposes to rescue the child from the backward culture of his parents by delivering him into the tender care of the state. The argument is sentimental above all in its assumption that the state can spare the child who does decide to break from his parents' traditions the pain, suffering, and guilt that such a break necessarily exacts—the confrontation with which, however, constitutes

2. MAINTENANCE OF RELATIONSHIPS

All Our Children, a new study of the family commissioned by the Carnegie Corporation in 1972, shows the influence of the new mood among welfare workers, government officials, social scientists, and social reformers. Until recently, most experts took the position that parents lacked the resources and the technical knowledge to provide for their children's needs and that their efforts had to be supplemented, or even supplanted, by a proliferation of social services. Keniston and his co-authors, conscious of belonging to "an emerging consensus," believe on the contrary that parents "are still the world's greatest experts about the needs of their own children." They recognize that many of the agencies ostensibly ministering to the family have undermined the family instead. These agencies have taken over much of the work of child rearing yet left parents with most of the blame for whatever goes wrong.

The experts, having assumed or undermined parental powers, still talk as if parents retained exclusive responsibility for the child's development. Parents thus exercise little authority over the young while experiencing most of the guilt that arises when the young fail to get ahead in life. The parental "malaise," according to Keniston, consists of "the sense of having no guidelines or supports for raising children, the feeling of not being in control as parents, and the widespread sense of personal guilt for what seems to be going awry."

The rehabilitation of parenthood, it appears, implies at the same time a thoroughgoing critique of professionalism and the welfare state. Unfortunately Keniston stops well short of such a critique. He takes for granted the family's dependence on experts and seeks merely to regularize and regulate this relationship. "Few people would dispute that we live in a society where parents must increasingly rely on others for help and support in raising their children." The family economy has disappeared, children represent a financial liability rather than an asset, the school has taken over the family's educational functions, and the medical profession has assumed most of the responsibility for health care.

These changes, according to Keniston, leave parents in the position of "executives in a large firm—responsible for the smooth coordination of the many people and processes that must work together to produce the final product."

This line of analysis leads to the conclusion, not that parents should collectively assert their control over child rearing, but that federal policy should seek to equalize the relationship between experts and parents. Yet Keniston's own reasoning shows that parents occupy a position closer to that of proletarians than of executives. As matters now stand, according to Keniston, "parents have little authority over those with whom they share the task of raising their children"; they "deal with those others from a position of inferiority or helplessness." The obvious reason for this is that the state, not the parents, pays the bill for professional services, or at least signs the paychecks. (The citizens, as taxpayers, pay in the end.) If parents organized and hired their own experts, things might be different.

It goes without saying that such solutions do not commend themselves to members of the policy-making establishment. Measures of this kind are too closely associated with populism, localism, and residual resistance to centralized progress. They have become doubly objectionable, and for reasons whose force even enemies of the establishment must acknowledge, in the wake of the Ocean Hill-Brownsville battle of the late Sixties, when "community control" degenerated into reverse racism and education into racial propaganda. The causes of this failure were not simple and a different result might have been possible in a more tolerant atmosphere, but the example is not promising. Yet the alternative to community control is more bureaucracy. I wish Keniston and other social democrats would squarely confront the choice. Instead they try to have things both ways. While advocating an expansion of government services to the family, a federal guarantee of full employment, improved protection of children's legal rights, and a vastly expanded program of health care, Keniston at the same time proposes to strengthen "parent participation" in all these programs.

Keniston has plenty of good intentions. Service workers, he believes, should take the needs of their clients into account (although the state pays the bills). The **government should "enable the simplest**

units **possible—individuals and families—to make their own choices and control the shape of their own lives."** Instead of always blaming the abuse and neglect of children on their parents, the law should recognize that neglect often arises out of intolerable living conditions. Accordingly, the state whenever possible should help the family to provide for its economic needs rather than remove the "neglected" child to an institution.

Yet the hope that the state can provide increased services to the family without undermining parental authority and competence even further remains unrealistic. Keniston himself admits that "people who provide services, at least those publicly funded, have had to account to their bosses, not their clients, for how well they are doing the job." In order to break this pattern, he wants to set up "consumers' councils" that would audit service agencies and "evaluate how well programs are actually alleviating the problems they were set up to solve." But the definition of parents as consumers of services already relegates them to a position of inferiority toward the services on which they depend. The experts' power rests on their claim to provide services the family cannot provide for itself, and this claim in turn rests on the experts' special access to technical knowledge allegedly indispensable to the job. Consumer education and participation in decision making—standard tactics of liberal reformers for years—make no assault on the monopoly of technical knowledge by experts and therefore do not alter the balance of power between experts and consumers, in this case between parents and the service agencies that have expropriated parental authority.

All Our Children, for all its laudable intent to restore authority to the family, bears the stamp of American social science, which has never been able to understand the role of power in social life or the way in which its own findings usually support the assumption of power by allegedly impartial, scientific experts. Social science treats the ascendancy of experts as an unavoidable condition of industrial society, even when it seeks to qualify this ascendancy by improving the position of consumers. In fact, however, the concepts of "industrial specialization" and "functional differentiation" conceal the expropriation of the workers' craft knowledge by modern management, just as the "transfer of functions" from the family to other agencies—the bland

---

the psychological and educative value of such an experience. In true paternalist fashion, Douglas would smooth away the painful obstacles to the child's progress, forgetting that progress consists precisely in overcoming those obstacles.

formula which social scientists use to describe the transformation of the family under industrialism—conceals the expropriation of parental authority by the so-called helping professions.

During the twentieth century, these professions have extended their authority over the care and nurture of the young by deriding maternal "instinct," stigmatizing parental services to the young as "home remedies," and ridiculing the "rule of thumb" methods used in the household. The medical and psychiatric assault on the family as a technologically backward sector complements the advertising industry's drive to convince people that store-bought goods are superior to home-made products.

The family's increasing inability to provide for its own needs does not in itself vindicate the experts' claims. Consumer advocates, who accept the inevitability of consumption as a way of life, have consistently deplored the shoddy quality of machine-made goods, and the same criticism extends to many of the services provided to the family by medicine and psychiatry. At one time the experts believed—and managed to convince their clients—that they had reduced child rearing to an exact science. The collapse of that faith calls into question the inevitability of professional dominance—of the increasing control exercised by the health, education, and welfare professions, and by the state, over the process of growing up in society.[3]

Social scientists assume that the requirements of a complex society dictate the triumph of factory production over handicraft production and the ascendancy of the "helping professions" over the family. It is significant that Keniston objects to the habit of blaming parents for everything that goes wrong with their children, not because it undermines the family's capacity for self-help, but because, on the contrary, it rests on "the myth of the self-sufficient individual and of the self-sufficient, protected, and protective family."

From his perspective—the one that prevails in all the social sciences—modern society constitutes a seamless web of interconnected, interdependent organisms. In such a society, "family self-sufficiency is a false myth," in Keniston's words. From his point of view, the consideration that "all today's families need help in raising children," instead of prompting questions about how experts came to put so many people in the position of needing "help," merely confirms the inevitability of professional ascendancy.

Recent studies of "professionalization" by historians have shown that professionalism did not emerge, in the nineteenth and early twentieth centuries, in response to clearly defined social needs.[4] Instead, the new professions themselves invented many of the needs they claimed to satisfy. They played on public fears of disorder and disease, adopted a deliberately mystifying jargon, ridiculed popular traditions of self-help as backward and unscientific, and in this way created or intensified (not without opposition) a demand for their own services. The case for the rise of the factory system in the nineteenth century, as Stephen Marglin has recently argued, rested not on its technological superiority over handicraft production but on the more effective control of the labor force it allowed the employer.[5]

Similarly the case for the "helping professions" rested not on their technical superiority over the family but on the control they exercised over the child, which made it possible, in the words of one reformer, "to rescue the child from irresponsible parents." What Durkheim said about the advantage of the school over the family applied to the whole apparatus of socialized reproduction, and laid bare the real motive behind the experts' drive to take over the functions of the family.

> We have through the school the means of training the child in a collective life different from home life. We have here a unique and irreplaceable opportunity to take hold of the child at a time when the gaps in our social organization have not yet been able to arouse in him feelings that make him partially rebellious to common life.

In Durkheim's view, the displacement of the family by the school and other agencies of socialized reproduction would facilitate the integration of the individual into society, "the nourishing mother from which we gain the whole of our moral and intellectual substance and toward whom our wills turn in a spirit of love and gratitude."

Against the hypothesis of professional self-aggrandizement, it has been argued that demands for professional services originate in "real advances of knowledge" and in the "conditions of modern society," which "place a high premium on esoteric knowledge."[6] But "conditions" do not in themselves generate social change. What counts is the way conditions are interpreted, and professionals have clearly interpreted them, and sold this interpretation to the public, in such a way as to increase the demand for their own knowledge. The evidence of their assiduous self-promotion can no longer be airily dismissed by reasserting the sociological truism that "modern society involves the individual in relations...that are vastly more complex than [those] his ancestors...had to contend with."[7]

[3]"We really know very little about how to raise a child to make him 'healthy'—however 'healthy' may be defined." This uncertainty, according to an argument that is beginning to find favor among lawyers, creates a "presumption in favor of parental autonomy" whenever the state attempts to transfer a child from his parents to a foster home or to some sort of asylum. See Michael Wald, "State Intervention on Behalf of 'Neglected' Children: A Search for Realistic Standards," *Stanford Law Review*, XXVII (1975), 992, 1037.

[4]See Burton J. Bledstein, *The Culture of Professionalism* (Norton, 1976); Robert H. Wiebe, *The Search for Order, 1877-1920* (Hill and Wang, 1967); Anthony M. Platt, *The Child Savers: The Invention of Delinquency* (University of Chicago Press, 1969); Joseph M. Hawes, *Children in Urban Society: Juvenile Delinquency in Nineteenth-Century America* (Oxford University Press, 1971); Robert M. Mennel, *Thorns and Thistles: Juvenile Delinquents in the United States, 1825-1940* (University Press of New England, 1973).

[5]Stephen Marglin, "What Do Bosses Do?" *Review of Radical Political Economics*, VI (Summer, 1974), pp. 60-112, VII (Spring, 1975), pp. 20-37.

[6]Thomas L. Haskell, "Power to the Experts," *NYR*, October 13, 1977, p. 33.

[7]Since Thomas Haskell has tried to equate criticism of the professions with a blind and willful opposition to the pursuit of truth, I do not wish my argument to be misunderstood as an unqualified condemnation of professionalism. Obviously professions uphold important values. In particular, they uphold standards of accuracy, honesty, verification, and service that might otherwise disappear altogether. But it is

2. MAINTENANCE OF RELATIONSHIPS

The work of Burton Bledstein, Anthony Platt, Robert Mennel, and other historians of professionalism is defective not because it underestimates the genuine need for professional services but because it treats professionalism as an independent, autonomous historical determinant, ignoring the connection between the rise of modern professionalism and the rise of industrial management. The same historical development that turned the citizen into a client transformed the worker from a producer into a consumer. The new historians of professionalism, by treating professionals as a separate class with their own interests and identity, repeat the mistake made by earlier students of the "managerial revolution," who argued that managers constitute a "new class." In reality, both the growth of management and the proliferation of professions represent new forms of capitalist control, which enable capital to transcend its personal form and to pervade every part of society.

The problem of strengthening the family has to be considered as part of the more general problem of control over production and over the technical knowledge on which modern production rests. The family's dependence on professional services over which it has little control represents one form of a more general phenomenon: the erosion of self-reliance and ordinary competence by the growth of giant corporations and of the bureaucratic state which serves them. The corporations and the state now control so much of the necessary know-how that Durkheim's image of society as the "nourishing mother," from whom all blessings flow, more and more coincides with the citizen's everyday experience. The "consensus of the competent," as Thomas L. Haskell refers to the professions in his book *The Emergence of Professional Social Science*, came into being by reducing the layman to incompetence.

As management extended its control over production, it appropriated the technical knowledge formerly controlled by the crafts and trades, centralized this knowledge, and then parceled it out piecemeal in a confusing, selective fashion guaranteed to keep the worker in a state of dependence. Similarly the "helping professions," by persuading the family to rely on scientific technology and the advice of scientifically trained experts, undermined the family's capacity to provide for itself and thereby justified the continuing expansion of health, education, and welfare services. Having monopolized or claimed to monopolize most of the knowledge necessary to bring up children, the agencies of socialized reproduction handed it back in the form of "parent education," "consumer education," and other devices intended to enable the citizen to shop more efficiently among proliferating professional services. As two child-guidance experts[a] put it in 1934, "Old functions of child welfare and training have passed over into the hands of sociologists, psychiatrists, physicians, home economists, and other scientists dealing with problems of human welfare. Through parent education the sum of their experiments and knowledge is given back to parents in response to their demand for help." Having first declared parents incompetent to raise their offspring without professional assistance, social pathologists "gave back" the knowledge they had appropriated—gave it back in a mystifying fashion that rendered parents more helpless than ever, more abject in their dependence on expert opinion.

What is to be done? Keniston's formulation—that policy should seek not to replace the family but to enable it to provide more efficiently for its own needs—can serve as a guide to social policy in general. Strengthen the citizen, not the state; above all, avoid the creation of new bureaucracies. Disenchantment with "institutional" solutions, together with a shortage of public funds, makes such proposals attractive right now. Unless access to knowledge can be made more radically democratic, however, reforms undertaken in this spirit may simply add to the family's burdens without adding to its power. In order to break the existing pattern of dependence and stop the erosion of competence, citizens must take the solution of their problems—the deterioration of child care, for example—into their own hands. They must create their own agencies of collective self-help, their own "communities of competence." This sounds utopian, but American society contains many traditions of localism, self-help, and community action, not yet defunct by any means, on which to base such a politics of decentralization. On the other hand, the well-meaning attempt to strengthen the family by improving the professional services that minister to it will merely strengthen the professions instead.

---

[a]Katherine Glover and Evelyn Dewey, *Children of the New Day* (D. Appleton-Century, 1934), p. 48.

not true, as Paul Goodman argued in his otherwise compelling defense of professionalism ("The New Reformation," cited by Haskell in his review of Bledstein), that "professionals are autonomous individuals beholden to the nature of things and the judgment of their peers, and bound by an explicit or implicit oath to benefit their clients and the community." The way in which professionals construe and discharge these responsibilities naturally reflects the social surroundings in which they operate. American professionalism has been corrupted by the managerial capitalism with which it is so closely allied, just as professionalism in the Soviet Union has been much more completely corrupted by the dictatorship of the Party.

In his book *The Emergence of Professional Social Science* (University of Illinois Press, 1977), Haskell writes: "Membership in a truly professional community [cannot] be based on charm, social standing, personal connection, good character, or perhaps even decency, but on demonstrated intellectual merit alone." Haskell does not appreciate how easily "intellectual merit" can be confused with the mere acquisition of professional credentials or, worse, with loyalty to any unspoken ideological consensus—how easily the indispensable ideal of professional disinterestedness can be warped and distorted by the social and political context in which it has grown up.

MARRIAGE AS A WRETCHED INSTITUTION

Mervyn Cadwallader

The author of this disturbing reflection on the mores and mishaps that increasingly afflict love and marriage among young Americans is a professor of sociology and the humanities at San Jose State College and director of its Experimental Program in Humanities and Science. He is forty, "has been happily married three times," and is the father of one child. (= poor child !!)

Our society expects us all to get married. With only rare exceptions we all do just that. Getting married is a rather complicated business. It involves mastering certain complex hustling and courtship games, the rituals and the ceremonies that celebrate the act of marriage, and finally the difficult requirements of domestic life with a husband or wife. It is an enormously elaborate round of activity, much more so than finding a job, and yet while many resolutely remain unemployed, few remain unmarried.

Now all this would not be particularly remarkable if there were no question about the advantages, the joys, and the rewards of married life, but most Americans, even young Americans, know or have heard that marriage is a hazardous affair. Of course, for all the increase in divorce, there are still young marriages that work, unions made by young men and women intelligent or fortunate enough to find the kind of mates they want, who know that they want children and how to love them when they come, or who find the artful blend between giving and receiving. It is not these marriages that concern us here, and that is not the trend in America today. We are concerned with the increasing number of others who, with mixed intentions and varied illusions, grope or fling themselves into marital disaster. They talk solemnly and sincerely about working to make their marriage succeed, but they are very aware of the countless marriages they have seen fail. But young people in particular do not seem to be able to relate the awesome divorce statistics to the probability of failure of their own marriage. And they rush into it, in increasing numbers, without any clear idea of the reality that underlies the myth.

Parents, teachers, and concerned adults all counsel against premature marriage. But they rarely speak the truth about marriage as it really is in modern middle-class America. The truth as I see it is that contemporary marriage is a wretched institution. It spells the end of voluntary affection, of love freely given and joyously received. Beautiful romances are transmuted into dull marriages, and eventually the relationship becomes constricting, corrosive, grinding, and destructive. The beautiful love affair becomes a bitter contract.

The basic reason for this sad state of affairs is that marriage was not designed to bear the burdens now being asked of it by the urban American middle class. It is an institution that evolved over centuries to meet some very specific functional needs of a nonindustrial society. Romantic love was viewed as tragic, or merely irrelevant. Today it is the titillating prelude to domestic tragedy, or, perhaps more frequently, to domestic grotesqueries that are only pathetic.

Marriage was not designed as a mechanism for providing friendship, erotic experience, romantic love, personal fulfillment, continuous lay psychotherapy, or recreation. The Western European family was not designed to carry a lifelong load of highly emotional romantic freight. Given its present structure, it simply has to fail when asked to do so. The very idea of an irrevocable contract obligating the parties concerned to a lifetime of romantic effort is utterly absurd.

Other pressures of the present era have tended to overburden marriage with expectations it cannot fulfill. Industrialized, urbanized America is a society which has lost the sense of community. Our ties to our society, to the bustling multitudes that make up this dazzling kaleidoscope of contemporary America, are as formal and superficial as they are numerous. We all search for community, and yet we know that the search is futile. Cut off from the support and satisfactions that flow from community, the confused and searching young American can do little but place all of his bets on creating a community in microcosm, his own marriage.

And so the ideal we struggle to reach in our love relationship is that of complete candor, total honesty. Out there all is phony, but within the romantic family there are to be no dishonest games, no hypocrisy, no misunderstanding. Here we have a painful paradox, for I submit that total exposure is probably always mutually destructive in the long run. What starts out as a tender coming together to share one's whole person with the beloved is transmuted by too much togetherness into attack and counterattack, doubt, disillusionment, and ambivalence. The moment the once-upon-a-time lover catches a glimpse of his own hatred, something precious and fragile is shattered. And soon another brave marriage will end.

The purposes of marriage have changed radically, yet we cling desperately to the outmoded structures of the past. Adult Americans behave as though the more obvious the contradiction between the old and the new, the more sentimental and irrational should be their advice to young people who are going steady or are engaged. Our schools, both high schools and colleges, teach sentimental rubbish in their marriage and family courses. The texts make much of a posture of hard-nosed objectivity that is neither objective nor hard-nosed. The basic structure of Western marriage is never questioned, alternatives are not proposed or discussed. Instead, the prospective young bride and bridegroom are offered housekeeping advice and told to work hard at making their marriage succeed. The chapter on sex, complete with ugly diagrams of the male and female genitals, is probably wedged in between a chapter on budgets and life insurance. The message is that if your marriage fails, you have been weighed in the domestic balance and found wanting. Perhaps you did not master the fifth position for sexual intercourse, or maybe you bought cheap term life rather than a preferred policy with income protection and retirement benefits. If taught honestly, these courses would alert the teenager and young adult to the realities of matrimonial life in the United States and try to advise them on how to survive marriage if they insist on that hazardous venture.

But teen-agers and young adults do insist upon it in greater and greater numbers with each passing year. And one of the reasons they do get married with such astonishing certainty is because they find themselves immersed in a culture that is preoccupied with and schizophrenic about sex. Advertising, entertainment, and fashion are all designed to produce and then to exploit sexual tension. Sexually aroused at an early age and asked to postpone marriage until they become adults, they have no recourse but to fill the intervening years with courtship rituals and games that are supposed to be sexy but sexless. Dating is expected to culminate in going steady, and that is the beginning of the end. The dating game hinges on an important exchange. The male wants sexual intimacy, and the female wants social commitment. The game involves bartering sex for security amid the sweet and heady agitations of a romantic entanglement. Once the game reaches the going-steady stage, marriage is virtually inevitable. The teen-ager finds himself driven into a corner, and the one way to legitimize his sex play and assuage the guilt is to plan marriage.

Another reason for the upsurge in young marriages is the real cultural break between teen-agers and adults in our society. This is a recent phenomenon. In my generation there was no teen culture. Adolescents wanted to become adults as soon as possible. The teen-age years were a time of impatient waiting, as teen-age boys tried to dress and act like little men. Adolescents sang the adults' songs ("South of the Border," "The Music Goes Round and Round," "Mairzy Doats" — notice I didn't say anything about the quality of the music), saw their movies, listened to their radios, and waited confidently to be allowed in. We had no money, and so there was no teen-age market. There was nothing to do then but get it over with. The boundary line was sharp, and you crossed it when you took your first serious job, when you passed the employment test.

Now there is a very definite adolescent culture, which is in many ways hostile to the dreary culture of the adult world. In its most extreme form it borrows from the beats and turns the middle-class value system inside out. The hip teen-ager on Macdougal Street or Telegraph Avenue can buy a costume and go to a freak show. It's fun to be an Indian, a prankster, a beat, or a swinging troubadour. He can get stoned. That particular trip leads to instant mysticism.

Even in less extreme forms, teen culture is weighted against the adult world of responsibility. I recently asked a roomful of eighteen-year-olds to tell me what an adult is. Their deliberate answer, after hours of discussion, was that an adult is someone who no longer plays, who is no longer playful. Is Bob Dylan an adult? No, never! Of course they did not want to remain children, or teens, or adolescents; but they did want to remain youthful, playful, free of squares, and free of responsibility. The teen-ager wants to be old enough to drive, drink, screw, and travel. He does not want to get pushed into square maturity. He wants to drag the main, be a surf bum, a ski bum, or dream of being a bum. He doesn't want to go to Vietnam, or to IBM, or to buy a split-level house in Knotty Pines Estates.

This swing away from responsibility quite predictably produces frictions between the adolescent and his parents. The clash of cultures is likely to drive the adolescent from the home, to persuade him to leave the dead world of his parents and strike out on his own. And here we find the central paradox of young marriages. For the only way the young person can escape from his parents is to assume many of the responsibilities that he so reviles in the life-style of his parents. He needs a job and an apartment. And he needs some kind of emotional substitute, some means of filling the emotional vacuum that leaving home has caused. And so he goes steady, and sooner rather than later, gets married to a girl with similar inclinations.

When he does this, he crosses the dividing line between the cultures. Though he seldom realizes it at the time, he has taken the first step to adulthood. Our society does not have a conventional "rite of passage." In Africa the Masai adolescent takes a lion test. He becomes an adult the first time he kills a lion with a spear. Our adolescents take the domesticity test. When they get married they have to come to terms with the system in one way or another. Some brave individuals continue to fight it. But most simply capitulate.

The cool adolescent finishing high school or starting college has a skeptical view of virtually every institutional sector of his society. He knows that government is corrupt, the military dehumanizing, the corporations rapacious, the churches organized hypocrisy, and the schools dishonest. But the one area that seems to be exempt from his cynicism is romantic love and marriage. When I talk to teen-agers about marriage, that cool skepticism turns to sentimental dreams right out of *Ladies' Home Journal* or the hard-hitting pages of *Reader's Digest*. They all mouth the same vapid platitudes about finding happiness through sharing and personal fulfillment through giving (each is to give 51 percent). They have all heard about divorce, and most of them have been touched by it in some way or another. Yet they insist that their marriage will be different.

So, clutching their illusions, young girls with ecstatic screams of joy lead their awkward brooding boys through the portals of the church into the land of the Mustang, Apartment 24, Macy's, Sears, and the ubiquitous drive-in. They have become members in good standing of the adult world.

The end of most of these sentimental marriages is quite predictable. They progress, in most cases, to varying stages of marital ennui, depending on the ability of the couple to adjust to reality; most common are (1) a lackluster standoff, (2) a bitter business carried on for the children, church, or neighbors, or (3) separation and divorce, followed by another search to find the right person.

Divorce rates have been rising in all Western countries. In many countries the rates are rising even faster than in the United States. In 1910 the divorce rate for the United States was 87 per 1000 marriages. In 1965 the rate had risen to an estimated figure of well over 300 per 1000 in many parts of the country. At the present time some 40 percent of all brides are between the ages of fifteen and eighteen; half of these marriages break up within five years. As our population becomes younger and the age of marriage continues to drop, the divorce rate will rise to significantly higher levels.

What do we do, what can we do, about this wretched and disappointing institution? In terms of the immediate generation, the answer probably is, not much. Even when subjected to the enormous strains I have described, the habits, customs, traditions, and taboos that make up our courtship and marriage cycle are uncommonly resistant to change. Here and there creative and courageous individuals can and do work out their own unique solutions to the problem of marriage. Most of us simply suffer without understanding and thrash around blindly in an attempt to reduce the acute pain of a romance gone sour. In time, all of these individual actions will show up as a trend away from the old and toward the new, and the bulk of sluggish moderates in the population will slowly come to accept this trend as part of social evolution. Clearly, in middle-class America, the trend is ever toward more romantic courtship and marriage, earlier premarital sexual intercourse, earlier first marriages, more extramarital affairs, earlier first divorces, more frequent divorces and remarriages. The trend is away from stable lifelong monogamous relationships toward some form of polygamous male-female relationship. Perhaps we should identify it as serial or consecutive polygamy, simply because Americans in significant numbers are going to have more than one husband or more than one wife. Attitudes and laws that make multiple marriages (in sequence, of course) difficult for the romantic and sentimental among us are archaic obstacles that one learns to circumvent with the aid of weary judges and clever attorneys.

Now, the absurdity of much of this lies in the fact that we pretend that marriages of short duration must be contracted for life. Why not permit a flexible contract perhaps for one to two or more years, with periodic options to renew? If a couple grew disenchanted with their life together, they would not feel trapped for life. They would not have to anticipate and then go through the destructive agonies of divorce. They would not have to carry about the stigma of marital failure, like the mark of Cain on their foreheads. Instead of a declaration of war, they could simply let their contract lapse, and while still friendly, be free to continue their romantic quest. Sexualized romanticism is now so fundamental to American life — and is bound to become even more so — that marriage will simply have to accommodate itself to it in one way or another. For a great proportion of us it already has.

What of the children in a society that is moving inexorably toward consecutive plural marriages? Under present arrangements in which marriages are ostensibly lifetime contracts and then are dissolved through hypocritical collusions or messy battles in court, the children do suffer. Marriage and divorce turn lovers into enemies, and the child is left to thread his way through the emotional wreckage of his parents' lives. Financial support of the children, mere subsistence, is not really a problem in a society as affluent as ours. Enduring emotional support of children by loving, healthy, and friendly adults is a serious problem in America, and it is a desperately urgent problem in many families where divorce is unthinkable. If the bitter and poisonous denouement of divorce could be avoided by a frank acceptance of short-term marriages, both adults and children would benefit. Any time husbands and wives and ex-husbands and ex-wives treat each other decently, generously, and respectfully, their children will benefit.

The braver and more critical among our teenagers and youthful adults will still ask, But if the institution is so bad, why get married at all? This is a tough one to deal with. The social pressures pushing any couple who live together into marriage are difficult to ignore even by the most resolute rebel. It can be done, and many should be encouraged to carry out their own creative experiments in living together in a relationship that is wholly voluntary. If the demands of society to conform seem overwhelming, the couple should know that simply to be defined by others as married will elicit married-like behavior in themselves, and that is precisely what they want to avoid.

How do you marry and yet live like gentle lovers, or at least like friendly roommates? Quite frankly, I do not know the answer to that question.

THE THREE STAGES OF MARRIAGE

LARRY NOBLE

Can the honeymoon last? Not forever—but even after a period of great difficulty, a marriage can become better, stronger and happier.

By DANIEL GOLDSTINE, SHIRLEY ZUCKERMAN, HILARY GOLDSTINE and KATHERINE LARNER

Daniel Goldstine, Shirley Zuckerman and Hilary Goldstine work at the Berkeley (California) Therapy Institute. Katherine Larner is a freelance writer.

An individual has a life cycle, a family has a life cycle and a couple relationship has a life cycle too. In doing therapy, we've observed that there is a definite sequence of stages in a marriage.

First of all, when two people discover that they love each other and wish to become partners, they tend to experience a harmony and mutual delight that we call Stage I. This phase of a relationship is characterized by openness, optimism and mutual engrossment. It's wonderful, but it doesn't last.

To a couple's distress, real life gradually impinges on their relationship. Conflict surfaces, failure intrudes and boredom casts its pall. Stage II arrives.

As therapists, we see a great many people who believe, at this point, that their couple relationships have failed and that this failure leaves them only two possibilities: to split up or to endure misery for the rest of their marriage. The trend toward divorce as a solution for a couple's unhappiness doesn't seem to have peaked yet. On the average, the length of a marriage has dropped to 7.2 years, and the stigma attached to ending a marriage is fading into irrelevance.

In fact, a kind of moral backlash seems to have set in. Divorce isn't just being sanctioned now, it's virtually being sponsored. A profusion of books and articles is making the argument that lasting commitments aren't viable, that the risks involved in splitting up are manageable and that people's personal selves are likely to thrive on dissolution.

Obviously, there are people for whom this is true. There *are* couple relationships that ought to be ended. But we've seen many more couples for whom splitting up is not only miserably painful but pointless and destructive. That's why we want to fortify people for the struggle against the difficulties inherent in a long-term partnership. It's a difficult but not impossible task to transform mutual attraction into lasting love and eventually to reach what we call the Stage III Accord.

Stage I—Happy Honeymoon

Falling in love creates an incontestable high. You feel good about yourself, good about your new partner, good about the world around you.

Stage I fosters trust; trust begets intimacy. One woman, Susan, said, "Always before, I felt I had all kinds of things inside me I could never let out. With Murray I feel like I can be completely open. I'm not scared with him. Anything that happens is okay, because there's nothing that I have to hold in."

As the couple nestles closer together physically and psychically, they develop a growing sense of us-ness. Just as each focuses on the other's merits and disregards the other's defects, so each experiences an overwhelming desire for closeness. Any ambivalence about intimacy yields temporarily to the simple childlike wish to be enfolded.

Stage I inclines people to treat each other with affectionate indulgence. They express their love by giving—and giving in—to each other. For example, rather than spoil the evening, one person relinquishes his preference to see a movie and goes along without complaint to the party his partner wants to attend.

When they are falling in love, people are deeply responsive to each other's needs. They often offer each other total backing and display an inexhaustible interest in each other's feelings. The alliance between them is deepened by interminable talk—about what's going on and how the pair of them should deal with things.

If problems too threatening to be discussed sometimes arise, they are likely to be avoided. And to a certain extent Stage I cushions individuals from external stress as well. A reversal at work or a spell of financial trouble doesn't pinch us as painfully when there's a newfound lover to kiss the hurt and make it well.

From *Family Circle*, May 1977. "The Three Stages of Marriage," by Daniel Goldstine, Shirley Zuckerman, Hilary Goldstine and Katherine Larner. Reprinted by permission.

2. MAINTENANCE OF RELATIONSHIPS

THE MARRIAGE CYCLE		STAGE I	STAGE II	STAGE III
	State of Partnership	Lovers—Couple falls in love and marries	Antagonists—Children are born, money and family pressures increase	Allies—Resentment changes to acceptance, disapproval to mutual acceptance
	Ambiance	Romantic	Resentful	Harmonious
	Certainty of Commitment	Untested	Uncertain—Periods of stress followed by periods of good will	Undoubted
	Conflict	Avoided	Constant—Overtly or covertly	Resolved—There is trust in each other, comfort in being together
	Perspective on Partner	Idealization	Disapproval—Couple may be going through individual crises about work or self-esteem	Acceptance

But the bleak fact is that Stage I is necessarily fleeting. Real-world obligations impinge on the relationship. As evidence of each other's shortcomings piles up, and as the relationship begins to exact visible cost, mutual idealization gives way to mutual disillusionment.

One phase of a long-term process, Stage I constitutes the romantic but not the most enduring version of coupled love. To have gone through Stage I bestows a valuable benefit on a couple's relationship as well as on them as individuals. In Stage I, two people learn how to enjoy themselves together. They discover pleasures they can share and ways to spend time together that make both of them feel good. Needless to say, a couple can't survive on a capacity to have fun together; and a couple can likewise make do without knowing how to be playful or joyful together. But a relationship that lacks this endowment is the poorer for it. Evanescent of itself, Stage I can leave a couple a valuable legacy—the knowledge that they can create pleasure together—that will help them to keep their relationship a source of satisfaction to them both.

Stage II—Conflicts and Regrets

Stage II of a couple relationship begins in disappointment. Conflicts and failures pile up, the letdown settles in and a couple begins to realize that their relationship isn't bringing them the fulfillment they'd hoped for. "The reality of living with her—it isn't good. It isn't working. We haven't been getting along for a long time," said one man of his eight-year marriage. "It's really getting me down."

In Stage I, a couple has the pleasure of discovering agreeable likenesses between them. In Stage II, however, as they try to integrate their values and their habits, a couple must come to grips with the differences that truly divide them.

They discover, for example, that he enjoys a pair of friends. "He wants to see them Friday night, Saturday afternoon, Saturday evening and Sunday afternoon." But as for her, well, "I don't have such a wonderful time over there," she says. Or she realizes that "doing the same thing every morning—getting up, making coffee, feeding the cats, eating granola—I kind of like that. It regulates my day. Every morning the same thing; it gets me going, but I think it gives him the doldrums." . . . It does!

It *is* difficult to be subjected to someone else's flaws and limitations without questioning the wisdom of the commitment to that person. It can also be difficult to keep from using such discreditable discoveries about a person as weapons against him. For example, one man told his wife, "It hurt me a lot when you said I was weak. It came from all those times I let you know I felt weak. That bothers me. Why should I want to tell you how I feel if you're going to use it against me?" Since disillusionment is a painful process all around, Stage II usually entails defensiveness about who you are as well as disenchantment about who your partner is.

Stage II also means mutual disapproval, the more painful because it's unexpected. The most concentrated dose of approval people usually get comes when they're falling in love. A major proof of the rightness of a new relationship is the fact that the partner "makes

me feel so good." But gradually the appreciation turns to criticism. One man said, "A million times she's made me feel like I never made the mark and I never would." Her retort: "In a lot of ways, I don't respect my husband. Am I supposed to lie about it?" It's difficult for most people to maintain their self-esteem in the face of such intimate, informed disapproval, and the characteristic Stage II complaint becomes, "You make me feel so bad."

What's more, the anxiety and the resentment that mark Stage II often provoke people to behavior they have trouble accepting in themselves. Brooded one woman: "I've become a bitch. The more he doesn't listen to me, the more I yell. And I don't like it. I'm always screaming—I'm sick of myself."

Usually a person holds his partner responsible for the various unappetizing changes that have been wrought in him. This woman invoked the fact that "I don't get into scenes like that with anybody else" to reassure herself that the fault for them lay with her partner.

The classic Stage II systems of behavior are mutual blame and mutual withholding. Mutual blame tosses the responsibility for a couple's unhappiness back and forth between them like a hot potato. For example, a couple was getting ready for a dinner party. The wife fussed with her hair, changed her clothing, and finally turned to her husband and wailed, "I look awful." Beverly's concern about her appearance was largely a symptom of her anxiety about the evening ahead, but Henry interpreted it quite literally. As he saw it, he came to her aid by suggesting, "Why don't you put on your blue pants suit?

That dress makes you look mousy."

"Oh, I see," she said coldly. And from there on the argument just started to snowball. She accused him of insensitivity and for failing to offer her the reassurance, "You look great, honey," she felt she deserved. He self-righteously maintained that he had acted from only the best of motives, had offered useful counsel and that she had spitefully picked a fight.

Beverly said, "What we were fighting about is not just that one thing, but what it means to both of us, what it reminds us of—all the things we dislike about each other and all the things we disagreed about in the past." Old injuries were dredged up, stock accusations were exchanged and the battle escalated. The more wronged each felt, the more ruthless each become.

To outgrow Stage II, a couple must learn to relinquish their suspicions as well as the resentments that nurture those suspicions. In Stage II, a person commonly blames his own unhappiness on his partner's indifference or malice. But in reality, couple relationships are far more complicated than this. A relationship is most likely to survive Stage II and thrive thereafter if each partner learns to judge the other's actions with charity: to remember that love can be felt far more often than it is expressed and that harm can be done unwittingly; that while each person bears responsibility for the consequences of his actions, he often didn't intend to cause the pain he inflicts.

For two people to succeed in outgrowing Stage II, they must develop an appreciation for their impact on each other. They must learn to balance concern for each other with respect for themselves.

Stage III—Reaching an Accord

The Stage III couple have brought their expectations for their relationship into some kind of equilibrium with their everyday lives. Frustrations and anxieties don't cease, but these no longer trigger doubts about their future as a couple. Each knows, and knows the other knows, that they're here to stay.

Beth said of her 13-year marriage to George, "Even those times when I'm angry with him, I have confidence. There's a reliability there that it's going to be good. We've seen too many good times not to live through the bad."

How does a couple learn to feel this way? Mainly by hard work. For a relationship to reach Stage III, changes on the level of behavior and feeling are invariably necessary, and changing isn't easy. In Beth's case, she learned to control her anger. Her husband had to outgrow the self-righteous posturing to which he retreated when he didn't get his way. During the past few years Beth has come to realistic terms with her deficient self-esteem, while her husband has rounded off the sharp edges of his arrogance. He has stopped taking so much responsibility for her,

and she has learned not to drop her troubles in his lap. All of these changes have been desirable for them as individuals as well as valuable as a couple.

In order for their relationship to flourish, a couple must relinquish threatening strategies like mutual blame —and they must learn some way of responding helpfully to each other's needs. As Beth said, "Instead of placing demands on my husband, instead of judgmentally saying, 'Why can't you do this?' or 'Why can't you do that?' I decided that I was going to go out and see what it was like in the business world. That was a big step. Instead of blaming him for my problems, I determined that I was going to change the situation myself."

A person can only accept and find satisfaction in a long-term relationship if his expectations for it are realistic. The relationship will continue to be more comfortable in some ways than in others and at some times than at others. And a couple relationship alone can't ensure a lifetime of happiness. Furthermore, a couple's troubles may often merely be the visible sign of problems in other areas of the partners' lives. "Some of my discontent with the relationship is discontent with myself," one woman, married 10 years, admitted.

If that's the case, the best tonic may be to stop focusing too intently on a relationship's deficiencies and instead to undertake the kind of independent activity that will make each partner's life more satisfying.

It's easy enough to suggest changes in behavior that are usually helpful in improving a couple's relationship. But it's far harder to actually venture these changes. And the process of change is almost never speedy or dramatic. For most couples, it's two steps forward, a step back, and a spell of foot-dragging. Even so, a Stage III relationship can relapse into a Stage II in a period of stress such as illness or financial reversal. But the same combination of realism, responsibility and attitude that enabled the couple to achieve an equilibrium in the first place can enable them to restore the balance to their relationship.

Stage III is an achievement and almost never a happy accident. Stage I can be a result of good fortune, but Stage III is a product of good work. A couple has to struggle to overcome the disillusionment and the mistrust that relationships often create. They have to believe that "there's a place beyond resentment" and persist in their efforts to reach it despite discouragement over the lack of change or the slow pace of change in their relationship

Basically, a couple moves toward Stage III when they discover that behavior that doesn't come naturally at first, that may be downright awkward, can nevertheless improve life for both partners. The husband who learns to offer his wife support and encouragement as well as advice; the woman who

can summon up her courage in the face of risk instead of shielding herself behind her husband whenever possible—both have enriched themselves and strengthened their relationship while extending their range of responses.

Although they are essential, persistence and good intentions won't suffice to reach Stage III. The essence of Stage III is mutual acceptance, the knowledge that with one's partner there's "no need to hurry, no need to sparkle, no need to be anybody but one's self." The partners trust and feel comfortable with each other. Beth expressed it this way, "Part of the success of our marriage is that we know we are a family, and a family is a kind of safety valve where you can express yourself in a way you can't anywhere else."

Stage III also means mutual accommodation. "Ten years ago or even five years ago," Beth's husband explained, "I would have been less happy with her slumps. It's a pain. It's so visible in her, in the way the house looks, in everything—it's striking. But now I'm better about saying, 'Well, I'll do it.' I can wait till her mood goes away without getting too upset. Basically, we're more sensitive to each other."

One of any couple's prerequisites for survival is enduring mutual attraction. Al, married 30 years, says, "How can I be in love with a 60-year-old woman? . . . But I am." And he adds, "We've always been able to have a good time together, just the two of us."

And for a relationship to survive over the long term, a couple must not only share a lively interest in each other, they must also share the inclination to seek each other out for pleasure. This kind of lasting mental, physical and emotional involvement creates a deep mutual knowledge that enlightens both partners.

The desire for "security" has taken some hard lumps of late; it has become synonymous with a lack of vision or a capitulation to anxiety. But in fact, men and women who are secure—who love and know they're loved in return—are likely to be far more venturesome and spontaneous than those whose emotional footing is insecure. Beth spoke to the point when she said, "We needed to be married to go ahead and do the rest of our lives. We needed that reassurance from each other. Then we could go out and develop the rest of our lives. I needed that successful relationship to be successful elsewhere."

The security of a Stage III relationship accomplishes an indispensable function for the couple. They have each other to rely on, and their mutual strength reassures them and reinforces them in their struggle through life. And, best of all, that exchanged strength truly enriches their experience of life.

The Inexpressive Male: A Tragedy of American Society

Jack O. Balswick and Charles W. Peek

The position is taken in this paper that inexpressiveness is a culturally produced temperament trait which is characteristic of many American males. It is suggested that in growing up, boys are taught that expressiveness is inconsistent with masculinity. Inexpressive males come in two varieties: the cowboy who, although he does have feelings toward women, does not or cannot express them; and the playboy who is a non-feeling man void of even unexpressed emotional feelings toward women. In light of the increase in importance of the companionship and affection function in marriage, across-the-board inexpressiveness of married males (that is, inexpressiveness toward all women, wife included) can be highly dysfunctional to their marital relationships, while selective inexpressiveness (that is, inexpressiveness toward women other than their wives) may be just as functional to maintaining these relationships.

The problem of what it means to be "male" and "female" is a problem which is faced and dealt with in its own way in every society. Through cross-cultural research one now surmises that culture rather than "nature" is the major influence in determining the temperamental differences between the sexes. It may be no accident that a woman, Margaret Mead, did the classic study demonstrating that temperamental differences between the sexes are explained very little in terms of innateness, but rather in terms of culture. In her book, *Sex and Temperament*, Mead reported on the differences in sex roles for three New Guinea societies. Using ethnocentric western standards in defining sex roles, she found that the ideal sex role for both the male and female was essentially "feminine" among the Arapesh, "masculine" among the Mundugumor, and "feminine" for the male and "masculine" for the female among the Tchambuli. The Tchambuli represents a society that defines sex roles in a complete reversal of the traditional distinctions made between masculine and feminine roles in the United States.

It is the purpose of this paper to consider a particular temperament trait that often characterizes the male in American society. As sex role distinctions have developed in America, the male sex role, as compared to the female sex role, carries with it prescriptions which encourage inexpressiveness. In some of its extreme contemporary forms, the inexpressive male has even come to be glorified as the epitome of a real man. This will be discussed later in the paper when two types of inexpressive male are examined.

The Creation of the Inexpressive Male

Children, from the time they are born both explicitly and implicitly are taught how to be a man or how to be a woman. While the girl is taught to act "feminine" and to desire "feminine" objects, the boy is taught how to be a man. In learning to be a man, the boy in American society comes to value expressions of masculinity and devalue expressions of femininity. Masculinity is expressed largely through physical courage, toughness, competitiveness, and aggressiveness, whereas femininity is, in contrast, expressed largely through gentleness, expressiveness, and responsiveness. When a young boy begins to express his emotions through crying, his parents are quick to assert, "You're a big boy and big boys don't cry." Parents often use the term, "he's all boy," in reference to their son, and by this term usually refer to behavior which is an expression of aggressiveness, getting into mischief, getting dirty, etc., but never use the term to denote behavior which is an expression of affection, tenderness, or emotion. What parents are really telling their son is that a real man does not show his emotions and if he is a real man he will not allow his emotions to be expressed. These outward expressions of emotion are viewed as a sign of femininity, and undesirable for a male.

Is it any wonder, then, that during the most emotional peak of a play or movie, when many in the audience have lumps in their throats and tears in their eyes, that the adolescent boy guffaws loudly or quickly suppresses any tears which may be threatening to emerge, thus demonstrating to the world that he is above such emotional feeling?

The Inexpressive Male as a Single Man

At least two basic types of inexpressive male seem to result from this socialization process: the cowboy and the playboy. Manville (1969) has referred to the *cowboy type* in terms of a "John Wayne Neurosis" which stresses the strong, silent, and two-fisted male as the 100 percent American he-man. For present purposes, it is especially in his relationship with women that the John Wayne neurosis is particularly significant in representing many American males. As portrayed by Wayne in any one of his many type-cast roles, the mark of a real man is that he does not show any tenderness or affection toward girls because his culturally-acquired male image dic-

* A revised version of a paper read at the meetings of the American Sociological Association, Washington, D.C., September, 1970.

** Jack O. Balswick, Ph.D., is Associate Professor of Sociology, Department of Sociology, University of Georgia, Athens, Georgia 30601, and Charles W. Peek, Ph.D., is Assistant Professor of Sociology, Department of Sociology and Anthropology, University of Georgia, Athens, Georgia 30601.

tates that such a show of emotions would be distinctly unmanly. If he does have anything to do with girls, it is on a "man to man" basis: the girl is treated roughly (but not sadistically), with little hint of gentleness or affection. As Manville puts it:

"The on-screen John Wayne doesn't feel comfortable around women. He does like them sometimes—God knows he's not *queer*. But at the right time, and in the right place — which he chooses. And always with his car/horse parked directly outside, in/on which he will ride away to his more important business back in Marlboro country." (1969, 111)

Alfred Auerback, a psychiatrist, has commented more directly (1970) on the cowboy type. He describes the American male's inexpressiveness with women as part of the "cowboy syndrome." He quite rightly states that "the cowboy in moving pictures has conveyed the image of the rugged 'he-man,' strong, resilient, resourceful, capable of coping with overwhelming odds. His attitude toward women is courteous but reserved." As the cowboy equally loved his girlfriend and his horse, so the present day American male loves his car or motorcycle and his girlfriend. Basic to both these descriptions is the notion that the cowboy does have feelings toward women but does not express them, since ironically such expression would conflict with his image of what a male is.

The *playboy type* has recently been epitomized in *Playboy* magazine and by James Bond. As with the cowboy type, he is resourceful and shrewd, and interacts with his girlfriend with a certain detachment which is expressed as "playing it cool." While Bond's relationship with women is more in terms of a Don Juan, he still treats women with an air of emotional detachment and independence similar to that of the cowboy. The playboy departs from the cowboy, however, in that he is also "non-feeling." Bond and the playboy he caricatures are in a sense "dead" inside. They have no emotional feelings toward women, while Wayne, although unwilling and perhaps unable to express them does have such feelings. Bond rejects women as women, treating them as consumer commodities; Wayne puts women on a pedestal. The playboy's relationship with women represents the culmination of Fromm's description of a marketing-oriented personality in which a person comes to see both himself and others as persons to be manipulated and exploited. Sexuality is reduced to a packageable consumption item which the playboy can handle because it demands no responsibility. The woman in the process, becomes reduced to a playboy accessory. A successful "love affair" is one in which the bed was shared, but the playboy emerges having avoided personal involvement or a

shared relationship with the woman.

The playboy, then, in part is the old cowboy in modern dress. Instead of the crude mannerisms of John Wayne, the playboy is a skilled manipulator of women, knowing when to turn the lights down, what music to play on the stereo, which drinks to serve, and what topics of conversation to pursue. The playboy, however, is not a perfect likeness; for unlike the cowboy, he does not seem to care for the women from whom he withholds his emotions. Thus, the inexpressive male as a single man comes in two types: the inexpressive feeling man (the cowboy) and the inexpressive non-feeling man (the playboy).

The Inexpressive Male as a Married Man

When the inexpressive male marries, his inexpressiveness can become highly dysfunctional to his marital relationship *if* he continues to apply it across-the-board to all women, his wife included. The modern American family places a greater demand upon the marriage relationship than did the family of the past. In the typical marriage of 100 or even 50 years ago, the roles of both the husband and the wife were clearly defined as demanding, task-oriented functions. If the husband successfully performed the role of provider and protector of his wife and family and if the wife performed the role of homemaker and mother to her children, chances were the marriage was defined as successful, both from a personal and a societal point of view. The traditional task functions which in the past were performed by the husband and wife are today often taken care of by individuals and organizations outside the home. Concomitant with the decline of the task functions in marriage has been the increase in the importance of the companionship and affectionate function in marriage. As Blood and Wolfe (1960, 172) concluded in their study of the modern American marriage, "companionship has emerged as the most valued aspect of marriage today."

As American society has become increasingly mechanized and depersonalized, the family remains as one of the few social groups where what sociologists call the primary relationship has still managed to survive. As such, a greater and greater demand has been placed upon the modern family and especially the modern marriage to provide for affection and companionship. Indeed, it is highly plausible to explain the increased rate of divorce during the last 70 years, not in terms of a breakdown in marriage relationships, but instead, as resulting from the increased load which marriage has been asked to carry. When the husband and wife no longer find af-

fection and companionship from their marriage relationship, they most likely question the wisdom of attempting to continue in their conjugal relationship. When affection is gone, the main reason for the marriage relationship disappears.

Thus, within the newly defined affectively-oriented marriage relationship male inexpressiveness toward *all* women, wife included, would be dysfunctional. But what may happen for many males is that through progressively more serious involvements with women (such as going steady, being pinned, engagement, and the honeymoon period of marriage), they begin to make some exceptions. That is, they may learn to be *situationally rather than totally inexpressive*, inexpressive toward women in most situations but not in all. As the child who learns a rule and then, through further experience, begins to understand the exceptions to it, many American males may pick up the principle of inexpressiveness toward women, discovering its exceptions as they become more and more experienced in the full range of man-woman relationships. Consequently, they may become more expressive toward their wives while remaining essentially inexpressive toward other women; they learn that the conjugal relationship is one situation that is an exception to the cultural requirement of male inexpressiveness. Thus, what was once a double *sexual* standard, where men had one standard of sexual conduct toward their fiancee or wife and another toward other women, may now be primarily a double *emotional* standard, where men learn to be expressive toward their fiancee or wife but remain inexpressive toward women in general.

To the extent that such situational inexpressiveness exists among males, it should be functional to the maintenance of the marriage relationship. Continued inexpressiveness by married males toward women other than their wives would seem to prohibit their forming meaningful relationships with these women. Such a situation would seem to be advantageous to preserving their marital relationships, since "promiscuous" expressiveness toward other women could easily threaten the stability of these companionship-oriented marital relationships.

In short, the authors' suggestion is that situational inexpressiveness, in which male expressiveness is essentially limited to the marital relationship, may be one of the basic timbers shoring up many American marriages, especially if indications of increasing extramarital sexual relations are correct. In a sense, then, the consequences of situational inexpressiveness for marital relationships do not seem very different from those of prostitution down through the centuries, where prostitution provided for extramarital sex under circumstances which discouraged personal affection toward the female partner strong enough to undermine the marital relationship. In the case of the situationally inexpressive husband, his inexpressiveness in relations with women other than his wife may serve as a line of defense against the possible negative consequences of such involvement toward marital stability. By acting as the cowboy or playboy, therefore, the married male may effectively rob extramarital relationships of their expressiveness and thus preserve his marital relationship.

The inexpressiveness which the American male early acquires may be bothersome in that he has to partially unlearn it in order to effectively relate to his wife. However, if he is successful in partially unlearning it (or learning a few exceptions to it), then it can be highly functional to maintaining the conjugal relationship.

But what if the husband does not partially unlearn his inexpressiveness? Within the newly defined expressive function of the marriage relationship, he is likely to be found inadequate. The possibility of an affectionate and companionship conjugal relationship carries with it the assumption that both the husband and wife are bringing into marriage the expressive capabilities to make such a relationship work. This being the case, American society is ironically short changing males in terms of their ability to fulfill this role expectation. Thus, society inconsistently teaches the male that to be masculine is to be inexpressive, while at the same time, expectations in the marital role are defined in terms of sharing affection and companionship which involves the ability to communicate and express feelings. What exists apparently, is another example of a discontinuity in cultural conditioning of which Benedict (1938) spoke more than 30 years ago.

Conclusion and Summary

It has been suggested that many American males are incapable of expressing themselves emotionally to a woman, and that this inexpressiveness is a result of the way society socialized males into their sex role. However, there is an alternative explanation which should be explored, namely, that the learning by the male of his sex role may not actually result in his inability to be expressive, but rather only in his thinking that he is not supposed to be expressive. Granted, according to the first explanation, the male cannot express himself precisely because he was taught that he was not supposed to be expressive, but in this second explanation inexpressiveness is a result of present perceived expectations and not a psychological condition which resulted from past socialization. The male perceives cultural expectations as saying, "don't express yourself to women," and although the male may be capable of such expressiveness, he "fits" into cultural expectations. In the case of the married male, where familial norms do call for expressiveness to one's wife, it may be that the expectations for the expression of emotions to his wife are not communicated to him.

There has been a trickle of evidence which would lend support to the first explanation, which stresses the male's incapacity to be expressive. Several studies (Balswick, 1970; Hurvitz, 1964; Komarovsky, 1962; Rainwater, 1965) have suggested that especially among the lowly educated, it is the wife playing the feminine role who is often disappointed in the lack of emotional concern shown by her husband. The husband, on the other hand, cannot understand the relatively greater concern and emotional expressiveness which his wife desires, since he does not usually feel this need himself. As a result of her research, Komarovsky (1962, 156) has suggested that "the ideal of masculinity into which . . .(men are) . . . socialized inhibits expressiveness both directly, with its emphasis on reserve, and indirectly, by identifying personal interchange with the feminine role." Balswick (1970) found that males are less capable than females of expressing or receiving companionship support from their spouses. His research also supports the view than inadequacy of expressiveness is greatest for the less educated males. Although inexpressiveness may be found among males at all socioeconomic levels, it is especially among the lower class male

that expressiveness is seen as being inconsistent with his defined masculine role.

There may be some signs that conditions which have contributed toward the creation of the inexpressive male are in the process of decline. The deemphasis in distinctiveness in dress and fashions between the sexes, as exemplified in the "hippy" movement can be seen as a reaction against the rigidly defined distinctions between the sexes which have characterized American society. The sexless look, as presently being advanced in high fashion, is the logical end reaction to a society which has superficially created strong distinctions between the sexes. Along with the blurring of sexual distinctions in fashion may very well be the shattering of the strong, silent male as a glorified type. There is already evidence of sharp criticisms of the inexpressive male and exposure of him as constituting a "hangup." Marriage counselors, sensitivity group leaders, "hippies," and certainly youth in general, are critical of inexpressiveness, and candid honesty in interpersonal relations. Should these views permeate American society, the inexpressive male may well come to be regarded as a pathetic tragedy instead of the epitome of masculinity and fade from the American scene. Not all may applaud his departure, however. While those interested in more satisfactory male-female relationships, marital and otherwise, will probably gladly see him off, those concerned with more stable marital relationships may greet his departure less enthusiastically. Although it should remove an important barrier to satisfaction in all male-female relationships via an increase in the male's capacity for emotional response toward females, by the same token it also may remove a barrier against emotional entanglement in relations with females outside marital relationships and thus threaten the stability of marriages. If one finds the inexpressive male no longer present one of these days, then, it will be interesting to observe whether any gains in the stability of marriage due to increased male expressiveness *within* this relationship will be enough to offset losses in stability emanating from increasing displays of male expressiveness *outside* it.

THE CONFUSED AMERICAN HOUSEWIFE

MYRA MARX FERREE

Myra Marx Ferree is an assistant professor of sociology at the University of Connecticut, Storrs. She received her Ph.D. in social psychology from Harvard University in 1976 with a dissertation on the effects of employment on working-class women's sympathy for the women's movement. With both her parents active in their respective unions, she feels that she has had a head start in studying social and political attitudes in a working-class setting and plans to continue her work in this area.

THE AMERICAN HOUSEWIFE feels herself to be besieged. On one side stand traditionalists, who tell her that her greatest pleasures come from satisfying the needs of others: making a home for her family, raising healthy children, and pleasing her husband. On the other side stand egalitarians, who tell her that her needs are important, too. A fulfilling career has generally come to mean one outside the home.

Betty Friedan's *The Feminine Mystique* made people aware that a career at home was difficult for middle- and upper-middle-class women to enjoy. Repetitive household chores were a great waste of their skills and education. These women compared themselves to their ambitious husbands, and felt trapped and uncomfortable. But at the same time, those who ventured forth to work outside the home did so knowing they were taking on the sunrise-to-bed burden of two full-time jobs.

The working-class woman was generally ignored. Many social scientists and laymen assumed that the housewife-career choice of her wealthier counterpart didn't apply to her. For one thing, housework may be boring, but surely better than carting heavy trays in a diner, scrubbing someone else's floors, or standing up all day selling hats. For another, working-class men do not have glamorous jobs, so there seemed little reason for their wives to envy them and covet their work.

Decades of research on job satisfaction, however, show that work, even low-status work, plays an important part in a person's self-image. Studs Terkel's book, Working, reports glowing examples of how people get self-esteem from a remarkable variety of occupations. People who are unemployed, retired, or incapacitated by illness feel considerable strain and anguish because they begin to see themselves as useless.

Social contact. Aside from the fact of working itself, a key cause of job satisfaction is social contact. For human beings, isolation is a devastating punishment, and the workplace is a clearing-house of friendships and camaraderie. For the blue-collar worker, male or female, friends help make the job pleasureable.

This research on the importance of work, along with the recent evidence on the dissatisfactions of housewives (see box), made me curious to see how working-class women saw their work. I interviewed 135 women living in a working-class community near Boston. I limited my sample to women whose youngest child was already in school, and for whom child-care was therefore only a part-time activity. Many of the women were high-school graduates; a substantial number (36 percent) had not finished high school and only three held college degrees. Slightly more than half of the women worked outside the home, and their jobs represented the typical occupations of women: most were supermarket and department-store clerks, waitresses, factory workers, typists, and nurse's aides, along with a few bookkeepers, banktellers, and beauticians.

These are not glamorous, exciting careers, but the wives who held such jobs were happier and more satisfied with their lives than the women who were full-time housewives. Almost twice as many housewives as employed wives said they were dissatisfied with their lives (26 percent to 14 percent) and believed that their husbands' work was more interesting than theirs (41 percent to 22 percent). More housewives claimed that they had not had a fair opportunity in life, and wanted their daughters to be "mostly different" from themselves.

Clear payoffs. As I talked to these women, it became clear that the reason for the housewives' dissatisfaction was not their personalities, but the characteristics of their work. A job has clear requirements and clear payoffs, in money, social life, and sense of accomplishment. A job takes a woman out of the house and gives her contact with other people—employers, co-workers and customers—and the regular paycheck is proof of work well done.

But a housewife's day is never done, and her tasks often bring neither tangible rewards nor social connections. Husbands and wives alike have an uncertain idea of how much of housework is work. Sociologist Hannah Gavron studied a group of British wives and found that when housework becomes an all-day, everyday affair, the distinction between work and nonwork blurs. The housewives expend great effort but don't get recognition for it: their husbands accuse them of "doing nothing all day" and in the next breath remind them that their duty is to stay home and keep house.

As a result, many housewives have an uncertain idea of what their occupation requires, and how well or poorly they are doing it. Of my interviewees, only one woman in 14 (about 7 percent) said she was extremely good at taking care of a home, and over half (57 percent) of these full-time housewives felt that they were not very good at it. Many of the employed wives also felt fairly incompetent as homemakers (67 percent), but their jobs gave them another source of self-esteem and feelings of achievement. Not one of the women with paid jobs said she was not very good at her job; in fact a majority (54 percent) said they were "extremely good." Paid work and housework are two roads to a sense of self-esteem, and the happiest women I talked to were those who felt competent in both activities. The least happy wives were displeased with their abilities as homemakers and did not have jobs to buck up their egos.

Obviously not all American housewives feel miserable and worthless, and it is important to understand why some women thrive in the role and others wilt and fade. If a woman is unhappy as a wife and mother, she tends to think there's something the matter with her. There usually isn't, I've found; there's something the matter with her environment.

It is not necessarily being a housewife that causes so many of these women to be unhappy, but certain aspects of the role. Not so long ago, housewives shared a social network that gave them mutual support, recognition and pleasure. Working-class women especially were likely to live near their mothers, other relatives, and close friends for many years and to establish close-knit groups. Within these groups there was

no doubt whether someone was, or was not, a good homemaker. In recent decades, however, the rise in numbers of people who move frequently and the millions of women going back to work, have made housewife networks less common and more difficult to maintain. Housework is more likely to be a solo pastime, and therefore a more lonely one. With husbands gone all day and children in school, wives became isolated. In PT's happiness survey, published last month, isolated wives who spent much of their days doing housework and watching television tended to feel worthless and despairing. Indeed, many of the women I interviewed said they felt they were "going crazy staying home," "not seeing anyone but four walls all day." Staying home all day, said one woman, "is like being in jail."

Painful isolation. No wonder that nearly half of the socially isolated housewives were unhappy, compared to fewer than one fourth of the housewives with daily social contacts. Most of the women described working outside the home as

> Not so long ago, housewives shared a social network that gave them mutual support, recognition and pleasure. Now, the rise in the numbers of people who move, and the millions of women who work, make housewife networks rare.

healthy because it meant "getting out and seeing other people." Working wives often mentioned the need to be with people as an important reason in their decision to get a job, along with the desire to feel useful and to have "something to do." Wives who had worked in the past missed the social contacts their jobs had offered, and for many the contrast with their current isolation was painful.

It is often assumed that working-class women work just for the money, that if

WOMEN: WORK ISN'T ALWAYS THE ANSWER

Doctors see her in their waiting rooms and read about her in their journals. She is the neurotic housewife, bored, depressed, anxious. She takes drugs to pep her up and Valium to calm her down. Psychologists and sociologists study her in interviews and surveys, and conclude, in Jessie Bernard's words, "Being a housewife makes women sick."

But is it true? Research by psychologist Linda Fidell and sociologist Jane Prather indicates that this stereotype can be just as distorted as the old picture of the happy homemaker. Housework by itself doesn't make women happy or unhappy. The difference lies elsewhere.

Previous research has put wives into two categories: those who have outside jobs and those who don't.

Fidell and Prather add a third group, women who want to work, but don't. These are the ones who fit the unhappy stereotype. They interviewed a random sample of 465 women living in a Los Angeles suburb. The women, who came from both working and middle-class families, were asked about their physical and mental health, their use of drugs, their attitudes about women and their families, and their self-esteem.

Fidell and Prather compared employed wives (53 percent of the sample), unemployed wives who wanted to work (18 percent), and housewives (29 percent). They found that many of the housewives are happy, healthy and comfortable in their role. These women don't want to work. They come from high-income families, so they don't need a salaried job, and they fill their days doing housework and spending time on themselves.

They have happy marriages, they feel in control of their lives, and they have the best physical and mental health of the three groups.

The women who are looking for jobs, in contrast, match Ferree's portrait of the unhappy housewife. These tend to be working-class wives, have the least education, and are the most dissatisfied with their

lives. They have low self-esteem, feel they are pawns of fate, and mask their loneliness and worry with drugs. Fidell and Prather describe them as trapped by circumstances they can't control. They aren't working either because of family responsibilities and a lack of child care, a bad job market, or illness.

Employed wives have a double burden, and in Fidell and Prather's group these women had the least time to spend on housework or themselves. They are less happily married than fulltime housewives but they have higher feelings of competence. These wives had the highest self-esteem and were most opposed to taking mood changing drugs.

This latest research on the "housewife syndrome" shows that we can't generalize about women's ambitions with confidence. This could explain why the women's movement was greeted with huzzas by women who felt stifled in the suburbs, and with boos by women who felt satisfied, thank you, to be caring for a home and family.
—Carol Tavris

Fidell and Prather are at California State University, Northridge.

they weren't in a financial pinch they would be happy to stay home. In truth, these women work for the same reasons men do—for the money, to be sure, but also for the pleasure. For example, a Portuguese immigrant factory worker told me, "I have to work. If I'm home I go crazy. I hit the children. When I work, I'm OK." Of course she works for the money; her husband is a bricklayer, frequently unemployed, and without her income the family would be on welfare. But there's no doubt that she is working for her own satisfaction too.

Not all of the housewives I spoke to felt that they were going crazy at home. A fourth of them are very happy with their lives. These are women who feel that their accomplishments are recognized and who are warmly involved with social support groups. Their mothers, sisters, friends and cousins are in and out of the house all day. Their husbands value their work, and think it is an important contribution to the maintenance of the family. They are not lonely and isolated, and they do not feel their efforts are wasted.

Family and job. Even though full-time workers are happier than full-time housewives, their lives are not featherbeds either. They have all the concerns of the job, plus the major responsibility for housework and child-care. In fact, one wife in three who worked full-time said she sometimes felt inadequate to meet the demands of her family and her job. Wives who work part-time, in contrast, have a somewhat easier time combining the two roles—only one in seven of them sometimes felt inadequate at doing both. Perhaps for this reason, part-time workers in this sample were even more satisfied with their lives than full-time workers.

Part-time work has its disadvantages, though. It neither warrants much help from husbands on home chores, nor offers enough chance for promotions and raises. Even so, part-time work may be seen as the best compromise by some of these women. When I asked one if she had ever been promoted, she said, "I've been asked, but I don't want the responsibility. I run a house, which is the most important thing. If I try to advance, it will harm my family life. I get out, and that's enough."

Not all wives, however, feel able to "get out" even if they may want to. Many working-class husbands are adamant that their wives must stay at home. A third of the full-time housewives I spoke with said it was their hus-

> **Full-time workers are happier than full-time housewives, but they have all the concerns of the job, plus the pressure of housework. One worker in three said she felt inadequate to meet both the demands of family and job.**

bands who made the decision whether they should work or stay home, compared to fewer than one in 10 of the working wives who attributed such power to their husbands. Of course, perceptions and attitudes change with events. Perhaps some of the housewives gave more responsibility for the decision to their husbands than was true. Perhaps some of the working wives, once they had taken jobs, found that their husbands' attitudes changed accordingly.

Marriage at risk. I asked the women whether a wife should take a job over her husband's opposition. While over half of the working women thought she should, only a third of the housewives agreed. But both groups believed that opposing the husband's wishes put the marriage at risk. Those who felt she should take the job anyway tended to feel, as one put it, that "she has a right to her own life. A marriage wouldn't be any good if this would break it up." Those who thought she should give in to her husband's wishes said, in one wife's words, "It only starts family troubles and you end up with a separation." All, however, seemed to agree with the sentiments of one woman, who observed, "She's gonna have to decide which is more important, the marriage or the job." It's a matter of just how badly she needs the job and "how much she's willing to pay for peace."

Many housewives pay a considerable price in personal unhappiness. A broken marriage also carries a high price tag, both financially and emotionally. The dilemma may be resolved when the husband's unemployment or other fi-

nancial emergency provides an opportunity to enter the labor force without jeopardizing the marriage. More than two thirds of the housewives, as well as the employed women, felt that a woman had an obligation to work to help support the family regardless of the husband's opinion. As one woman put it, "He wasn't working. What could he say? We had to eat." Once working, she can "show him it doesn't hurt anything" and "he'll come around."

People who think that housework is a naturally gratifying activity for most housewives, while blue-collar work is invariably dull and stifling, need to reconsider that assumption. But others who argue that housework is invariably dull and stifling, while paid work is naturally gratifying, are also missing the boat. We have to look at the circumstances of a person's occupation that make the work satisfying or alienating, that build self-esteem or destroy it.

For the women—and, increasingly, the men—who wish or need to stay home, housework can be structured in ways to assure homemakers a sense of accomplishment and a set of social contacts. For those who wish or need to go to work, the responsibility for housework and child-care can be shared so that one spouse does not have the burden of two jobs.

In my interviews with working-class women, I found that a paid job frees more often than it confines. I found more captive housewives than happy homemakers. There are women who enjoy the role of housewife because it does provide them with the social support and interaction they, like all people, need. Still, in the present conditions of our society, full-time housework is becoming a job that is difficult to enjoy.

For more information read:

Ferree, Myra Marx. "Working Class Jobs: Paid Work and Housework as Sources of Satisfaction" in Social Problems, forthcoming.

Gavron, Hannah. The Captive Wife, Routledge and Kegan Paul, 1966, $7.25.

Kanter, Rosabeth Moss. "The Impact of Hierarchical Structures on the Work Behavior of Women and Men" in Social Problems, Vol. 23/4, April 1976.

Komarovsky, Mirra, Blue-Collar Marriage, Vintage, 1964, paper, $2.45.

Oakley, Anne, The Sociology of Housework, Pantheon, 1975, $10.00, paper, $3.95.

Banking on women

When the roles are switched and wives support their husbands, both resort to subterfuge to protect that vulnerable national resource: male pride

Joan Frazier

Twenty years ago Jules had a top job in the music business. Today, if you ask Jules what he does for a living, he'll tell you: "I make love."

Jules is no gigolo. He's a married man who happens to depend on his wife for most of his keep. Are there many men like Jules? It's not easy to find out.

The U.S. Bureau of Labor Statistics, whose consciousness has yet to be raised, assumes that wherever husband and wife are living together, the man is the chief provider. Jules, for instance, is nominally proprietor of a business—a small record company that produces no records but through which Jules funnels his total income, $2,000 to $3,000 a year in royalties from records made when his career was at its peak. Jules' wife earns more than 10 times as much. Even so, government statisticians consider Jules the primary source of provender.

The latest census reveals that 47 million men are married and living with their wives. Of that number, 7 million men are retired, totally disabled, or unemployed and for one reason or another—possibly discouragement—not seeking employment. About 20 million wives work, and different polling organizations have determined that about 19 million of them work because they need the money—not for any glorious notions of personal fulfillment.

How many of those 19 million wives earn substantially more than their husbands or support them in toto? No one knows.

Doing my own loose sort of polling, I discovered that everyone I asked is acquainted firsthand with at least two or three families in which the wife earns most of the money. Even if my cross section was skewed by locale (New York City and suburbs), that could easily work out to 5 million families nationwide.

So Jules is no isolated case. The only thing unusual about Jules is that he isn't ashamed of his dependency. Like most jazz musicians, he doesn't spend a lot of time worrying about status and the Protestant work ethic. His friends, in fact, envy him. To them, Jules has it made.

But most financially dependent husbands—and the wives they depend on—hide the male's dependency, even if it's only temporary, as if it were a sin on a par with incest. "You're not going to use our names, are you?" I heard right along. No, I'm not. Most of the names here are fictitious, though the situations are real. I recognize that camouflage is both kind and necessary.

The stigma attached to dependent husbands is not limited to the ranks of ordinary folks. The famed and the wealthy also find it necessary to dissemble. Gary Morton, for example, was a second-string stand-up comic when he married Lucille Ball in the early '60s. She was so embarrassed by the gaucheries of his act that she quickly yanked him off the stage and awarded him with the title of executive producer with her Desilu Productions. Although, in time, Morton became involved in the job in fact as well as in name, during those first few years his chief responsibility was to warm up the studio audience in anticipation of Lucy's antics.

High-income women are married with suspicious frequency to men who call themselves public relations or business managers. There are, of course, bona fide managers married to well-heeled wives, but the job titles have become disguises for dependent husbands. Former *77 Sunset Strip* co-star Roger Smith's acting career was apparently plummeting when he married Ann-Margret, whose star was rising just as quickly. Now he is her full-time manager. Often as not, when she is invited to appear on talk shows, he comes along for the ride. And when the conversation turns to her happy present—she just opened to strong reviews in *Tommy*—and her shiny future, it is he who waxes eloquent, while she looks respectfully on. "The pity of it," notes one show business observer, "is that he has talent too. If the breaks had gone differently, he could be out promoting himself."

Sometimes the husband and wife invest heavily in stage props to support the disguise. Everyone in the ad business knows someone like our former neighbor, Martin M., whose wife is a well-paid ex-

Reprinted from *New Times*, April 18, 1975.

ecutive secretary. When Martin lost his job at one of the big agencies and couldn't get situated elsewhere, he decided to set himself up as a creative marketing consultant. He rented a small office in a Fifth Avenue building, had stationery and business cards printed, and arranged for a telephone-answering service. In his mind he was legitimately starting a new business, and he and Ellen were truly excited about it. Yet in the two years his "business" existed, he failed to sign up a single account or earn a dollar in income.

I often run into Ellen in the supermarket on Saturday mornings. One Saturday, because at the time I was going through something similar, I asked Ellen what finally made them decide to give up on Martin's attempt at self-employment.

"We didn't decide," she said. "We just ran out of money."

I knew they had had to sell their house and were now living in an apartment with their two teenage children.

"Is Martin doing anything now?" I asked.

"He's found somebody else." She concentrated her on the shelves of canned goods. "We're getting divorced."

Despite her emotionless tone, Ellen's bitterness was tangible. Women have grown up expecting their husbands to be at least self-supporting, if not the sole provider. When that expectation is betrayed, the entire marital relationship almost inevitably suffers. A wife may resent carrying the added responsibility and express that resentment by withholding the money she now controls from the mate she feels has burdened her so unjustly. He, in turn, may retaliate by seeking understanding and affection elsewhere.

Being dependent is especially hard to bear for the middle-class, middle-aged professional. After all, if you could make it through medical school or law school, you're assumed to be earning a sizable income. What if you aren't? What if your income is less than your wife's? It usually becomes very important for you to conceal the truth.

Even though a husband's dependency may be caused by forces over which he has no control—poor health, economic recession—the weight of social disapproval is so heavy that it is virtually impossible for him to maintain his self-esteem. What happened to Stewart B., a lawyer, follows a familiar pattern.

Stewart held a top political office in upstate New York for more than a dozen years. He and Marge went to lots of parties and he began to drink more and more. When he was unexpectedly voted out of office, his world was shattered and his heavy drinking turned into alcoholism. He became unable to attend to even the few law clients he still had.

Luckily, while Stew was an officeholder, Marge had bought a part interest in a gift shop, more as a hobby than anything else. With Stew out of the running both as politician and provider, Marge turned all the energy she had formerly devoted to furthering his career to making a financial go of the gift shop. Today, their children grown, Marge goes to the shop every day. Stew stays home, walks their Yorkshire terrier once in the morning and once in the early evening, watches TV and drinks himself into a stupor by bedtime. It's been years since they've had sex.

Most of their friends know the tragic turn Stew's life has taken. When strangers inquire, Marge downplays her contribution. "Stew's health hasn't been good and he's had to cut way back on his law practice," she says, as if he were daily besieged by clients. As for herself: "Me? I run a little shop in town. It's so boring to stay home." She tells anyone who will listen how much they still love each other.

Alcoholism seems to be a disability frequently associated with male dependency, but whether it is cause or effect is unclear. When I asked a Family Service social worker in Westchester County about cases of dependent husbands, she told me: "If you have fifteen cases, you have fifteen different reasons." But then she added, in seeming contradiction: "Of course the great majority are psychopaths taking advantage of some good-natured woman."

Dr. Robert Counts, Manhattan psychiatrist and family therapist, does not believe a man must be emotionally disturbed to depend financially on his wife. In 30 years of practice, not a single man has come to him for treatment because of problems connected with being dependent on his spouse. On the other hand, many women have become his patients because of poor adjustment to the role of dependent wife.

The explanation is not difficult. Even if being dependent disturbs a man profoundly and threatens to ruin his relationship not only with his family but with the world at large, he is unlikely to seek therapy since it would only confirm the fact of his dependence and bring his manhood further into question. This correlates with Phyllis Chesler's observation in *Women and Madness* that women are much more likely to seek treatment than men because it is part of the woman's traditional role to rely on figures in authority for help and self-definition. Not so the man.

Dr. Counts thinks that in younger couples there is less insistence that the husband be the chief or only provider. "I know an artist whose wife has a small income of her own. They both lived on this income—a kind of hippie, spartan existence—and were quite happy." The young husband had no difficulties in accepting his financial dependency until, Dr. Counts says, "the wife had a baby. At this point the husband behaved in a rather self-defeating way and caused a lot of unhappiness all around, besides filling himself full of guilt. When we looked into it, we found that what was bothering him were the vestiges of his middle-class upbringing, which suddenly surfaced when he became a father." Dr. Counts wonders whether the continuing social pressure for the male to climb the career ladder will eventually affect those young couples who so far have managed to liberate themselves from the work-success drive that he's seen ruin so many marriages.

The sad truth is that basic attitudes haven't changed for most people, even though in many younger marriages today both husband and wife work. The white male pays a high psychological price for his many privileges, since the exaggerated need for success can lead to an exaggerated sense of failure.

Eight years ago my husband lost his job as director of sales promotion when his company changed hands. Although he was in his late 40s, his associates assured him that he'd have no trouble landing another job since he had a record of solid achievement and fine references. Yet a year of job-seeking brought only one result—a sure knowledge that the term "overqualified" was a code word for "too old."

I had not worked since the first year we were married, but our finances were in desperate shape. Tom had no objections to my getting a job—we really had no other choice. I found an entry-level spot that paid about a quarter of Tom's salary.

Tom, meanwhile, began his second year of seeking employment. And subtly, he lost hope. More and more often, after the children and I had gone, he went back to bed. I would come home from work to find him still in robe and slippers. He complained of severe shoulder pain, from an old football injury.

The doctor took X-rays and found nothing wrong. He asked to speak with me privately and told me that Tom was suffering from depression. I remember shouting at him, "Of course Tom's depressed. He'd be crazy if he wasn't!" In those days I was still capable of getting angry. The doctor thought psychotherapy would help, and we found a therapist who was willing to wait for payment until after Tom found a job.

That therapist was never paid. My career bloomed alongside the ashes of Tom's. On occasion he gets a low-paying sales job. Since he is a good salesman, his spirits improve remarkably. During these periods we are both happy. He is again performing as the man of the family should. But at the slightest disappointment—a dip in the sales curve, an ambiguous remark from a co-worker—his pain returns and he takes to bed. I threaten, "If you don't get up, I'm leav-

When the husband becomes dependent, the wife is held responsible for the damage to his ego

ing—for good." Sometimes the threat works, sometimes it doesn't. I am heartsick and bitter—bitter at having to be the family's breadwinner, a role that brings me more hostility and ridicule than praise, bitter at having to dole out dollars not only to the children but to a grown, able-bodied man now in his 50s, bitter at our lack of social life because Tom seldom feels up to seeing people. It does no good to tell myself that Tom is sick and that, given the circumstances, I should be grateful our family is still together and fairly well off. Somehow I feel cheated.

Like Tom, many dependent husbands are the victims of age discrimination or career obsolescence.

Jules, for instance, made it big when he was in his early 20s, and supported a wife and children for many years. But when his career began to go sour, his wife divorced him to marry an older man with money. Jules, faced with the fact that at 42 there was no longer any place for him in the music business, found that the prospect of being loved and supported by Ann was not the worst thing in the world. As marriages go, theirs is relatively happy. "A lot better," Jules says, "than my first. In bed, too."

If Jules' attitude became more common, much misery might be avoided. But even Jules' wife is affected by the almost universal view of dependent husbands as sponges and parasites. To counteract this, she tends to exaggerate Jules' present participation in the music scene and to see herself as a kind of patron-of-the-arts. And at times, undeniably, she is irritated by Jules' lack of financial independence, complaining that he has squandered his limited funds on foolish extravagances while leaving her to pay for all the necessities.

The great majority of dependent husbands have little in common with the comic-strip stereotype of the lazy slob in T-shirt, slouched in front of the TV, beer can in hand, who wouldn't wield a broom or boil an egg if his life depended on it. The women's movement has seen to that. One of the side benefits of feminism has been that men are more willing to take a hand in cooking, cleaning and child care. Such activities are much less virility-threatening than they were even five years ago.

Another recent development, also a by-product of the feminist movement, has been career competition between husband and wife—something movie stars have experienced for decades, with results we all know. With a different view of the male role—and the work/success syndrome—Barbra Streisand might still be married to Elliott Gould. After all, when they wed in 1963, Gould was the star—in *I Can Get It for You Wholesale*—and Streisand was the bit player. Perhaps if his ego had been less threatened when her career shot into the stratosphere, they might never have had to split.

Some people seem to believe that a woman makes it big only by climbing up the backs of recumbent men. They point to Mary Wells of Wells, Rich, Greene advertising agency, probably the top-paid woman executive in the world. She's now married to Harding Lawrence, head of Braniff International Airlines, who isn't starving either. But for 16 years she was married to Burt Wells, who was also in advertising and today runs a small agency in Connecticut. The fact that her career went farther and faster than his ought to say nothing about Burt Wells' standing as a human being, but unfortunately, too many people think it does.

Often, when the husband becomes dependent, the wife is blamed. She is held responsible for the damage to his ego caused by his decline in status. In cocktail party chatter, she's a "castrating bitch,"

one of male chauvinism's more punitive concepts.

I asked Dr. Counts if he thought there was any truth to that picture. "I haven't seen it in economic terms," Counts said. And he doubts that psychological dependence correlates with financial dependence. In one couple he knows, the wife is a psychiatrist and the husband is a writer. The husband admits to earning less than his wife, but Counts saw no signs that this troubled their marriage. "He told me he spent more time in the park babysitting than any of the nursemaids." Counts said. "He was genuinely proud of it."

Conceivably, writers, artists and musicians are special cases. The odds on the gamble may be long, but many a wife has supported her husband for years in the hope that one day his achievement will make him—and, by extension, her—famous. There is no aphrodisiac like fame, or even the promise of it.

Bob Smith, husband of literary agent Claire Smith, quit his job in advertising some years back to concentrate on writing. He recouped handsomely for his years of dependence when Simon & Schuster published his lighthearted novel, *Sadie Shapiro's Knitting Book*. Each such success makes other nurturers of talent take heart.

In any case, creative artists of either sex need sturdy egos to persevere. Being financially dependent seldom does damage to their self-images.

The dependent husband who suffers the most is not a creative artist or counterculturist but someone who believes in the system and has a traditional regard for the man's responsibilities. When such a man reaches 45 and finds himself unemployed and unemployable, his whole life comes under attack. Most younger men reading this will shrug and figure that nothing like that will happen to them. Yet the Labor Department reports that a stretch of joblessness is experienced by half the men in the work force at some time during every five-year period.

Of course, the 32-year-old ad agency creative director and the 28-year-old rock record promoter, each pulling in over 50 grand a year, don't want to think about that day, maybe a decade hence, when they'll be as obsolete as the engineers after the space program was slashed. If something forces them to think about it, they run a little faster on the treadmill.

What has to change is society's attitude toward the male role. But to date, even in the vanguard—women's consciousness-raising groups—the notion that the husband must be the main breadwinner is firmly fixed. In the CR sessions I attended for two years, I was pitied by all—and no doubt pitied myself—because I remained married to a man who was no longer able to support the family. No matter what her personal success in a career, a woman who even partially supports her husband is held to be somehow less fortunate than the woman whose husband is a lavish provider, no matter what his other failings.

I've frequently heard divorcees who receive alimony and child-support express contempt for the woman who stays with a man who doesn't support her. Their attitude reveals the chains on their own thinking since, economically speaking, they are still slaves willing to be sold to the highest bidder. To them, the wife with a dependent husband has been found wanting on the auction block.

In two popular feminist novels, Doris Lessing's *Summer Before the Dark* and Erica Jong's *Fear of Flying*, the heroines are married to successful professional men. In fact, the husbands are doctors—one a neurologist, the other a psychoanalyst—which reminded one jaundiced reader of the Jewish mother's definition of paradise: "My daughter married a doctor!" There are unsuccessful *ex*-husbands but no unemployed acting husbands in feminist novels. In seeking equal pay and economic independence for women, NOW and other feminist organizations repeatedly point to the fact that most women are "only one man away from welfare." But the feminists are not willing to take the next step—to allow men true economic independence, or dependence, if that is their need.

There are good historical and social reasons for this. Throughout the Western world laws require the male to support his offspring, and no laws have proved harder to enforce. The poorest families, as we all know, are those headed by women. Women, on the average, earn less than 60 percent of what men earn. Certainly the main effort must go, for the present, toward bringing women's pay and job opportunities more nearly in line with men's.

But even in the current state of economic inequality, thousands if not millions of families would be helped if our attitudes toward the male role could be transformed. Unemployed fathers, instead of being regarded with suspicion by social workers and hounded by the welfare bureaucracy, might stick around and help bring up their kids if their self-esteem weren't destroyed by doing so. Disabled men—such as my grammar-school principal's husband, a carpenter who fell from a ladder and was crippled for life—might be able to live longer, fuller, less apologetic lives. Divorce among high achievers might become less inevitable.

Graduate students today are making the longest strides toward this goal. Whereas 10 years ago it was always the husband who was helped through law school or medical school, and always the wife who did the helping, the current pattern is for them to take turns and help each other. It makes economic sense, both in the short and the long run.

Norman Mintz, associate dean of Columbia University's Graduate School of Arts and Sciences, says that, in awarding fellowships based on need, "We assume that an employed spouse contributes to the support of the spouse in school." He doesn't specify male or female.

He was eager to tell me about his "very, very able administrative assistant." She had been supporting her husband, who had just graduated from Columbia Law School. Now it was her turn. Since her husband was taking a job with the government in Washington, she was leaving Columbia to enter Georgetown Law School.

Their pattern may be the pattern of the future, not only for the purposes of education but throughout married life. More and more couples are devising ways to relieve the man of a lifetime of financial responsibility and the woman of a lifetime of household drudgery. Trade-off and sharing allow for richer, more varied marriages and greater personal fulfillment. On the day when it is no more demeaning for a man to be dependent on a woman than for a woman to be dependent on a man, sexual equality will have taken a large step toward realization.

MARRIAGE COUNSELING

- Private and group counseling
- Male-female therapy teams
- The three-generation approach
- Sex therapy

"Despite all the divorce talk, most people I know are sticking, dammit, and finding ways to make marriage work." So says a Boston textile executive, 45, who recently completed a series of marriage counseling sessions with his wife. "We had invested over 20 years together, but when the kids went to college, there was an awful lull at home," he adds. "We found a blank space in our marriage." The executive, a marketing manager, feels that the marriage therapy "kept us together." And he adds: "Now we are doing a repair job. It takes time."

His story is a common one today, and—despite rising divorce rates, particularly among couples under 35—it highlights a growing countermove that is aimed at saving marriages instead of ending them. "Counseling is becoming more acceptable, and more people are using it to prevent serious problems from building to a crisis," says Dr. Mark H. Bernstein, director of the Marriage Council of Philadelphia at the University of Pennsylvania.

The number of licensed marriage counselors is rising fast (from 5,000 to 12,000 in five years), and the American Psychiatric Assn. reports that far more psychiatrists are doing marriage therapy than ever before. At least part of the reason for this increase is a growing reaction against cynicism about marriage. The other part is that marriage counseling therapies have been greatly expanded and improved:

- Group marriage counseling is spreading rapidly, partly because of the lower cost ($20 to $30 per session, compared with the $40 to $60 common for private sessions). Also, such groups can often reach and help resolve the emotional conflicts in a marriage much faster.
- Male-female therapy teams are a new trend, and some say they are the most effective method yet devised to help solve difficult marriage problems. The cost is high (often $80 for a private session), but the group approach helps to keep it in line ($30 to $40 per couple).
- Three-generation therapy, designed in part to tackle difficult parental relationships, also is spreading. Says a Providence (R. I.) businesswoman: "You get the teenagers and your own parents to attend the sessions, and somehow you reach amazing solutions."
- "Marriage enrichment" weekends, similar to religious retreats, are growing in popularity. In many cases, the prerequisite is that couples who attend must be undergoing marriage counseling. The weekends are an outgrowth of the so-called marriage encounter, a similar, but less skilled, approach that is often conducted without professional guidance. Marriage enrichment sessions last from Friday night to Sunday night, involve highly specific techniques, and cost about $200 per couple.
- Sex therapy is now out of the hush-hush stage and is available at 100 or so qualified clinics (though there are many more offering the service). The benefits can be great: With 10 to 20 weekly sessions, the cure rate is over 60%.

Whatever the therapy method needed, many executives are plagued by conflicts between their career and their marriage, with dual-career marriages heading the list of trouble areas. According to New York City psychiatrist Henry I. Spitz, a noted marriage therapist, dual-career couples are often so obsessed with their professional lives that they forget their marriage. "These couples have to set aside careers for a moment and take preventive measures to stave off marriage troubles," says Spitz.

Indeed, prevention is the trend. Says the Boston textile executive: "I'll say that had we seen a counselor 10 years ago, we'd have saved many heartaches."

The therapy team approach

Of the newer methods, group counseling led by male-female therapy teams probably offers the brightest prospect for those seeking help. "It adds to the basic advantages of the group method," notes Harvard psychologist George Goethals. In a group of as many as six couples, he explains, each couple provides moral support for the others. "And the open discussion of marriage conflicts lets the couples unburden themselves and get more quickly to delicate subjects," Goethals adds.

The male-female team, often a married couple, works in a free-discussion style. And the team approach combats the sense of imbalance couples often feel in a session led by a single therapist of one sex or the other. With the male-female team, there is an equal number of men and women in the room as well as a "working model" for the group.

Says Spitz, who teams with his therapist wife: "We are able to illustrate how cooperation can work between married people, as we conduct the sessions, week to week. It rubs off on the group."

In a recent series of sessions held by a married male-female team in Hyannis, Mass., one couple in the group began to vent bitterness over the 44-year-old husband's habit of driving two hours to Boston on weekly business trips and often not returning home until Saturday. As the male member of the team relates: "The husband, an affluent business owner, at one point shouted to his wife, 'Your suspicions are petty and revolting!'" Adds the therapist: "This set off an intense discussion of business travel because two others in the group travel away from home.

"Finally it came out that the businessman stayed in Boston on Friday nights to unwind and have a quiet dinner because he knew that at home he would face some unwanted social obligation that his wife had arranged." As the therapist explains: "He'd developed a deep resentment over her 'foolishness in planning forced friendships' with people he barely knew. Two wives in the group then jumped to her defense, saying they understood her loneliness at home." The therapist team guided the discussions so that the group would stick to the basic problems.

"The couple are still working at all this, and they have uncovered some incompatibilities," he says. "It also became clear that the husband was not 'playing around' in Boston, as his wife had feared, and this is a positive point."

The male-female team is effective, though, only if the team's skills are equally strong and if one member is not subordinate to the other. "The team has to know how to overcome their own disagreements," cautions Atlanta counselor Donald H. Highlander. Group sessions are usually 1½ hours long and last from six to eight weeks, or sometimes even a year and longer.

Three generations talking

Three-generation marriage therapy usually brings together the couple, their teenage children, and grandparents who either live with the family or maintain close ties. "Unresolved conflicts of the couple's parents tend to throw over to the next generation," notes Donald S. Williamson, a Houston psychologist. One object, he explains, is to free the troubled spouse from this inheritance.

A professional woman, one of Williamson's marriage-therapy patients, says that she was able to explore successfully the relationship with her parents in sessions at which they were present. "It freed me to develop my own values in marriage, as a career woman, rather than modeling myself after mother's traditional views," she says.

A Westwood (N.J.) therapist notes that in working with an executive and his wife in their late 30s, their 13-year-old son, and the wife's 70-year-old mother, it soon became clear that there was great hostility over the mother-in-law's living with the family. "The husband, who was 39, was almost in tears at one session," says the therapist. "He was with his wife, without the boy or grandmother, and he said 'I'm tired of sharing my wife with her mother.' He let himself go."

The therapist explains that as weeks went by, the tension ebbed. "We got around to some calm talks about aged parents and their feelings, as well as their children's feelings," he adds. "Then, in a later session, it came out

that the husband's mother had been an abusive alcoholic. I began to see the husband privately, concurrently with the family sessions, and I think the solution will come soon."

"Some couples don't realize that an aged parent, or a teenager, can help solve their conflict," says the therapist. "In this case, the willingness of the wife's mother to attend the sessions and do her best made a lot of difference." The teenager, by being at four sessions, added to the strength of the therapy.

Says Frederick G. Humphrey, a psychologist at the University of Connecticut: "Yes, the aged parent can help many times. But basically, the feelings of the couple are the crux of it. If they can achieve closeness, they can shoulder problems involving the young and old."

A highly personal approach to marriage dilemmas is the "marriage enrichment" weekend as an adjunct to counseling. The technique was conceived in part by Larry Hof, an instructor at the University of Pennsylvania medical school. "It in no way replaces therapy for couples who need therapy," says Hof. "But it is helpful and, I think, shortens the therapy required."

When couples who are undergoing counseling at the medical school center agree that they want to salvage their marriage, they can sign up for an enrichment weekend. The program, a model for similar sessions being developed elsewhere, is held at a conference center outside Philadelphia, and its basic aim is to help the couples participating gain greater mutual respect and confidence.

On Friday evening the couples hear an introductory talk and are encouraged to set "personal goals" for the upcoming weekend. The idea is to "share" goals with one's spouse, then with others in the group. The evening ends with what Hof says is a group circle, with the couples entering into "a very light physical-touch experience." For example, they might sit in a wide circle and meditate on the possibilities of a better marriage, as they touch hands. The idea is to provide a sense of intimacy.

Saturday starts with a "marriage lifeline session" in which the couples tell about their marriage and about where they feel they are heading in it. There are more exercises, such as writing down individual marriage objectives and responsibilities as well as a "marital intimacy checklist" to help achieve greater closeness.

The weekend closes with a renewal of a couple's marriage vows. "It can help troubled people who still care," says Thelma Dixon-Murphy, a New York City marriage therapist. "Some couples come back with an emotional 'high'—the question is, can they sustain it?"

Problems with sex

Sex therapy clinics are becoming popular, but successful senior executives have less reason to seek them out than most people, say the experts. "The truly successful businessman on the top rung has fewer sex problems than most," says leading specialist Dr. Helen Singer Kaplan, a psychiatrist and sex therapist at Cornell medical school in New York. "It is the striving second-line man and the workaholic who have trouble with sex," she adds.

Kaplan also notes that successful businesswomen, contrary to myth, "have better sex lives than quiet, passive women." She adds: "They aren't cold, as some think."

The three major sex problems of married couples are a lack of desire on the part of either partner, a widespread difficulty among people of 30 and older; troubles with physical performance, mainly among middle-aged men; and ejaculation and orgasmic troubles. "Lack of desire is curable in 10% to 15% of the cases, with 10 to 20 sessions," notes Kaplan. Most cases, however, require extended therapy. "Performance problems of middle-aged men can be cured 50% to 60% of the time, within 20 sessions, and ejaculation problems, in 80% to 90% of the cases," she says.

These three major problems occur in normal, nonneurotic people, and they usually are stress-related. Only 15% of all cases are caused by a physical problem such as alcoholism or drugs taken for hypertension.

To locate a reputable sex therapist, you should contact a local medical society or a university medical school. The average psychiatrist or psychologist does not perform sex therapy. And the cost for a specialist in this area is usually $75 to $100 per session, with some overall fees as high as $3,000.

Rethinking the marriage

Executives over 40 who are suffering dire marriage problems often fall into a common trap, notes Yale psychologist Daniel J. Levinson, author of the new book, *The Seasons of a Man's Life*. "The executive and his wife have an unspoken agreement at the start," Levinson explains. "He will climb the ladder in business, and she will raise the children. But when the kids are older, on their own, trouble starts. He finds that climbing the ladder is no longer so important to him, and his wife senses that her life is empty. Now both need the marriage more, but they turn to it and find it wanting."

2. MAINTENANCE OF RELATIONSHIPS

Fixing up the marriage at this stage is hard, Levinson says. And when a man is battling his way through a midlife transition from early to middle adulthood, the task of righting the marriage "can be monumental." New York psychiatrist Spitz notes that "executives have wide exposure to women, and a man under this midlife pressure sometimes seeks a younger woman as an escape from the prospect of old age." The drive to prove that youth has not fled takes other forms. "Some businessmen use work as an escape, and others take up sports obsessively," Spitz adds. "If it is a driven effort to stay young, the marriage suffers."

He notes that female executives also try desperate ways to stay young at certain times in their lives, and again the marriage suffers. Spitz explains that he tries, first, "to get executives to put the brakes on the frantic activity, and then to understand what it is they are doing." In marriage therapy, the couple involved is then encouraged to develop mutual pursuits and interests, including a reemphasis on sex.

The dual-career marriage may be faced with even harder problems when both husband and wife rise to the executive level. At that point, the entire marriage contract needs to be renegotiated. Among other things, a couple in counseling will be encouraged to understand and rise above any new feelings of career competition and to accept that each other's career efforts will benefit both of them.

"In our therapy, we arrived at all the practical points like budgeting the money we earned and who would fix meals when that was necessary," says a New Haven finance executive, 35, whose wife is an assistant corporate counsel. "I didn't think much of marriage therapy, and frankly, it was painful," he adds. "But we've overcome antagonisms."

Junior executives still forming their careers and marriage relationships should try some preventive medicine, advises Connecticut's Humphrey. "Many young couples, particularly dual-career couples, ought to discuss the whole thing the minute one of them gets on a career track," he says. "Whether they'll have children, whose career will justify moving out of town, whether they go for the idea of a weekend marriage because of work—all these things need to be aired," Humphrey says.

If all else fails, predivorce therapy can help dull the pain occasioned by the prospect of separation. When a divorce decision is made in counseling, the rejected spouse ("there usually is one," says Humphrey) can be given support and guidance in private sessions.

Says Dr. Martin Blinder, a San Francisco psychiatrist and family therapist: "People come here to get better. It should be understood that one of the possible outcomes is to get rid of the marriage."

Sex Therapy: Making It as a Science and an Industry

CONSTANCE HOLDEN

The rapid spread of the human potential movement in America today—which encompasses a wild assortment of new techniques, psychotherapeutic and otherwise, for individual self-exploration and the enhancement of the joys of being human—has provided a fertile environment for what may be the fastest-growing field of all—the exploration of human sexuality and treatment of sexual problems.

Sex research, sex training, sex education, and sex therapy programs are blooming profusely around the country, but amid the blossoms there are a good many weeds. People with little or no qualifications are getting into the act—some "educational seminars," for example, offer little more enlightenment than a weekend of dirty movies. There is particular confusion and concern over what constitutes proper training of a sex therapist, and what measures should be taken to curb the abuses that flourish in the name of therapy.

Alfred Kinsey was the first American to pierce through the clouds of puritan ethics and Victorian morality which have shrouded the subject in this country and have exempted it from the mainstreams of scientific and behavioral research. The sex research team of William Masters and Virginia Johnson, who this year celebrated their 20th anniversary of professional association, is largely responsible for giving the investigation of sexuality and the treatment of "sexual dysfunction" credibility and scientific respectability.

Particularly significant is the fact that courses in sexuality have rapidly become standard fare in medical schools throughout the country. This is part of the new humanistic approach to learning in medical schools, where there is less concentration on pathology and more on the whole person. This is also reflected in the fact that more and more students are turning to family medicine rather than to specialties, and that gynecologists are learning to help women gain a better understanding of their own bodies. Also there is a new recognition of the importance of physicians in helping patients and their families face death and dying.

Since Masters and Johnson's second book, *Treatment of Sexual Dysfunction*, appeared 4½ years ago, hundreds of "clinics," "foundations," and "study centers" run by individuals with varying qualifications have sprouted up. Professional intervention in sexual problems is not new—marriage counsellors in particular have been giving advice for years. What is new is that sex therapy has emerged as a discipline of its own, thanks to the discovery that it is possible, with the use of behavioral techniques, to alleviate a sexual problem by focusing on the symptom. This means that it is not necessary to overhaul an entire relationship or personality to achieve successful sexual functioning. The idea is that sexual dysfunction is learned, and, with proper guidance and practice, it can be unlearned. This is in sharp contrast to the traditional psychoanalytic view, which holds that underlying psychological conflicts are responsible for the symptom and have to be straightened out before the sex problem can be eliminated. The virtue of sex therapy, as viewed by its practitioners, is that it is relatively short term, and for many people it can be a low cost substitute for years of psychotherapy, which may fail to relieve the symptoms anyway.

Responding to the rocketing demand for help in sexual problems, a great many people, some clinically trained and some not, have embraced the handy techniques developed by Masters and Johnson and have opened thriving practices as sex therapists. Since offering such services is legal and not unethical by any existing professional code, there is now no way of controlling or even getting reliable statistics on the phenomenon.

There are no official estimates of the number of sex clinics operating in the country today. Masters thinks there are 3500 to 5000, most lacking any institutional affiliation, and only about 100 of which are run by properly trained professionals. Many sex therapy programs are offered by practitioners in medicine and other clinical disciplines whose sex training begins and ends with reading Masters and Johnson, but who offer to treat dysfunction at astronomical prices ranging from $2500 (the standard set by Masters and Johnson who use their fees to support their research program) to $4000.

Then there are sex therapy clinics that are based at universities and teaching hospitals and that are usually part of a broader set of interconnected programs of sex instruction, training, and research. These generally offer the lowest cost services—between $300 and $400 for a course of treatment—to the widest number of people. Their institutional connections generally ensure that therapy will be conducted in a responsible manner by properly trained counsellors.

Since there remains much to be explored and discovered concerning sexual response, it is impossible to define what is legitimate sex therapy other than to say it is that which enhances people's sex functioning and attitudes. Certain practices, such as sexual interaction between therapist and client, are out.

A few programs are briefly described here. There are different roads to the mountaintop, but most start from the base camp established by Masters and Johnson who, in these telescoped times, have already become to sex therapy what Freud is to psychotherapy.

Masters and Johnson believe in the

man-woman therapeutic approach, preferably with one member of the team a physician and the other a behavioral scientist. They deal only with couples (although they can be homosexual as well as heterosexual), and during an intensive, expensive, 2-week program with the couple quartered in a hotel in St. Louis with nothing to distract them from their homework—"sensate focus" exercises that are the core of the treatment—the problem is zeroed in on. Unlike mental health professionals who are also trained as psychotherapists, they deal with the dysfunction* and if psychiatric problems are apparent, they are then referred to a therapist.

Helen Singer Kaplan, psychoanalyst in the psychiatry department of Cornell Medical Center and head of the sex therapy unit at New York Hospital, is well known for her work in placing sex treatment more firmly in a psychiatric framework. She has expanded techniques developed by Masters and Johnson and adapted them for use on an outpatient basis. She deals with individuals as well as couples, uses group techniques—one example being a group of husbands and wives working on the problem of premature ejaculation. Rather than driving solely for symptomatic relief, the program deals with emotional problems that have disabled marital communication. Kaplan believes her philosophical model—the integration of behavioral sexual tasks with psychodynamics—has implications for the whole field of psychiatry because it shows how behavioral and analytical techniques can be complementary rather than discrete alternatives. Kaplan is also involved in the training of sex therapists, all of whom must be skilled psychotherapists to begin with.

On the other side of the country, in Long Beach, California, are the team of William Hartman, marriage counsellor and sociologist, and his associate Marilyn Fithian. This pair is regarded by some as the "Masters and Johnson of the West Coast." They run a private therapy and training outfit called the Center for Marital and Sexual Studies. Starting with a basic Masters and Johnson approach, they have added a number of twists, including films of people having healthy sexual interac-

tions, hypnosis, and a "sexological" exam, where a couple is given detailed guided tours of each other's bodies. The pair also conducts a 6-week training program for dual therapy teams, and they make periodic tours around the major cities of the nation offering 1-day lecture-and-film seminars.

One program that is generally held in high esteem by sex people is the Sex Advisory and Counselling Unit at the University of California Medical Center in San Francisco. There, attempts are being made to tailor therapy to the limitations of low-income people, and people who can't take much time off from the job. Work is also being done with groups of inorgasmic women, which combines women's movement consciousness-raising with new sexual awareness. This program is part of a major trend in the field—an effort to make responsible sex therapy available to the needy and not just those who can afford the exotic prices charged by private practitioners. The main schism in the field, in fact, is not so much the matter of correct approaches to dysfunction, but between private practitioners and those who work in connection with institutions. The academics think the private operators are too often ill trained and high priced, and they look askance at fancy brochures sent out to advertise treatment programs and seminars.

Another approach that deserves mention is that developed by Ted McIlvenna, a clergyman, sexologist, and psychologist at the National Sex Forum in San Francisco. This organization takes an educational approach, says McIlvenna, in the belief that sex problems should not be regarded as pathological but as manifestations of negative attitudes and misinformation. So the National Sex Forum has developed a multimedia blitz weekend program for "sexual attitude restructuring." Anyone can come (it costs $75 per couple). They sit around on pillows and are subjected to simultaneous slides and movies accompanied by running explanations from a staff member. Every possible sex practice—including bestiality, sadism, masturbation, and practices of other cultures—is depicted and discussed at length. That is "desensitization." Viewers go home somewhat appalled, says McIlvenna, but then they sleep on it and end up thinking "so what." So they come back for "resensitization" the next day, where with

more movies and talks they find out how good and normal sexual expression is. Individuals and couples can then come back and work out a program to cope with their particular problems.

The National Sex Forum makes its own films which it distributes to hundreds of institutions, including medical schools, here and abroad. The use of films, both pornographic ones and ones depicting sexual anatomy and activity, has become standard fare in training, education, and therapy. They are used widely in medical schools, where courses on sexuality, unusual a half a decade ago, are now routine. They are particularly useful in changing people's attitudes toward sex, a function which a recent survey showed is probably the primary goal of sexuality courses in medical school. Most doctors are not only unskilled in confronting a patient's sex problem, but many are too uptight about the subject to try. James Maddock, who runs the human sexuality program at the University of Minnesota medical school, suggests that physicians have particularly high anxiety levels when it comes to sex because of the type of personality that is drawn to doctoring. Many have "obsessive compulsive" personalities which make it difficult for them to deal with an emotion-laden and ambiguous subject that requires a tolerant, sensitive, and, above all, relaxed approach. They also find it difficult to explore the subtleties of sex relationships when they are keyed up to making daily life-or-death decisions, he notes.

Harold Lief, who heads the 6-year-old Center for the Study of Sex Education in Medicine at the University of Pennsylvania, is a pioneer in sex education for medical students. In the early 1960's, he says, only three schools offered any instruction in sexuality. In 1968 there were 30. Now, according to a survey he recently completed with his colleague David Reed, 106 of the country's 112 medical schools teach it, and in 60 percent of these the courses are required as part of the core curriculum. Medical students overwhelmingly favor such courses, the survey finds, and are even more enthusiastic about them than faculty members. The content of the courses includes instruction on normal sexual behavior, its variations and deviations, sexual disorders, psychosexual development, and treatment of disorders, including rudi-

---

*Dysfunctions are defined as impotence, premature ejaculation, retarded ejaculation, inorgasmic potential in women, vaginismus (constricted vaginal muscles), and dyspareunia (painful intercourse).

mentary counselling skills. Half the schools invite spouses or "significant other partners" to attend with the students. While sex instruction is particularly relevant to the fields of gynecology and psychiatry, new emphasis is also being placed on counselling people partially disabled by disease (diabetes, for example, can produce impotency), heart attacks, operations, or advanced age. A cardiac patient, for example, is no longer vaguely told to "take it easy," but is treated to a frank discussion of safe levels of exertion. Old people also stand to benefit. Despite Masters and Johnson's affirmation that sex can enhance life up to the last minute, a recent study of doctor-patient relationships showed that most physicians felt inadequate when it came to dealing with sex and the senior citizen, that most of the doctors regarded it as "unimportant," and even gerontologists agreed that for old people it was "just a memory."

Of all the sex projects springing up across the land, one of the newest, and most ambitious sounding, is the research, therapy, and training program being set up at the State University of New York at Stony Brook. The impetus has come from Stanley Yolles, head of the department of psychiatry there and former head of the National Institute of Mental Health, where, before his departure several years ago, he unsuccessfully sought to establish an in-house sexual research project. Yolles has been gathering together an interdisciplinary team of educators, clinicians, and researchers with the object of establishing an "international academy of sex research," a mecca for sex researchers from around the world. At present, according to Joseph LoPiccolo, head of the sex therapy and research unit, Stony Brook is one of very few places where research is being done on new behavioral techniques for alleviating sexual dysfunction. LoPiccolo is well known in sex circles for his explorations of the potentials of masturbation. His innovations include a detailed program of masturbation for inorgasmic women, and a routine, involving pornography and masturbation, that has enabled homosexual men to respond sexually to their wives. (To LoPiccolo's surprise, these men, rather than learning to favor women as sex partners, learned instead to become firmly bisexual—one indication of the malleability and continuing mysteries of human sexual response.) The Stony Brook group is also developing video cassettes and booklets for at-home use by dysfunctional couples. The effectiveness of this method, or lack of it, will help resolve a still unanswered question of how much can be done by instructional materials and how much needs interaction with a therapist.

While Middle America may quail at such frontal assaults on the privacy and taboos surrounding sex, there are, within the educational, medical, and research establishments, few overt traces of the resistance that met the work of Alfred Kinsey or the early research of Masters.

The chief controversy now going on among those concerned with training and clinical work on sex, and the one that has brought Masters and Johnson out of their laboratory and into such forums as the "Today" show, is the matter of quality control in sex counselling. If sex were a drug, it would top the list of abused substances, so it is hardly surprising that some pretty gross exploitation is going on. Some "sex therapists" treat their clients to sado-masochistic practices, homosexual seduction, sexual participation by the "therapist," and thinly veiled prostitution under the label of "surrogate partners." On a less flagrant level, many academics are distressed about the number of ill-trained private operators who in addition to doing high-priced therapy are fond of running weekend "seminars" largely composed of a barrage of pornographic films that purport to train professionals in sex therapy.

No one is agreed on exactly what constitutes proper training for a sex therapist and there are raging debates on what the proper accreditation and licensing procedures should be. Terminology, too, remains to be sorted out. Some people use the term "therapist" and "counsellor" interchangeably; others say the former deal with deep-seated problems, while the latter are only equipped to deal with relatively simple anxieties and communicational difficulties. There is general agreement that a would-be sex therapist should start with a degree in a discipline requiring clinical and counselling skills and should then undergo a course of specialized training, lasting perhaps 6 months to a year. The obvious candidates for advanced training are doctors, psychiatrists, psychologists, marriage and family counsellors, psychiatric nurses, social workers, and clergymen. Full-fledged training programs (as opposed to weekend or longer seminars and workshops) are now conducted in upwards of half a dozen places, most of them university-based. They include "desensitization," familiarization with variations of sexual functioning and dysfunctioning, methods for dealing with dysfunction, relationship counselling, and supervised on-the-job training. Training facilities nowhere near begin to fill the growing demand for sex counselling, so not even strict legislation would presently prevent unqualified individuals from getting into the business.

The American Association of Sex Educators and Counsellors (AASEC), which has been accrediting sex educators since 1967, plans to become the first organization to accredit sex counsellors, starting in November.

Concern Spreading

Other organizations have started actively worrying. The newly formed Eastern Academy of Sex Therapy, whose membership is mainly drawn from medical schools, will be addressing itself to the questions of proper training and qualification. The National Association for the Scientific Study of Sex will address the issue in its meeting in November. The American Medical Association (AMA) also has a task force on sex therapy, with representation from mental health professionals, which is trying to figure out what the role of physicians should be in seeing that clinics have appropriately trained personnel and programs. Masters, who compares the state of affairs now ("god-awful") with medical education at the time the Flexner report came out in 1910, is pinning his hopes on the AMA committee to make recommendations that will guide states in proposing licensing law for sex therapists. Many observers think it is too soon for one organization, such as AASEC, to set itself up as the arbiter of what constitutes adequate qualifications. Others think accreditation by a private organization doesn't mean much and that it is up to states to develop licensing procedures.

Everyone thinks things have to get

2. MAINTENANCE OF RELATIONSHIPS

organized, not only for the protection of the public and the integrity of the field, but so that people will be able to obtain insurance reimbursement for sex therapy. Currently, insurance carriers will not reimburse any "relationship" counselling, whether it is marriage counselling or 2 weeks at Masters and Johnson's. Reimbursement is generally available if sex therapy is done by a qualified health provider, provided that the diagnosis is something other than sex dysfunction. This leads to some silly dilemmas—one Washington-area psychologist who is also a trained sex therapist says her patients never had trouble getting reimbursed until the insurance carriers found out her specialty. They don't want to pay for the sex part so "they ask in each case whether sex therapy was involved." She finds this differentiation absurd. "A person who is not healthy sexually is not a healthy person." The status of

sex therapy, like that of clinical psychology, will probably remain murky until national health insurance rolls around.

As the clouds of Victorianism and misinformation continue to lift, it is becoming increasingly apparent that sex therapy, while hardly a life-or-death matter, can contribute significantly to emotional health. One's sexual identity, after all, is inseparable from one's identity. Some people, who function reasonably well themselves, may regard sex therapy as a luxury, perhaps even decadent, but as any sex counsellor will testify, the amount of sexual misery across the land, suffered in secret because of guilt, anxiety, shame, ignorance, and the belief that "that's how things are," is incalculable. Masters and Johnson estimate that 50 percent of married couples (and by extension, all people) suffer from sexual problems that significantly affect the relationship.

While many are the logical products of rotten relationships, others—learned responses from the past—can poison good ones.

James Lieberman, a Washington, D.C., psychiatrist who also does sex therapy with married couples says "The nice thing about sex therapy is that it involves touch, intimacy, vulnerability, and trust. Many people have never experienced these in childhood. A great many of the adults walking around today are probably incapable of genuine intimacy because their parents had been themselves deprived of love in their early years, and didn't know how to transmit it to their children. Hopefully this picture is changing because now for the first time, thanks to contraception, most children born were planned and are wanted. There is no way to learn intimacy just by talking or reading books, you have to learn it by early experience, education and practice."

The Eight Myths of Marriage

William J. Lederer and
Don D. Jackson, M.D.

Almost everyone suffers severe disappointment within a few months after marriage. A study conducted with couples married for an average of one year indicated that they felt marriage was different from what they had expected.

One young woman said, "Marriage is not what I had assumed it would be. One premarital assumption after another has crashed down on my head. I am going to make my marriage work, but it's going to take a lot of hard work and readjusting. Marriage is like taking an airplane to Florida for a relaxing vacation in January, and when you get off the plane you find you're in the Swiss Alps. There is cold and snow instead of swimming and sunshine. Well, after you buy winter clothes and learn how to ski and learn how to talk a new foreign language, you can have just as good a vacation in the Swiss Alps as you can in Florida. But I can tell you it's one hell of a surprise when you get off that marital airplane and find that everything is far different from what one had assumed."

This realistic and candid young woman is now happy in her marriage. But for her to reach this point required two years of patient working and changing. She learned that the institution of modern marriage is based on many false assumptions and untrue beliefs.

Whenever a decision or a system is based on false assumptions it is almost certain to be a failure. If women and men were acquainted with the realities of marriage before they entered it, and if they accepted these realities, the divorce rate in the United States would diminish markedly.

To understand the realities of the marital relationship it is essential first to recognize the unrealities. What follows is a discussion of eight of the major myths of marriage.

Myth No. 1. The belief that people get married because they are "in love." It is extremely difficult to define love satisfactorily.

A very practical definition of love has been given by the great American psychiatrist Harry Stack Sullivan: "When the satisfaction or the security of *another person becomes as significant to one as is one's own satisfaction or security, then the state of love exists.*"

The state of love described by Sullivan is possible in marriage — but few spouses are prepared for it, or capable of experiencing it, right after the wedding. Its coming, if it comes at all, is the result of luck or of years of hard work and patience — as we hope to demonstrate later. Observation of hundreds of married couples shows that very few experience love. *They like to think of themselves as being in love;* but by and large the emotion they interpret as love is in reality some other emotion — often a strong sex drive, fear or a hunger for approval.

If they are not in love, then why are they impelled to marry? There are several reasons.

1. *During courtship, individuals lose most of their judgment.* People who believe themselves to be in love describe their emotion as ecstasy. "Ecstasy" — from the Greek *ekstasis*, which means "derange" — is defined as the "state of being beside oneself; state of being beyond all reason and self-control." When an emotional courtship starts, the woman and man appear to relinquish whatever sense of balance and reality they ordinarily possess.

2. *People often marry because society expects it of them.* Society encourages marriage in many ways and for many reasons. For example, marriage is — to put it crudely — good for business. It gives employment to ministers, justices of the peace, caterers, florists, dressmakers, printers, jewelers, furniture manufacturers, architects, landlords, obstetricians, and so on almost endlessly. Whenever there is a wedding hundreds of cash registers tinkle. Therefore members of the profit-making multitude smile and applaud, frequently in honest approval. This approval adds to the myth that the very act of marriage is a good thing; it brings prestige in society's eyes to the young couple.

3. *The pressures and the maneuverings of parents often push their children into premature and careless marriages.* Parents maneuver and manipulate claiming they meddle for their children's benefit. And since parents are seldom fully honest to their children about their own relationships, most young people believe that their parents are or were in love, and that they must be emulated in this respect.

4. *Romantic literature, tradition and movies have given marriage false values which the excited male and female often accept as true.* They enter wedlock expecting a high level of constant joy from that moment on. Although they take an oath to love and cherish each other throughout all adversity, in fact they do not expect any serious adversity. They have been persuaded that love (which they cannot even define) automatically will make it possible to solve all problems.

5. *Loneliness often drives people into marriage.* Many individuals simply cannot bear to be alone. They get bored and restless, and they think that having somebody of the opposite sex in the house will stop them from being miserable. Thus they marry because of desperation, not love.

6. *Some individuals marry because of an unconscious desire to improve themselves.* Almost all human beings have a mental image — called the ego ideal — of what they would like to be. In reality an individual seldom develops into this ideal person. But when she meets someone of the opposite sex who has the qualities which she desires, then up pops another false assumption. The individual unconsciously concludes that if she marries, she will, without effort, acquire the missing desirable characteristics or talents. After the marriage the spouses learn that intimacy does not bring about the desired self-improvement. Each blames the other and the discord begins.

7. *Many marriages are motivated by neuroses.* Certain individuals pick as mates those who make it possible for them to exercise their neuroses. These people do not wish to be happy in the normal sense. If they enjoy suffering, they unconsciously choose partners with whom they can fight, or who will abuse or degrade them. Some of these marriages endure for a considerable

time because the partners get pleasure from discord, but this type of perversion can hardly be called an expression of love.

8. *Some people miss their father or mother and cannot live without a parental symbol.* Therefore they find — and marry — a person of the opposite sex who will play the parental role.

In summary, then, it may be said that people generally enter matrimony thinking they are in love and believing that marriage will bring them "instant happiness," which will solve all problems. Actually, in most instances they are swept into marriage on a tidal wave of romance, not love. Romance is usually ephemeral; it is selfish. Romantic "lovers" are distraught and miserable when separated, and this misery is caused by selfishness of the most egocentric type. The "lover" is sorry for herself and is grieving over her loss of pleasure and intimacy. This state of mind is closely related to another selfish emotion — jealousy. Romance is exciting — but it is no relation to love, no kin to that generous concern for someone else which Harry Stack Sullivan defines as love.

Most people believe they are marrying for love. This is a false assumption and a dangerous myth.

Myth No. 2. The belief that most *married people love each other.* Spouses who have been married for more than three or four years rarely state spontaneously that they are in love with one another. Yet in many marriages, especially discordant ones, each partner tenaciously and stubbornly believes that she is a loving individual — trying, with courage and self-sacrifice, to make the marriage work; and that if there is friction, the other partner is causing it. Each may cite specific episodes which demonstrate that she is loving, patient and good (and that the other is selfish, unkind and unreasonable).

Myth No. 3. The belief that love is necessary for a satisfactory marriage. Even though people are reluctant to admit it, most husbands and wives are disappointed in their marriages.

Evidently the dreamed-of marriage often does not materialize. There are unexpected shortcomings, bickerings, misunderstandings. Most spouses to varying degrees are frustrated, confused, belligerent and disappointed.

One reason for this marital disenchantment is the prevalence of the mistaken belief that "love" is necessary for a satisfying and workable marriage. Usually when the word "love" is used,

reference is actually being made to romance — that hypnotic, ecstatic condition enjoyed during courtship. Romance and love are different. Romance is based usually on minimum knowledge of the other person (restricted frequently to the fact that being around her or him is a wonderful, beatific, stimulating experience). Romance is built on a foundation of quicksilver nonlogic. It consists of attributing to the other person — blindly, hopefully, but without much basis in fact — the qualities one *wishes* him or her to have, though they may not even be desirable, in actuality. Most people who select mates on the basis of imputed qualities later find themselves disappointed, if the qualities are not present in fact, or discover that they are unable to tolerate the implication of the longed-for qualities in actual life. It is a dream relationship, an unrealistic relationship with a dream person imagined in terms of one's own needs.

Romance is essentially selfish, though it is expressed in terms of glittering sentiment and generous promises, which usually cannot be fulfilled.

Romance — *which most spouses mistake for love* — is not necessary for a good marriage. The sparkle some couples manage to preserve in a satisfying marriage — based on genuine pleasure in one another's company, affection and sexual attraction for the spouse as she or he really is — can be called love.

If romance is different than love, then what *is* love? A devotion and respect for the spouse that is equal to one's own self-love.

We have already shown that people usually marry on a wave of romance having nothing to do with love. When the average American (not long from the altar) lives with the spouse in the intimacy of morning bad breath, of annoying habits previously not known, when she and he are hampered by the limitations of a small income (compared with the lavishness of the honeymoon), or encounters business frustrations and fatigue, a change in attitude begins to occur. The previously romantic person begins to have doubts about the wonderful attributes with which her or his spouse has been so blindly credited.

Not very long ago, after all, the spouse believed that "love" (romance) was heavenly, all-consuming, immutable and that beautiful relationships and behavior were *voluntary* and *spontaneous*. Now, if doubts and criticism are permitted to intrude upon

this perfect dream, the foundations begin to shake in a giddy manner. To the husband or wife the doubts seem to be evidence that one of them is inadequate or not to be trusted. The doubts imply that the relationship is suffering from an unsuspected malignancy.

To live with another person in a state of love (as defined by Sullivan) is a different experience from whirling around in a tornado of romance. A loving union is perhaps best seen in elderly couples who have been married for a long time. They need and treasure companionship. Differences between them have been either accepted or worked out. In such instances each has as much interest in the well-being and security of the other as she has in herself. Here is a true symbiosis: a union where each admittedly feeds off the other. Those who give together really live together!

The Chinese have a saying, "One hand washes the other." That sort of describes it.

But it is possible to have a productive and workable marriage without love (although love is desirable) as well as without romance. One can have a functioning marriage which includes doubts and criticism of the spouse and occasional inclinations toward divorce. The wife or husband may even think about how much fun it might be to flirt with an attractive neighbor. Such thoughts can occur without being disastrous to the marriage. *In many workable marriages both spouses get a good deal of mileage out of fantasy.*

How, then, can we describe this functional union which can bring reasonable satisfaction and well-being to both partners? It has four major elements: tolerance, respect, honesty and the desire to stay together for mutual advantage. One can prefer the spouse's company to all others', and even be lonely in her absence, without experiencing either the wild passion inherent in romance, or the totally unselfish, unswerving devotion that is basic in true love.

In a workable marriage both parties may be better off together than they would have been on their own. They may not be ecstatically happy because of their union, and they may not be "in love," but they are not lonely and they have areas of shared contentment. They feel reasonably satisfied with their levels of personal and interpersonal functioning. They can count their blessings and, like a sage, philosophically realize that nothing is perfect.

We must return once again to the meaning of the word "love," for no other word in English carries more misleading connotations.

Sullivan's definition of love is important: "*When the satisfaction or the security of another person becomes as significant to one as is one's own satisfaction or security, then the state of love exists.*" It describes not a unilateral process, but a two-way street, a bilateral process in which two individuals function in relation to each other as equals. One spouse alone cannot achieve this relationship. The necessity for both spouses to "give" equally is one of the reasons that a marriage built upon mutual love is so rare.

It is not possible to live in a permanent state of romance. Normal people should not be frustrated or disappointed if they are not in a *constant* state of love. If they experience the joy of love (or imagine they do) for ten percent of the time they are married, attempt to treat each other with as much courtesy as they do distinguished strangers, and attempt to make the marriage a workable affair — one where there are some practical advantages and satisfactions for each — the chances are that the marriage will endure longer and with more strength than the so-called love matches.

Myth No. 4. The belief that there are inherent behavioral and attitudinal differences between female and male, and that these differences cause most marital troubles.

Ever since history was first well recorded people have based their behavior on an unprovable belief that women and men are vastly different emotionally, intellectually and spiritually. They have considered each other almost as different species of *Homo sapiens*. Here are some examples: (1) Women are more emotional than men. (2) Men are better at abstract thinking than are women. (3) Women are more intuitive than men. (4) Men are more skillful with their hands (and in using tools) than women. (5) Women are more hypochondriacal than men, but men are little boys at heart, especially when they're ill. (6) It is almost always the man who indulges in infidelity and breaks up the marriage. (7) Homosexuality is practiced more by men than by women. (8) The female usually snares the male. (9) Women are slier and more cunning then men. (10) Men are bolder, more physically vigorous, more courageous than women. (11) Women are more loving than men.

Myth No. 5. The belief that the ad-

vent of children automatically improves a difficult or an unfulfilled marriage.

It is easily observed that some spouses are totally child-oriented: they live for their children. In return, the children keep the marriage alive by providing the parents a *raison d'etre* for the marriage and help fill the emotional and physical distance between the spouses, so that the expression of tension and friction between them is kept at a minimum. When the children leave home, these marriages typically are in serious difficulties — unless the parents are fortunate enough to have developed outside interests sufficient to maintain the protective distance between them.

In Puerto Rico, India and other countries where devices preventing pregnancy have been in use for five or more years, statistics are becoming available. These indicate that there is a higher percentage of happy, productive marriages among couples who have no children. Recent research suggests that the same situation exists in the United States, and that the parents of five or more children who so proudly point to their huge brood may be putting on an act. Our picture of the large, happy family (the poor and shoeless) was based on myth.

These facts do not mean that the presence of children reduces the chance for success of any particular marriage. However, it is clear that the begetting of children is not a magic which will improve an already shaky marriage; instead, it will help to destroy it even further.

Myth No. 6. The belief that loneliness will be cured by marriage.

Once upon a time there was a well-received television drama (it later became a motion picture) called *Marty*. At the conclusion of the performance, the viewer experienced a feeling of satisfaction and general good feeling, the same sense of well-being and joy that a person has when she has read a fairy tale.

The story of *Marty* concerns a lonely, shy boy, Marty, who finds, or is found by, a lonely, shy girl. They supply each other's needs, decide to marry, presumably live happily ever after. It could be wonderful if such events could take place frequently in the lives of lonely people. But the action in *Marty* represents — for most people — fantasies, not reality. Lonely people who marry each other to correct their situation usually discover that the most intense and excruciating loneliness is the loneliness that is shared with another.

There are several types of loneliness.

First is the loneliness of individuals who have a limited behavioral repertoire. The "behavioral repertoire" is the accumulation of behavioral acts that have been learned since birth and are at the individual's command. People afflicted with this type of loneliness find themselves to be strangers in a more than normal number of situations involving relationships. They yearn to be on a cheerful, or perhaps competitive, or perhaps collaborative, action-interaction basis with other people. But they have difficulty because their behavioral repertoire is limited and therefore in many cases they do not understand other people and other people do not understand them. So they are strangers — and lonely.

When such lonely people marry one another, each has expectations of the spouse, and neither realizes that the other is paralyzed by a limited behavioral repertoire. Neither of these individuals has much to give to the other, unless the behavioral repertoire is enlarged and developed. If lonely spouses recognize this problem, they may have a chance for a workable marriage; if they are cognizant of their limitations, perhaps they can form a team and slowly and painfully increase the range of their behavior. Usually, however, each expects behavior from the other which is beyond her or his capability. As a result, both of them end up more lonely than ever before. And to this loneliness, a bitterness frequently is added. Thus the distance between the two quickly increases.

A second type of loneliness frequently characterizes the individual who has been denied love as a child and unconsciously seeks "triumphs" over others as a love substitute. He or she cannot get along with anyone over whom she cannot triumph in some way, or except in some rare instances in which she collaborates with someone else to triumph against society.

Within this category we find many "successes" in the arts, in industry and in business. These are the perfectionists, the people who are obsessed with becoming champions or innovators, or the top person in a field. Such people have limited emotional repertoires. Usually they can be loving and kind and considerate only to those who are useful to them; and they define usefulness only in terms of their drive for perfection or success. In the marriage of such a person nothing which the spouse does is ever good enough. She or he is constantly critical of the spouse's performance level. People of this sort trust no one to do anything well. They suspect that almost everyone will impede their gallop toward success. They require almost everything to revolve around themselves; and as this seldom happens in married life, these individuals drift from one marriage to another, always looking for the impossible, and becoming more and more suspicious and more and more lonely.

The third type of loneliness is perhaps the most painful of all. It is usually experienced by individuals who are obsessed with the desire to be popular and well thought of. They have bright personalities and well-developed social skills. Frequently they are glib talkers and good dancers, and dress attractively. Often they are excellent saleswomen, advertising personnel and social leaders, and they tend to be gossips. By gossiping (transmitting malicious information about somebody else) they bribe others to approve of them. A high percentage of these people give the appearance of being flirtatious and "sexy," but really are sexually unskilled, and often frigid, even though they act passionate and may have had more than the normal number of affairs. This type of individual finds it difficult to be intimate with anyone unless their mutual behavior results in her being the center of attraction. This can happen only if she marries a passive person, probably her inferior. But the fact is that in marriage — and in relations with people in general — unless one can participate in behavioral interactions which are characterized by equality, one is lonely despite the appearance one may give of being very gregarious and a great mixer.

Loneliness cannot be cured by marriage. Loneliness is better tolerated by those who live alone; they have no expectations, and thus no disappointments. Lonely people who live together have about the same chance of realizing their expectations as the host who insists that everybody have a good time at his party.

Myth No. 7. The belief that if you tell your spouse to go to hell you have a poor marriage.

Most of us in this country are taught diplomacy, decorum and the art of self-restraint. Many husbands and wives believe that politeness, consideration and benevolence are important in a marriage and not wishing to be rejected, they may attempt to practice these arts unremittingly.

If spouses are thoughtful of each other on all occasions, the likelihood is that they have a sick marriage. It is obvious that individuals have competing tendencies — different interests, different ways of using time, different biological rhythms, and so on — and they cannot always have the same desires, needs, wishes or whatever at the same time. The problem then is: What should they do when conflicts arise?

There are several possible answers, but the most important one is that the individual should do *what she or he feels she has to do* at this particular moment, and should believe enough in the durability of the marriage to withstand even a period of hate from the other spouse. When such conflicts do not ever arise, it must be concluded either that the spouses are peculiarly lucky in having chosen partners with exactly the same values, tastes, needs and so on, or that somebody is sacrificing quietly and will unwittingly pay the other spouse back.

It is obvious that human behavior seldom is constant for long. An individual may be cheerful one morning, irritable the next. She or he may be generous and benevolent one afternoon, stingy and mean the next. A person may feel amorous one evening and frigid the following night.

When a husband and wife go out together and meet other people, their behavior patterns are different from what they are when the two are alone. The presence of others feeds new stimuli into the joint wife-husband team and it becomes *a different team* as long as the other persons are present. Husbands and wives often wonder why they behave differently in public than when they are home alone. This apparent inconsistency often causes trouble. Each spouse notices the changes in the other but not in herself. An objective observer would see that they both change.

In a marriage, each partner tries to maintain behavioral patterns which provide herself with maximum satisfaction. Sometimes the satisfaction assumes neurotic dimensions, such as finding pleasure in illness because it can be used as a weapon against the spouse. When both partners are in a state of satisfaction, there is present an emotional and psychic balance, a homeostasis. That is what they strive for. But human behavior changes frequently and radically, and every action and mood of one spouse begets a reaction from the other. Therefore, to remain in balance, the marriage always is in a state of flux. The forces in it move

this way and then that way, go up and down to various levels.

Even Silence Is Communicating

When people marry, the first important action which takes place is the attempt of each spouse to determine the nature of the relationship; that is, each wants the marriage to be satisfying to herself/himself and would prefer to achieve this end without changing her already established behavioral pattern. Each wants the other partner to make the accommodations. Usually a spouse approves of her/his own ways of behaving, her own mannerisms, habits and performances, and finds fault with those of the other. For this reason almost all marriages — at least at first — have friction.

People in our culture believe that the most important communications are spoken or written. This view is erroneous. Scientists have estimated that fifty to a hundred bits of information are exchanged *each second* between individuals communicating actively. Everything which a person does in relation to another is some kind of message. *There is no* NOT *communicating. Even silence is communication.*

If one partner asks another, "What are you thinking?" she/he may answer by looking at her/him tenderly and smiling. The message here is, "I am thinking of you, darling." The tender look and the smile are more eloquent than speech.

One of the necessary ingredients of a workable marriage is trust. "Trust" is defined as "confidence in or reliance on some quality or attribute of a person or thing, or the truth of a statement."

The word "trust" originally came from the Scandanavian language and meant "to comfort," "to console," "to confide in." It seems to have first appeared about the ninth or tenth century in a Nordic society in which men and women lived, in a state of relative equality, in an environment requiring a desperate struggle for survival. To "trust" then meant to give comfort and cheer when needed. It had nothing to do with estimating another's behavior. This original definition of the word represents the first step toward Sullivan's definition of love.

An Extra Dividend

The practice of honesty and clear communication in marriage is likely to result in an extra dividend, for it encourages spouses to be generous, comforting and consoling. If the spouses can be truthful and open about themselves — for example, if a spouse can admit she/he is afraid that she is failing at her job instead of attacking the other for spending too much money — mutual support and helpfulness are possible. Tolerance and generosity in relation to others' mistakes become easier when one learns that others can be generous in return. If a person can be honest enough to recognize and admit her/his own weaknesses — and finds she is forgiven by others for her lapses — it then becomes possible for her to be tolerant in relation to the weaknesses of others.

There is a place in the best of marriages for occasional bluntness or even rudeness. Occasionally, even an out-and-out fight may be in order; as long as it falls short of homicide, it will probably leave both spouses refreshed. At times we all let relationships become complacent and limited by incomplete transactions. Our auto mechanic, for example, may take us for granted, and for a while we accept his/her "Sure, sure, I'll take care of it," but often she does not take care of it, and makes endless reasonable excuses instead. Finally, one day we blow up and say, "God damn it, Catherine, get that carburetor fixed or I'll take my business elsewhere." As a result of this explosion the mechanic has more respect for us, we have more respect for ourselves, and the limits of the relationship have been clarified.

Similarly, in marriage there is no miraculous method for carving out a relationship without occasional struggles. One cannot make an omelet without breaking eggs, and one cannot make a marital relationship without breaking some of the other spouse's

expectations and built-in preconceptions, and forestalling his/her very human tendency to try for a foot when a few inches have just been offered.

Unfortunately, our American notions of romance, chivalry and "nice" behavior make it difficult for couples to believe that fighting is permissible — and may even be necessary. If husbands and wives are to clarify what each other's limits are, there is no alternative to frank talk or action, even at the risk of temporarily damaging the relationship.

To put it simply, the motto of two people trying to work out a relationship should be, "If you can't tell someone to go to hell, you can't love him/her very much." It takes courage to shake the status quo, but if the relationship isn't worth a risk to improve it, it is bound to be forever limited and burdened by its own stagnation.

Myth No. 8. The belief that unsatisfactory sexual relations are the major cause of bad marriages.

The speciousness here is clear. Unsatisfactory sexual relations are a symptom of marital discord, not the cause of it. It is difficult for the victims to see this because of the mass of propaganda about sex that attacks them day and night, on the street, in the home, in the office. We are such an absurd culture that even mouthwashes and Lysol are related to the sexual aspects of marriage.

The reason people keep asking where sex fits into marriage is that they have been hoodwinked, bamboozled, pressured, conned and persuaded that the sexual act is compulsory in their lives and *must be performed alike by everyone;* the "standards" are established by advertisers, publicity for sexpot motion-picture stars, literature, movies, plays,

television, and so on. But these are standards of fantasy. Therefore people ask silly questions: How often should we have sex? What is the best position? How intense should it be? Perhaps even worse off are the myriads of couples who don't dare ask questions and just assume they *must* be abnormal because their own practice differs from some so-called standard.

The problem is obvious. In sex, trying to keep up with the Joneses is the road to disaster. To decide where sex fits into their particular marriage, a couple must look inward at the marriage not outward at the deceptive advice and make-believe standards set by others. There are no standards, and most "advice" from friends or family is misleading, for few people can speak honestly about their own sex life. Rather than admit their own sex problems and misgivings, friends often let one assume that their sex experiences are indeed superior; otherwise, the implication is, they wouldn't be giving advice.

Can women and men live without sex and still stay healthy?

Yes, they can. People cast away on isolated islands have gone for years without sex and have not experienced any physiological or psychological breakdowns or deficiencies as a result.

Is sex important in married life? Yes, it is. It is *one* of the cements which hold the bricks of married life together. But the when, the how, the now often, and the quality can only be determined by the people involved. But if sex is not up to culturally created expectations, is the marriage a failure?

It need not be a failure. It can be a good marriage even if the partners don't find heaven in bed.

3 Change as a Function of Relationships

A relationship is an ongoing process of interaction between individuals and is therefore, by definition, in a constant state of dynamic change. The individuals sharing a bond must perpetually adapt to and accomodate one another. A relationship must provide for change and for periodic evaluations of self and others in order to permit personal growth.

A life-style that is conducive to growth for one person may be stagnant or harmful to another. A couple who is living together, married or unmarried, intimate or casual, will periodically evaluate their life-styles and goals. They will examine their personal and mutual satisfaction and dissatisfaction, ask what sort of changes would improve their relationship, determine how much motivation there is to change, and eventually either acknowledge a need for change or confirm their desire to continue in the same style. In order to succeed, this kind of evaluation must be a process of sharing feelings and thoughts. Conducted in isolation, without open communication, it places stress on the relationship. Real change requires cooperation and an honesty that is as difficult as it is rewarding.

One of the most basic areas requiring examination is that of sex roles. Virtually from birth, we are taught in countless subtle ways what is expected of us as a man or a woman. A woman is expected to care for the home and children, be physically weak, highly emotional, passive, and dependent on the male. Men are expected to be strong and independent providers, protectors, and decision-makers. But it should be the task of the individual to determine, and the task of the relationship to accommodate the needs of its members—the male who chooses childcare or the female who chooses a career. In some human societies it is expected that the men gather and prepare food and tend children while the women manage the wealth and law of the culture. Sex roles are not inborn, they are culturally determined. Current investigations, on both academic and personal levels, are forcing individuals to take a closer look at the inequalities in relationships between women and men. The view, held by most sectors of our society, that men are superior to women is continually being challenged, and this changes both relationships that are already formed and the social climate within which new relationships will be formed.

The nature of sexual interaction is also under examination. New attitudes toward freedom of sexual expression have evolved. The pioneering efforts of Masters and Johnson have stimulated the helping professions to deal effectively with the treatment of sexual problems. The new sexuality has repercussions as diverse as the "singles" life-style and the diminished birth rate.

The articles in this section of *Annual Editions: Readings in Marriage and Family 79/80* are organized into four subsections. The first subsection addresses issues such as the consequences of a stabalizing birth rate, the advantages and disadvantages of the single life-style, and the economic consequences of changing population and family composition. Two views of the childbearing probabilities of American women are examined in the second subsection. Subsection three examines various options in the area of parenting, which include alternatives available for child care, the importance of fathering, adoption, and the effect on children of working parents. The final subsection examines the unfortunate reality of violence in the family and takes into account child-beating, wife-beating, and husband-beating.

Looking Ahead: Challenge Questions

What are the hopeful signs for the American family?

Does violence in the family portend the disintegration of certain values? Which ones?

Do children benefit from the adoption of untraditional sex roles by their parents?

Is the importance of fathering generally neglected by society?

Is the single life-style a valid and equal alternative to married life?

Do the advantages to the family of both parents working outweigh the disadvantages?

What are the causes for family violence in the United States? What solutions are viable?

Whatever Happened to Ma, Pa and the Kids?

Divorce rates, remarriages, number of dependents, sex and age of household heads — they are all changing a $2 trillion economy.

Eli Ginzberg

Eli Ginzberg is A. Barton Hepburn Professor of Economics and Director of the Conservation of Human Resources Project at Columbia University. He is also Chairman of the National Commission for Manpower Policy and the author of more than 50 books primarily in the field of human resources and manpower.

"*If you visit an old New England cemetery and look around, you will find John Smith buried alongside his four wives. And then, if you visit Woodlawn cemetery in New York, you will find Jane Smith buried alongside her four husbands.*"*

Vast changes are occurring in the structure of American families which are bound to have a significant impact on the American economy in the next few

*This is the way Roswell McCrea, a former dean at both Columbia and Wharton, once summarized his feelings about studying the family.

years. The recent upward spiral of divorce rates, for example, might seem to indicate that family instability is on the rise, but it actually shows that divorce has simply replaced death as the principal – although temporary – source of family dissolution. The fact is that most divorced men and women remarry soon after their initial separation; this phenomenon has raised the proportion of the population that is married to an all-time high.

Of course, vast changes in the economy also will have their impact on the family. Given our increasing propensity to quantify increasingly complex and changing human behavior, any economic analysis of the family must recognize that it is not solely an economic unit; sociological, psychological and anthropological perspectives are important in a clear economic picture of the family. So in order to assess the mutual impact of the economy and the changing American family, one should look at some recent developments as a basis for some speculation about the future.

MEDIAN income for all families in the United States today is about $15,000. In families where wife and husband work (41 percent), the median income is about $19,000; in families where the wife does not work it is about $14,000. To give these basic figures fuller dimension requires the answer to a key question about American families: among how many dependents must this family income be divided?

From 1960 to 1975 – a period during which family income grew steadily – there was an increase of about 6 percent in childless and one-child familes, from 62 million to 66 million. More important, there has been a decline of about 33 percent in families with four or more children. So disposable famiy income per family member has certainly increased.

However, the costs of raising children

have grown as a result of an increased desire of parents to improve the "quality" of their children. The current average cost for a middle-class family to raise one child from birth through college is more than $100,000. This does not include sending children to camp, orthodontia, an occasional trip to Europe in adolescence, or some psychoanalysis along the way. So $100,000 is a modest figure.

Another increase in disposable family income comes from the vast growth in employment of women over 18 – up from about one in three in 1950 to one in two in 1978. But this change also has had a muted effect on the stability of the family. Men now have less guilt about walking out of a marriage if they think that their wives are not totally dependent upon them – both financially and socially. And women do not have to put up with miserable husbands if they are able to support themselves.

People just could not do that in the old days. The cost of walking out of an intolerable family situation was prohibitive, socially as well as financially. The loosening of attitudes does not necessarily mean that family stability is crumbling – options for walking out of a marriage also carry along options for entering a new marriage. Five out of six divorced men remarry, and so do three out of four women.

Myths about the sumptuous lives of women receiving alimony are wildly exaggerated. Two out of every five divorced women never receive alimony; the average amount paid to those who do receive alimony is about $2,000 annually. If divorced women lived on alimony alone, only 3 percent of their families would be above the poverty level. The economic incentives for women to become divorced, on the average, are minimal.

One further disincentive for women to walk out of a marriage is that most are badly positioned to reenter the labor market, especially if they are middle-aged and unprepared for a career. There is one major proposed bill – The Displaced Homemakers Act – now in Congress which has singled out this new disadvantaged group for special assistance.

Furthermore, there are about 7.2 million female-headed households, an increase of approximately 50 percent between 1940 and 1975. The fact that such a high proportion of these households are at or below the poverty level is indicative of the difficulties that many women face in entering or reentering the job market.

One of the most significant changes in family structures since World War II has been the improvement in the plight of lower income families. The federal government has spent large sums on transfer efforts; a major, but rarely considered, outlay has been transfers in kind, which include about $5 billion annually in food stamps, about $20 billion in Medicaid, plus additional billions for housing allowances and day care facilities. With the exception of certain benighted states, mainly in the South, fewer families live below the poverty level each year. In fact, one cost of a welfare reform package is that some people who work full-time at low-skilled jobs cannot make as much as they could get for nothing.

Perhaps the most significant gain of all has been for elderly families. The improvement of social security benefits, including indexing for inflation, has lifted most older persons out of poverty. The social security system has aged, which means that workers now becoming eligible for benefits have a longer record of earnings and therefore will receive more. More also have spouses who have worked, which adds further to benefits. There is also a larger total pot of pension money to which retired persons have claims – about $200 billion in private and Civil Service pension money in the United States today. And there is a legislative reform brewing which will permit people who receive social security benefits to earn more money from work without suffering deductions. Finally, we are likely to get some postponement of compulsory retirement. The income problems for the elderly have been brought reasonably under control, unless we mess up the whole social security system through underfinancing or inflation, which is possible but unlikely.

The creation of Medicare in the 1960's and the proliferation of private health insurance have had an enormous impact on the financial viability of older families. One can get pretty good insurance up to a quarter of a million dollars at relatively low group rates. The consequent growth of the health industry to a current level of $175 billion (FY 1978) has affected everyone. Health services are also the largest employer in America today with 5 million jobs. (My new book, *The Limits of Health Reform: The Search for Realism*, Basic Books, reviews the large-scale infusion of monies into the health arena and some of its implications for poor and near-poor families.)

BY and large, regional differences in real family income have been narrowed. It takes about $28,000 in New York City to achieve the same standard of living one could attain in Houston for $21,000. However, in terms of disposable income, the two figures are remarkably similar. Most of the difference is absorbed in direct and indirect taxes of all kinds, mostly New York State income taxes.

A great deal of misconception exists about income inequality among families in the United States. Although there has been practically no change in the relation between the top fifth and the lowest fifth over the last 30 years, people in the lowest fifth are not the same families year after year. Professor James Morgan of the University of Michigan found in his research that over a five-year sample period, one-third of all people on welfare in any one year never went back on welfare. Furthermore, only one-third of the welfare recipients remained on welfare for the entire five years. That is a very important finding about the fluidity of changing family compositions and changing economic circumstances.

The narrowing of the income differential between whites and blacks has been substantial but the gap remains wide. From 1947 to 1975, the ratio of non-white to white median family income rose from 51 percent to 65 percent. But median family income is not a truly representative measure because it includes so many individuals and families who are past the age at which they can benefit from recent policies designed to ameliorate racial inequalities. If greater changes in society occur, they will be found in the future experiences of young people.

Consider some current differences between white and minority young families (25 to 34 years) in which the husband works full-time and the wife also works. On the West Coast, the black family has only about $1,000 less earnings per year than the comparable white family ($18,000 vs. $19,000). In the rest of the country, where discrimination is more entrenched, the differential is in the $4,000 range.

In New York, where the income differential between whites and minorities is relatively large, if both the husband and wife in a black family work at relatively low-level jobs, the family's income will be in the $20,000 range. Given the opportunity of women to work, minority families are in a much better position to make money than they ever have been. But if the wife does not work, it is an entirely different matter.

To sum up recent developments related to family income:

☐ There has been a steady increase in real income for families up until 1973 (it has since leveled off), primarily as the result of greater participation of women in the labor market.
☐ This rise in disposable income has been supplemented by a reduction in the number of dependents in American families since 1960.
☐ Increased divorce rates have left many women heads of households in a vulnerable economic position.
☐ Progress has been made to raise older families out of poverty and to reduce income inequality between younger white and black families as well as among families living in different regions.

BY 1990, the number of households in the United States is estimated to increase from roughly 72 million to 90 million, of which only about half will be husband-wife households; the remainder will consist of a household headed by a male or a female without a spouse or single persons living alone. But the annual rate of increase in households will slacken, from about 1.5 million new households now to about 1 million in 1990.

Household and family size should decrease by about 20 percent from the current levels of 2.8 and 3.5 respectively to around 2.4 and 3.0 persons. Even if real income per capita were not to grow during the next 15 years, disposable income would be pushed up merely by these decreases in family size.

The age distribution of heads of households will become more flat: there will be relatively fewer old and very young wage earners compared with the number in the middle age span. Since the age at which individual earnings peak tends to be in the 45-51 range (there is a 25 percent difference in earnings between the peak and the lifetime average), family earnings should increase. This forecast is predicated on continued reasonable job creation in the future, but no one can be absolutely certain about that factor.

Continued increases in labor participation rates among women should also add to disposable family income. Moreover, a sub-group of affluent two-worker, career families is emerging. For example, two law school graduates, starting at their first day of work in New York City, earn a minimum of $45,000 annually. Even those with only undergraduate degrees can be expected to produce a combined family income of about $30,000 after several years of work.

This educated subgroup, with its attendant lifestyle, may have a significant effect on revitalizing our cities, because women who are interested in careers need to work in a large labor market which offers a wide range of job opportunities. Once the ball starts rolling, there should be enough income among dual-career families to support decent housing in urban areas. The ghetto areas in large cities will remain depressed, but the long-term movement of families away from upper income urban areas could be arrested and turned around.

Despite improvements in the real standard of living of lower income families, it is not clear that our economy can keep up the same pace in the future. If the prosperous post-World War II period could not reduce income inequalities substantially, it is doubtful that the prospective slower-growth period ahead will be able to accomplish much. From 1973 through 1977, there was no increase in real family income due to inflation and recession. Low income families were hurt the most.

The world scramble for strategic raw materials keeps on pushing up the price of our imports; oil and coffee are only part of the picture. Also, we are becoming much more environmentally sensitive, which certainly adds to the cost of production. Finally, the balance between production of goods and production of services has reached an ominous point: big gains in worker productivity can be made mainly in the *goods* sector, where capital can be invested and labor can be reduced. But in the United States, two-thirds of all jobs are in the *service* sector, and the proportion keeps growing. In New York City, manufacturing and construction provide only 17 percent of the jobs available; the remaining 83 percent are in services. (A disproportionate share of the nation's service output, as in the case of medical care, is directed toward older people, many of whom have completed their working years. But a society in which old persons are cared for, not eliminated, has no option but to deflect resources this way.)

If our economy is entering a period of slower growth at a time when the expectations of many groups for better jobs and higher incomes remain unmet, one of the few balancing factors in sight is the developing changes in family structure – the facts that more women are working and that there are fewer dependents per family. But even these "favorable" trends will bring consequences, not all of which are likely to be favorable. The effect on the next generation of the children of busy parents is unclear and the shortened longevity of career women is a warning sign.

As I stated at the outset, to consider the impact of the American family on an annual economy of $2 trillion requires consideration of a constantly changing social and cultural tapestry.

Suggested Reading

ELI GINZBERG, *"The Broadening of Options,"* *Chapter 15 of* The Human Economy, *McGraw-Hill, 1976. Points out some of the interactions between greater affluence and enhanced human satisfaction.*
LESTER THUROW, Generating Inequality, *Basic Books, 1975. The best single introduction to the inequality issue.*
ELI GINZBERG, *Ed.*, Jobs for Americans, *Prentice-Hall, 1976. The chapters by Andrew Brimmer and Robert Lampman deal comprehensively and authoritatively with income trends among black Americans and employment versus income maintenance.*
KENNETH KENISTON AND CARNEGIE COUNCIL ON CHILDREN, All Our Children, *Harcourt, Brace and Jovanovich, 1977. A well-written tract which argues that only strong families can produce strong children.*

Looking to the ZPGeneration

Worship Cupid, but Don't Be Stupid! advises a press release put out by Zero Population Growth, Inc. A Valentine received by some Americans last week, inscribed *Love . . . Carefully,* was equipped with a red condom. But few young couples in the U.S. today need antinatalist exhortations or equipment. Since 1957 the fertility rate has dropped from a peak of 3.76 children per woman to a record low of 1.75 last year. Though it may rise in the next 30 years, it is highly improbable that Americans in the foreseeable future will again engage in the great procreational spree of the postwar years. The baby boom has become a bust.

The nation is seemingly on its way to the long-debated goal of Zero Population Growth (ZPG), the theoretical point at which deaths and births balance out. If present fertility and mortality rates remain constant, the U.S. population may stabilize around the

year 2025 at between 260 million and 270 million (up from 216 million today).

A few—very few—demographers think that there will soon be a mini-boom in the U.S. birth rate, as couples who have deferred parenthood decide to start families. Most experts, however, discount an end to the birth dearth. With the exception of the aberrant twelve-year postwar fertility surge, they point out, the birth rate has been declining in the U.S. since 1800.

Pleasure Principle. In parts of the critically overpopulated Third World, birth rates are also tapering off. "Sometime near the beginning of this decade, the rate of world population growth reached an all-time high and then began to subside," notes Lester Brown, president of Worldwatch Institute, an international research organization. "In 1970 human numbers grew by an estimated 1.90%, an annual increase of 69 million. The most recent data show a marked decline since then, to 1.64%, an increase of 64 million a year."

Americans nowadays are painfully

aware that resources may be increasingly short and expensive in coming years. Inflation has already made the cost of rearing a large family (now estimated at more than $250,000 for four children from cradle through college) all but prohibitive. The pleasure principle may be a factor too. Richard Brown, manager of population studies for a General Electric think tank in Washington, observes: "Children are competing with travel, the new house and professional standing. Once the checkbook is balanced and all other desires have been indulged, a couple will think of having a child—or, indeed, that child may have its place in the list of Wants & Goals."

The biggest, if least predictable, element in the fertility rate is the attitude of the American woman. As the eco-

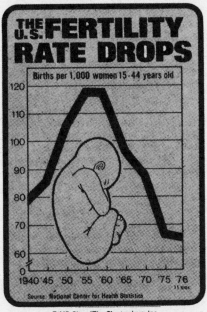

TIME Chart/The Chartmakers, Inc.

nomic, social and political status of women has improved, the desirability and mystique of motherhood has declined. Says Princeton's Charles Westoff, a world-renowned demographer: "There is a very pronounced change in the attitude of women toward marriage, childbearing and working, and all these attitudes seem to lead in one direction: they don't want three or four children." As Berkeley Demographer Judith Blake Davis puts it succinctly: "You won't find those sacrificial mothers any more."

Thus—if the U.S. is indeed headed for ZPG—people will for the first time in history be consciously forging their own destiny.

Not all sociologists, demographers and economists agree that a stable population is necessarily desirable. Some worry about the social and cultural implications of a markedly older popula-

tion. By the year 2020 there will be almost twice as many people over 65 (43 million) as there are today, exerting immense new pressures on the Social Security, pension and Medicare systems. To Columbia University Sociologist Amitai Etzioni, "ZPG spells a decadent society, à la France in the '30s, à la Berlin in the early '30s. This means a less innovative society, a society in which fewer people will have to attend, care, feed, house and pay for a larger number."

Most futurists, however, agree that a better life is in store for a stabilized population. Among those who believe in the beneficial effects is Demographer Westoff: "ZPG will reduce pressures on the environment and on resources. It will probably increase per capita income. It will reduce pressure on governmental services. And it will give society an opportunity to invest more in the quality than the quantity of life."

Less Pollution. Other experts point out that with fewer children, families will have more discretionary income to spend on the pursuit of pleasure—and for better health care and education. Air, water and noise pollution should be reduced. With a drop in the number of youths in their teens and twenties, the segment responsible for most crime today, the cities may be safer.

With an older and less adventurous population, demographers predict, there will be less pressure on the nation's congested beaches, lakes, waterways, hiking trails, ski slopes and wilderness areas —while sales of art supplies, mah-jongg, backgammon, b̶ ̶d endless variations of electro̶ ̶ld soar. The station wa̶ suburbia, may cars. The auto̶ of the hand̶ part of the y̶ recreationa̶ campers, ̶ cles and ̶ ly get be̶ improve̶ of the California Institute of Technology: "I think ZPG is going to be a very good thing for higher education. There will be an end to overcrowding."

There will be a continuing increase in the demand for adult education, with the emphasis on practical skills and crafts rather than abstract knowledge. Says Vincent Ficcaglia, an economist at the Cambridge-based Arthur D. Little think tank: "What is changing is the type of learning people want. It's much less formal: they don't want or they already have a liberal arts degree. What they do want is to acquire skills to satisfy their own creative urges or help them survive—plant-growing and plumbing, for instance." Colleges and universities will have to adjust swiftly to this developing educational market —even if tenured professors of medieval English have to be retrained to teach ceramics and auto repair.

Smaller families of course can live in smaller houses. Experts also foresee a greater demand for town houses, condominiums and apartments as suburbanites move back into the cities to take advantage of the cultural opportunities clustered in urban centers.

All Americans will be affected by the new lifescape:

CHILDREN tend to be physically and psychologically healthier when there are fewer of them in a family—and when they are wanted. The University of Michigan's Robert Zajonc, a psychologist who studies educational trends closely, already notes a marked rise in the IQs of the ZPGeneration now in primary school. Verbal and linguistic skills, he finds, increase in inverse proportion to the size of the family; smaller families, as he puts it, are "more adult-oriented than sibling-oriented." Education may revert in part from classroom to living room. Children may again receive wisdom from respected, caring elders.

THE MIDDLE AGED will, more than ever, tote society's Sisyphean boulder. They will not need to spend as much time and money on so many offspring, but they will increasingly have new dependents—the old. By 2020, it is estimated that only one out of three Americans will be a taxpayer, and that liened group should be more heavily composed of the middle aged. In contrast to the whiz-kid

executive syndrome of the '70s—a direct result of the baby boom—the reins of power will revert to older hands. For the middle-age, middle-management sector, there will be fewer shots at the top, though there will be more titular promotions and merit raises to reward the faithful. On the positive side, lessened competition may result in heightened creativity. People may concentrate on doing what they know best, rather than aspiring to levels at which they may prove incompetent, or be bored, or both.

THE ELDERLY, as a much bigger and therefore more influential segment of the population, with longer life expectancy, will almost certainly insist on filling a more productive role in society than they occupy today. With a smaller work force, the mandatory retirement age within the next quarter-century will have to be advanced to 70. Indeed, many social critics have long argued that the nation is spinning off an incalculably valuable resource by relegating robust, creative people to senior citizens' ghettos. The graying of America will offer new opportunities for the retired. There is already a crying need in the U.S. for day-care centers and kindergartens where working couples may safely leave their children; they could ideally be —and may have to be—staffed by older people. Some futurists have suggested that the elderly may form a class of "professional parents" for children of working couples. Some demographers, including Australia-based Lincoln Day, have proposed that retired couples be given state subsidies to take over abandoned small farms, where they could help increase the food supply. A report on the future of agriculture, published last week, strongly advocated a revival of small farms, located near cities, that could provide food more cheaply than agribusiness can in the face of the enduring, expensive energy shortage. Many retired people could find new and rewarding lives as small-scale producers of food.

One of the most heartening aspects of the new society, Stanford University Biologist Paul Ehrlich believes, is the speed with which it has come about. "It indicates that attitudes and customs are not so deeply ingrained that they cannot change rather quickly," he notes. "Ten years ago, we believed that the attitudes of women and the kinds of lives

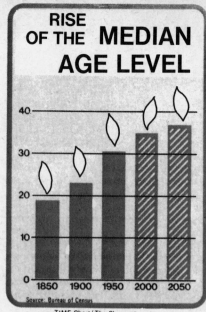

RISE OF THE MEDIAN AGE LEVEL

Source: Bureau of Census

TIME Chart/ The Chartmakers, Inc.

they lived would be something that had to change slowly, over decades. Actually there was a remarkably swift change between 1968 and 1970. It indicates that other attitudes we believe to be deeply held could also change quickly. Like the attitude that Americans must consume energy and other resources out of proportion to their needs."

Already, from Ithaca, N.Y., to Evanston, Ill., from Kalamazoo, Mich., to Livermore, Calif., empty elementary and now high schools are being converted to make room for shops, restaurants, arts workshops, Headstart programs, day-care centers, concert halls, studios, ballet schools, adult classes, seminars for unwed mothers, vocational training and housing for the elderly. Young doctors trained as pediatricians or gynecologists are increasingly transferring to the lamentably neglected area of public health. The transformation from growthmania to a less-is-more society will demand greater adjustments and some painful decisions. Nevertheless, demographers point out, a controlled population will allow the U.S. to reorder its priorities and reassess its values before they are dictated by scarcity.

Not least, the joy of having children may be enhanced.

Going It Alone

It was billed as Singles Expo '78, and at first it looked like the old meet market as 1,200 unattached people swarmed into Los Angeles's Bonaventure Hotel on an August weekend. But there was a difference. Besides the familiar lonely-hearts seminars, covering such topics as "How to Survive Rejection" and "Finding That Perfect Mate," there were workshops on "Government Loan Programs to Help Singles Start Businesses" and "Estate Planning for Singles." Among the booths selling video-dates and travel clubs, there were sales pitches from Merrill, Lynch stockbrokers eager to handle other types of extramarital affairs. "It used to be that being single was what you were when you were divorced or widowed, but these people are looking at being single as more than just passing through a stage," says Stephen Bay, who organized the Expo. "They came to the convention saying, 'If this is a way of life, give me more information to make it better'."

Only five years ago, the single life was regarded at best as a temporary existence, inhabited by post-adolescent swingers who lived in singles complexes, luxuriated in singles bars and waited anxiously to get married. Today, more people are committing themselves to being single—at least for a while—and in the process, many of the old stereotypes and stigmas of the single life have disappeared. For one thing, as more separated, divorced and widowed people live alone, the single population is growing older and settling down. For another, unmarried adults have more money and opportunities than ever before, and many of them are single by choice rather than chance. Living alone is not only becoming more socially acceptable, it may, in some cases, even be desirable. "Clear across the board, it's easier to be single," says Arlene Skolnick, a psychologist at the University of California, Berkeley. "They are losing the image of being life's lonely losers."

With more mobility, more spendable income and fewer responsibilities, the single life has also come to represent substantial sales. Last year, 17 per cent of all home buyers were single, 25 per cent of all new-car purchasers were single and unmarried adults between the ages of 18 and 40 took three times as many vacation trips as the rest of the adult population. Bankers, brokers, retailers, restaurateurs and real-estate agents are all trying to capitalize on the lucrative market. "Singles have become increasingly important in the marketplace," explains Bank of America economist Eric Thor. "It's a misconception to continue thinking of the traditional American unit as a family of four."

Striking Out: At present, there are 52 million single adults in the U.S., and record numbers of them are striking out on their own. The number of people living alone has jumped from 10.8 million in 1970 to 15.5 million in 1977, about 21 per cent of total U.S. households. Of those 15.5 million, 9 per cent are separated people living alone, 17 per cent are divorced, 44 per cent are widowed and 30 per cent never married. And if the projections of Donaldson, Lufkin & Jenrette, a New York securities firm, are actually borne out, people who live alone may well account for 25 per cent of all U.S. households by 1985.

Part of the increase in numbers is due to the baby boom, those children born between 1947 and 1957 who are now between the ages of 20 and 30 and likely to be living alone. But even if the numbers eventually decrease, due to the drop-off in births in recent years, some experts believe that the ratio of singles to marrieds will remain high. "More and more people will find themselves single at some time," says Arthur Norton, chief of the marriage and family statistics branch of the Bureau of the Census. "Proportionally, more and more will be living independently, and more and more will be breaking up their marriages. And many think that if they do get married now, it will be tough economically."

Freedom: In San Francisco, where single people are in the majority, 33-year-old Lee Grygo has found that going it alone is better than her six-year marriage. A legal secretary who is about to receive a master's degree in psychology,

Grygo happily goes to the theater, ballet and movies by herself, dines alone—insisting on a table up front—and finds she has more friends now than when she was married. "I didn't know I could enjoy being single," she says. "I like my freedom." Lise Mauer, a 32-year-old New York film producer who owns her own distribution company, is equally content with the single lot. In the last two years, Mauer has got her pilot's license, spent four months on a farm in France, rafted down the Colorado River, bought and sold a car and is now looking for a co-op. "I'm glad I never married," she says. "Not having responsibilities feels great. I don't even have any plants."

Such contentment doesn't always come easily. Georgia Johnstone, a 41-year-old interior decorator from Los Angeles, found single life quite difficult immediately after her divorce ten years ago. Not wanting to take money from her ex-husband, she sold her clothes and antiques and set off on her bicycle to scout run-down neighborhoods for property she could afford. "I had to go through hell even to get a credit card," she recalls. "Master Charge turned me down three times, because they couldn't check my credit rating. As a divorcee, I had none." She does not plan to remarry as most marriages strike her as "stifling." Now, Johnstone has everything she wants—including a vintage Mercedes. "That car," she says, "is a $60-an-hour psychiatrist."

Problems: But if the singles life has its rosy aspects, it is not without serious drawbacks. There is still the overwhelming loneliness, the problems of meeting people and maintaining lasting relationships. Larry Ross, 32, is a restaurateur who lives in suburban Chicago with two dogs. Although he enjoys his single life on the whole, he admits that he would indeed prefer to be married. "There's a real motive to be away from the house unless you're entertaining," he says. "You're all alone."

The problems are especially acute for those on the low end of the socioeconomic scale. Carol Silva dropped out of college at 18, married, had four children in six years and got divorced ("The stigma that a single mother was a 'loose woman' was very heavy then," she recalls). Moving into a public housing project in Somerville, Mass., Silva worked first as a waitress, then at a mental-health center. Now, ten years later, she has gained her master's degree from Harvard's School of Education and is finally off welfare. But, she says, there is still the social stigma and still the difficulty in securing well-paying jobs and decent housing. "Ten years ago, landlords used to turn me down because my kids were toddlers and therefore likely to be loud and unruly," says the 38-year-old Silva, who spends two-thirds of her income on housing, utilities and food for her family. "Now they turn me down because I have three adolescent boys who are therefore also likely to be loud and unruly."

Life is considerably easier for the more affluent singles, but it is also very expensive. As an investment and a hedge against inflation, more and more single people are buying condominiums, town houses and single-family houses in suburban and urban areas.

'Asset Base': At Lexington Village, a booming development of $55,000 coach-house condominiums outside Chicago, 50 per cent of the sales are to professionals who are single. In the San Francisco suburb of Fremont, the L.B. Nelson Corp. put up two- and three-bedroom fourplexes, for $55,000 and $65,000, and 80 per cent of the units were sold to single people. "With my apartment I'm building up my asset base," says Judy Bowman, a Chicago banker in her mid-30s who has owned three condominiums. "I'm preparing for my old age."

With recent legislation prohibiting credit and mortgage discrimination on the basis of sex and marital status, singles have become the fastest-growing segment of the housing industry. And single women are a new force on the market. Lynn Johnson, a Shell Oil employee in Houston, purchased a

Nettles of Errands Unlimited: Serving singles
Frank Armstrong

town house as a financial and psychological investment. "It's mine—and it's a good feeling to know. that anything I put into fixing it up is not just money thrown away," says the 34-year-old divorcee. For the divorced woman in particular, says Bob Harper, director of sales for Fox and Jacobs, a Dallas construction firm, "a house seems to signify to the world that she's making it on her own. It may be smaller than the house she had before, but it is a visible symbol that she's standing on her own."

Reversal: To accommodate the singles' needs, the shape of housing is changing. In New York City, where rents for studio and one-bedroom apartments have increased 35 per cent in the past four years, the formula for constructing residential buildings has reversed. The Sheffield, a new building under construction in midtown Manhattan, will be 60 per cent studio and one-bedroom apartments; two years ago, 60 per cent would have been two-bedroom apartments. San Francisco architect Pat Coplans is designing new condominiums for two singles to share. The floor plans are the size of a three-bedroom house, but instead she has made large two-bedroom suites, each with a sleeping area, bath and sitting room—and no family room.

With smaller-housing needs and one-person family units, a whole new breed of appliances and mini-food products has also been born to serve the singles crowd.

Even though singles spend up to 63 per cent of their food dollar eating out (three times what marrieds spend), there is often a night in, and manufacturers have rushed to capture the tea-for-one market.

Presto jumped in first with its single-hamburger cooker, followed by its miniature deep-fryer and wee-fry skillet. Sunbeam has entered the market with a pint-size cooker-fryer, a single hot-dog steamer and a two-slice toaster with an energy-saving switch to shut off one slot. Mirro Aluminum is offering its new Eggory (for one omelet) and Watta Pizzaria Jr., which doubles as a mini-oven. Campbell's soup has added Chunky to its six-flavor line of Soup for One, while the A&P chain offers

Tea-tor-one market (clockwise): Presto's fryer, Sunbeam's cooker, beverage maker, frank steamer

single-serving cans of chicken, tuna and corned-beef hash, half-loaves of bread and half-cartons of eggs.

Some entrepreneurs have begun services for busy singles who don't have the urge—or the partners—to do the chores. In Austin, Texas, working singles pay Shirley Nettles $8 an hour to do two weeks' worth of their supermarket shopping. The owner of Errands Unlimited, Nettles also picks up prescriptions and mail, buys clothes and keeps track of weddings, birthdays, and anniversaries for her clients—the majority of whom are single. In Houston, attorney Elizabeth Burke found a dry cleaner who will come by her office to get her car keys, pick up the dirty clothes from the back seat and hang up her clean ones before relocking the car. "I do that for a lot of singles," says the cheerful cleaner. "They know me and they can trust me."

Function: No matter how content they are, singles still have the need to meet and be with other people. But as the single population has matured, a new, less blatant version of the old singles club has come into existence. The brochure for the New York travel club, Singleworld, formerly Bachelor Party Tours, explains that the service "is not a lonely-hearts club, not a matrimonial bureau, not a tour with equal numbers of men and women . . ." The main function of Boston's Bien Vivre Society is not to meet mates but to match singles as roommates so they can travel at lower rates.

Most of the new groups are special-interest clubs, which offer something to singles beyond one another. Among the 50 singles groups in the Bay area of San

Francisco, loners can join the Intelligent Singles in San Rafael (IQ permitting), eat with the Mid-Peninsula Supper Club, which meets four times a week at different restaurants, or discuss the classics once a month with the Oldest Established Permanent Floating Book Club in San Francisco. Singles are even showing up at the Council on Foreign Affairs in Chicago to meet and mingle; every dinner lecture is sold out.

Narcissism: While the freedom, affluence and acceptability of America's single population represents significant changes in life-style and attitude, there are social critics who believe that the celebration of being single has dangers contained within it. David Riesman, professor of social sciences at Harvard, thinks that the trend to living alone is an expression of the new narcissism. "Something's missing and that is connectedness," he says. "Both sexes are more dependent than they admit. Jealou-

sy is inadmissible and inevitable. We want fidelity. We want bonds—even though they may strangle us at times."

University of Pennsylvania sociologist Frank Furstenberg thinks that what is now emerging is "the institutionalization of singledom" as in Soup for One, "the symbolic recognition of the right of someone not to share his meal with someone. Instead of the module of society being the family, you see the individual also emerging as a module," Furstenberg adds. "Some view it as society's liberation—and others as society's dissolution. It's a double-edged sword."

Whether the new singleness will remain an institution or be replaced once more by the family remains to be seen. The divorce rate appears to be finally leveling off. And many experts believe that the delaying of first marriages will result finally in marriage stability.

Sacrifice: But some wonder whether young men and especially young women will readily give up their newfound emo-

tional and financial independence to take on the inevitable compromises marriage demands. "People are looking for more out of life, particularly young people," says sociologist John Mogey of Boston University. "They want satisfying work. They want to travel. They want a variety of social experiences. They expect more out of marriage. But in this climate of elevated expectations, it becomes more and more difficult to maintain a long-term relationship." That, perhaps, is the crux of the problem. For a while the pressure to couple is powerful and although the great majority of singles say they would prefer to be married, many are now unwilling to sacrifice living alone for anything less satisfying. "Being single is not the greatest thing in the world," says 38-year-old Nadyne Oakley of San Diego, "but it is better than being married unhappily."

—LINDA BIRD FRANCKE with PAMELA ABRAMSON in San Francisco, PAMELA ELLIS SIMONS in Chicago, JEFF COPELAND in Los Angeles, LISA WHITMAN in New York and bureau reports

Are Children Going Out of Style?

"To say one was a mother—that was past a joke: it was an obscenity."
—Aldous Huxley,
Brave New World

As recently as a generation ago, motherhood ranked as one of the few subjects an American politician could expect every one of his constituents to favor. But today, in the United States and other highly industrialized countries, more and more people are adopting—or at least proposing—life-styles in which children are regarded as a liability.

Signs of the trend away from motherhood include:

• *Declining Birthrates:* The general fertility rate in the U.S. (that is, the number of live births per 1,000 women aged 15-44) dropped from 82.3 in 1971, to 73.4 in 1972, and again to 69.3 in 1973. Although there were one-third more potential mothers in 1972 than in 1946, there were actually 4% fewer children born (3,256,000 in 1972 versus 3,411,000 in 1946).

• *New "Image" for Women:* Advertising and the mass media increasingly depict the "model woman" as glamorous, active, and seductive, but essentially self-sufficient—very often financially independent—and successful in direct competition with men, rather than in the roles of housewife or mother.

• *Alternatives to Marriage:* College-educated women in particular are entering the labor market in search of career-oriented positions, not just one or two-year interim jobs, and many are putting off marriage and child-rearing (whether temporarily or permanently remains to be seen).

• *Population Pressure Fears:* Forecasts of potentially catastrophic famines, resource depletion, and overcrowding due to unchecked population growth have had their greatest impact in the affluent, industrialized countries where social security makes parents less dependent on children for support in old age and where quality-of-life expectations are the highest.

• *Rising Economic and Social Costs:* In 1972, the Presidential Commission on Population Growth and the American Future reported that it cost an average American family around $60,000 to raise and educate a child from kindergarten through college. Today, the costs are even higher and still climbing. Moreover, the opportunities now available for travel, entertainment, education, and other activities—both as individuals and as a couple—seem more attractive to many potential parents than do the traditional joys (and attendant responsibilities) of parenthood. The concept of childless or "childfree" marriage is growing both in popularity and in respectability.

• *More Pressure, Less Patience in Marriages:* While intimate relationships are being formed more quickly today than in the more formal society of the past, evidence suggests that deep emotional commitments between individuals are becoming rarer. There appears to be less tolerance for the strains that come from living together. In fact, today's increased freedom from social restraints creates conflicts and decision-making situations that seldom arose when social roles were fixed by tradition. Divorces are becoming easier to obtain, but it is becoming harder to maintain a secure and stable marriage. Uncertainty about the present combines with uncertainties about the future to discourage many couples from committing themselves to having children.

Implications for the Future

In *Retreat from Motherhood* (New Rochelle, New York: Arlington House, 1975), author Samuel L. Blumenfeld examines many of the competing desires and pressures that combine to discourage parenthood in the United States today. Though his own views on such issues as abortion, experimental marriage, and sexual fidelity would class him as a conservative in the eyes of many readers, Blumenfeld's book contains enough articulate statements by spokesmen for other viewpoints to serve as a general introduction to the subject.

If the trend away from parenthood continues in the U.S., Blumenfeld speculates, it could have far-reaching effects on the future life-experience of American citizens:

It is already creating a lot of empty classrooms in our primary schools. It is also forcing manufacturers of baby products to change their lines or go out of business. And it means that in 30 years a diminished young population will be heavily taxed to pay the retirement benefits of the aging majority. It also means that we will have a society of many "only children," that is, a lot of people who won't know what it's like to have a brother or sister. The rich, overflowing attachment stimuli that came with large families will be missing from our national experience. Parents will have fewer children, but more emotion will be invested in each one of them. People in general will have fewer blood relatives, making the loss of one of them a severe loss indeed. Family gatherings will be shadows of their former selves. Will this be good or bad? Will the quality of mothering improve as the number of children decreases? Who can say? But I have a feeling that a lot of our present childless couples are going to produce a lot of late children when they've had all the fun and games they can take and then decide that a future generation is not such a bad idea after all.

In Aldous Huxley's *Brave New World*, the concept of parenthood had been made obsolete by the development of artificial birth processes that could turn out chemically and psychologically pre-determined human beings ideally suited to fill a particular role in society. Even without such processes, however, parenthood may well lose much of its attraction—and perhaps even its respectability— in many countries within the next few years.

From *The Futurist*, August 1977, published by the World Future Society, P.O. Box 30369 (Bethesda), Washington, D.C.
20014

The Coming Baby Boom

Linda Wolfe

One day last month an editorial assistant at a venerable New York publishing house brought her four-month-old baby into the office and caused an elaborate work stoppage. I was told the story by a man who sits at the desk next to the young mother. According to him, every female editor, publicist, and editorial assistant on the company's two floors stopped by to have a look at the baby and then lingered, picking it up, pecking at it, patting its cheeks, probing its plastic panties. The man who told me about the incident said, "They hung around all morning. Every woman in the place. Some of them were the very ones I've been dating, the very ones who have been telling me that I'm not to get serious, that they *know* what they want and it's only one-nighters and none of the marriage-and-family business. But there they all were, bending over this damn baby in its Guatemalan sling, gawking at it and gossiping about it as if it were a celebrity. Or a new triumph of technology."

This kind of scene has been occurring all over the city lately as babies, once plentiful and therefore boring, become more and more scarce, and therefore intriguing. But the meaning of such scenes is causing great controversy among demographers and social scientists.

One group asserts that no matter how women fuss over the occasional baby they see, they will never again turn to having children in the numbers they used to. Another group insists that they will, and soon. A fever of fertility, they say, will shortly be sweeping the nation and pregnancy will once again become chic. A generation ago, during the height of the post–World War II baby boom, women were producing an average of 3.5 babies apiece. Then the figure began to descend, reaching in 1972 the rate of 2.08. Since 1972 it has continued to plummet, dipping as low this year as 1.8. But, say those who are bullish on babies, by 1980 family size will be up again and by the mid-1980s women will once again be producing babies in volume. Around that time women will be having close to three babies apiece, and by the start of the next decade they will be averaging even more than three, thus giving us another colossal baby boom.

At first it seems difficult to believe. If anything, we are right now deep in the throes of a baby bust. All over the country federal hospital administrators are urging obstetrical units to close—and doing it not merely to save money but because the people working in many such units are on the verge of becoming dangerously out of practice. We are becoming a nation of the elderly: Gerber's baby foods has had to diversify; in Washington, D.C., this fall, an event unique in the nation's history was announced—the number of abortions performed in the capital had matched the number of births. Yet no matter, say the baby-boom theorists, the boom is coming. Indeed, it is the very fact and depth of the bust that is going to produce the boom. One will beget the other, they assert; every thesis contains its antithesis; every social swing in one direction impels a pendulum rush backward.

To understand the boom theory, one must first appreciate the depths of the bust. Fertility has been falling all over America, in all classes, among all ethnic groups. There have been dramatic declines in the birthrates of black, Puerto Rican, and Mexican women, and reductions during some years of the seventies among welfare women. But among middle-class women, fertility seems almost to have dried up.

Most of us are dimly aware of this. We find ourselves staring when we see a pregnant woman on a bus, and we may think to ourselves that no one we know seems to be having babies anymore. Of course, this is merely an impression. But social scientists who monitor statistics confirm our impressions. They know some facts we don't and one of the facts they know is enough to give something of a jolt to the nervous system, a present shock more tingling and disquieting to the brain than any amount of future shock. The fact is: Among some groups of educated women, fewer than 1 percent of potential childbearers are having babies.

The figure turned up this year in an obscure, little-circulated book entitled *A College in Dispersion: Women of Bryn Mawr 1896–1975*. There, buried in the back among the endless tables of Bryn Mawr women's career choices, college satisfaction, and foreign languages read and spoken, was a startling piece of information: There had been only three babies born to the 70 percent of Bryn Mawr women who had graduated from the college between 1971 and 1975 and had participated in the poll. In 1971, when close to 70 percent of Bryn Mawr graduates from the classes of 1966–1970 had been polled about *their* baby production, a total of more than 70 babies had been racked up. In a five-year period, the baby production of recent Bryn Mawr graduates had gone from over 10 percent to under 1 percent.

The baby bust has, of course, affected all segments of American society and it has been in progress since 1957, the year that is considered the official climax of the post–World War II baby boom. From that date forward, family size began to shrink, as did the national birthrate, which fell from 25.3 in 1957 to 17.5 in 1968 to 14.8 in 1975. Thus, given the precedents, one might predict that the future of babies in America is dim, that American women will simply continue in the direction already established and have ever fewer and fewer children. But according to the boom theorists, this is far from what is going to happen. Demographer Richard Easterlin, professor of economics at the University of Pennsylvania and father of today's most accepted baby-boom theory, says, "The trend is now going to reverse itself."

Easterlin's theory is based on the importance of the size of a cohort—the number of people born in any particular year—to earning power and consequently to the wish to procreate. His is, of course, an economic theory—but not one that draws the usual simple ratio of "good times equals more

Vintage Years for People: How Lucky Was Your Cohort?

Most people tend to think of demography as an abstract, impersonal subject. But actually it is of great personal significance. It can help us determine not only which careers we would be wise to pursue, but it can even, like a branch of psychology, help us understand our personalities and abilities to adjust to society. If we are born into a year in which many others are born, chances are that we will live and age competitively and always feel somewhat tense, wary, and unsuccessful. If we are born into a year when few people are born, opportunities will seem to shine and we will feel not just economically but psychologically secure. The chart below lists U.S. births from 1910 to 1976. The years in which births were relatively low can be said to have been vintage years for people. They are indicated by asterisks—one asterisk for the vintage year in each grouping of five years; two asterisks for the best year within each grouping of two decades. If you were one of the cohort born in a starred year, you should, according to some demographers, be more self-confident and optimistic than people you know who were born in the nonvintage years.

—L.W.

Live Births in the U.S., 1910—1976

*Best year (fewest births) within each span of five years.
**Best year (fewest births) within each span of two decades.

Year	Total Births	Year	Total Births
1910*	2,777,000	1945*	2,858,000
1911	2,809,000	1946	3,411,000
1912	2,940,000	1947	3,817,000
1913	2,869,000	1948	3,637,000
1914	2,966,000	1949	3,649,000
1915	2,965,000	1950*	3,632,000
1916	2,964,000	1951	3,820,000
1917	2,944,000	1952	3,909,000
1918	2,948,000	1953	3,959,000
1919*	2,740,000	1954	4,071,000
1920	2,950,000	1955*	4,097,000
1921	3,055,000	1956	4,210,000
1922*	2,882,000	1957	4,300,000
1923	2,910,000	1958	4,246,000
1924	2,979,000	1959	4,286,000
1925	2,909,000	1960	4,257,000
1926	2,839,000	1961	4,268,000
1927	2,802,000	1962	4,167,000
1928	2,674,000	1963	4,098,000
1929*	2,582,000**	1964*	4,027,000
1930	2,618,000	1965	3,760,000
1931	2,506,000	1966	3,606,000
1932	2,440,000	1967	3,520,000
1933*	2,307,000**	1968*	3,501,000**
1934	2,396,000	1969	3,600,000
1935	2,377,000	1970	3,731,000
1936*	2,355,000	1971	3,556,000
1937	2,413,000	1972	3,258,000
1938	2,496,000	1973*	3,137,000
1939	2,466,000	1974	3,166,000
1940*	2,559,000	1975	3,193,000
1941	2,703,000	1976	3,128,000
1942	2,989,000		
1943	3,104,000		
1944	2,939,000		

babies and bad times equals fewer." In the Easterlin theory, people do not have babies or avoid having them because times are good or bad. They have them or avoid having them because of how well off they feel in either good or bad times. And the subjective feeling depends on one essential: the number of people in their cohort.

Easterlin speculates, "One of the factors that seem to have been important in the last baby boom was the relative number of young people in the labor market. In the forties and fifties, there were relatively few of them and they were thus relatively well off. These people then had lots of children—the baby-boom cohorts—so that in the sixties and seventies there was a relative glut of young people on the market and they've had a somewhat rough time. They had fewer children than their parents had had, and now some of their children—the first of the post-baby-boom cohorts—will soon be entering the labor market. And when they do, there are going to be relatively few of them and they are going to find themselves relatively well off, and thus the baby trend is going to swing upward again."

At the University of Michigan, economist and demographer Ronald Lee subscribes to the Easterlin theory. Lee explains, "Children born into a small cohort are bound to feel, when they mature, that there are economic opportunities for them, even if there has not been a sudden surge forward in the economy. The reason for this is that our society always has a number of low-end-of-the-totem spots that must be filled, can only be filled, by those just entering the work world. Small cohorts need not compete for these positions the way large ones must, and thus they feel secure." (See chart of vintage cohort birth years on page 102.)

But Lee goes Easterlin one step farther. Stressing early childhood and sounding as much like a psychologist as an economist, Lee says, "It isn't the economics of one's maturity that determines whether or not one will have a large or a small family, but the way in which the economics of one's maturity differs from one's childhood expectations. Depression children expected the worst but when they grew up they discovered they were better off than they had expected to be and thus they had lots of babies. Their children grew up in affluent times and expected the best—yet when so many of them descended on the work world, they did poorly. As a result, they had few babies. Now their children, expecting hard times, are about to look for work—and are

about to discover that, by virtue of their small numbers, things aren't so bad after all."

So certain is Lee of the boom around the corner that he has even dated it and predicted its dimension. "Fertility will start to rise around 1980, will increase steadily through the mid-1980s, and in the nineties it will peak, with women once again having an average of more than three children apiece."

Can the baby-boom theorists be correct? It would seem that more than economics is involved in an increase in family size, that for a boom of such magnitude to occur, we would have to experience a cataclysmic change in social attitudes. And such a change seems inconceivable right now, when the urge of most American women is to work rather than to rear. Motherhood has not only decreased but it has also declined in status—so much so that while only a few years ago mothers who went to work complained that they were viewed as social pariahs, women who today stay at home with children and do not work beef that it is *they* who are constantly denigrated. Even those women who have combined childrearing with careers feel that motherhood has low status; to speak of their jobs over lunch or at a party is acceptable, they say; to speak of their children is to ask to be snubbed. Regina Karp, a former schoolteacher who retired from work in order to devote her full energies to her two young children, gives an example of how the snub is administered. Karp met Shirley MacLaine at a party and offered some opinions on child care in China. MacLaine asked Karp her occupation; learning it was full-time mother, the actress said, "What do *you* know?"

Under the circumstances, with motherhood no longer appearing altogether respectable, it is difficult to imagine the monumental shift in values that a baby boom would require. Yet there *was* such a shift in values in the 1960s, a change in the climate of opinion concerning maternity that seemed, in its own time, even more unlikely. That shift required the acceptance not only of birth control and careers for women but of abortion as well. Nevertheless, that shift occurred, and when it did, it coincided with the baby bust. And now, according to boom theorists who are oriented toward social philosophy rather than economics, we are in for a new shift that will coincide with the coming boom. Basing their opinions on analyses of social trends as well as population figures, demographers June Sklar of the University of California at

Berkeley and Beth Berkov of the California State Department of Health have also begun predicting that "the decline in the nation's birthrate is coming to a halt and an upturn is in the making."

Sklar and Berkov made this pronouncement in 1975 after observing that despite legalized abortion and no rise in the marriage rate, fertility had gone up in California in 1974. The two demographers attributed the rise in the California birthrate to an increase in babies among married and previously childless women who were now having the children they had earlier chosen not to have. Then the demographers predicted a national-birthrate rise, citing recent surveys of American women which revealed aversions to childlessness and even to the one-child family. Although "the proportion of young married women who are childless is now very high," Sklar and Berkov wrote, "there is evidence that very few of them wish to remain childless."

Certainly there is such evidence even among the Bryn Mawr childless. "I'm looking forward to having children. Maybe even lots of them," said Marian Scheuer, lawyer, class of '70. "I want babies," said Roslyn Schloss, administrative assistant, class of '70. "But I'd rather find a father for them first."

If these women and others like them —those who have decided not so much to avoid babies altogether as to delay them until their careers are established —were now to begin to produce their postponed offspring, it is certainly possible that they could bring about a mini-run on dying day-care centers and neglected nursery schools. But they could not, in and of themselves, produce a national baby boom. That could result only if women who are just now getting out of college or into the work force also begin to have children—only, in other words, if postponement itself goes out of fashion. Yet on this point too, Sklar and Berkov made a boom forecast. It is possible, they said, that women just now entering their early twenties may "not continue the present pattern of postponing marriage and childbearing." It has happened before, they said, that attitudes toward marriage and childbearing changed suddenly, and they predicted that such swings "may well occur again."

Still, if the swing comes, it is not likely to be a swing back to former attitudes. Women are unlikely ever again to turn to motherhood as an occupation satisfactory in and of itself, or as a conventional, hidebound aspiration. If a baby boom comes, it will stem from

The Sexual-Chase Ratio

If the baby bust should continue, we can expect widespread social as well as economic changes. Amitai Etzioni of Columbia University predicts, for one thing, that we will undergo "an extreme flip-flop in the chase ratio." His pronouncement is based on the still common tendency of men to seek their sexual partners among women who are younger than themselves. But since there has been a general decline in births since 1957 (and thus fewer women), men have of late had to reach down into even smaller pools of young females in order to find partners. Etzioni maintains that if the bust continues we may at last see the older-man/younger-woman dyad give up the ghost, since men will be forced, by virtue of the numbers, to seek partners among their own age-mates or even to reach upward into the pools of older women. In the long term, however, if the baby *boom* theorists prove to be right, the more conventional sexual dispensation will prevail.

—L. W.

values altogether different from those that prompted the past boom. These new values are already becoming manifest.

One young mother from Antioch College told me, "I'm viewed as unconventional now that I've had my baby. I married a man I thought was rather boring at first, but decided that having a family sounded fascinating. I expected my friends to scoff but actually they think I've done something original, even quaint. Everyone likes to sit around and watch me nurse the baby or change diapers—some of my friends have never seen these things done before—and now I'm considered the class bohemian."

Faith Greenfield-Lewis, linguist, Bryn Mawr '70, one of the 1966–1970 baby-postponers but now a brand-new mother, reports that, for her, having a baby was exotic if not bohemian. She decided to give birth after going to Africa with her husband and absorbing there a whole new set of attitudes. "We went to Mali," Lewis explains. "My husband was studying the Bambara. We lived with them and I made friends with the women. I discovered that to them having children made you liberated. They used to say, 'When you have a baby, then you can *travel*.' They meant it both literally and figuratively. When they have babies, they go places, go trading in the other villages. And they are not allowed to do that before they have given birth. But they also meant travel in the sense of *develop*. I learned how important a baby could be to my development as a person by going to Africa."

Amitai Etzioni, professor of sociology at Columbia University, says, "I can see babies becoming popular again. But they'll be that way because of some back-to-nature urge that so many young women experience today."

Most of us tend to feel more than a little disconcerted at the prospect of a baby boom, and fear that population expansion is ecologically unsound. This notion, promulgated by the Club of Rome and other prestigious organizations, has come to seem gospel among lay people, but some social scientists have begun to doubt its validity. Etzioni says, "The idea of limiting population growth began as propaganda for countries like India, and the only reason the word was spread here too was that the proponents of limited growth were afraid to be accused of elitism. But it's clear now that we don't need to limit population growth in the United States. We can easily continue expanding. Have you ever flown to Washington or driven to Boston? The growth-limiters keep saying our country is overcrowded, particularly here in the Northeast, but if you've kept your eyes open on the routes to Washington or Boston you can see that there are miles and miles of open space. Believing we're overcrowded, believing we have to stop expanding, is what I consider an extreme case of sheepishly accepting what's printed in a newspaper instead of accepting the evidence in front of one's own eyes."

Of course, proponents of baby reduction aren't all social planners with eyes on the future. Some are simply everyday hedonists, people preoccupied with a pleasurable present, those who feel the quality of current life is enhanced by the absence of babies. And in some respects they seem right. We have, as a nation, enjoyed the baby bust, have found it liberating, even sexy. Two national surveys of sexual frequency conducted in recent years both revealed that as population shrank there was a copulation explosion.

One study, executed by Princeton's Office of Population Research but funded by the federal government, is jokingly referred to by demographers as the GNL—the Gross National Love index. In 1970 the GNL revealed that there had been a 14 percent increase in marital lovemaking across the nation in the years since 1965; the 1975 figures are not yet available, but they are expected to show a continuation of the trend. The other study, funded by the Playboy Foundation, found not only a monumental increase in coital frequency in 1972 when compared to Kinsey's two-decades-earlier data, but also a "major and historic" increase in oral sex. Andrew Hacker, professor of polit-

ical science at Queens College and author of *The New Yorkers*, a demographic study of our city, says, "There is no aphrodisiac in the world as powerful as the absence of babies."

But some people have suffered as a result of the bust. Teachers, children's-book publishers, and others who sell baby products have obviously suffered, but so too have learning-disability psychologists and life-insurance salespeople. Eventually, according to some social scientists, the bust will make us all suffer economically. Etzioni asks, "What does it mean to have ever fewer children and ever more old persons proportionately? It means more people who need services and fewer people able to work. It means a lot of wheelchairs and few baby carriages, and it means the rest of us having to foot the bill for more and more people in nursing homes and hospitals."

Hacker says, "Babies are a liability. A drag. And the notion that people will ever stop viewing them that way is ridiculous."

Still, according to Hacker, there are serious dangers ahead when the baby bust causes the inevitable tilt in the ratio of working, productive, taxpaying individuals to retired individuals. "How many of us, age 35 to 45, will have to carry how many retired people on our backs? Take a person 80 to 85. Think how much it costs to keep that person alive—and I'm not even talking about when he gets sick and has to have elaborate modern medicine. I'm talking just about his ordinary daily life. Who pays for it? We do, with the money we pay out for Social Security. It doesn't go into our own little private accounts, but goes to pay for the currently retired, since the money they paid in has already been spent. Okay.

When you and I are up to age 85, it will be people age 35 who are supporting us, but since there are going to be so few of them—given the current birthrates—and so many of us, they are going to have to pay fantastic amounts!"

There is also the fear that a society with many aged and few young people will be lacking in innovation. A young society is a creative one; an old one is a conservative one. Scientific and technological achievements are the province of the young, maintaining standards is the province of the old. A French writer has characterized a baby-bust society as a silent world, one in which there will be "old people ruminating over old ideas in old houses." Thus, while the thought of a baby boom is distressing to many of us, it is possible to take some comfort in it.

Of course, no one knows for sure if the boom is really going to come or if the bust is simply going to deepen. As Charles F. Westoff, associate director of Princeton's Office of Population Research, says, "There's only one sure thing about predicting population trends and that is that whichever you predict, you're probably going to be wrong." Nevertheless, financial advisers and furriers, college presidents and congressmen, publishers and perambulator manufacturers are all nervously studying the end-of-the-year demographic figures and attempting to make sound forecasts. And perhaps all of us would be wise to do so, since it is inevitable that one way or the other, whether 1977 marks the burrowing in of the bust or the burgeoning forth of the boom, we are headed for major social changes as the population trend finally makes itself clear.

WHO TAKES CARE OF THE CHILDREN?

For working mothers of young children this is the key question. The solutions women find—day-care centers or sitters, fathers or grandmothers, the woman down the block or working mothers themselves—are many and varied. But how good are they? And how can one judge? Here is a comprehensive (and controversial) report in which psychologists, pediatricians and other experts offer their opinions. When you've read them all, it is still you who will have to make the often hard choices. This guide should help you make them with a good deal more confidence.

THE DEBATE OVER DAY CARE

Should mothers of young children work? There is a certain quaintness to the question. It harks back to the closing years of World War II when the soldiers were returning, when young women were only too glad to give up their wartime jobs and tend to their husbands and homes and babies. It is a question that recalls 'the baby boom of the 1950s, the renaissance of the large family and breast-feeding and the appearance of Dr. Benjamin Spock's classic. Should mothers of young children work? Certainly not, said Dr. Spock—and almost every woman who possibly could manage not to, agreed with him.

Today the question seems largely irrelevant. Whether prompted by rising career expectations, or by the need for two incomes to keep afloat financially, or by the spiraling divorce rate that has increased the number of one-parent households, more and more women with preschool children are working or seeking employment, and it is, indeed, the women with very young children who are entering the labor market at the fastest clip. More than a third of all youngsters under six now have working mothers. The so-called "average" American family, made up of a working husband, a homemaker wife and two children accounts for only 7 percent of all husband-wife families. And, the Bureau of Labor Statistics predicts, that kind of "average" family will be increasingly unrepresentative of American families in the future. Should mothers of young children work? More and more of them do.

Still, few mothers of infants and toddlers go blithely off to work without qualms (even though Dr. Spock has changed his mind on the question). They may decide that, on balance, what they are doing is best for their family, yet there is no certainty in their minds that all will be well with the children. Disturbed by the problems involved in getting good substitute child care, confused and anxious even if their decision to work is based on need, not choice, mothers continue to worry about whether their children will thrive without their constant attention. Working mothers can and do take comfort in their numbers, but they still look to the experts—not for advice on whether or not to work, since that is not an issue for most of them —but for guidance in finding the right kind of child care and for reassurance that entrusting their youngsters to other caretakers at least will not harm them. That's not what they are getting this year, however.

This year's book about children was written by a University of Michigan psychiatrist, Selma Fraiberg. It is called *Every Child's Birthright: In Defense of Mothering,* and it is reassuring—for the 1950s woman. The title is the message, and the message is loud and clear: "Stay home!" The contents go beyond the title; they not only suggest that women stay home, but they are enough to scare the daylights out of any woman who doesn't stay home. Fraiberg, who calls herself an "advocate for children" and who is, to be sure, a sensitive and eloquent spokeswoman for them, raises the specter of "hollow" human beings, incapable of love, emerging from the "baby banks" that, she writes, care for many of the infants and toddlers of

Reprinted from McCall's *Working Mother,* October 1978.

working mothers. Rarely, she holds, do the housekeepers available to upper-middle-class mothers; the baby-sitters, commercial "baby parks" or neighborhood homes used by middle- and working-class families; or the government-subsidized day-care centers catering to the poor; provide what she considers to be the proper care to "ensure stable human partnerships for every baby." And without these partnerships, she suggests, the child's emotional, social and intellectual growth could be retarded.

The theoretical underpinnings of Fraiberg's thesis come, in part, from a landmark study made more than 40 years ago by Dr. René Spitz of infants in an antiseptic orphanage—an institution that was the prototype of an impersonal, cold, hygienic, routinized hospital. In this classic case of what has come to be called "maternal deprivation," the babies were neither held, not talked to, nor smiled at, nor cuddled, nor, in any way at all, mothered. By the time they were two years old they were virtually imbeciles.

Fraiberg also notes some well-known experiments of the early 1960s made at the University of Wisconsin. A group of monkeys ("Harlows' monkeys," they are called, from the name of the researchers) instead of being raised by their mothers or in the company of their peers, were isolated and reared by a wire monkey that had a feeding contraption attached to it. These monkey children turned out terribly! When they grew up, they were aggressive and had rotten sex lives. Like the orphans, they never made a real attachment to a principal care giver—a mother or mother substitute—that is so crucial to a child's healthy development.

In the mind of the unwary reader, the connection seems obvious—if women go out to work when their children are still young, they will contract these diseases of nonattachment and turn into morons and/or aggressive adults who cannot love. They will become "hollow" human beings.

To other child-rearing experts, this, of course, is sheer nonsense. The equating of institutionalized, un-mothered-in-any-way children (or monkeys) with the children of work-

ing mothers is simply indefensible. So indefensible that even Selma Fraiberg, in an interview, disowns the concept.

"I do not think that a mother who is working is, under ordinary circumstances, grossly neglecting her child's welfare," she says mildly.

"I was not in any way trying to create guilt," she explains. "Rather, I was trying to share a dilemma with mothers. The alternatives to her caring for the baby are so lousy. One set of arguments in the book belongs to the 'hollow men,' to the severe form of deprivation. Another set of arguments belongs to the question of what babies need for their fullest development.

"I don't give any advice," she insists. "I don't think that's any of my business. I think every woman should choose. And I would just like her to have very good options in choosing. Some women choose to stay at home, and they are being overlooked. I know some middle-class women who have to apologize to their women friends because they choose to stay at home. Again, one has the right to choose."

Double-talk? Perhaps. Can a person of Fraiberg's sophistication naïvely write a book, one half of which is devoted to scary tales about orphans and antisocial animals and the other half of which is devoted to working mothers and their sorry substitute caretakers (sitters, day-care centers and other wire-monkey types), without wishing to suggest that a working mother spells disaster for her young child?

And while Fraiberg denies taking the role of advice giver, what is the working mother of a two-year-old to make of a sentence such as this: "Around the age of three, but sometimes later, most children can tolerate separation from the mother for half a day, morning or afternoon, without distress when a good and stable substitute care plan is provided."

In fact, what is a *non*working mother of a two-year-old to make of that sentence? For the crux of what Fraiberg is saying is that it is *intolerable* for a child under three to have anything less than the nonstop, round-the-clock presence of Mother. The extremity of Fraiberg's position —the leap she makes from nonat-

tached children to mothers who are absent half the day; the picture of the fragile, anxious, porcelain child, on the one hand, and the tireless, cheerful, smiling 24-hours-a-day "ideal" mother, on the other hand— may grossly underestimate the strengths of children and grossly overestimate the strengths of mothers, other experts say. And the caricatures she draws make it difficult even for those who find merit in some aspects of her position—her criticism of public policy, for example, toward poor women who wish to stay home but are asked to work in order to collect welfare—to support her thesis entirely.

Burton L. White, author of *The First Three Years of Life,* shares some of her reservations. A specialist in the development of learning processes, White believes that only a parent or grandparents or some one person who is especially orientated and devoted to that one child can provide the necessary stimulation for intellectual growth during these pivotal years.

"On balance," Dr. White says, "I think children do best when, in those first years, taking their first form as human beings and learning their first learnings about what life is all about, they are reared by people who care for them more than anyone else in the world does." He believes that it is "altogether unwise and reckless to take anything but a very careful attitude toward what it is children are learning and experiencing in those first years."

Burton White, though, does not insist that this careful attitude requires full-time attention from no one but a mother. As a matter of fact, he endorses the nice upper-middle-class practice whereby a mother does not go out to work but, nevertheless, has part-time help so that she can escape the confinement of constant life with a young child.

Fraiberg and White, however, constitute a distinct minority in child-development circles today. Most authorities would agree with Dr. Alexander Thomas, a psychiatrist at New York University-Bellevue Medical Center, who says: "I challenge anyone to produce evidence that working mothers adversely affect their children's development. There isn't anything in the current literature or research to support that contention." Since 1954 Dr. Thomas and his associates have been conducting an ongoing study of a group of 130 children. They have found no difference in behavior between the children whose mothers worked and those children whose mothers stayed home.

The absence of any contemporary research pointing to a negative impact is further documented by a Carnegie Council on Children Report. Echoing the results of a similar study done in 1963, Alison Clarke-Stewart, a University of Chicago education professor, examined 350 child-care studies and "found no clear results relating to working alone. You just can't compare maternal employment to maternal deprivation." Indeed, in reviewing Fraiberg's book for the New York *Times,* Kenneth Keniston, chairman of the Carnegie Council on Children, took her to task for "her easy linking of maternal employment, less-than-perfect child care and the 'diseases of nonattachment.' On the contrary, research suggests that children of mothers who freely choose to work outside the home are better off, other things being equal, than the children of mothers who decide to stay home but are discontented with full-time mothering and homemaking."

Putting what Dr. Thomas calls "outdated theories" aside, the big guns in the field have moved on from the question, "Should mothers work?," to a consideration of how parents and public policy can best assure the welfare of children when, for whatever reasons, a mother chooses to work—or not to work.

Jerome Kagan, professor of psychology at Harvard University, poses an important case in point. Just seven years ago, he was adamantly opposed to even the concept of day care for children under three. Involvement in an experimental "ideal" nursery made him change his mind. "It isn't a question of whether mothers should work," he says. "That's a moral, an ethical question, not a scientific question." And scientifically, he says, the available objective evidence indicates that if a child is cared for by a conscientious, nurturing caretaker he or she will not be harmed. This is sec-

onded by T. Berry Brazelton, a practicing pediatrician and associate professor of pediatrics at Harvard Medical School, who says that even infants in day care know their mothers. (See box.)

Dr. Kagan's own experience bears this out. In his university-run day-care center in Boston, he saw that infants and toddlers were developing the same way a carefully matched control group was developing at home.

Last spring Gregory Jackson, host of "Help Yourself," a program produced by WNET/Thirteen for Public Television, interviewed Dr. T. Berry Brazelton:

JACKSON: Virtually everyone agrees that the decision to leave a child in a day-care center is not an easy one. But what do you do? What are the alternatives? We put the question to Dr. T. Berry Brazelton, a renowned, practicing pediatrician and Harvard professor.

What can the mother who feels guilty about leaving her child to go to work do?

BRAZELTON: For one thing, once she knows that feeling guilty about it is normal, maybe she won't have to feel so guilty. Also, if she's doing a decent job raising her child when she's with her, that may be enough. I really do not believe that you need to feel you're doing a lousy job just because you have to share your child with a day-care center.

J: When, exactly, is a woman doing a lousy job?

B: When she gets home at night and she is really still back at work or still split from her child, or is just not available to the child, because she is feeling so guilty. That is when I think you are damaging the child.

What we started doing was looking at babies, first at a year, then at eight months and then back at four months. And, we found that babies could defend themselves pretty well. When they were left, say at an eight-hour day-care center—which is a long time for a baby that age—they would never get very wide awake, or sleep very deeply during those eight hours. They would get mildly excited about the day-care operator, or the toys, or what have you. But they would never get *really* excited until their mothers came at the end of the day and then, whammo!—they'd

blow up, and start screaming and crying. And then the mother would say, "My God! What have I done by leaving my baby. It's my fault." And she would blame herself.

J: This happens to a four-month-old baby?

B: Yes. The four-month-old baby knew when her mother or father was there, and responded that way. We began to realize that the baby was saving up all the important stuff until the parent got there and was then throwing it at him. After the blowup, the baby would be very alert and excited. So what is waiting for the parents is the blowup, and then all the exciting material.

J: Dr. Brazelton, you say that the first three months of any infant's life is often a very cranky time, followed by happier moments when there are signs of response, smiles and laughter. You urge a mother to stay with her child at least for these first six months so that she can share those rewards before she gives the child over to someone else's care.

B: If you give the child to somebody else while it's cranky and while you're just feeling tortured and ready to strangle it half the time, then when it starts smiling and cooing, you will feel like, "Gee, the day-care person did that. Not me." And so you never feel as if all those goodies are your doing.

J: So a mother should stick around long enough to pick up the goodies?

B: That's what I would like to see happen—and it has already happened this way in Russia, China and Israel. They automatically give mothers a six-month leave of absence from their jobs, and fathers a three-month leave. This is saying, implicitly: "You're important to that child for that long, and you shouldn't give your baby up so soon." I think we ought to be doing that in this country.

Furthermore, though separated from their mothers five days a week from eight thirty A.M. to four P.M., the youngsters still displayed strong bonds of attachment to their mothers. At the least, he concludes, quality day care is "harmless." Another five-year study at Syracuse University was even more positive, with psychologist J. Ronald Lally finding that good day care can effectively upgrade the intellectual level of children from deprived backgrounds.

These, of course, were textbook nurseries where the child-caretaker ratio was perfect (three children to every adult) and where the caretakers had been trained carefully to be sensitive to their charges' needs. But even "average" care can be worthwhile and not merely custodial. By closely examining 400 children scattered throughout 31 different day-care centers and family-care homes that ranged from excellent to poor, the New York City Infant Care Study recently found that infants fared better in these facilities than comparable samples at home.

Still, the experts insist, there is room for improvement. For though almost three quarters of the pre-school children of working mothers are actually cared for by their fathers, or mothers who work at night, or by other relatives, those outside the umbrella of the family are often in informal arrangements where no controls exist. Only about one sixth of the 6.4 million preschool children of working mothers are currently in licensed centers or family-care homes. And here, Fraiberg's book may bear its most negative fruit. For, says Professor Lally, it could be used as ammunition by people who do not support the concept of day care.

This would be tragic, according to Professor Ed Zigler, former director of the U.S. Office of Child Development and currently Sterling Professor of Psychology at Yale University, who wants the federal government, which spends about $1.6 billion a year on various types of day care, to upgrade the chaotic system by establishing and then enforcing standards that would insure quality care. Despite a Congressional directive to come up with such a policy, the Department of Health, Education and Welfare has failed to carry through, year after year delaying action. At the very least, Zigler would like the United States to join all other industrial nations in the world and pay subsidies that would allow mothers (or fathers) to stay home with their children for six months if they choose.

The Carnegie Council on Children too has called for guidelines to improve existing care. In addition to supporting an increased governmental role in defining and then maintaining high standards for services that basically would be parent directed, the Council also would like the government to encourage "a pluralistic system of child care" by permitting a broader tax-credit system.

"We know what the good standards should be," says Zigler. What the ratio between care giver and child should be; how the care giver should be trained; the need to monitor family day-care homes where HEW estimates that most of the children who aren't cared for by relatives are placed. "All we have to do is make the commitment."

Ideally, this commitment would produce high-quality day care that would satisfy experts and anxious mothers alike. It would be a boon to mothers of very young children whose jobs don't lend themselves to part-time employment in an economy not geared to flexibility and to millions of mothers who, as heads of households, desperately need a full-time salary. But are these mothers to feel guilty until concrete aid appears?

Dr. Thomas says no. "There is no reason why an affectionate, giving relationship can't develop between mother and child, even if the mother isn't around twenty-four hours a day," he insists. "It's a matter of quality making up for quantity. And the mother doesn't have to be triply psyched-up, trying to squeeze too much into her limited time with the baby. All she has to do is be normally involved with the baby.

"Sure, ten minutes a day isn't enough. But few mothers spend only ten minutes a day with their babies. Feeding them and dressing them in the morning; feeding and bathing them at night; playing with them before they go to sleep. That's time well spent. The quality which is what counts is not necessarily lost when the quantity is reduced."

—BARBARA DELATINER
AND VIVIAN CADDEN

WHEN GRANNIES ACT AS NANNIES

It's been a year and a half since I returned to work and started leaving my infant son, Marky, with my mother-in-law each morning. Though things haven't always gone smoothly, I'm still very pleased with the arrangement—confident that no one else could give him more loving, attentive care.

Some psychiatrists and social workers believe grandmothers may not have the patience or flexibility to cope with the demands of small children. Yet Marky's grandmother handles him beautifully and at times is a lot more patient with him than I am. Having raised children of her own—and learned from her mistakes—she seems to understand more quickly just what my baby needs, and why.

She lets him explore and "make a mess." Often I'll find him seated in the middle of her kitchen floor, busily banging away on the pots and pans strewn around him. *I* can't stand the noise, but his grandmother smiles and gently says, "Oh, he's having such a good time." (When we're home and he heads for *my* pots, I cry, "Oh, no. Please play with something else." I feel guilty, but Mommy's nerves just can't take it.)

My mother-in-law reprimands Marky when he's naughty, but spanks him only when it's absolutely necessary—usually when he insists on doing something dangerous, like running into the street. Conscious of the importance of letting a child know he's loved, she hugs him often and calls him by endearing nicknames (his two-year-old vocabulary is already punctuated with the words sweetheart and darling). One day, overhearing me call Marky "a little monster," she admonished, "If you keep telling him he's a monster or a bad boy, he'll believe you and act like one. Tell him he's a nice boy!" So now I call him Pumpkin and hope he doesn't grow plump and round.

My mother-in-law has also taught me not to be too quick to scold. "He's a little boy and just acting like one," she's often said. "They're curious and mischievous and need plenty of space to get into things. That's how they learn." (A house-proud woman, she works hard to keep her home attractive and orderly. I'm grateful that she nevertheless gives Marky full rein.)

Besides fielding the troubles, my mother-in-law shares in the triumphs. She enjoys watching my son grow and develop as much as his father and I do. Aware of all the new little things he does and says, she proudly reports each daily accomplishment, and so, though I may not be with my baby for most of his day, I can still share many of his growing experiences.

Fortunately, my mother-in-law and I have similar views on raising children; she may disagree with me at times, but she respects my wishes. For example, I believe a car seat is mandatory whenever a baby or young child travels in an automobile. Although she finds it a nuisance and prefers to hold Marky in her lap if someone else is driving, she straps him in his seat anyway. I try to make things easier for her by securing the seat in her car before leaving for work if I know she plans to go out.

Most importantly, we're comfortable with each other and have learned to express what we feel even when we're angry or hurt. If this hadn't been the case, things wouldn't have worked out as well as they have.

Not that we didn't have our share of problems.

In my eagerness to have my mother-in-law play nanny, I thought only of how beneficial it would be for my son and how convenient for me. I didn't stop to think that it might be a difficult undertaking for a woman her age.

Many an evening I was greeted by a very weary mother-in-law. What's more, she suffers from back trouble and picking up a 20-pound baby was strenuous, sometimes painful. There were days when I resented coming home to the tune of "Your-son-gave-me-a-hard-time-today." To be constantly reminded that caring for my baby was difficult made me feel guilty, and I resented that feeling, since I had no alternative for child care at the time. I even found myself wishing Marky were old enough for a day-care center so I wouldn't have to deal with a sitter on a personal basis. But I knew those were selfish thoughts. Marky's welfare comes first, I reminded myself, and being cared for by his grandmother is best for him.

But caring for an infant is not only physically hard on my mother-in-

law, it is psychologically binding, too. It keeps her tied to the house, and she prefers being active in projects that will take her outside of her home. "I sure get tired of just having one-year-old company all day," she once remarked to me. "Sometimes I think I'll go crazy if I don't get some adult conversation."

Having my mother-in-law as baby-sitter is sometimes hard on me, too —particularly when she gets carried away with advice-giving. I bristle (to myself): "So I make a few mistakes? Didn't you learn with your children? Well, I will, too, and I'm sure my baby will survive quite nicely, thank you."

I've learned the hard way to be tactful and to let unimportant issues slide. One incident, which now seems silly, occurred when Marky was learning to get around in his walker. Usually he went shoeless, and his white socks would become so dirty that I'd have trouble getting them clean. I asked my mother-in-law to put on his old or dark-colored socks before letting him run about; that way, he'd have a few nice pairs when I took him out.

One day she forgot, or simply didn't feel like taking the time to change the socks. When I brought it to her attention, she blew up: "I'll wash them if you find it's too much trouble," she said curtly, adding, "I can't follow him around all day."

Her outburst was uncalled for, and I was hurt. But in a moment I realized something besides the socks was bothering her—that caring for my son was an immense strain at that point. Instead of saying something, I should have simply bought a few extra pairs of socks and put them aside. And I should have immediately asked my mother-in-law what was troubling her so we could have discussed the *real* problem.

Insecurity—mine—is another problem I've learned to contend with. It breaks my heart when I rush to my in-laws' house to pick up my son and he's reluctant to go home. He'll struggle when I try to put on his jacket, or he'll make me chase him around the house when I say it's time to go. At other times, we'll arrive at our apartment, and he'll whine

for his grandma. I wonder, then, if he really knows I'm his mother. After all, his grandmother feeds him, changes his diapers and comforts him when he hurts himself during the day.

My mother-in-law, bless her heart, tries to reassure me. Marky often asks for me during the day, she says, and when it's time for me to come home, he insists on looking out the window for me. Sure enough, when I walk up the driveway most evenings he's there, with his face pressed against the pane, grinning and waving.

I treasure the memory of one evening, just a few months after I'd started working again, when Marky, my mother-in-law and I were in her kitchen. I was depressed about being a working mother and worried about how it would affect my relationship with my child. Suddenly, Marky started to cry. Since his grandmother was closest, she reached to comfort him—but he wouldn't go to her. He cried for me. I felt comforted, knowing my baby still needed and wanted me.

Marky is thriving under his grandmother's care. He's happy and affectionate. And though he still runs his grandmother ragged with his newfound independence, they get out more often now that he can walk, which makes them both happier. Occasionally I'll hear a complaint or two from my mother-in-law, but she admits she really enjoys caring for her grandson. "I won't stop," she says, "until he's old enough to tell us if someone mistreats him."

If I had to do it over again, I would make the same decision. But I realize that if I wanted to have another baby, I'd have to be willing to stay at home for a time. I couldn't expect my mother-in-law to sacrifice so much more time and energy to help raise another child.

Each day I leave for work confident that my baby is getting everything he needs. Do I ever feel sad and guilty about leaving him? Sure —there are moments. But they pass quickly, because I know that working is necessary for me. And I'm certain that my son is a very happy, very-well-cared-for little boy.

—LINDA CLINTON

DO FATHERS MAKE GOOD MOTHERS?

Can men care for the children when women go off to work? Can fathers handle what has been traditionally seen as the mother's job?

More and more fathers are choosing to do just that, and are doing it well. That's the conclusion I reached after traveling throughout the country, talking with, and sometimes even living with, families in which men have taken on the major child-rearing role.

To research my book *Who Will Raise the Children?: New Options for Fathers (and Mothers)* (Bantam), I interviewed married men who stay at home full time while their wives are out breadwinning, as well as those who purposely work part time —as do their wives— in order to be more fully involved with their children. I also talked to single men and to divorced fathers who had won custody of their children.

It is not just men in such special situations, though, who have substantial daily responsibility for child care. For many two-parent families, economic necessity, split-shift jobs or an unemployed father mean that Daddy takes care of the children during the day while Mommy is at work. Indeed, according to the most recent statistics from the Bureau of Census, some 350,000 children, ages three to six, are cared for at home during the day by their fathers. That's 6.6 percent—or one in every 15—of all children in this age group with working mothers.

What do fathers in all these different arrangements do? To a large extent, the same things that mothers have always done. They wipe spaghetti sauce off upper lips (and off the floor), wander through shopping malls looking for snowsuits and shoes (and sometimes their children), make emergency runs to the pediatrician or hospital, play peek-a-boo and patty-cake, and sing naptime lullabyes. Men can nurture, and

children accept that as something entirely natural. In fact, they don't question it until they run into someone with the notion that fathers shouldn't do the same things as mothers.

One 11-year-old girl I met felt enormous pressure from her classmates because her father was at home with her baby brother—and several other neighborhood children —while her mother was out working. It took lots of talking together to help her feel comfortable and even proud of her "different" type of family.

Of course it's not easy for men to find support when they choose or are cast in nontraditional fathering roles. One New York police officer, for example, wanted to share fully in caring for his newborn daughter. Since he was on the four to 12 P.M. shift, he could easily take care of the baby from nine A.M. to three P.M., while his wife was at work. The minute he announced his plans, however, his "buddies" began making fun and questioning his virility. To make matters worse, his in-laws and parents got on him for "making his wife work," even though she wanted to continue at her job. It took considerable strength for him to claim his rights as a father.

Any significant increase in the number of men taking care of children will depend on changes in a complex set of factors including the economic status of women, the structure of work and the attitudes we have and pass on to our children about men and women. Such changes won't come easy. But as more and more mothers work outside of the home, it seems highly probable, for a variety of reasons, that more and more fathers will work inside the home. **—JAMES A. LEVINE** *(James A. Levine is a Research Associate at Wellesley College Center for Research on Women.)*

KIDS MINDING KIDS

Leaving young children in the care of their older brothers and sisters is common in many parts of the

world. In fact, learning how to take care of children can be an important part of growing up. It teaches both boys and girls how to be good parents. It teaches them that working together and helping to take care of one another are part of family living. But how much responsibility for young children can you safely give to the older ones?

It depends a lot on the maturity of the child. Safety regulations, the kinds of situations to watch out for, can be taught pretty easily to a responsible ten-year-old—but there are also 15-year-olds who are totally irresponsible. My husband and I set the arbitrary age of 12 as the time when our oldest son (he's 27 now) could start to baby-sit for the three younger children. And 12 is probably a good age for most children to begin baby-sitting for short periods— an evening or two or three hours in the afternoon before the parent comes home. You don't want to cramp the style of the older child, to keep the child from having his or her own recreation and after-school activities. I don't think even a few hours three or four days a week is too much, as long as the child does not have to baby-sit all weekend, too.

You also have to consider the age of the younger child. Infants are fairly easy to take care of. A 12-year-old can do a pretty good job with a baby if he knows what to feed him and when to feed him and how to change diapers. He should also be comfortable playing and talking with babies. Toddlers, on the other hand, are the most difficult to watch. Toddlers are insatiably curious and get into everything. You need a fairly mature early teenager, around 14 or 15, to take good care of one. Children who are old enough to go to school are much easier to supervise —a 12-year-old could certainly manage a first grader and a child as young as eight could pinch-hit in an emergency.

Another factor is the number of children you are asking your youngster to watch. As a rule, I think that below the age of 14 no child should be responsible for more than one brother or sister. A 12-year-old could probably look after two or three younger ones at night if they were already in bed and not likely to wake up, but during the day the children would be better off with an older baby-sitter.

Of course, none of this should happen suddenly. From almost the time that a baby is born, there is something that older children can do to help, to make them feel part of the family and part of the baby's care-taking. My children used to help me change the diapers, bathe the baby and feed him. I would read a story to an older child while I was nursing the baby. It gave the children a feeling of closeness and belonging, and they were concerned for the younger ones, which is very important. I did this with each of my children, not just the oldest one, and by the time they were ready to baby-sit they knew what to do.

You also have to prepare your younger children to accept the authority of an older brother or sister as a baby-sitter. The best thing to do is sit down and talk about it. You might ask the child, "Would you be willing to have your sister baby-sit for you?" Then explain what it will mean. "No, she can't hit you if she wants to"—that's the first question you'll get—"but you have to tell her where you are going if you leave the house."

Set up some basic rules about what the children are allowed to do until a parent gets home. You should establish how far away they can go, make sure that the older child won't just go off with her friends without watching the younger one and that the younger child has to call his older sister if he goes to a friend's house to play, or whatever. If you're going out for the evening, bedtime and TV rules should be set beforehand.

Safety is, of course, every parent's biggest worry. Long lists of telephone numbers can confuse children, but you should post by the telephone the number of a neighbor who has agreed to help out and of the family doctor. If you or your husband can be reached at work, these numbers should also be on the list. We always told our children that, in case of fire, they should leave the house at once and call the fire department from the house of a neighbor. But whatever advice you give your children, it's important to re-

hearse what to do in an emergency, not just tell them about it. Make up situations ("What would you do if Janie fell down and cut herself?"), and ask the child how he or she would handle it if you weren't around. That's the only way to find out if the child really understands what you said to him.

In our hospital, we see a lot of home-accident victims in the emergency room—adults as well as children. If you have small children, your house is probably already child-proof, but check extra carefully if you're going to leave them in the care of an older child. Poisons and sharp objects should be locked away, matches removed and electrical sockets protected against curious little fingers. Be sure that the windows are fixed so that a child can't fall out of them and that there are gates across the stairs if you have toddlers. If your child has been watching you take care of his younger brother or sister, he probably already knows how to keep them out of mischief. A responsible older child can be one of the best baby-sitters around.

—SUSAN G. GORDON, M.D.
(Dr. Gordon is an associate professor of clinical pediatrics at Columbia University College of Physicians and Surgeons.)

WHAT ARE THE CHOICES YOU HAVE?

Roughly seven out of ten of the children of full-time working mothers in this country are taken care of during the day by one of their parents or by other relatives; still, that leaves many parents looking elsewhere for solutions. If you are among them, and are wondering what kinds of child care are available, here is a guide.

It may seem too obvious, but the best place to begin is the Yellow Pages of your telephone book under Day-Care Centers or Day Nurseries. Depending on the size and resources

of your community, you will find many of the following facilities.

GOVERNMENT-FUNDED DAY CARE

Publicly funded day-care centers—which you can also find by calling your city or state or department of social services—may be located at or near the neighborhood elementary school. Some programs provide hot lunches for children in full-day programs. Fees and eligibility are determined by individual states and are based on parents' gross incomes. Priority in public day-care centers often goes to single mothers who are receiving government financial aid.

A *family day-care home* can be found through the county social services department. This is a licensed facility, usually run by a mother in her own home, that meets certain federal and state standards for health and safety. It usually serves no more than six children ages three through six (including the operator mother's own children), fewer if there are infants in the group. Fees vary from state to state but are usually low for the low-income women who are eligible and rise on a sliding scale for others.

PROPRIETARY (FOR PROFIT) DAY CARE

Unlicensed family day-care homes are usually run by neighborhood women who, for a fee, care for several children and have never sought to be licensed. (In most states, anyone caring for a certain number of children is supposed to have a license, but few states have the facilities or personnel to enforce these requirements.) Recommendations from friends are often the only way to locate these homes.

Independent proprietary centers are usually begun by mothers who have become aware both of a community need and a business opportunity. The number of children at such centers is generally small, although the operator may hire a staff if necessary. Independent centers can be located by writing the NACDE. (National Association for Child Development and Education, a trade association of proprietary centers, at 500 12th Street, S.W., Washington, D.C. 20024, enclosing a stamped, self-addressed envelope.)

The largest providers of day care, however, are proprietary *chains,* and they thrive —from coast to coast. Of approximately 18,000 centers in the country, which enroll roughly 900,000 children, 30 percent are for-profit centers, totally supported by parents' fees. A few are: Living and Learning Centers, in Massachusetts and Connecticut; Kinder-Care, in the South and Midwest; and Mini-Skools, Ltd. (which operates 82 centers in California, Colorado, Georgia, Kentucky, North and South Carolina, Ohio, Texas and Canada). The only day-care franchise in the United States is Mary Moppet in the Midwest and West. Fees in these centers range from about $24 to $40 (higher for infants) per child per week. Centers vary in size—and there is generally one teacher for every seven or eight children. For a list of member centers in your area, you may also write to NACDE.

NONPROFIT PRIVATE DAY-CARE CENTERS

These receive no government funding, but operate as a community service and do not earn profits. They can have a variety of sponsors.

Often, *churches* and *synagogues* offer day-care services. But if you are considering a program in a church or synagogue solely because of its religious affiliation, determine whether the church runs the program or merely rents out space.

Companies have begun day-care programs, primarily for the children of employees, although these are not widely available. One company—Stride Rite in Boston, Massachusetts —has been operating a center for seven years. (See article which appears on page 47, "The Factory as a Nursery.")

Hospitals are another provider of nonprofit day care. Priority is usually given to children of the nursing and other staffs. Centers are generally administered by members of the hospital's nursing service, who may hire a staff to operate the program. Many programs admit infants and, because of their in-hospital location, may be better equipped than the average facility to handle a handicapped child's needs.

Colleges and universities often provide day care; these centers are usually run by teachers and students in early-childhood education programs. Students' children have priority, but centers frequently admit children of faculty, staff and members of the community. Fees are often based on a sliding scale according to family income; sometimes you will find that these facilities are free.

OTHER OPTIONS

Nursery schools are seldom a solution for women who work full time; they're usually open half a day for children under three years old, and until 2:30 or three P.M. for four-to-five-year-year-olds. They can be helpful to women who can accommodate their hours or in combination with other kinds of care. And, if approached by a group of parents, some nursery schools are willing to adapt their programs to parents' needs. Good nursery schools, however, are usually very expensive—often running from $2,000 to $2,500 a year.

Play groups are informal cooperatives operated and organized by parents. These may be located in members' homes on a rotating basis, or in a rented facility; parents may share staff duties or hire a teacher.

Sitters, of course, can be hired to care for your child in your home or in theirs. For high-income families in certain places, there is still the old-fashioned nurse or nanny to be hired.
—HOLLY HYANS

HOW SCHOOLS CAN HELP PARENTS

When a child starts school, it would seem a woman's day-care worries are over, but that's not quite true. If she works full time, there are still those hours between three P.M. and when she gets home—time enough for a child to get into trouble, or a perfect opportunity for him to finish his homework. What can be done about those few hours?

There are several options for after-school care: baby-sitters, letting the child stay alone, a group-care arrangement at someone's home, or even a group that rotates among different homes. Or the child could simply stay longer in school, using the building for after-school activities. Which is exactly what's going on in an increasing number of cities.

New York City, for example, has allocated $15 million for keeping 300 of its 600 elementary schools open until five P.M. weekdays for remedial classes and recreation. "The school program which we're resurrecting wasn't designed with the working mother in mind, but it might serve her well," says Edward L. Sadowsky, chairman of the City Council's Finance Committee. "It's a place where a mother knows her child can go after school." The students don't sign up in advance, and the program is not structured, but gyms and other school facilities are supervised for student use.

In Brookline, Massachusetts, a group of parents hired trained teachers to staff an after-school program in the eight neighborhood schools. The setup includes arts and crafts, snacks and local outings, and the older children can sign up for a variety of art courses.

Fairfax County, Virginia, and the Fairfax County public schools cosponsor a program in 13 of the 109 elementary schools during the week. The organizers are also planning supplemental holiday schedules. There's a session from seven A.M. until school starts, and one from noon to six P.M. for kindergarteners. Older children can come after school until six P.M. Fees are on a sliding scale, and the county subsidizes part of the cost. The highest price is $100 a month—for a kindergartener who attends the preschool and noon-to-six sessions. Children can get their own lunches at the school cafeteria, and snacks are also provided for them.

Other schools are sponsoring similar activities. Arlington and Montgomery Counties in Virginia run programs like the one in Fairfax. Oakland Children's Centers in Oakland, California, are district-operated programs, serving infants through children 14 years old. South Carolina has facilities in 20 of its 92 school districts, and there are a variety of programs. For instance, one district, Anderson 5, serves infants and children up to five years old, while another in Pickens County is for kindergarteners and five-year-olds who require after-school care.

"There's obviously a growing number of working parents, and the need for child care has been accelerated," says Millicent Grant, coordinator of the Fairfax County program. According to James A. Levine, author of the upcoming book *Day Care and the Public Schools: Profiles of Five Communities,* the key issue is "who is going to be in control of the programs."

"Parents really have to decide if an after-school program in the schools is what they want for their youngsters," says Nellie Quander, president of the National Association of Elementary School Principals. "The schools can do lots of things if the community is willing to pay for the extra hours."

—ANDREA I. BURTMAN

THE FACTORY AS A NURSERY

Industry-sponsored day care is not new, but most of the companies that opened child-care centers in the late 1960s have, for various reasons, dropped their programs. That's why the Stride Rite Children's Center in Boston is unique. Started in 1971 by one of the country's leading manufacturers of children's footwear, the center is not only still functioning—it's thriving.

Parental participation and careful staffing are chiefly responsible for its success. Ten dedicated staff members (eight are certified teachers), plus a number of volunteers, including students from nearby high schools and universities, run the center between seven A.M. and five P.M. weekdays. During the last seven years there has been little turn-over in staff, a fact that has helped win parents' confidence and enabled the center to maintain a stable program. Today 43 children between the ages of 2¾ and six are enrolled in the 50-week program. Twenty of them have parents employed by Stride Rite; the balance live in the community.

Lunchtime is a high point of the day. Parents are encouraged to eat with their children, though only about one quarter of them do, because, as Ms. Kertzman says, factory work is strenuous and parents need peace and quiet during their breaks. A number of parents do stop in during the day to say hello and kiss their children. Others attend supper meetings so they can meet socially with the staff and participate in program planning. Of course, the chief advantage to the women who work for Stride Rite in having a day-care center on the premises is that they save time—not having to make a detour to and from work to drop off or pick up their children each morning and evening.

Since children's needs vary, depending on their age and stage of development, the center divides its youngsters into three age groups in which activities are designed to meet specific needs in emotional, intellectual, physical and social development. The emphasis always: to establish a sense of security and self-esteem in each child. Stride Rite physicians provide medical and mental-health care when needed, and the children are taken for regular dental checkups to the nearby Boston University Graduate School of Dentistry.

To meet the costs of maintaining the center—about $60 a week per child—a three-way funding plan was set up among Stride Rite workers (who pay 10 percent of their gross weekly salaries as tuition for each child enrolled), the Massachusetts Department of Public Welfare (which provides $50.60 a week for each of the community children) and the Stride Rite Charitable Foundation (which contributes the balance of the funds). The Massachusetts Bureau of School Food and Nutrition Services also supplies 78 cents a day per child to cover the cost of breakfasts, lunches and two daily snacks. The staff ingeniously uses factory scraps (pieces of leather and lumber, for instance), designer samples, bottle caps, and so on, to keep the costs of learning and play materials at a minimum.

The center has proved to be a valuable investment for the Stride Rite Corporation. "Sure it makes economic sense," says Arnold Hiatt, president. "It's helped us to attract and keep desirable personnel. But we feel it's a form of preventive medicine, too. We want to demonstrate the advantages and feasibility of industry-sponsored day care, to spark national recognition of the need for child-care facilities." Plans are in the works for similar child-care centers at Stride Rite plants in three other Massachusetts cities, as well as in Maine and Missouri.

HOW CAN YOU TELL IF IT'S GOOD?

How do you actually go about choosing a program or a person you'll feel comfortable entrusting your child to? The key to it is taking your time and following your own instincts. Ideally, you would find the child-care arrangement first and the job second, but even if it doesn't happen that way, don't be stampeded into a decision. There are some generally accepted guidelines about what to look for that will help you choose—and here they are —but remember you are the best judge of what is best for your child.

• Visit each child-care facility that you are considering for as long and often as your schedule will allow. Go alone for your first visit; bring your child along the next time.

• Even if the first person you interview, or the first place you visit, seems perfect, check out several other possibilities for comparison.

• Try to choose a program that will offer your child consistency and predictability: In a center, this means that the staff is fairly constant and that the same person is always responsible for certain children; in a home situation, it means having one steady baby-sitter.

• Will travel to and from the facility be convenient? Is it close to your home or office?

• Is the home or center aesthetically pleasing and comfortable? Is it well-lit? Is there adequate heating in winter and good ventilation in summer?

• Is there a safe, fenced-in area out-of-doors where children can run about and play?

• If the facility is a day-care center or family day-care home, is it licensed?

• Are there adequate provisions for caring for a sick child?

• Is the caretaker a healthy person, who has a good reputation or references?

• Does the caretaker seem to be a warm, open and flexible person? Is she/he affectionate with the children. Does she/he console and comfort them?

• Does the caretaker respond to the children? Does she/he listen to them? Talk to them? Encourage curiosity and answer questions, or mainly concerned with keeping order?

• For a very young child, look for a caretaker who will be interested enough and experienced enough to anticipate his needs and understand his signals; someone who will recognize when he's fussy because he's sleepy or teething or, perhaps, developing a cold.

• Do the children in the group appear involved and busy, or do they wander aimlessly and seem bored?

• Note how the children react when arriving and departing and how the caretaker greets them and bids them good-bye. Are they eager or hesitant? If you are interviewing a sitter, note how she greets your child and what kinds of approaches she makes to him.

• How does the caretaker respond to a child who has difficulty adjusting to his or her parent leaving him or her? Is she sympathetic and kind?

• Can a child pursue activities that she's interested in? Can boys play with dolls and girls with trucks?

• Will your child have a special place to keep his or her own things?

• Do you feel comfortable with the way discipline is handled; how toilet accidents are handled?

• Will there be a variety of stimulating materials available to him or her—games, puzzles, books, music, water, sand, etc.

• Will the program be varied, allowing your child the opportunity to encounter new experiences? For example, are the children taken on outings around the neighborhood?

• Is there a quiet place with cots for rest or naptime?

• Will well-balanced and nutritious meals and snacks be served regularly—with mealtimes made pleasant and relaxing?

• Are parents encouraged to visit at any time? Can they participate in program planning and suggest changes? Are they kept informed about what goes on each day?

• On balance, even if all is not exactly as you would hope, do you like, trust and feel comfortable with the caretaker? If the setup feels right to you, it probably will be right for your child. If your child's response to the caretaker and the place is positive, that will be an important signal, too.

—LINDA CLINTON

FIFTEEN IS A GOOD NUMBER

As the largest single purchaser of day care in the United States, the federal government has a special interest in finding "the best buy" in terms of quality day care and the number of children who can be served. Because of that interest, the Department of Health, Education and Welfare, at the behest of Congress, commissioned in 1974 a massive four-year study of how variations in the size of the group, the ratio of care givers to children and the qualifications of the staff affect both the cost and the quality of care for preschoolers in a center.

Prepared by ABT Associates, a private Cambridge, Massachusetts, research organization under the direction of Dr. Richard Ruopp, the National Day Care Study, as it is called, has just been released. Much

of it, of course, is principally of interest to professionals in the field of early-childhood education, to organizations concerned with child care and child development and to the government seeking to set guidelines for federally-funded care.

But one very clear finding gives parents seeking any kind of group care—whether in a nursery school, a proprietary center or a publicly-funded center—a simple rule of thumb for judging the probable quality of the care: Small groups are best.

Even more specifically, Dr. Ruopp says, "A group of fifteen or sixteen preschoolers with two caretakers seems to be the ideal situation for children."

Confounding what has been the conventional wisdom that it is the ratio of staff to children that is the key to quality in child care, Dr. Ruopp notes that, if the group is too large, adding another staff person won't help.

"Twenty-four children with three care givers just isn't as good as fifteen or sixteen or even seventeen with two."

In classrooms with more children, the study found, grown-ups spent a much greater proportion of their time managing and controlling children and keeping order. In classrooms with few children, care givers spent more of their time responding to children and answering their questions and enlarging their horizons.

"When the group is too large," Ruopp says, "it is too easy for some children to 'get lost' and 'tune out,' harder for some of them to form relationships with other children."

Interestingly enough, centers—both those that are supported by parents and those that are publicly funded—seem to have discovered the advantages of the small group solution. For example, the average size of the group for three-year-olds in both parent-funded and subsidized centers is 14.

In a substudy on infant and toddler care, the researchers found that both a high ratio of care givers to children (one care giver to, say, three or four children), as well as a small group (six to eight children), worked best for the children and for the staff.

ADOPTION

David Cohen

David Cohen is a British journalist who writes on psychology for magazines in Britain, France, Germany, and the United States and is also active in television. His most recent book is *Psychologists on Psychology: Modern Innovators Talk About Their Work* (Taplinger). He has received a grant from the Leverhulme Trust in London to study the development of laughter.

Two widely accepted "truths" in psychology are that early experiences are crucial to a child's development and that his natural parents are almost always the best ones to raise him. John Bowlby in Great Britain and René Spitz in the United States both have argued that a child who suffers maternal deprivation up to the age of two will be irreparably harmed. For Bowlby, maternal care has to be given by the biological mother; he once told me that he had found a few cases in which substitute mothers had been effective, but they were rare. Other psychologists, including Margaret Mahler in the United States, believe that a substitute mother can be just as good, provided that one person consistently cares for the child. A series of substitutes will not do.

Even psychiatrist R. D. Laing has taken pains to set the record straight and affirm that natural families are good, healthy, and fun. Laing, who made his reputation arguing that the games some families play lead to schizophrenia, told me in a recent interview: "You're interviewing me in the midst of my family. I enjoy living in a family. I think the family is still the best thing that exists biologically as a natural thing."

The belief that blood ties make good parents of us all has strongly influenced the way children are treated in both the United States and Great Britain. Social workers usually assume that the best solution is to get a child back to his natural family, whatever the circumstances. Moreover, it has been taken for granted that if a child suffers maternal deprivation during the first two years of life, he or she will be forever a stunted creature, emotionally and intellectually. Didn't that happen to the monkeys in Harlow's experiment that had contact only with "wire mothers" that provided little warmth? Why should babies do any better?

A recent British study of children adopted and later restored to their natural parents casts doubt on both these assumptions. In 1970, psychologist Barbara Tizard of London's Thomas Coram Research Foundation started looking at how institutional care affected children who were placed soon after birth in orphanages and residential nurseries. Most of the children in these nurseries are orphans, but some have living parents who give them up for various reasons. Their mothers may be unmarried, and unable or unwilling to care for them. Or the mother may be married but have too many other children to care for.

Tizard started with children who had not been adopted by the age of two, and followed their emotional, intellectual, and social development over the next six years. By the age of four and a half, 24 children had been adopted and 15 had been restored to their original mothers. By examining how each group had fared, Tizard hoped to determine the effects of late adoption. Her work also would cast light on just how important the biological mother was, as well as how critical and permanent were the effects of institutionalization. As a control, she compared their development with that of 30 working-class children in ordinary families.

She found marked differences among the two groups of formerly institutionalized children at age four and a half. On an IQ test, the 24 adopted children had an above-average mean score of 115, compared with a mean of 100 for the restored children. Tizard also felt that the adopted children concentrated better on the tasks the psychologists set for them, and used language more imaginatively.

(The difference in IQ scores might be explained partially by the fact that the adoptive parents were able to choose their children and therefore may have picked the brighter ones. On the other hand, all the adopted children had natural parents who were manual workers, while three of the restored children had parents who were either professionals or skilled workers—two factors that could be expected to produce higher IQ scores, on the average, among the restored children.)

She also asked the parents what problems they had with the children. The adoptive parents reported few behavior problems. The children tended to be exceptionally obedient. Most of them ate well and slept well, although two children wet their beds occasionally. Only four of the 24 had temper tantrums—fewer than among the working-class children in the control group.

Overall, the adoptive parents found only one consistent flaw in their children. They tended to do anything to get attention—anything, that is, except to be naughty. This hunger for attention, coupled with a reluctance to be bad, was a legacy of their lives in the residential nurseries. Tizard found that the nurseries are rather like old-fashioned homes. Meals are formal and good table manners are expected. The children are played with and read to at least once a day. They get perfectly good care, with one exception: since the nursery staff changes frequently, staff members are warned not to form a close bond with any child; so the children get little personal mothering or fathering. Thus, the competition for the attention of adults.

The restored children had considerably more problems. Many wet themselves by day, had tantrums regularly, and fought constantly. They clamored for attention even more than the adopted children. Half of them climbed into the psychologists' laps during the interviews, hungering for affection. Only a few of the adopted children did that—and none of the working-class controls.

The anxieties of the restored children were perfectly rational. Many of the natural mothers expressed ambivalence toward their children. Only six of the 15 mothers who took their children back had maintained a close relationship with them at the nursery. Sometimes, they claimed that because the children were not in their care as babies, they were not capable of loving them properly. As one mother put it, "I didn't want him, I didn't want the responsibility. I wanted him adopted. The society kept on asking me what I was going to do with him. I'll be glad when he grows up. Often he irritates me just by being in the room. I used to thump him a lot, but now I can't be bothered. I just keep out of his way."

In such circumstances, there is nothing surprising about the pathetic behavior of one four-year-old girl who kept asking her mother if she loved her. Her mother told the psychologists that this was rather embarrassing if it happened in a bus or a shop.

Other natural mothers threatened to send their children back to the nursery. Indeed, four of the children threatened to return to the nursery themselves, although legally the institution could not have taken them back. Parents may abandon children, but children can't abandon parents at will.

Tizard worked up a check list of problems (tantrums, bed-wetting, constant seeking of attention) and rated each child against it. Adopted children had far lower problem scores than the restored children. Clearly, at the age of four and a half, the adoptees were doing better than those who had been returned to their natural families. The reasons are easy to see.

Adoption standards are strict in Great Britain, as they are in the United States. Unless a husband and wife are stable and have a good income, they can't adopt a child. As a result, the adopted children have more toys, more books, outings, and more stimulation in general. But Tizard believes that the adoptees' higher IQ scores and lower problem scores reflected differences in attitude as well as wealth.

The adoptive parents very much wanted to be parents. They had been through considerable bureaucratic rigmarole before being given a child. (In one case, a couple had to undergo eight medical examinations.) They were willing to spend a lot of time playing with their children. Often, they were teachers or professional people who played in ways that fostered intelligence and verbal skills.

The restored children, on the other hand, went into environments that were generally poorer than those of their nurseries. Their parents had less time and energy to devote to playing with their children. They had ambivalent feelings about them and so less motivation to play and "be" with them.

Another consistent difference illustrated the contrast between the natural and adoptive family environments. The adoptive mothers and fathers always insisted on meeting with the psychologist together, since the child's development was a joint concern; no natural mother insisted on the father's being there. In fact, many demanded clandestine meetings with Tizard and her colleagues: they would cooperate only if their man would never find out. (Only two of the mothers were still living with the child's natural father; eight others were single parents; four were living with another man; and one father who reclaimed his child was living with a woman.)

Why, then, did mothers take their children back? Tizard points to several causes. Despite the glories of the swinging 60s and the women's movement, most people in Great Britain still consider a mother who does not look after her own children a personal failure. It marks a woman as incompetent and unfeeling—even unnatural. There is much social pressure for her to take the child back.

Many of the real mothers were misled by what they saw when they visited their children in the residential nurseries. There, the children were well looked after and appeared charming, lovable, and easy to handle; on impulse, the mothers took them back. Only after a few weeks at home did they learn what it really meant to care for them.

These mothers did not have to get to know their youngsters before being allowed to take them home—in contrast, ironically, to those who wanted

to adopt a child. Once a British couple have been accepted as adoptive parents, an elaborate ritual begins. They visit the child at the nursery and can take him on outings. Then they may take him home for a weekend to see how well they get along. There may be a number of such visits to ease the child into his new home.

There is no such courtship when a child is returned to his natural mother or parents. What usually happened, Tizard found, was that the mother would simply turn up at the nursery and say, "You're coming with me." Since British and American laws hallow the blood bond, this was usually enough for the authorities. The mother simply assumed the child would be delighted to come home, not realizing that the sudden change might cause problems and confusion.

Tizard tells of one girl who was suddenly reclaimed by her mother—"repossessed" might be a better word—and had to fit into a family with five other children, all of whom had spent some time in institutions. The girl wet and soiled herself day and night. She quarreled with all her siblings and was particularly adept at inventing ways of infuriating her mother. Just before the family was visited by Tizard, the child had flooded the mother's flat by turning on the water taps in the sink, destroying everything they owned.

The researchers revisited both groups of children several years later (when they were about eight) to check on their progress. They could see only 20 of the 24 adopted children, since one family had emigrated and three refused interviews. They were able to see nine out of the 15 families with children who had been restored.

For children in those families who were interviewed, earlier differences had been accentuated by the age of eight. The adopted children still scored higher on IQ tests, and, more important, they were doing well at school.

Their teachers did say that many of them had problems. Some, for instance, were described as unpopular with classmates and considered quarrelsome, but their academic progress was good. The restored children did poorer schoolwork than their IQ scores promised, and they had more behavior problems both at school and at home. All but two of the adopted children helped regularly around the house, while only about half the restored children were helpful. (Tizard believes the difference between adopted and restored would have been more marked if she had been able to interview all of the families. For example, the six restored children who were "lost" had the highest problem scores at age four and a half. Tizard, however, also points out that any such small sample can provide only impressions and not statistical evidence.)

Researchers asked the mothers how they felt about their children and how the children felt about them. Only three of the adoptive mothers seemed to dislike their children or doubt their feelings for them. More than half of the natural mothers, on the other hand, felt there was not much of a loving bond between them and their children. To make matters even more difficult for the restored children, few of them had developed any relationship with the man their mother was living with.

By the age of eight, six of the nine restored children had been referred to a child-guidance clinic for psychiatric help. This figure is even more striking considering that it was the six children Tizard could *not* follow up at the age of eight who had the most problems three years earlier.

Tizard found that the restored children who fared the best had returned to a home in which the mother lived alone or with teen-agers who could help care for them. Other children suffered when they were suddenly thrown into a new home where no one really wanted them.

As her research developed, Tizard studied six other children who had been adopted between the ages of four

THE AMERICAN EXPERIENCE IS DIFFERENT

As in Great Britain, the guiding maxim of adoption in the United States is that blood ties count most. "The laws of most states make a presumption in favor of the biological parents," says Albert Solnit, director of Yale University's Child Study Center. "That's why there's a waiting period between placement and legal adoption. If the natural parents decide they want the child back, they can appeal."

The most famous case of this type was the dispute over "Baby Lenore" in 1970-72. New York State courts were prepared to return the child to the natural mother, who had voluntarily given up rights and then changed her mind before the decree was final. The prospective adoptive parents fled with the child to Florida, where the courts found in their favor.

Once the adoption procedure is complete in the U.S., the rights of the natural parents have been terminated, in theory. But, up to that point, the courts, under the blood-is-best presumption, have allowed natural parents to reclaim their children, even when the children have never been in their care.

Because so many babies on the U.S. adoption market have been black, Hispanic, or Asian, more attention has been given in research here to the effects of transracial adoption than to testing the blood presumption. These hard-to-adopt children, along with handicapped children and the emotionally disturbed, make up much of the remaining institutional population here. "The trend is away from orphanages, toward foster care," says Jane Fairbanks of the Council on Adoptable Children. "It's generally agreed that's better, with individual attention for the child. Kids in institutions now are generally the emotionally disturbed, kids from messed-up homes with chronic problems."

These factors have prevented studies such as Jane Tizard's from being done in the United States: follow-up studies of institutionalized children would involve the complicating factors of race or handicap. Following the progress of children through foster homes to adoptive parents would mean generalizing about vastly differing experiences. In most states, such care is regarded as temporary; children may be shuttled between foster homes several times. This creates an unsettled situation for both children and foster parents. The temporary arrangement can lead to a lack of emotional involvement, or one that may be painfully disrupted at any time.

The system acknowledges that children need to form attachments; but these bonds are, in practice, often broken. "If the natural parents have ongoing problems," says Jane Fairbanks, "kids end up in supposedly temporary foster care for years. The goal is to get the family back together, but it's not done—and the rights of the natural parents aren't terminated."

In many cases, foster homes may be the most permanent family a child has known. Court decisions in the past have basically ignored this fact, equating the "best interests of the child" with the natural family. According to Steve Shapiro of the New York Civil Liberties Union's Children's Rights Project, though, the situation may be changing somewhat: "In the absence of abandonment, neglect, or present unfitness, the natural parents could always get custody. That's still true. But courts are beginning to question that, in extreme cases, if it means lifting kids out of a long-term foster family."

Last June, the U.S. Supreme Court avoided the issue of whether foster parents are entitled to a review of their interest in a child. The Court upheld the New York State procedures for removing children from foster homes, which entitle the foster family to a hearing only in certain cases. Says Solnit: "The Supreme Court's interpretation of the law says that if a child has been with foster parents for a year and a half or longer, he may not be removed summarily. A hearing is necessary to establish two things: if removal is in the best interest of the child, and if it is, whether placement with the biological parents is in the child's best interest."

In their 1973 book, *Beyond the Best Interests of the Child*, Solnit, Joseph Goldstein, and Anna Freud argued that the child's "real" parent is the one with whom he or she establishes a bond, the "psychological" parent who is supportive on a day-to-day basis. "The child's best interests," says Solnit, "require a guiding, protective parent who wants him and gives him a feeling of being wanted."

—Debra Cohen

and a half and eight, and seven others who had been restored to their mothers between the same ages. Their development was similar to the children in the other groups. Again, the adopted ones did better at school and had fewer emotional problems. In these cases, too, the adoptive parents made greater efforts to ease their children's way into new lives. While they tolerated immature behavior (such as the demand by one six-year-old that they always dress him), the natural parents were less forgiving. Several complained that the child didn't really love them—couldn't love them, in fact, because they had spent all those years apart. It was as if the parents' roles had been reversed. The adoptive parents thought of the child as their own, while the natural parents often saw the child as not really theirs.

Tizard thinks adoption can be successful even if a child is two, four, seven, or older, if the adoptive parents are willing to face the difficulties. She doesn't believe in the maternal-deprivation hypothesis accepted by many social agencies.

In the residential nurseries, the children received no personal mothering. By the age of two, each had been cared for by about 25 adults, and by the age of four, by 40 adults. If early loving care is as essential as many theorists believe, the children's emotional and intellectual growth should have been stunted, with little hope for improvement. Yet, in Tizard's study, the children who were adopted late did quite well.

Indeed, they had been eager to make friends with any adult at the nursery and were fickle in their affections. But given a good home, they developed a very strong natural feeling for their adopted parents. They learned to love by being loved and cared for, even though love didn't start until the age of four, five, or, in the case of one child, seven.

Tizard would like to see foster parents given a better chance to adopt or become guardians of a child they have cared for. She also feels strongly that social workers and others who deal with the children must accept the fact that there are times when a mother shouldn't be pressed to take her child back. Many social workers in England seem to be dogmatic in their belief that a child is better off with his natural mother. In the groups studied by Tizard, social workers often fostered the guilt that drove mothers to reclaim their children, even when the mothers expressed a great deal of ambivalence and weren't really prepared to care for them. As a result, there were strong feelings of hostility between parents and social workers.

Tizard recognizes that her findings were strongly influenced by economic factors. All the restored children she studied returned to families that were, often, quite poor. The adoptive families were better off. Does this mean that children should not be returned to poor people but should be given up for adoption to the rich? Tizard argues that although money helps, it is not merely a question of money but rather of the feelings and attitudes of the natural parents. Far too often, they are badgered into raising a child they don't want and can't handle. In such circumstances, they are unlikely to be sensitive to the needs of children who have been through a lot in their first years and consequently need a lot of devoted care. Paradoxically, the authorities tend to see a child restored to his family as a happy ending.

It is easy to pick scientific holes in Tizard's research. She used a small sample. She relied a good deal on what parents said about the children, believing that questioning the children directly might create more problems in their relationships with their parents. Despite these limitations, the picture that emerges from the study is clear and consistent. It seems obvious that families should not be forced, subtly or otherwise, to take children back simply because we assume that blood is best. And, important as the first two years of life may be, we need not give up on children who may not have been given much love and attention in those years.

Fathering: It's a Major Role

Fathers bring a
special dimension to infant care,
according to recent studies.
In the way they play, and
in the way their kids respond.

Ross D. Parke and Douglas B. Sawin

Ross D. Parke is professor of psychology at the University of Illinois at Champaign-Urbana. Educated at the University of Toronto and the University of Waterloo, Parke is a former associate editor of *Child Development*, and currently serves on the editorial boards of several other journals. He is coauthor of *Child Psychology: A Contemporary Viewpoint*, editor of *Readings in Social Development* and *Recent Trends in Social Learning Theory*, and coeditor of *Contemporary Readings in Child Psychology*.

Douglas B. Sawin received his graduate training at the Institute of Child Development at the University of Minnesota and was awarded his Ph.D. in 1974. He has collaborated on research with Ross D. Parke at the Fels Research Institute for Human Development in Yellow Springs, Ohio, and is now an assistant professor in the Department of Psychology at the University of Texas at Austin. Sawin is currently studying ethnic differences in paternal and maternal roles and their effects on infant development during the first year.

"FATHERS ARE A BIOLOGICAL necessity but a social accident," Margaret Mead once observed. Contemporary women might take issue with this traditional image of the father as the helpless parent with little talent for or interest in child-rearing. They are likely to argue that the father is just as capable of caring for babies as the mother, and ought to at least share the burdens.

Interestingly, research by developmental psychologists tends to support their view. Our studies of fathers confirm that they are not a social accident at all. They contribute significantly to an infant's social and intellectual growth, although in ways that are different from the mother's. The father is not just a poor substitute for the mother; he makes his own unique contribution to the care and development of infants and young children.

Our observations began seven years ago, in Madison, Wisconsin, with the assistance of Sandra O'Leary, after we convinced reluctant maternity-ward personnel that fathers should be permitted to handle their newborns and not just admire them through a glass window. The fathers were allowed to join mothers and infants in their hospital rooms, where trained observers watched and recorded a wide variety of parenting behaviors in the first two days after delivery. We concluded that the fathers clearly were just as involved with their babies as the mothers—looking and smiling at them, holding and kissing.

There were several questions that remained from this early study. First, since both mother and father were in the room, the high degree of father-infant interaction might have been due to the supporting presence of the mother, who might encourage the father's involvement and provide physical assistance and verbal instructions. Second, most of the fathers had attended Lamaze childbirth classes and had been present during the delivery. They therefore might have been more interested in their parental role and more likely to involve themselves with their infants than other fathers. Third, the men we observed were middle class and well educated; perhaps fathers in lower-income families, who tend to define parental roles more rigidly, would have behaved differently.

To address these questions, we next studied 82 lower-class fathers who had not participated in childbirth classes and were not present during delivery. Fathers and mothers were observed when they were alone with their infants and when both parents were present.

Again, the fathers were interested and active participants in the days after delivery. When alone with their infants, the fathers were just as nurturant and stimulating as the mothers. In fact, they were more likely than the mothers to hold the infants and to look at them. Mothers exceeded fathers in only one kind of stimulation—they smiled more at their babies, a difference that may simply reflect the established fact that women smile more often than men do in general.

Our studies also suggest that both mother and father show more interest in their baby when they are together with the infant. They both examine the infant more carefully (count toes, check ears, and so forth), and smile at him more.

Our subsequent studies have confirmed that fathers, when given the opportunity, become actively involved with their newborns. While mothers and fathers are equally involved with their infants, they are involved in different ways right from the start. When they have the chance, fathers are more visually attentive and playful (talking to the baby, imitating the baby), but they are less active in feeding and caretaking activities such as wiping the child's face or changing diapers. We considered the possibility that mothers took over these duties simply because they were better at them. When we tested the hypothesis, we turned out to be wrong, as shown below.

In our view, parental competence is a question of how sensitively parents interpret, and react to, infant cues and signals. Success in caretaking and playing depends largely on reading the subtle changes in the infant's behavior correctly and reacting properly.

In feeding, for example, the parents' job is to make sure that the feeding process goes smoothly and that the infant receives enough milk. One way to measure how good a job parents are doing is to see how quickly they modify their behavior in response to the infant's distress signals: sneezing, coughing, or spitting up.

We found that mothers were only slightly more responsive, and that the amount of milk infants drank for their mothers was only slightly more than when their fathers were doing the feeding. Considering that mothers usually have had more contact with babies than fathers—as baby sitters, mothers' helpers, sisters, and so on—it seems that fathers do very well at the traditional feminine tasks of child care.

When we followed parents home and watched them interact with their children at the ages of three weeks and three months, we saw that differences between mothers and fathers persisted. Other researchers, using reports from parents on routine activities in the home, confirm these results. In a recent Boston study of middle-class families, mothers spent an average of one and one-half hours a day feeding their year-old infants, compared with 15 minutes for the fathers. Of course, most of them weren't around during the day. But that is not the only reason for the difference. Nearly half the fathers said that they had *never* changed the baby's diapers, and 75 percent said that they had no regular responsibilities for taking care of the child.

The birth of a baby seems to lead even egalitarian parents back to traditional roles. In a recent study of California couples, researchers found a marked return to the customary division of labor for a variety of functions, from decision-making to baby care and housework.

Other studies convince us that in most families, the father's main role is that of a playmate to the infant. Indeed, fathers spend four to five times as much time playing with their infants as taking care of them. Michael Lamb has found that fathers are also more likely to hold babies simply to play with them, while mothers are far more likely to hold them for caretaking purposes.

Fathers not only play more than mothers, but their style of communication and play is also different. Harvard pediatricians Michael Yogman, T. Berry Brazelton, and their colleagues recently explored these differences in detail by studying five infants from the ages of two weeks to six months. They observed how each child interacted with its mother, its father, or a stranger for two-minute periods. Through slow-motion analyses on video tapes, they made detailed records of the play patterns of various adults with the infants. They found that the mothers spoke softly, re-peating words and phrases frequently, and imitating the infants' sounds. The usual pattern was what Yogman calls burst-pause: a rapidly spoken series of words and sounds, followed by a short period of silence.

The fathers were less verbal and more tactile than the mothers. They touched their infants with rhythmic tapping patterns more often than mothers or strangers. Father-infant play shifts rapidly from peaks of high infant attention and excitement to valleys of minimal attention, while mother-infant play includes more gradual shifts.

Observers have found the same differences in normal home situations for both infants and older children. Fathers engage in more physically arousing and unusual activities; for instance, such rough-and-tumble play as tossing the infant in the air. Mothers usually play conventional games, such as peekaboo. They also tend to stimulate their children verbally rather than physically.

In most cases, researchers have found, the infants' responses were more positive to play with their fathers than to play with their mothers. In one study, K. Alison Clarke-Stewart found that most children from seven to 30 months picked their fathers rather than their mothers as playmates.

How much and how well fathers interact with their infants has a strong effect on the child's development, particularly if the child is a boy. Babies as young as five months are more at ease in social situations when their fathers help take care of them and play with them. For example, they prove to be calmer and happier when left alone or with strangers. Perhaps egalitarian families not only share caretaking more, but also expose the infant to a variety of other people, so the child becomes accustomed to strangers. Cross-cultural studies tell a similar story: whether in Guatemala or Uganda, babies cope better with unusual social situations and strange people if the father is an involved parent.

Studies suggest that fathers and mothers contribute to their child's intellectual development in different ways. The father's greatest contribution to the infant's cognitive progress comes from the quality of his play with the child. In the case of the mother, it is her verbal stimulation that is the best predictor of the infant's cognitive level.

As fathers take greater responsibility for the care of their children, it becomes more important for them to do the job right. As far back as 1925, the national PTA was advocating that parenthood training be included in the high-school curriculum. It is still an excellent idea, which is only slowly taking hold.

Hospitals are changing their visiting policies to give fathers more contact with their newborn infants. In New York City, 60 percent of the hospitals permit fathers to visit with their newborns. The importance of this change is highlighted by the innovative work of pediatricians Marshall Klaus and John Kennell of Case Western Reserve University School of Medicine, who have provided evidence that the mother-infant attachment is strengthened by extended contact between the two immediately after birth. Some evidence from Sweden suggests that the same is true for fathers. In these studies, men who were given a chance to learn and practice basic caretaking skills right in the hospital were more involved in the care of the infant and in household tasks three months later.

One innovation that should be given wider support is paternity leave, not just immediately after birth but during pregnancy as well. Other suggested changes at the workplace that would permit a larger role for the father in infancy include shorter work weeks, more flexible working hours, and "split jobs" (in which father and mother each work part-time at a given job).

These and similar ideas would all be helpful to families that want such equality. In many families, though, increased participation by the father may cause conflict and disrupt family life by threatening well-established and satisfying roles. Our goal should be to acknowledge that the father makes an important contribution to infant care.

Fathers are clearly not forgotten. Nor is Mead's famous claim that "fathers are a biological necessity but a social accident" still valid. Fathers are alive, well, and playing an active and important role in infancy—a role that is likely to increase in the future.

For further information, read:

Lewis, M. and M. Weinraub, "The Father's Role in the Infant's Social Network, in *The Role of the Father in Child Development*. Michael E. Lamb, ed., Wiley 1976 $17.95.

Parke, R.D., "Perspectives on Father Infant Interaction" in *Handbook of Infancy*, J. Osofsky, ed., Wiley 1978 in press.

Parke, R.D. and D.B. Sawin, "The Father's Role in Infancy. A Re-evaluation." *Family Coordinator* Vol. 25 No. 4, 1976.

Parke, R.D. and S.E. O'Leary, "Family Interaction in the Newborn Period, Some Findings." "Some Observations and Some Unresolved Issues, in *The Developing Individual in a Changing World*. Vol. 2, K. Riegel and J. Meacham eds. Mouton 1976.

When Mommy Goes to Work...

What happens to her kids' emotional development... her husband's ego... her own self-esteem?

SALLY WENDKOS OLDS

Sally Olds has three daughters, aged 15, 18 and 20, and has worked part time or free lance in public relations and journalism ever since her youngest was a year old.

It used to be easy to diagnose the problems of children whose mothers worked outside the home—a group of youngsters that today totals more than 27 million in this country alone. Is Mary overly dependent and whiny? That's because she doesn't see enough of her Mommy. Does Billy do badly at school? Poor thing, he doesn't have the loving attention of a mother who could help him with his homework. Is Freddy stealing candy bars from the corner store? He wouldn't if he had Mom's guidance at home!

Such assumptions may seem logical, but they just don't hold up when scrutinized under the research microscope. As social scientists delve more deeply into the effects on children of their mothers' working, their findings are turning out to be quite different from long-accepted beliefs.

Let's take a moment for a brief history lesson. Twenty-five years ago, only 1.5 million mothers were in the labor force. Today, 14 million are. As late as 1940, only one female parent in ten worked outside the home. Today, four in ten do. Before 1969, most women with children between the ages of 6 and 17 spent their days at home. Today, the United States Department of Labor reports that a record nine million women with children 6 to 17 years old are working. In fact, nearly three million have little ones aged three to five, and over two and half million have babies under three!

With employment patterns shifting so dramatically, it's only logical that we reevaluate our long-held beliefs about child care and babies' needs in general—beliefs that for years have kept mothers tied to their babies' cribs for fear of sparking emotional and psychological traumas later on. Most of our baby-care gospel (example: "children need a loving mother at home") is based on studies of hospitalized youngsters conducted during the 1940's and 50's. Not surprisingly, researchers found that infants in understaffed institutions, who were cut off from familiar people and places and who were cared for by a bewildering succession of hospital nurses, eventually suffered severe emotional problems. Valid as these studies may be, they tell us nothing about babies who, though looked after by competent babysitters or day-care workers during the day, are reunited with their own loving parents come evening. Fortunately, studies of the last decade have sharpened and reinforced this distinction.

In 1973, for example, Harvard University pediatrician Dr. Mary C. Howell surveyed the voluminous literature on children of working mothers. After poring over nearly 300 studies involving thousands of youngsters, she concluded: "Almost every childhood behavior characteristic, and its opposite, can be found among the children of employed mothers. Put another way, there are almost no constant differences found between the children of employed and nonemployed mothers." To wit: Researchers found both groups equally likely to make friends easily or to have trouble getting along with their peers, to excel at their studies or to fail, to get into trouble or to exhibit model behavior, to be well adjusted and independent or to be emotionally tied to the apron strings, to love and feel loved by their parents or to reject them.

Just recently, Harvard psychologist Jerome Kagan and two researchers from the Tufts New England Medical Center, Phillip Zelazo and Richard Kearsley, zeroed in on the possible effects of day care on the emotional and developmental progress of infants whose mothers worked, as compared to children raised by their mothers at home. As the yardstick for his evaluation, Kagan used three characteristics considered "most desirable" by parents: intellectual growth, social development and ability to achieve a close relationship with the mother. His results? Provided the center was well staffed and well equipped, Kagan and his colleagues were unable to find *any* significant differences between the two groups of children.

Since a mother's working per se is no longer considered a crucial factor in a child's development, what factors *are* important? To find out, let's examine the problem from a different perspective. Instead of thinking in terms of working and stay-at-home mothers, we'll divide women according to whether or not they *enjoy* whatever it is they are doing, and here we can see the differences emerge.

Back in 1956, psychologist Jack Rouman traced the progress of 400 California school children and found that the emotional problems they suffered were related not to their mothers' employment status but, rather, to the state of their mothers' emotions. He concluded: "As long as the child is made to feel secure and happy, the mother's full-time employment away from the home does not become a serious problem."

Take Linda Farber, a Philadelphia city clerk who hates her job, is bitter at her ex-husband for leaving her, making it necessary for her to work, and who feels tied down by her six-year-old son, Greg. He, in turn, is wetting his bed again, gets stomachaches every morning before school and is withdrawing from other children. On the other hand, Marjorie Gorman would love to return to the personnel office where she worked before her kids were born, but her husband insists, "It's your duty to stay home with the children."

According to anthropologist Margaret Mead, who has examined child-rearing patterns around the world, the notion that a baby must not be separated from its mother is absurd.

Marjorie is bored and restless. Annie, her oldest daughter, has run away from home three times, has thrown a kitchen knife at her parents and is habitually truant.

Of course, these children's problems are not triggered simply by their mothers' attitudes about work. But maternal unhappiness and resentment is easily communicated to other members of the family, and can, indeed, influence the quality of home life.

Studies undertaken by University of Michigan psychologist Lois Wladis Hoffman bear this out. She found that employed women who enjoy their jobs are more affectionate with their children and less likely to lose their tempers than mothers who are disenchanted with their daily work. Furthermore, those who are content with their situations are more likely to have sons and daughters who think well of themselves, as measured on tests of self-esteem, than are resentful workers or unhappy homemakers. Following a 1974 review of 122 research papers on working mothers and their children, Dr. Hoffman concluded, "The dissatisfied mother, whether employed or not and whether lower class or middle class, is less likely to be an adequate mother." Norwegian psychologist Aase Gruda Skard agrees: "Children develop best and most harmoniously when the mother herself is happy and gay. For some women the best thing is to go out to work, for others it is best to stay in the home."

For Ellen Anthony, staying at home to care for her small baby was stifling. "I need to work," she insists. "Without some outside stimulation and a way to discharge pent-up energy, I become bored and aggressive. Now that I'm back at my public relations post, I don't overpower my daughter and husband so much and we're all happier." Carol Brunetti, on the other hand, left a good job as a department store buyer to devote full attention to her infant son. "I haven't missed my job for a minute," she says. "I love the flexibility of making my own hours. And whenever I want to go somewhere, I just take Jason along with me."

But Mom's attitude is not the only one that must be taken into consideration. No one will argue the fact that the happiness of both mother and chil-dren also depends on the father: How a husband feels about his wife's working is crucial to the emotional climate within the home. And his attitude is a distillation of many things—whether he considers himself a success or a failure at his own profession, what the basic marital relationship is like and how willing he is to assume a fair share of the management of the household and the children if his wife takes a job.

Obviously, the woman whose husband approves of her working is lucky: Balancing job and family is never easy, but when a wife has to do the juggling herself, as well as contend with a husband's opposition, it's twice as difficult.

Happily, many a man who was originally opposed to his wife's working has discovered that he likes spending more time getting to know his children, that money problems have lessened and that he and his wife have more to talk about now that she's also exposed to new people and situations.

Although many psychoanalysts continue to stress the need for an exclusive relationship between mother and baby, recent research has shown that such relationships are probably the exception rather than the rule, even in families where the female parent does not go out to work. For one thing, most fathers today are vital figures in their children's lives. A 1974 study by Milton Kotelchuck of Harvard University found that one- and two-year-olds are just as attached to their fathers as to their mothers. And for another, the typical baby in our society is cared for by several other people in addition to its parents.

According to anthropologist Margaret Mead, who has examined child-rearing patterns in societies around the world, the notion that a baby must not be separated from its mother is absurd. Babies are most likely to develop into well-adjusted human beings, she says, when they are cared for "by many warm, friendly people"—as long as most of the loved ones maintain a stable place in the infants' lives.

There's the rub. For many working mothers, finding these "warm, friendly people" to care for their children on a long-term basis is often a frustrating and expensive proposition. Experts agree that the following scenarios are probably the most stable (and, in turn, most successful), especially for babies and toddlers:

• A father who is able to dovetail his work schedule with his wife's so that their child can be looked after by one parent or the other.

• A grandmother, other relative, friend or neighbor who cares for a child in his or her own home.

• Family day care—an arrangement similar to the one above but between people who have not previously met, often arranged by a public agency.

• A full-time babysitter who comes to the house five days a week and may perform housekeeping chores, too.

• A well-run, well-staffed day-care center.

But once the parents have made the decision that Mommy should work, what about the kids? How will *they* take to their mother's new role—and if they don't, what can you do to make them understand?

Most likely, children will have mixed feelings about Mommy's new job. David, nine, whose mother is the only working mother on the block, sometimes asks her, "Why can't you be home when I get home from school like Mark's mother? She always gives us milk and cookies." But the day David's class visited the dress factory where his mother works, he proudly explained her role in designing the clothes they saw being produced.

One woman met her child's resentment head-on. After ten-year-old Lisa had asked for the umpteenth time, "Oh, why do you have to work, anyway?" her mother stopped what she was doing, sat down with her daughter and explained just how important her job was to her. She let Lisa know that she understood the child's annoyance but she made it clear—without getting angry—how unhappy, bored and restless she would be staying home.

A group of 11-year-olds told an investigator that they loved the responsibility of using their own keys to let themselves in and out and they relished the privilege of having the house to themselves for a few hours after school.

What can both parents do to help children more readily accept their mother's employment? Child-care experts suggest that you:

• Plan your schedules so that at least

one parent is with the baby for half his or her waking hours during the first three years of life.

• Institute new child-care arrangements a week or so before you start a job, so that your child has a chance to get used to the new set-up.

• Don't take a full-time job for the first time or make a big change in child-care arrangements when your baby is between six months and a year old, or between one-and-a-half and two-and-a-half. Try to wait a couple of months after any major upheaval—such as a move to a new home, a long illness or the break-up of a marriage.

• Keep in close touch with whoever is caring for your child and consider her or him a partner in nurturing.

• Plan "child time" into your schedule when your youngsters can depend on having some uninterrupted time with you. It need not be long, but it should be regular.

• Let your children know how much they mean to you, and that they mean more to you than your job.

"The mother who obtains satisfaction from her work, who has adequate arrangements so that her dual role does not involve undue strain, and who does not feel so guilty that she overcompensates, is likely to do quite well and, under certain conditions, better than the nonworking mother," insists Dr. Hoffman.

In other words, it's not a matter of "whether" or "where"—but of "how" the woman who works balances the seemingly conflicting elements in her life. As one magazine editor explains, "I feel I have the best of both worlds— I love my family and I love my work, and every day in every way I feel a little better about being me."

The Family as Cradle of Violence

Lizzie Borden took an ax
And gave her father 40 whacks.
When the job was neatly done
She gave her mother 41.

Suzanne K. Steinmetz
and Murray A. Straus

Although intrafamily violence like that attributed to Lizzie Borden is occasionally reported, such behavior is considered totally out of the ordinary—families are supposed to be oases of serenity where love and good feeling flow from each parent and child.

Unfortunately, that lovely picture is not accurate. In fact, the grizzly tale of Lizzie Borden may not be unique. Violence seems as typical of family relationships as love; and it would be hard to find a group or institution in American society in which violence is more of an every-day occurrence than it is within the family. Family members physically abuse each other far more often than do nonrelated individuals. Starting with slaps and going on to torture and murder, the family provides a prime setting for every degree of physical violence. So universal is the phenomenon that it is probable that some form of violence will occur in almost every family.

The most universal type of physical violence is corporal punishment by parents. Studies in England and the United States show that between 84 and 97 percent of all parents use physical punishment at some point in their child's life. Moreover, such use of physical force to maintain parental authority is not confined to early childhood. Data on students in three different regions of the United States show that half of the parents sampled either used or threatened their high school seniors with physical punishment.

Of course, physical punishment differs significantly from other violence. But it is violence, nonetheless. Despite its good intentions, it has some of the same consequences as other forms of violence. Research shows that parents who use physical punishment to control the aggressiveness of their children probably increase rather than decrease their child's aggressive tendencies. Violence begets violence, however peaceful and altruistic the motivation.

The violent tendencies thus reinforced may well be turned against the parents, as in the case of Lizzie Borden. Although most intrafamily violence is less bloody than that attributed to Lizzie, some family abuse does go as far as ax murder. Examination of relationships between murderer and victim proves that the largest single category of victim is that of family member or relative.

Homicide at Home

The magnitude of family violence became particularly obvious during the summer heat wave of 1972. Page 1 of the July 22, 1972 *New York Times* carried an article describing the increase in murders during the previous few days of extreme heat in New York City and summarizing the statistics for murder in New York during the previous six months. Page 2 held an article totalling deaths in Northern Ireland during three and a half years of disturbances. About as many people were murdered by their relatives in one six-month period in New York City as had been killed in three and a half years of political upheaval in Northern Ireland.

Murder, though relatively rare, gets far more attention than less violent abuse. Even though more murders are committed on family members than any other type of person, and even though the United States has a high degree of homicide, the rate is still only four or five per 100,000 population. What about non-lethal physical violence between husband and wife? While accurate statistics are hard to find, one way of estimating the magnitude of the phenomenon is through the eyes of the police.

Just as relatives are the largest single category of murder victim, so family fights are the largest single category of police calls. One legal researcher estimates that more police calls involve family conflict than do calls for all criminal incidents, including murders, rapes, non-family assaults, robberies and muggings. "Violence in the home" deserves at least as much public concern as "crime in the streets." The police hate and fear family conflict calls for several reasons. First, a family disturbance call lacks the glamour, prestige and public appreciation of a robbery or an accident summons. More important, such calls are extremely dangerous. Many a policeman coming to the aid of a wife who is being beaten has had a chair or a bottle thrown at him or has been stabbed or shot by a wife who suddenly becomes fearful of what is going to happen to her husband, or who abruptly turns her rage from her husband to the police. Twenty-two percent of all police fatalities come from investigating problems between husband and wife or parent and child.

One cannot tell from these data on police calls just what proportion of all husbands and wives have had physical fights, since it takes an unusual combination of events to have the police summoned. The closest published estimate is found in the research of George Levinger and John O'Brien. In studying applicants for divorce, O'Brien found that 17 percent of his cases spontaneously mentioned overt violent behavior, and Levinger found that 23 percent of the middle-class couples and 40 percent of the working-class couples gave "physical abuse" as a major complaint.

Both of these figures probably underestimate the amount of physical violence between husbands and wives because there may well have been violent incidents which were not mentioned or which were not listed as a main cause of divorce. Even doubling the figure, however, leaves us far from knowing the extent of husband-wife violence. First, there is a discrepancy between the O'Brien and the Levinger figures. Second, these figures apply only to couples who have applied for divorce. It may be that there is a lower incidence of physical violence among a cross-section of couples; or it may be, as we suspect, that the difference is not very great.

A survey conducted for the National Commission of the Causes and Prevention of Violence deals with what violence people would approve. These data show that one out of four men and one out of six women approve of slapping a wife under certain conditions. As for a wife slapping a husband, 26 percent of the men and 19 percent of the women approve. Of course, some people who approve of slapping will never do it and some who disapprove *will* slap—or worse. Probably the latter group is larger. If that is true, we know that husband-wife violence at the minimal level of slapping occurs in at least one quarter of American families.

Our own pilot studies also give some indication of the high rate of violence in the family. Richard Gelles of the University of New Hampshire, who has done a series of in-depth case studies of a sample of 80 families, found that about 56 percent of the couples have used physical force on each other at some time.

In a second study, freshman college students responded to a series of questions about conflicts which occurred in their senior year in high school, and to further questions about how these conflicts were handled. Included in the conflict resolution section were questions on whether or not the parties to the disputes had ever hit, pushed, shoved, thrown things or kicked each other in the course of a quarrel.

The results show that during that one year 62 percent of the high school seniors had used physical force on a brother or sister and 16 percent of their parents had used physical force on each other. Since these figures are for a single year, the percentage who had *ever* used violence is probably much greater. How much greater is difficult to estimate because we cannot simply accumulate the 16 percent for one year over the total number of years married. Some couples will never have used violence and others will have used it repeatedly. Nevertheless, it seems safe to assume that it will not always be the same 16 percent. So, it is probably best to fall back on the 56 percent estimate from the 80 earlier interviews.

The fact is that almost all everyday beating, slapping, kicking and throwing things is carried out by normal Americans rather than deranged persons.

Since a vast amount of family violence can be documented, what accounts for the myth of family nonviolence? At least one basis for the rosy, if false, view is that the family is a tremendously important social institution, which must be preserved. In Western countries one supportive device is the ideology of familial love and gentleness, an ideology which helps encourage people to marry and to stay married. It tends to maintain satisfaction with the family system despite the stresses and strains of family life. From the viewpoint of preserving the integrity of a critical social institution, such a mythology is highly useful.

Other simplifications and generalizations also block knowledge and understanding of the nature of violence in the family. The psychopathology myth, the class myth, the sex myth and the catharsis myth must be exposed and examined if the true nature of intrafamily abuse is to emerge.

A growing number of sociologists and psychologists have suggested that a focus on conflict and violence may be a more revealing way of understanding the family than a focus on consensus and solidarity. Most members of this group, however, recognize that family conflict is legitimate, but still consider physical violence only as an abnormality—something which involves sick families. The facts do not support this *psychopathology myth*. According to Richard J. Gelles, only a tiny proportion of those using violence—even child abusers—can be considered mentally ill. Our own studies reveal that physically abusive husbands, wives and children are of overwhelmingly sound mind and body.

The fact that almost all family violence, including everyday beating, slapping, kicking and throwing things, is carried out by normal everyday Americans rather than deranged persons should not lead us to think of violence as being desirable or even acceptable. The important question is, Why is physical violence so common between members of the closest and most intimate of all human groups?

Although social scientists are still far from a full understanding of the causes of violence between family members, evidence is accumulating that family violence is learned—and learned in childhood in the home. This fact does not deny the importance of the human biological heritage. If the capacity for violence were not present in the human organism, learning and social patterning could not produce it.

If a child actually observes and experiences the effects of violence, he will learn to be violent. Husbands, wives and parents play out models of behavior which they learned in childhood from *their* parents and from friends and relatives. Rather than being deviant, they are conforming to patterns learned in childhood. Of course, in most cases they also learned the opposite message—that

family violence is wrong. However, a message learned by experience and observation, rather than the message learned Sunday-school-style, has more force, especially when social stresses become great—and family stresses are often very great. The high level of interaction and commitment which is part of the pleasure of family life also produces great tensions.

Another widespread but hard-to-prove belief is the *class myth*, the idea that intrafamily violence occurs mainly in lower- and working-class families. Studying divorce applicants, George Levinger found that 40 percent of the working-class wives and 23 percent of the middle-class wives indicated "physical abuse" as a reason for seeking divorce. If almost one out of four middle-class women can report physical abuse, violence hardly seems absent from middle-class families. The nationwide sample survey conducted for the United States Commission on Violence reveals that over one-fifth of the respondents approve of slapping a spouse under certain conditions. There were no social-class differences in this *approval* of slapping, nor in reports of having ever spanked a child. At the same time, almost twice as many less educated respondents spank *frequently* (42 percent) as more educated respondents (22 percent).

Class Differences

Other research on physical punishment is also contradictory. Most studies report more use of physical punishment by working-class parents, but some find no difference. Howard S. Erlanger undertook a comprehensive review of studies of social-class differences in the use of physical punishment and concluded that, although the weight of the evidence supports the view of less use of this technique among the middle class, the differences are small. Sizeable differences between social classes show up only when the analysis takes into account differences within social classes of such things as race, the sex of the child and of the parent, parental ambition for the child and the specific nature of the father's occupation. Differences *within* social classes are at least as important as differences *between* classes.

Despite the mixed evidence, and despite the fact that there is a great deal of violence in middle-class families, we believe that research will eventually show that intrafamily violence is more common as one goes down the socioeconomic status ladder. Many social scientists attribute this to a lower-class "culture of violence" which encourages violent acts, and to an opposite middle-class culture which condemns violence. Although these cultural elements are well documented, we see them not as a cause, but as a response to fundamental social structural forces which affect families at all social levels but press harder and more frequently on the lower and working classes.

3. CHANGE AS A FUNCTION OF RELATIONSHIPS

Compensatory Violence

Willingness and ability to use physical violence may compensate for lack of other resources such as money, knowledge and respect. If the social system does not provide an individual with the resources needed to maintain his or her family position, that individual will use violence if he is capable of it. John E. O'Brien asserts that "... there is considerable evidence that ... husbands who ... displayed violent behavior were severely inadequate in work, earner, or family support roles." While lack of the occupational and economic resources needed to fulfill the position of husband in our society is more characteristic of lower-class families than others, it is by no means confined to that stratum. The 1970-72 recession, with its high rates of unemployment among middle-class occupational groups (such as aerospace engineers) provides an opportunity to test this theory. The *resource theory* of violence would predict that unemployed husbands would engage in more intrafamily violence than comparable middle-class husbands who have not lost their jobs.

Some indication that the predicted results might be found is suggested by statistics for Birmingham, England, which showed a sharp rise in wife-beating during a six-month period when unemployment also rose sharply. A 1971 *Parade* report characterized these men as "frustrated, bored, unable to find a satisfying outlet for their energy, Britishers who are reduced to life on the dole meet adversity like men: they blame it on their wives. Then, pow!!!"

In a society such as ours, in which aggression is defined as a normal response to frustration, we can expect that the more frustrating the familial and occupational roles, the greater the amount of violence. Donald McKinley found that the lower the degree of self-direction a man has in his work, the greater the degree of aggressiveness in his relationship with his son. McKinley's data

also show that the lower the job satisfaction, the higher the percentage using harsh punishment of children. The same relationship was found within each social class.

Both husbands and wives suffer from frustration, but since the main avenue of achievement for women has been in the family rather than in occupational roles, we must look within the family for the circumstances that are frustrating to women. Both residential crowding and too many children have been found to be related to the use of physical punishment. As with men, frustrations of this type are more common in the lower class, since lower-class wives are unlikely to have sufficient equipment and money for efficient, convenient housekeeping.

Although intrafamily violence probably is more common among lower-class families, it is incorrect to see it as only a lower-class or working-class phenomenon. What we have called the class myth overlooks the basic structural conditions (such as lack of adequate resources and frustrating life experiences) which are major causes of intrafamily violence and are present at all social levels, though to varying degrees. Some kinds of intrafamily violence are typical of all social classes—such as hitting children—even though the rate may be lower for middle class—while other kinds of intrafamily violence are typical of *neither* class—like severe wife-beating—even though the rate is probably greater for the working class and especially the lower class.

The *sex myth* is the idea that sexual drives are linked to violence by basic biological mechanisms developed in the course of human evolution. Violence in sex is directly related to violence in the family because the family is the main way in which sex is made legitimate. To the extent that there is an inherent connection between sex and violence, it would be part of the biological basis for violence within the family.

There is abundant evidence that sex and violence go together, at least in our society and in a number of others. At the extreme, sex and warfare have been associated in many ways, ranging from societies which view sex before a battle as a source of strength (or in some tribes, as a weakness) to the almost universally high frequency of rape by soldiers, often accompanied by subsequent genital mutilation and murder. In the fighting following the independence of the Congo in the early 1960s, rape was so common that the Catholic church is said to have given a special dispensation so that nuns could take contraceptive pills. More recently, in the Pakistan civil war, rape and mutilation were everyday occurrences. In Vietnam, scattered reports suggest that rapes and sexual tortures have been widespread. Closer to home, we have the romantic view of the aggressive he-man who "takes his woman" as portrayed in westerns and James Bond-type novels. In both cases, sex and gunfights are liberally intertwined.

Frustrated, bored, unable to find a satisfying outlet for their energy Britishers who are reduced to life on the dole meet adversity like men: they blame it on their wives. Then, pow!!!

Sexual Repression

Then there are the sadists and masochists—individuals who can obtain sexual pleasure only by inflicting or receiving violent acts. We could dismiss such people as pathological exceptions, but it seems better to consider sadism and masochism as simply extreme forms of widespread behavior. The sex act itself typically is accompanied at least by mild violence and often by biting and scratching.

Nevertheless, despite all of this and much other evidence which could be cited, we feel that there is little biological linkage between sex and violence. It is true that in our society and in many other societies, sex and violence are linked. But there are enough instances of societies in which this is not the case to raise doubts about the biological linkage. What social conditions produce the association between violence and sex?

The most commonly offered explanation attributes the linkage between sex and violence to rules of the culture which limit or prevent sex. Empirical evidence supporting this sexual repression theory is difficult to establish. Societies which are high in restriction of extramarital intercourse are also societies which tend to be violent—particularly in emphasizing military glory, killing, torture and mutilation of an enemy. But just how this carries over to violence in the sex act is not clear. Our interpretation hinges on the fact that sexual restriction tends to be associated with a definition of sex as intrinsically evil. This combination sets in motion two powerful forces making sex violent in societies having such a sexual code. First, since sex is normally prohibited or restricted, engaging in sexual intercourse may imply license to disregard other normally prohibited or restricted aspects of interpersonal relations. Consequently, aggressively inclined persons will tend to express their aggressiveness when they express their sexuality. Second, since sex is defined as evil and base, this cultural definition of sex may create a label or an expectancy which tends to be acted out.

By contrast, in societies such as Mangaia, which impose minimal sex restrictions and in which sex is defined as something to be enjoyed by all from the time they are first capable until death, sex is nonviolent. In Mangaia, exactly the opposite of the two violence-producing mechanisms just listed seem to operate. First, since sex is a normal everyday activity, the normal standards for control of aggression apply. Second, since sex is defined as an act expressing the best in man, it is an occasion for altruistic behavior. Thus, Donald S. Marshall says of the Mangaia: "My several informants generally agreed that the really important thing in sexual intercourse—for the married man or for his unwed fellow—was to give pleasure to his partner; that her pleasure in orgasm was what

gave the male partner a special thrill, separate from his own orgasm."

There is little evidence to show direct linkage between sex and violence. It is true that they are socially linked in many cultures, but there are enough societies where this is not the case to raise doubts about the biological linkage.

Socially patterned antagonism between men and women is at the heart of a related theory which can also account for the association of sex and violence. The sex antagonism and segregation theory suggests that the higher the level of antagonism between men and women, the greater the tendency to use violence in sexual acts. Since, by itself, this statement is open to a charge of circular reasoning, the theory must be backed up by related propositions which account for the sex role antagonism.

In societies such as ours, part of the explanation for antagonism between the sexes is probably traceable to the sexual restrictions and sexual denigration mentioned above. The curse God placed on all women when Eve sinned is the earliest example in our culture of the sexually restrictive ethic, the placing of the "blame" for sex on women, and the resulting negative definition of women—all of which tend to make women culturally legitimate objects of antagonism and aggression. The New Testament reveals much more antipathy to sex than the Old and contains many derogatory (and implicitly hostile) statements about women.

The present level of antagonism between the sexes is probably at least as great as that in biblical times. In novels, biographies and everyday speech, words indicating femaleness, especially in its sexual aspect (such as "bitch"), are used by men as terms of disparagement, and terms for sexual intercourse, such as "screw" and "fuck," are used to indicate an aggressive or harmful act. On the female side, women tend to see men as exploiters and to teach their daughters that men are out to take advantage of them.

It would be a colossal example of ethnocentrism, however, to attribute antagonism between the sexes to the Western Judeo-Christian tradition. Cultural definitions of women as evil are found in many societies. Obviously, more fundamental processes are at work, of which the Christian tradition is only one manifestation.

3. CHANGE AS A FUNCTION OF RELATIONSHIPS

Catharsis Myth

A clue to a possibly universal process giving rise to antagonism between the sexes may be found in the cross-cultural studies which trace this hostility back to the division of labor between the sexes and other differences in the roles of men and women. This sex role segregation, gives rise to differences in child-rearing practices for boys and girls and to problems in establishing sexual identity. Beatrice Whiting, for example, concludes: "It would seem as if there were a never-ending circle. The separation of the sexes leads to a conflict of identity in the boy children, to unconscious fear of being feminine, which leads to protest masculinity, exaggeration of the differences between men and women, antagonism against and fear of women, male solidarity, and hence back to isolation of women and very young children." This process can also be observed in the matrifocal family of the urban slum and the Caribbean, the relationships between the sexes have been labeled by Jackson Toby as "compulsive masculinity" and vividly depicted in Eldridge Cleaver's "Allegory of the Black Eunuchs." Slightly more genteel forms of the same sexual antagonism are to be found among middle-class men, as illustrated by the character of Jonathan in the movie *Carnal Knowledge*.

Obviously, the linkages between sex and violence are extremely complex, and many other factors probably operate besides the degree of restrictiveness, the cultural definition of sexuality and antagonism between the sexes. But even these indicate sufficiently that it is incorrect to assume a direct connection between sexual drives and violence, since such an assumption disregards the sociocultural framework within which sexual relations take place. These social and cultural factors, rather than sex drives *per se*, give rise to the violent aspects of sexuality in so many societies.

The *catharsis myth* asserts that the expression of "normal" aggression between family members should not be bottled up: if normal aggression is allowed to be expressed, tension is released, and the likelihood of severe violence is therefore reduced. This view has a long and distinguished intellectual history. Aristotle used the term "catharsis" to refer to the purging of the passions or sufferings of spectators through vicarious participation in the suffering of a tragic hero. Both Freud's idea of "the liberation of affect" to enable reexperiencing blocked or inhibited emotions, and the view of John Dollard and his associates that "the occurrence of any act of aggression is assumed to reduce the instigation of aggression" are modern versions of this tradition.

Applying this approach to the family, Bettelheim urges that children should learn about violence in order to learn how to handle it. Under the present rules (at least for the middle class), we forbid a child to hit, yell or swear at us or his playmates. The child must also refrain from destroying property or even his own toys. In teaching this type of self-control, however, Bruno Bettelheim holds that we have denied the child outlets for the instinct of human violence and have failed to teach him how to deal with his violent feelings.

Proof of the catharsis theory is overwhelmingly negative. Exposure to vicariously experienced violence has been shown to increase rather than decrease both aggressive fantasy and aggressive acts. Similarly, experiments in which children are given the opportunity to express violence and aggression show that they express more aggression after the purported cathartic experience than do controls.

Theoretical arguments against the catharsis view are equally cogent. The instinct theory assumptions which underlie the idea of catharsis have long been discarded in social science. Modern social psychological theories—including social learning theory, symbolic interaction theory and labeling theory—all predict the opposite of the catharsis theory: the more frequently an act is performed, the greater the likelihood that it will become a standard part of the behavior repertory of the individual and of the expectations of others for that individual.

Cultural Beliefs

In light of largely negative evidence and cogent theoretical criticism, the sheer persistence of the catharsis theory becomes an interesting phenomenon. There seem to be several factors underlying the persistence of the catharsis myth:

□ *Prestige and influence of psychoanalytic theory*. Albert Bandura and Richard Walters suggest that the persistence of the catharsis view is partly the result of the extent to which psychoanalytic ideas have become part of both social science and popular culture. Granting this, one must also ask why this particular part of Freud's vast writing is unquestioned. After all, much of what Freud wrote has been ignored, and other parts have been dropped on the basis of contrary evidence.

Whenever an element of cultural belief persists in spite of seemingly sound reasons for discarding it, one should look for ways in which the belief may be woven into a system of social behavior. Certain behavior may be least partially congruent with the "false" belief; various social patterns may be justified by such beliefs.

□ *Justification of existing patterns*. Intrafamily violence is a recurring feature of our society, despite the cultural commitment to nonviolence. It is not far-fetched to assume that, under the circumstances, the catharsis theory which in effect justifies sporadic violence will be attractive to a population engaged in occasional violence.

☐ *Congruence with the positive value of violence in non-family spheres of life.* Although *familial* norms deprecate or forbid intrafamily violence, the larger value system of American society is hardly nonviolent. In fact, the overwhelming proportion of American parents consider it part of their role to train sons to be tough. The violence commission survey reveals that 70 percent of the respondents believed it is good for boys to have a few fist-fights. Thus, a social theory which justifies violence as being psychologically beneficial to the aggressor is likely to be well received.

☐ *Congruence with the way familial violence often occurs.* Given the antiviolence norms, intrafamily physical abuse typically occurs as a climax to a repressed conflict. As Louis Coser points out:

> Closely knit groups in which there exists a high frequency of interaction and high personality involvement of the members have a tendency to suppress conflict. While they provide frequent occasions for hostility (since both sentiments of love and hatred are intensified through frequency of interaction), the acting out of such feelings is sensed as a danger to such intimate relationships, and hence there is a tendency to suppress rather than to allow expression of hostile feelings. In close-knit groups, feelings of hostility tend, therefore, to accumulate and hence to intensify.

At some point the repressed conflict has to be resolved. Frequently, the mechanism which forces the conflict into the open is a violent outburst. This is one of the social functions of violence listed by Coser. In this sense, intrafamily violence does have a cathartic effect. But the catharsis which takes place comes from getting the conflict into the open and resolving it—not the releasing effects of violent incidents *per se*, but on the ability to recognize these as warning signals and to deal with the underlying conflict honestly and with empathy.

☐ *Confusion of immediate with long-term effects.* There can be little doubt that a sequence of violent activity is often followed by a sharp reduction of tension, an emotional release and even a feeling of quiescence. To the extent that tension release *is* produced by violence, this immediate cathartic effect is likely to powerfully reinforce the violence which preceded it. Having reduced tension in one instance, it becomes a mode of behavior likely to be repeated later in similar instances. An analogy with sexual orgasm seems plausible. Following orgasm, there is typically a sharp reduction in sexual drive, most obvious in the male's loss of erection. At the same time, however, the experience of orgasm is powerfully reinforcing and has the long-term effect of increasing the sex drive. We believe that violence and sex are similar in this respect. The short-term effect of violence is, in one sense, cathartic; but the long-term effect is a powerful force toward including violence as a standard mode of social interaction.

While the assumptions outlined in this article in some ways contribute to preserving the institution of family, they also keep us from taking a hard and realistic look at the family and taking steps to change it in ways which might correct the underlying problems. Such stereotypes contain a kernel of truth but are dangerous oversimplifications. Although there are differences between social classes in intrafamily violence, the class myth ignores the high level of family violence present in other social strata. The sex myth, although based on historically accurate observation of the link between sex and violence, tends to assume that this link is biologically determined and fails to take into account the social and cultural factors which associate sex and violence in many societies. The catharsis myth seems to have the smallest kernel of truth at its core, and its persistence, in the face of devastating evidence to the contrary, may be due to the subtle justification it gives to the violent nature of American society and to the fact that violent episodes in a family can have the positive function of forcing a repressed conflict into the open for nonviolent resolution.

Battered Women

Marina had been home from the hospital for only two days after giving birth to her second child when her husband, an unemployed drug addict, stumbled into the bedroom and began to beat her and kick her in the stomach. Several weeks later, he was at it again—this time pummeling her head and face with his fists. Bruised and shaken, Marina fled to the Washington, D.C., Citizens Complaint Center, where an assistant U.S. attorney declined to press criminal charges because there was no evidence of a dangerous weapon. A sympathetic social worker and lawyer spent hours phoning local agencies trying to find temporary shelter for Marina and her children. There was no space. "We had to send her right back to the same place where she had been beaten and brutalized," said Nancy Dorsch, an assistant corporation counsel. "I felt like a rat."

Marina is one of thousands of women who are regularly beaten, tortured and sometimes killed by their husbands and boyfriends. But she is one of the few who tried to seek help. Traditionally, battered women have suffered in silence— gagged by the shame of the admission, the fear of losing financial support and the indifference of a judicial system that is reluctant to interfere in family disputes. Now, prompted by the feminist movement, women are beginning to speak out about bedroom brutality. The incidence of wife-beating is not necessarily on the rise, but the protests of the women are starting to attract attention to the problem and stir some change in its treatment. Police departments are attempting to re-educate cops on the beat. Social workers and women's groups are establishing "hot lines" and "rap sessions" to offer aid to women in danger. And feminists are campaigning for emergency havens to shelter the victims and their children.

Alcoholism: Considered by law-enforcement officials to be the single "most unreported" crime in the country, wife-beating is almost impossible to document since it is often listed under "assault and battery" or "disputes." But as special-interest groups begin to investigate the violence, much of it the result of alcoholism and drug abuse, their findings are astonishing. In Dade County, Fla., the Citizens Dispute Settlement Center has handled nearly 1,000 cases involving beatings of women since last May, and a wife-abuse task force in Montgomery County, Md., one of the nation's most

affluent areas, reported an estimated 650 incidents of assault by husbands in a year.

"Wife-beating has been categorized as a lower-class crime, but that's wrong," says commander Joseph DiLeonardi, head of the homicide/sex division of the Chicago police department. "A lot of men are under the same frustrations whether they're rich or poor." Enid Keljik, now an administrative assistant on Wall Street, was beaten by her husband, a restaurateur, over a three-year period—but never dared admit it. "It was just something nice people don't do," she says.

But in all classes, the plight of the battered woman remains suspended in bureaucratic red tape and the historical concept of women as men's property. Complaints about police indifference abound. "The police don't seem able to differentiate between a woman in danger and a woman just trying to put a scare into her spouse," says Brooklyn divorce attorney Marjory D. Fields, who estimates that about 40 per cent of her 700

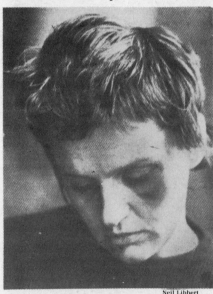

Neil Libbert

Casualty: A London victim

low-income clients have been beaten.

To combat the problem, several police departments are now forming family-crisis-intervention units. In Atlanta, cops are taught through role-playing to defuse family fights by projecting a calm, mediating force rather than the aggressive posture of an arresting officer. In Hayward, Calif., three-year-old Project

Outreach has teamed family counselors with police, thereby reducing the recurrence of domestic-quarrel complaints from 50 per cent to 20 per cent.

Shunted: For those who seek court protection, there is little relief. State laws vary widely and women find themselves shunted between civil, criminal and family court—and often advised not to bring a complaint at all. In severe cases, the court will issue a restraining order forbidding the man to assault his wife again for a period of up to a year. If the order is violated, the woman can have the man arrested. If the wife has obtained an arrest warrant, however, the husband can be released on his own recognizance—to return home even madder.

Taking the situation into their own hands, women across the country have begun to lobby for funds to open emergency shelters for battered women and their children. While England has 28 such shelters with 83 more being formed, only a handful have opened in the U.S. One is Haven House in Los Angeles County, which has counseled 652 women since May 1974. The women are usually housewives with no job skills. "Their average age is 36," says director Ruth Slaughter. "They have been abused or beaten for years and they usually come to us after their husbands have threatened to kill them."

"When we were young, I thought things would change and I stayed with him," says Betsy Warrior, 35, a janitor in Boston who was 17 when her husband first hit her. "I was accustomed to seeing a certain amount of male hostility expressed toward women so I took it for granted." After years of being beaten, even during a pregnancy that produced a stillborn child, Betsy finally started assault proceedings. "If I had had some place to go," she says, "I think I would have left him years earlier."

Many battered women feel the same way. At New York City's AWAIC (Abused Women's Aid in Crisis), which opened last February, the "hot line" has pulled in more than 800 calls, even though the office is open two hours a day. And in Washington, D.C., 70 women recently called a referral number broadcast on a local television show on wife-beating. That was on a Saturday night. Monday morning, the hot line picked up 100 more calls from women who had memorized the number—then waited to call until their husbands were safely off to work.

The Battered Husbands

Wives aren't always the victims

A doctor in the Chicago area is severely beaten by his attorney wife once or twice a year. He keeps cosmetics at home and in his office to cover up the bruises and face bites. An Army veteran and multiple amputee living in Georgia says his wife routinely socks and kicks him "just for being so useless, I guess." A former Virginia television personality endured a 26-year marriage to a woman who regularly punched him in the groin and face while he was driving. Once she bashed his head open with two cans of Campbell's pepper-pot soup.

These men are all members in good standing of a newly recognized fraternity of victims: the battered husbands. Though jokes about rolling-pin-wielding wives have long been a male staple, researchers are now finding increasingly that such bittersweet humor is all too often a black-and-blue reality. Says University of Delaware Sociologist Suzanne Steinmetz: "The most unreported crime is not wife beating—it's husband beating."

Steinmetz is the author of a book on family fighting called *The Cycle of Violence*. Extrapolating from her studies of domestic quarreling in Delaware's New Castle County, she estimates that each year at least 250,000 American husbands are severely thrashed by their wives. University of New Hampshire Sociologist Murray Straus projects an equally grim picture of this battle of the sexes. On the basis of his 1976 national survey of violence in 2,143 representative American families, he concludes that about 2 million husbands and about the same number of wives commit at least one serious attack a year on their mates. These range from kicks, bites or punches to murderous assaults with knives and other deadly weapons. Says University of Rhode Island Sociologist Richard Gelles, another student of domestic combat: "Men and women have always been equal victims in family violence. Fifty percent of the killings are men. Fifty percent are women. That hasn't changed in at least 50 years."

Hard statistics are admittedly impossible to come by, and the estimates infuriate some feminists, who feel that these figures distract from what they believe with considerable justice to be the far more serious problem of the battered wife. Indeed, it is women who are usually on the receiving end of the worst batterings in the home. Says Straus: "When there is a fight, the woman, on the average, comes out the loser."

Yet both Steinmetz and Straus point out that women are as prone as men to use violence on their mates. Whatever the result, most battered wives—and husbands—fight back. But about 600,000 husbands and 600,000 wives do not retaliate.

Some of the pummeled husbands are too old or sick to defend themselves, but most are able bodied. One type of victim is the baffled he-man who is afraid of unleashing his own violence. Says Steinmetz: "There is a feeling among beaten men: 'If I ever let go I would kill her.'" Another type is the passive, dependent man who has sought out a strong wife to shield him from worldly problems. Barbara Star, a professor of social work at the University of Southern California, finds that battered spouses are usually people who feel overwhelmed by life, repress all strong feelings and tend to blame themselves for whatever goes wrong. Most, she explains, are convinced that fighting back is useless.

At first battered husbands may overlook their wives' occasional outbursts of physical punishment and simply hope they blow over. But before long a flurry of wifely fists is part of the domestic routine. Says Family Therapist Norman Paul of Boston: "They think their wives' violence is part of family life. They have come to accept it." Paralyzed by shame and guilt, they are reluctant to seek help from anyone—family, friends, counselors or the cops. Explains Steinmetz: "Police are a symbol of manhood, and it is simply too much to approach a policeman and say, 'The little woman has just beaten me up.'"

Nor are the courts likely to seem helpful. When the Virginia TV personality, now divorced, finally retaliated and knocked his wife unconscious with a single punch, he was ostracized as a wife beater, lost his TV show and was ordered by the court to stay away from his home for three months. Says Straus: "Some people figure it would be worse if they hit back. They need the good things the marriage has to offer and put up with the violence because they don't have much alternative." Others restrain themselves because they have been brought up never to strike a woman. One such husband, says Gelles, was so determined not to strike back that "he virtually gave her a license to kill him."

Many battered men manage to convince themselves that their marriages are sound and their beatings are trivial. The British social worker Erin Pizzey, founder of a refuge for battered women in London, notes that abused men are so good at self-deception that they often refuse to acknowledge the beatings at all. "Mostly they don't see themselves on the receiving end," she adds, "even though they're scratched and bitten or hit by instruments." In fact, she says, many of the men who show up at her center are originally reported as wife beaters, but turn out to be beaten husbands.

Though only a few men are now willing to seek aid, some social agencies believe that the beaten male needs the same kind of counseling and support as that given to abused women. Adina Weiner, chief counselor at Atlanta's Council on Battered Women, even wants to change the name of her group to the Council on Battered People. Pizzey set up a house for battered men in London. She had to close it last year for lack of funds, but hopes to open another, staffed by nuns (because she feels they would be especially sympathetic). Says Pizzey: "These men are frightened by women. They need gentleness."

4 Termination of Relationships

Most of us are familiar with the myth of marriage: the handsome young man falls in love with the beautiful young girl; he kneels and asks for her hand in marriage; they vow to honor and cherish until death do them part; and they live happily ever after with their obedient, pink-cheeked children.

But we learn very little about those frightening things that aren't supposed to happen such as death, separation, and divorce. And the less we know, the less capable we are of dealing with them when they do occur. And occur they do—nine out of ten of us will marry, at least one third of us will divorce, and all of us will die.

Usually accompanying termination of relationships are feelings of guilt, hurt and anger, loneliness, and anxiety. Anxiety, for example, often arises after the death of someone close if conflicts have remained unresolved. Investigators, particularly Dr. Elizabeth Kubler-Ross, have identified five stages that people who are dying often experience. These five stages—denial, anger, bargaining, depression, and finally, acceptance—can probably be generalized to any extremely negative situation or disaster, and often can help explain how to deal with the termination of a relationship.

The various aspects of terminating relationships are examined in this section. It includes a discussion of divorce both from the personal level (what kinds of traits are common to those who divorce), and the social level (to what extent is divorce socially contagious.) Also explored in this section are the different alternatives regarding the care of the children of divorced parents. Finally, selections that concern aging and coping with death conclude this section.

Looking Ahead: Challenge Questions

What constraints does society place on its members about expressing their feelings when relationships end?

Can rituals help ease sorrow? How?

What might be done to help ease the pain of divorce for the couple involved and their children?

To what extent is our high divorce rate due to personal traits, breakdown in interpersonal relationships, and/or societal changes?

What are the advantages and disadvantages of various options for care of the elderly in our society?

PERSONALITY & DIVORCE

Jack Horn

Jack Horn is an associate editor of Psychology Today.

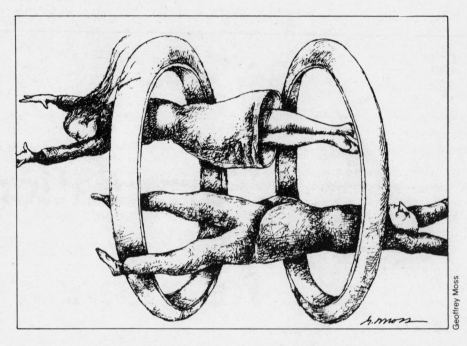

Geoffrey Moss

IS DIVORCE A SIGN of personal weakness and failure? Or is it an indication of strength and independence which reveals basic weaknesses in marriage itself?

Tsipora Peskin of the University of California's Institute of Human Development in Berkeley has taken data from a long-range study started by the Institute 40 years ago to examine the paths young men and women follow on their way to marriage and divorce. Institute researchers observed a group of Berkeley girls and boys born between 1928 and 1930 over a long period, interviewing them every six months until the age of 17.

Based on the interviews, psychologists rated the adolescents' personality and behavioral traits, using the California Q-sort method. In the Q sort, a rater takes 100 statements describing traits and behaviors and puts them in order from the most to the least characteristic of the person being studied. The result is a picture of the individual's personality, intellectual development, and other characteristics.

Institute researchers interviewed the same people again in 1960 and 1970, when they were about 30 and 40 years old, to see what had happened to them. Peskin analyzed this information for differences among the men and women who were still married, were divorced, or had never married. She found little to distinguish the 46 married men from the 17 who were divorced, but she uncovered considerable difference between them and the eight unmarried men.

As adolescents, the singles had been rated as less compliant and conventional, more independent and negativistic than the others. The married and divorced men had been seen as more gregarious, warm and giving, more liked and more liking than those who never married.

The women presented a different picture. The eight single women were indistinguishable as adolescents from the later-divorced or married, but the 58 married and 15 divorced women were markedly different from each other. The married ones had been described as more productive, ambitious, and prone to intellectual pursuits, and, at the same time, as more submissive and conventional. The later-divorced adolescents had been rated as more nonconforming, rebellious, negativistic, and self-indulgent. This constellation of traits, Peskin believes, relates to a quest for personal development and identity.

She interprets these sex differences between married and divorced people as reflecting the fact that marriage is two worlds, his and hers. Men and women reach these worlds by different developmental paths.

Traditionally, marriage has been the most important part of a woman's life, the main job even if she works outside the home. Men, in contrast, have been taught to see marriage as merely a companion to their career and other interests. Peskin illustrates the point by quoting a career woman on her impending marriage: "I have to cut down *my* work to build *our* relationship."

In preparing for marriage, women learn to merge seemingly contradictory traits: being productive and aspiring, on one hand, and submissive on the other. Peskin puts it this way: "The narcissism of the self...is transformed to the narcissism for the marriage. Of all the resources that one might think of as helping to sustain marriage, this changeover...may be the most important. It is not for herself any longer but for her marriage that the woman prepares herself to be capable and accomplished." Women who can't or won't make this switch are strong candidates for divorce.

Peskin found support for her interpretation by comparing adolescent Q-sort ratings of the most happily married women with those whose marriages had lasted less than two years. The happiest wives had been rated lowest in self-assertion and independence, most submissive and conventional, and least self-indulgent. Women who divorced quickly scored at the opposite end of the scale on these traits, leading Peskin to conclude that "quests for personal identity and happy marriage follow very different life paths."

Married and divorced men didn't show this same personality split in adolescence. Their preparation for marriage did not require them to make the young woman's choice between what Peskin calls "personal growth and relationship-making."

As a result, personality differences had little effect on the success or failure of the men's marriages. For them, golden anniversaries or early divorces depended on other factors, such as economic success, job satisfaction, and their wives' forbearance.

The ground rules for marriage and divorce change with the times. The men and women Peskin studied grew up in a world much different from today's. The women's movement, more available abortion, equal pay, no-fault divorce, and other changes create a different climate for marriage itself and for the way young men and women grow up preparing for it. Exactly how this climate will affect marriage is a guess. That it will be affected is suggested by another study.

Peskin compared the 152 individuals in the Berkeley group with a similar group from Oakland, California, also studied by the Institute of Human Development. These men and women were 10 years older than the Berkeley sample. They were adolescents during the Depression of the 1930s; the Berkeley group grew up during the prosperous 1940s. The divorced and married women in the two groups were much the same. Those with a strong push for personal development got divorced, while those who developed a "narcissism for marriage" stayed married

The men, affected much more by the disparate economic climates of the two eras, were quite different. While it was hard to tell the Berkeley adolescents who would eventually get divorced from those who stayed married, their Oakland counterparts were different types. The Oakland adolescents who were rated high in personal competence, risk-taking and self-confidence were likely to get divorced, while the men who were rated as dependent, indecisive, and uncomfortable with complexity were likely to stay married.

Peskin concludes that the Oakland men who grew up in the Depression learned to look upon marriage as a refuge from the failure they faced in the outside world. The young men who grew up in the 1940s (the Berkeley group) developed a freer, less dependent attitude toward marriage, reflecting the optimistic mood of the times.

It seems likely that today's sweeping changes in attitudes of women and attitudes toward women will have a similar strong effect on how both sexes learn to regard marriage and the parts they play in a relationship.

Is Divorce Contagious?

Sally Wendkos Olds

How to keep your marriage together when everybody else's is breaking up.

In the Long Island suburb where I live, there is a winding street that looks much like many other streets in many other towns. The maple trees that were young and spindly ten years ago now shade the children careening down sidewalks on skateboards. The houses, surrounded by trim lawns, alternate among three styles of split-level construction, their identifying numbers spelled out in neat script over garage doors.

In other respects, too, this street is like many others around the country. Of the 15 couples who moved into the brand-new houses ten years ago, only nine are still married to each other. The other six marriages have broken up, one after another, like falling dominoes. People who still live on this street joke about the dangers of "catching it"—the divorce fever that seems to pick off marriages like some medieval plague. But underneath the banter is a chilling thought: If it happened to them, will it happen to us?

For it's happening to marriages in suburbs, in little towns, in big cities all over America. It's happening to marriages in every ethnic group, every economic stratum, every social level. Over the past 12 years, the number of divorces has doubled, reaching an all-time high of over a million in 1975. It is projected that half the marriages celebrated today will undergo a separation, and one out of three will end in divorce.

What is happening with divorce in our country? Is it contagious? Is a sociological chain reaction involved? Sociologist Dwight Dean of Iowa State University thinks so. He plotted the incidence of divorces in one Midwestern city and found what he calls a "measles pattern." Several blocks would have no divorces, then sud-denly there would be three or four in one block.

Amazingly, no one else seems to have studied the ways by which the ripples from one divorce may spread out to lap at other marriages. If any research literature exists on this subject, it is unknown to authorities at the American Sociological Association, the American Psychological Association, the National Council on Family Relations or the United States Census Bureau.

Yet all the experts I spoke to concede that the more people travel in circles where divorce is common, the more likely they are to sunder their own marriages.

Ben, 40, says, "Two years ago, when my wife went back to school for her master's degree, she told me that one-third of her class was divorced. I said, "Hey, is divorce a course requirement, or something you catch in graduate school? We used to joke about it. But ever since she kicked me out of the house so she could find herself, it's not so funny any more."

Sociologist Marvin Sussman has conducted extensive studies of people in the process of separation and divorce. "My gut feeling," says Dr. Sussman, chairman of the department of medical social science and marital health of the Bowman-Gray School of Medicine in North Carolina, "is that people don't break up intimate relationships just on the ground that 'Gee whiz, Mary's doing it—why don't I?' Nevertheless, a kind of group principle *is* in operation. For example, studies of working mothers have shown that their problems vary depending on where they live. When the working mother is an accepted part of the community lifestyle, she has group support, feels less guilty and does very well with her kids."

He suspects the same principle may apply to divorce. If people don't get snubbed, or fired from their jobs when they divorce, there's less pressure against it. Says Dr. Sussman: "Where divorce is a sizable minority phenomenon, and you can find other people you can share your problems with, the contagious principle may be operating to make divorce a more possible option."

And there is less pressure against divorce today in almost all sectors of society. True, the romantic, idealized version of marriage still exists; we are essentially a religious, marriage-centered, happy-ending-loving country. But increasingly, we consider it sensible and proper to get out of an intolerable union. Even in "Can This Marriage Be Saved?", this magazine's most popular feature, separation is sometimes seen as the best solution.

In the news, divorce is commonplace. Betty Ford and Nelson Rockefeller, both divorced, brought the issue to the threshold of the nation's highest office. The pediatrician of us all—Dr. Benjamin Spock—dissolved his marriage of 48 years in search of a more rewarding one. Advice columnist Ann Landers shocked her millions of newspaper readers when she announced that her 36-year marriage had joined the divorce statistics she once had only written about.

"Hard to resist"

In certain circles divorce has even become chic. Cathy, 35 whose marriage broke up after 11 years, says, "It's almost as if you have to keep up with what everyone else is doing. First you feel you should have multiple orgasms because everybody else is having them. Then you need a couple of affairs. Then a part-time job, then a full-time career. And then, to be up to date, you have to have a divorce. You feel maybe you're missing something, some special experience that all these other people have gone through. And you keep telling yourself, "I shouldn't be influenced by this. This isn't the way I want to live my life.' But it's all around you—and it's sometimes hard to resist."

The arguments for divorce are part of our current rhetoric, and there is surely truth in those arguments for many people: To attempt to establish interminable peace is to move towards deadness. Children are often better off with one reasonably satisfied parent than in a home filled with discord. Self-actualization for both sexes is a legitimate goal.

As further encouragement, all sorts of

From *Ladies' Home Journal*, February 1977. ©1977 LHJ Publishing, Inc. Reprinted with permission of the author and LADIES' HOME JOURNAL.

societal supports are springing up for the formerly married. No suburban adult education brochure is complete without its course on "Going It Alone." Of nine parent counseling workshops offered by one suburban child guidance association, five deal with divorce. A writer forms The National Association of Divorced Women. Divorced Catholics form their own group. Books on divorce abound. A therapist produces a cassette series to comfort distraught people in the throes of separation.

Even some professional counselors encourage change. A few years ago, Diane and Ed went into therapy separately. "Since both our therapists had been divorced," Diane says now, "I wonder whether they may have been subtly leading us in the direction of splitting rather than staying together. I also think that seeing that these two psychologists could leave their marriages and come through okay made us feel we could do it, too."

Seeing that people could leave their marriages and come through okay . . . The women's movement has been criticized for just this "role-model" element of divorce contagion. "Those women are sitting around in their groups selling discontent and divorce to each other," charges one separated man. Counters Elizabeth Spalding, former coordinator of the marriage and divorce task force of the National Organization for Women, "The women's movement didn't create bad marriages. What it may have done is help a woman define what had already troubled her in marriage and gave her the support to get out of it."

Social set role

Whether or not the women's movement bears a major responsibility for the divorce statistics, some believe that divorce is especially communicable when people have a strong tie to the group, when their fundamental loyalty is not to the spouse but to the social set. As New York psychiatrist Stephen L. Zaslow explains, some people seem to get married because all their friends are getting married and stay together because everyone in the group is doing the same thing at the same time in life. When one marriage in this kind of close group cracks, the fissure spreads and you hear of cases such as that of three friends who graduated from school together, got married within months of each other, wheeled their babies around together and are now using the same divorce lawyer.

The heady excitement that seems to surround the newly separated person can be seductive. Divorce, we think—overlooking the anguish we know is there—is being on one's own after years of having to consider another person's preferences,

moods, idiosyncrasies. Divorce is getting to know new sexual partners after years of getting to know every curve and wrinkle and mole on one person's body. Divorce is showing the world how independent you are, that you are the kind of person who can take risks and make it on your own.

This need to "make it on your own" is another important divorce catalyst. According to psychiatrist Zaslow, there is an intense interest today in the development of the individual. This is sometimes called the "New Narcissism" or the "Me Decade." Many of the new therapies, says Zaslow, "are intent on developing the self, and their concept of self often does not include another person in intimate and enduring give-and-take."

When one is intent on self-realization, it is often hard to remember that the person on the other side of the bed has a self, too. When the needs of that other person interfere with the pure white flame of one's own search for personal growth, that interference is often seen as a crushing burden weighing down the seeker. Or as Dr. Ray Fowler, executive director of the American Association of Marriage and Family Counselors, puts it: "We rarely ask ourselves, 'Am I a self-fulfilling person?' Instead we ask, 'Hey, is this jerk I married fulfilling me?' Instead of looking into ourselves to find the source of our unhappiness, we're more likely to shuck our partner and look for fulfillment with someone else."

Divorce is like surgery. It cleaves a marriage the way a scalpel parts the flesh. As operations save lives and improve health, divorces also can save spirits and improve well-being. But just as critics charge that our medical system is too knife-happy, resulting in needless operations, it sometimes seems as if a couple rushes into divorce when less drastic therapy could heal the schism between them. These are the partings which are later regretted and that lead not to a new life script for both partners, but right back into a repeat show of the same series, with a different cast.

Of course, no one who is not a party to a marriage can ever know just when a troubled bond becomes so painful that it chokes the life out of one or both partners. There are marriages that seem calm and untroubled even to the spouse's closest friends, but which damage body and spirit every day. The wrenching decision facing those in pain is whether they need the operation they see so many others getting—or whether they can restore life to their aching marriage.

How then can we know when a marriage is salvageable? How can we prevent a needless divorce? How can we avoid having something happen to us almost against our will?

First, we must acknowledge that strong forces are at work. We need to recognize our vulnerability to what is happening around us. We need to guard against the way the epidemic itself can stir our fantasies.

Second—and perhaps most important —we need to learn the difference between personal and marital problems. "It is very difficult to differentiate between personal and marital crises," admits New York marriage counselor Tilla Vahanian, "because any significant emotional upheaval in one partner is bound to have some impact on the marriage." But it's vital to try.

The deep feelings aroused by a personal trauma—such as the death of a parent—can spill over and profoundly affect the couple relationship. Marital tension may also spring from a woman's turmoil over her changing life goals or a man's depression over growing older. Instead of jumping to the conclusion that a spouse's unhappiness must mean there is something wrong with the marital relationship, people need to ask, "What is *really* wrong here?"

Adults experience certain common life patterns, says Gail Sheehy in her book *Passages,* and the patterns of husband and wife often do not coincide. "No two people can possibly coordinate all their developmental crises," Sheehy writes. "Each one has an inner life structure with its own idiosyncrasies." Couples who recognize the seesawing of their individual needs can balance them out, according to Sheehy, "if they come to recognize that each of them will have periods of inner turmoil, and that it is not evidence of one partner's badness nor the fault of the other."

Certain periods in a marriage are especially perilous. The famous "seven-year-itch"—when husband and wife grow restless, a time that typically coincides with Sheehy's passage to the thirties—is a statistical reality, a peak year for divorce. Then there is the crisis of middle age, when men and women are apt to be heading in different directions. The wife is likely to be newly interested in the career she postponed to raise a family—precisely at a time when her husband wants to spend more time at home after having devoted years to his work. Add to this the presence of teenage children who are stirring their parents' long-buried adolescent fantasies, and the result is a strain on any marriage.

When something seems to be wrong with a marriage, don't panic, says Dr. Vahanian. "Panic pushes people into negative thinking, hasty conclusions and rash activity. A marriage must be expected—and allowed—to have some ups and downs."

4. TERMINATION OF RELATIONSHIPS

Early communication is the key. Sometimes people are so frightened about what is troubling them that they do not share their worries with their spouses. But isolation is risky. When people hold back their feelings, each partner may be seized with awful thoughts that are wildly incorrect interpretations of what is going on.

Says Ellen, divorced at 38, "It hurts me that I couldn't get Ralph to work through a critical time in our marriage. I think he was finding a lot of things wrong in our relationship when they really had more to do with his own feelings about himself and his life. I can't help feeling that we could have worked it out if both of us had been willing to give the time to do it."

Solve problems together

Troubled couples need to share their problems without blaming each other for them. A man or a woman needs to say, "This is what's happening with *me*. I don't know where the trouble is. Let's look for a solution together." It doesn't always work, but with every disagreement a couple confronts and truly resolves, new strength can surge into the relationship. If we let too much go by, then the job of dealing with every issue may seem so overwhelming that we're tempted to start all over with someone new.

Couples in turmoil need to look closely at themselves, at each other, and at the bond between them. Can they rescue their connection? Is there a solid base beneath the tempest? What of the love? Can it inspire them to work things out? Are they flexible enough to change—and to accept change in each other? Can they seek professional help to guide them and to work through the angers and fears that have buffeted them?

There is no foolproof vaccination against divorce. But there may be preventive medicine. If husbands and wives recognize that they are vulnerable, if they can learn from their friends' trials, if they can steadfastly face up to the conflicts between them, perhaps many more of us can infuse our marriages with the strength to combat the epidemic raging around us.

DIVORCE

The first two years are the worst

An in-depth study of divorced parents and their children examines the
problems and changes they face in the two years following separation

ROBERT J. TROTTER

Divorce American Style
Divorce for the Unbroken Marriage
Creative Divorce
Divorce in the Progressive Era
Divorce: Chance of a New Lifetime
Divorce: The Gateway to Self Realization
Divorce: The New Freedom

As these current book titles suggest,
divorce is becoming increasingly popular
in the United States. They also suggest
that divorce can be an exciting and fun
thing and that it can open the door to
liberation and new possibilities. The first
suggestion is true. In fact, if the 1974
trend continues (about one million divorces per year) 40 percent of all new
marriages will ultimately end in divorce.
The second suggestion is more difficult to
evaluate. Divorce can be a positive and
liberating solution to certain family problems, but it can also be a time of crisis
that results in stress, conflict and trauma
for the divorcees and for their children.
Some of the problems that follow in the
wake of divorce were described at the
recent meeting of the American Psychological Association (SN: 9/18/76, p. 186)
by E. Mavis Hetherington of the University of Virginia.

Most divorce research in the past has
focused on mothers and children and has
been largely descriptive. The characteristics of divorced mothers and their
children have been described and compared to those of mothers and children in
intact homes. Hetherington's research,
conducted with Martha Cox and Roger
Cox, is one of the first studies to concentrate on the entire family system. It makes
an in-depth analysis of changes in family
interaction and functioning in the two
years following divorce.

A total of 96 white, middle-class families took part in the study. They consisted
of 24 boys and 24 girls and their divorced
parents and the same number of children
and parents from intact families. The
children were all about four years of age
at the start of the study. In all divorced
families custody of the children had been
granted to the mothers (as is the case in

more than 90 percent of divorces involving children). A multimethod, multimeas-
ure approach was used in the investigation
of family interactions. The measures used
included interviews of and diaries kept by
the parents, observations of parents and
children interacting in a laboratory setting
and at home, checklists and parent ratings
of children's behavior and a battery of
personality tests of the parents. In addition, observations of the children were
made in nursery schools, and ratings of
the children were obtained from their
peers and teachers. Parents and children
were evaluated by these measures two
months, one year and two years after the
divorce.

As would be expected, some of the first
problems faced by divorced parents were
those related to household maintenance
and economic and occupational difficulties. Many of the men, particularly those
from marriages in which conventional sex
roles had been maintained and in which
the wife was not employed, experienced
considerable difficulty in running a household and reported a "chaotic life style."
Although the men had more problems, the
households of both divorced men and
women were more disorganized than those
of intact families, especially in the first
year following divorce. Members of separated households were more likely to eat
at irregular hours. Divorced mothers and
their children were less likely to eat together. Bedtimes were more erratic, and
children were more likely to be late for
school. Divorced men slept less, had more
erratic sleep patterns and had more
difficulty with shopping, cooking, laundry
and cleaning. These problems sometimes
interfered with job performance and were
further complicated by the economic
stress associated with maintaining two
households.

Divorce also led to changes in self
concept and emotional adjustment. Two
months after the divorce about one third
of the fathers and one fourth of the
mothers reported an ebullient sense of
freedom, but by one year this had largely
been replaced by depression, anxiety or

apathy. One of the most obvious changes
in divorced parents in the first year following divorce was a decline in feelings
of competence. They felt they had failed
as parents and spouses and expressed
doubts about their ability to adjust well
in any future marriages. They reported
that they functioned less well in social
situations and were less competent in heterosexual relations. Nine of the divorced
fathers reported an increased rate of sexual
dysfunction.

Social life and the establishment of
meaningful, intimate interpersonal relationships also present problems for divorced parents. Almost all complained
that socializing is organized around
couples and that being a single adult,
especially a single woman with children,
limits recreational opportunities. Divorced
mothers reported having significantly less
contact with adults and often commented
on the sense of being locked into a child's
world. Several described themselves as
prisoners and used terms like "walled in"
and "trapped." This was less true, however, of working women who had social
contacts through their co-workers. Divorced men had a restricted social life two
months after divorce, followed by a surge
of activity at one year and a decline in
activity to the wife's level by two years.
In contrast with the women, divorced men
complained of feeling shut out, rootless
and at loose ends and of a need to engage
in social activities even if they were not
pleasurable. Both men and women spoke
of intense feelings of loneliness.

Happiness, self-esteem and feelings of
competence in heterosexual behavior increased steadily during the two years following divorce for males and females, but
they were not as high even in the second
year as those of married couples. Frequency of sexual intercourse was lower
for divorced parents than married couples
at two months, higher at one year for
males and about the same frequency at
two years. Divorced males particularly
seemed to show a peak of sexual activity
and a pattern of dating a variety of women
in the first year. However, the stereotyped

image of the happy, swinging single life was not altogether accurate. Many males, but few of the females, were pleased with the increased opportunity for sexual experiences with a variety of partners, but by the end of the first year both men and women were expressing a need for intimacy and a lack of satisfaction in casual sexual encounters.

Six of the 48 divorced couples had sexual intercourse with each other during the two months following divorce, but the relationship between all but four of the divorced couples was characterized by acrimony, anger, feelings of desertion, resentment and memories of painful conflicts. Considering the stress involved, it is not surprising that at one year after divorce 29 of the fathers and 35 of the mothers reported that they thought the divorce might have been a mistake and that they should have tried harder to resolve their conflicts. By the end of the second year only 12 of the mothers and 9 of the fathers felt this way.

Poor parenting on the part of divorced parents was apparent in most cases during the two years following divorce. The researchers found that divorced parents make fewer maturity demands of their children, communicate less well with their children, tend to be less affectionate and show marked inconsistency in discipline and a lack of control over their children when compared with parents in intact families. Poor parenting is most apparent when divorced parents, particularly mothers, are interacting with their sons. These parents communicate less, are less consistent with and use more negative sanctions with sons than with daughters. In addition, in the laboratory situation, divorced mothers exhibited fewer positive sanctions and affiliation and more negative

behaviors, such as negative commands and opposition to requests, with sons than with daughters. Sons of divorced parents seem to have a harder time of it, says Hetherington, and this may explain why previous studies have shown that the effects of divorce are more severe and enduring for boys than for girls.

The interviews and observations showed that the lack of control divorced parents have over their children was associated with different patterns of relating to the child for mothers and fathers. The mother tries to control the child by being more restrictive and giving more commands that the child often ignores or resists. The father wants his contacts with his children to be as happy as possible. He begins by being extremely permissive and indulgent with his children but becomes increasingly restrictive during the two-year period, although never as restrictive as fathers in intact homes. The "every day is Christmas" behavior of the divorced father decreases with time, and the divorced mother decreases her futile attempts at authoritarian control and becomes more effective in dealing with her children by two years.

Divorced mothers may give their children a hard time, but mothers, especially divorced mothers, get rough treatment from their children. In most cases, children are more likely to oppose their mothers and comply with fathers. They also more frequently make negative complaining demands of the mother. Boys tend to be more oppositional and aggressive and girls more whining, complaining and compliant. The divorced mother is harassed by her children, particularly her sons. In comparison with fathers and mothers in intact families, her children in the first year don't obey, affiliate with or

pay attention to her. They nag and whine, make more dependency demands and are more likely to ignore her. The aggression of boys with divorced mothers peaks at one year and then drops significantly but is still higher than that of boys in intact homes at two years. Some divorced mothers described their relationship with their child one year after divorce as "declared war," "struggle for survival," "the old Chinese water torture" or "like getting bitten to death by ducks." As was found in the divorced parents' behavior, one year following divorce seemed to be the period of maximum negative behaviors for children, and great improvement occurred by two years, although the negative behaviors were longer lasting in boys than in girls. In almost all areas, the second year appears to be a year of marked recovery and constructive adaptation for both parents and children.

These findings, of course, represent averages. There were wide variations in coping and parenting within intact and divorced families. However, of the families studied, there were none in which at least one family member did not report distress or exhibit disrupted behavior, particularly during the first year following divorce. Previous research has shown that a conflict-ridden intact family may be more harmful than divorce for family members, but this does not mean that divorce itself does not represent a crisis.

"We did not encounter a victimless divorce," says Hetherington. Since this seems to be the rule rather than the exception and since statistical evidence suggests that the rate of divorce is likely to increase, Hetherington concludes that "it is important that parents and children be realistically prepared for problems associated with divorce that they may encounter."

THE CASE FOR
JOINT CUSTODY

The notion that the children of divorced parents are best consigned to the exclusive care of the mother is a relatively recent one. Given changing social patterns, the authors argue, it's time for a reappraisal.

Mel Roman and William Haddad

Mel Roman is a professor in the department of psychiatry at the Albert Einstein College of Medicine, and director of family studies at the Bronx Municipal Hospital Center.

William Haddad is a journalist and former associate director of the Peace Corps. He is currently director of New York State Office of Legislative Oversight.

On Manhattan's Lower East Side, six-year-old Morgan Gillette divides her time between two households that are within blocks of each other. Half the week is spent with her mother, Lena, and the other half with her father, Al. Weekends are alternated. In each apartment, Morgan has her own bedroom, and both rooms are filled with her presence—her clothes, drawings, and all sorts of toys. Morgan's school is situated near the two apartments so each parent can pick her up there on days when a shift takes place. On occasions when the drop-off point has been one of her parents' apartments, Morgan maneuvers Al and Lena into her room and expresses her wish that the parents, who separated when she was just over three, could live together again. But she seems increasingly aware that they won't.

Observing Morgan and talking with her parents and teachers, one concludes that she is, by and large, a happy child. She has many friends, does well at school, and seems to accept comfortably the biweekly shift in households. By a negative standard, she shows none of the disturbing symptoms (behavioral problems or poor sleeping or eating habits) that have been uncovered in so many divorced families in which one parent has sole custody of the child and the other has only visitation rights.

The Gillette joint-custody agreement was worked out in the New York State courts in 1976. It is typical of postdivorce custodial arrangements in which parents agree to share child care—to develop a pattern for dividing the child's week, routines for picking up and dropping off, and consultations on major decisions, such as schooling and summer camp.

Many forces today are at work on men, pushing them to play a greater role in family life, and, according to the magazine *Student Lawyer* (May 1978), "the women's liberation movement has made men more conscious of their equal role in family life. 'I think it's changing because fathers are realizing they have an equal right to custody,' says Judge Charles Fleck. 'Men are coming out of the woodwork.' . . . Nevertheless," *Student Lawyer* concludes, "their speed is hardly mind-boggling. National Center of Health Statistics figures show that, between 1970 and 1976, the percentage of American fathers keeping custody of their children under 18 remained just over one percent of *all* family living arrangements. However, that still makes 780,000 children living with their fathers nationwide." And as best we can determine at least an equal number of children, if not more, share their fathers through joint custody.

F or the last three years, one of us, Mel Roman, has been looking at such arrangements to see how they work out. Roman's studies at the Albert Einstein College of Medicine have shown that it is not profitable to seek to understand one family member in isolation, as, for example, in the case of Morgan Gillette. Family interconnections have to be closely analyzed. Roman has studied 40 families who are presently practicing joint custody, as well as 60 fathers who have various degrees of custody.

While none of the families has found joint custody to be trouble-free—and most are involved in continuously questioning its effects—there is no doubt that joint custody *is* working for them all. In most instances, the children are thriving, not merely "adjusting," and the parents themselves are working out new and, they believe, productive lifestyles.

All this contradicts the notion that once a divorce occurs, the children are best off in their mother's exclusive care. The father, by popular belief, cannot wait to enjoy his "freedom." Therefore, one objection to joint custody is the theory of the "weak father." Two other objections are often raised. First, it is argued that parents who could not reconcile conflicts while living together are even less likely to be accommodating to one another while living apart. (Unaccountably, this argument is sometimes paired with its opposite, the view that parents in a joint-custody arrangement are unable to separate in a healthy way and are using this arrangement—and by implication, their children—to stay together in some fashion.) Second, it is felt that joint custody is too disruptive: the "child as yo-yo" is put in an untenable position, in which both his loyalties and even his physical surroundings are split. As a consequence, it is felt that the child's sense of continuity and stability are undermined.

While these objections sound plausible, they do not square with the available evidence that joint-custody couples show reduced conflict and that their children are quite well adjusted. Looking first at the issue of parental conflict, we see one pattern emerging as true of nearly all joint-custody couples. When couples want to share custody of their children, they are able to isolate their marital conflicts from their parental responsibilities. In fact, it is not uncommon for joint-custody parents to frankly admit their antipathy toward one another, but, at the same time, to maintain that they do not intend to harm their children because they

---

"New studies refute the theory of the 'child as yo-yo,' with loyalties split between parents."

---

might like to harm one another.

In the case of Morgan, her parents still do not relish one another's company, yet both feel that joint custody is working out. Her father, an anthropologist, is especially positive about it. He feels that the real problem for Morgan was never the form of her postseparation living arrangement, but the fact of the separation itself. And even though Lena initially sought sole custody because she did not want to deal with what she saw as her husband's overwhelming anger, she now agrees with Al about what is truly important for Morgan. "Maybe," she says, "sole custody was

an illusion. Any parent who cares at all about the other parent or that parent's relation with the child will not make decisions unilaterally."

Having been coparents for two and a half years now, Al and Lena are surprised that their anger has somewhat diminished. While they do not communicate much with each other, they feel that a "basic trust" has begun to grow and that they have evolved a good working relationship when it comes to Morgan. If she is ill and at Lena's home, for instance, she will remain there; or if Lena, who is a writer, must be elsewhere, Al will stay with Morgan at his ex-wife's apartment. Occasionally, they disagree about specific decisions that affect Morgan: for example, each chose a different summer camp for her. Generally, they do not have many big child-rearing decisions to make.

For each of them, joint custody has proven a means to be closer with, and to learn to communicate with, their daughter. For Lena, the arrangement intensifies her relationship with Morgan. "When something goes wrong, we have to work it out ourselves. . . . Neither of us can turn to Al anymore as a go-between," she says. Al also feels that the best part of the postseparation relationship is that "I can appreciate Morgan more. It's easier one-to-one. I can see her more clearly, who she is."

A Brooklyn couple whom we interviewed, Frank and Jody Vanda, also arranged a split-week custody pattern. Their two daughters, Amy, 11, and Sarah, seven, spend half the week in their mother's large, comfortable apartment and the other half in their father's smaller apartment a few blocks away. For this family, their four years of shared parenthood have been very good ones.

Asked to explain why joint custody has worked out so well for them, Frank and Jody both say it's because the commitment to shared parenthood is strong, stronger than any differences they've had. (As it happens, many of their quarrels had concerned their divergent lifestyles. Now that they lead separate lives, they no longer feel compelled to attack each other's different ways.) Jody and Frank are, in fact, unusually close. They talk with each other often, meeting for lunch to discuss the children and their lives in general. They

still celebrate all four birthdays together and, on occasion, visit relatives as a family.

Jody feels that joint custody has posed no difficulties for her children. They accept the split living "totally." "There is," says their mother, "no issue of shuttling, just that there is time to be with Mother and time to be with Father. In fact, the girls were relieved to learn that they'd be with us both."

Jody also perceives that Frank, who recently joined the local school board, is now more involved with the children than prior to the separation, and that she has become—in a healthy way—less involved. "I have," she says, "let go more. I have time to myself . . . it's delicious." Both girls lead active, full lives and feel altogether free to express how they feel to both parents. Amy has said that she wishes her parents had stayed together, but as this is not possible, she likes living with them both separately.

If the Vandas have managed to maintain a close relationship, Marge and Bill Langley share custody of sons Edward, seven, and Bruce, four, while having virtually nothing to do with each other. Edward and Bruce together change homes every Monday, when one of their parents drops them off at school, and the other parent picks them up. The weekly rotation seems to be fine with the boys. The shift from the Langley house, in Brooklyn, where their father still lives and conducts his business, to their mother's apartment some 12 blocks away is no problem. The boys have friends in both neighborhoods and are doing well in school. Bill remarks that unlike other children of separated parents, "My kids don't visit, they *live* here; it's much more natural. The *other* way is unrealistic. It puts unrealistic pressure on parent and child to compress everything into five or six hours. I've seen it—the fathers walk the children in the park like dogs."

What is a problem is that Bill wants to move to the country in upstate New York and work out a new arrangement under which he would have custody of the boys one year, his wife would have them the next, and so on. Marge refuses to separate that long from the children, and they are at an impasse; other than talks with a therapist about the custody issue, months can go by when they do not speak to each other. "We don't," Marge says, "have a working relationship. Bill is unhappy about staying in the city. He wants to get out and have as little to do with me as possible. I feel at times it would be easier if he were out of my life . . . but to be completely honest, I don't want the children all the time."

Bill says he would take the children full time. This, too, is unacceptable to Marge. Given the commitment both parents show toward their sons, and their belief that joint custody is working out well for the boys, it is difficult to know how they will resolve Bill's desire to move. For most couples, geographic closeness is a *sine qua non* of joint custody. As Marge expresses it, "In our situation, where both of us want custody of the children, I can't see a better setup unless one of us would bow out. Even with a power play—if one of us fought for custody and won—it would lead to so much bitterness it would be terrible."

These New York families represent but a few of the many arrangements adopted by joint-custody parents. Across the continent, in the San Francisco Bay area, four joint-custody families are the subject of a recently

---

"According to available evidence, children of joint-custody couples are well adjusted."

---

completed doctoral dissertation by Alice Abarbanel, at the California School of Professional Psychology. These four families are all quite different from one another: the amount of conflict that the parents experience varies from household to household. Each household, too, has a different division in the length of the child's stay in each household, ranging from relatively long periods (a nine-to-five-day split, for instance) to shorter periods (a four-to-three-day split). The families differed, too, in their preseparation households: in one marriage, the husband was always fully in-

volved in child care, while in another, the husband did very little with the children before the divorce.

Clearly, joint-custody families conform to no one pattern; and just as living arrangements vary from one family to the next—splitting custody by days, weeks, months, and even years—so also do the kinds of communication that prevail between ex-spouses. Some ex-spouses are supportive of each other and maintain a close relationship, while others see as little of each other as possible; and, in between, every imaginable permutation exists—from the close to the distant. Within this wide range, however, there is at least one thing that joint-custody families all have in common: by placing the child's need for both parents first, the parents themselves work out—in different ways—a *modus vivendi*.

Only in the past few years have some courts in the country begun to recognize the importance of the two-parent principle. Before the 19th century, when custody of children arose as an issue, the response was simple: children belonged to their father. By the early years of the 20th century, customs gradually began to change, until, in the 1920s, the rights of the father were no longer recognized. From the 1920s on, mothers were virtually assured of the custody of their children, even though the women's paramount claims were not then, nor are they now, based on the law. Today, mothers receive custody in more than 90 percent of all contested cases. In at least an equivalent percentage of cases that never reach the courts (by far the greater number), the divorced woman also assumes sole custody.

In large part, the bias in favor of mothers has merely accommodated social reality. Industrialization, which separated the wage labor of men from the private labor of women, is behind the glorification of motherhood and the "maternal instinct." That is, society's stress on the maternal instinct came along precisely when it was required, making a virtue out of what seemed to be a necessity. Its enshrinement parallels the development of a new family form that we have come to call the nuclear family, the social—but not economic—center of personal life and a refuge

from the world. As our culture became both urban and industrialized, the father worked away from the house and left the raising of children, for all practical purposes, in the hands of the mother.

The inevitable tendency of psychoanalysts and other researchers has been to concentrate attention upon the mother as the influential parent and to minimize, as a result, the influence of fathers, peers, and the larger social network. The legal system has pursued the same course. Although from time to time children are awarded to the father, this occurs only under the most extreme circumstances. In the absence of any real guidelines, the parents' characters are inevitably scrutinized when judging the child's best interests. It's almost inevitable that such scrutiny becomes character assassination. As the writer Joseph Epstein put it, the father "must prove his wife either an emotional cripple or a moral leper, and, should he wish to maximize his chances, preferably both."

A few isolated cases in recent years have appeared to signal a shift in the courts' attitudes. Most of these cases, however, are deceptive. In 1975, the Lee Salk case provoked wide press coverage because Salk, a renowned child psychologist, won custody of his two children, even though the court explicitly acknowledged that their mother was in no way "unfit." However, Salk's profession and the flexible hours that it allowed him made his case the exception that proves the rule. For the courts, it would appear, a child psychologist is the vocational equivalent of a biological mother.

A second case that also aroused considerable interest did, initially, appear to herald significant change. The contested suit known as the *Watts* case took place in 1973 and involved custody of three children, ages 11, nine, and five. When the ex-husband sued for custody, the children had been living with their mother, who was pregnant by the man she lived with and intended to marry. Custody was awarded to the father—but not because of the mother's way of life (unconventional lifestyles no longer have anything like the negative weight they once had in court), but because the judge, Sybil Hart Kooper, was not satisfied that the husband-to-be could assume the responsibilities of parenthood. The court's ruling against the mother, in what was in any event a melodramatic case, was bound to create attention. What was significant about the case, though, was the judge's written argument. Taking exception to the bias in favor of the mother, Judge Kooper identified some of its pertinent flaws. She pointed out, among other things, that it was "the acts and not the facts of motherhood" that determined most court practice and that the courts were guided by prejudice, not law. Kooper stressed that the law unequivocally stipulates that both parents have an equal claim when forced to turn to the courts for a determination about the children's future. Further, a child's "tender years" should not create any legal, let alone psychological, presumption toward either parent. Citing several states that specifically disallow any prejudice on the basis of sex, Judge Kooper added, "The simple fact of being a mother does not, by itself, indicate a capacity or willingness to render a quality of care different from that which the father can provide. The traditional and romantic view, at least since the turn of the century, has been that nothing can be an adequate substitute for mother love."

Judge Kooper further remarked that

"Only recently have courts begun to accept the logic of the two-parent principle."

"studies of maternal deprivation have shown that the essential experience for the child is that of mothering—the warmth, consistency and continuity of the relationship rather than the sex of the individual who is performing the mothering function." Finally, she added, "Application of the 'tender-years presumption' would deprive respondent of his right to equal protection of the law under the 14th Amendment to the United States Constitution."

Unfortunately, despite the soundness of her arguments, Judge

Kooper's decision does not appear to have had much impact. She has said that she expected it to be more influential than it has been, and that her views have been received with considerable hostility by both male and female judges.

The 14th Amendment, which guarantees that no one shall be discriminated against on the basis of sex, has recently been used to challenge the mother's overwhelming courtroom advantage. Lately, there has been talk of appointing a special lawyer, or the equivalent, for the child in a contested-custody case. Although this seems to further the recognition of the child's "best interests," there are as many reasons to be suspicious of court-appointed mediators as there are reasons to be suspicious of experts in general. It was, after all, as recently as 1955 that sociologists Talcott Parsons and Robert Bales popularized the idea that in the family, the father served an "instrumental" role and the mother an "expressive" one. What these terms connoted was an appalling reconfirmation of patriarchal assumptions in the new language of sociology; the "instrumental" father is seen as directing the child's development in serious ways, while the "expressive" mother "soothes" with all the feeling and nurturing the father is too busy and too inexpressive to give.

In any event, leaving aside the dubious value of increased court involvement in custody cases, those decisions that the most optimistic observers invoke as signs of progress are still ones that endorse an either/or view of custody. The Levy case, decided in 1975 in New York State, is a conspicuous exception. In that instance, the husband was awarded a divorce on the basis of his wife's adultery, but both parents were awarded custody of their 11-year-old son. Regarding his decision, Judge Guy R. Ribaudo wrote that joint custody would serve "to give that measure of psychological support and uplift to each parent which would communicate itself to the child in the measure of mutual love, mutual attention and mutual training."

The judge also ruled that "it is basic law that the father of a son is responsible for his support until he reaches a majority," and that, for the initial two

years, the boy should live with his mother, after which he would choose between the two homes himself. Judge Ribaudo concluded that "although there is little New York case authority as to the concept of joint custody in matrimonial actions, there is no doubt that the courts will adopt a liberal attitude with regard to this type of custody whenever the facts of each particular case may so indicate."

So far, we have seen little evidence of this "liberal attitude." Without changing so much as a syllable, what was modestly opined in 1850 might well be repeated today: "The state of the law relating to the custody of the persons of infants is not very satisfactory. Not only are there defects which can, perhaps, be remedied only by the authority of the Legislature; but there prevails an uncertainty in the application of the law, as it exists, to the difficult cases which frequently arise in connection with the disposal of minor children."

A liberal attitude is certainly not evident in the influential book Beyond the Best Interests of the Child, written in 1973 by Joseph Goldstein (Yale law professor), Anna Freud (child psychoanalyst), and Albert Solnit (child psychiatrist and director of Yale University Child Study Center). Their book advances the position that divorced couples cannot get along and invariably use the child as a battleground. The authors strongly recommend not only that there be one custodial parent, but also that that parent have complete and exclusive control over all aspects of custody: "Once it is determined who will be the custodial parent, it is that parent, not the court, who must decide under what conditions he or she

---

"Joint custody should increasingly be the pragmatic, and hence American, choice."

---

wishes to raise the child. Thus, the noncustodial parent should have no legally enforceable right to visit the child, and the custodial parent should have the right to decide whether it is desirable for the child to have such visits."

Moreover, the authors are quite clear that such visits, even if allowed, are not worth much. In their view, "a 'visiting' or 'visited' parent has little chance to serve as a true object of love, trust and identification, since this role is based on his being available on an uninterrupted day-to-day basis."

The stature of its authors has assured the book considerable attention and may well have influenced those lawyers and judges whose knowledge of child development is limited. If so, we believe this to be extremely unfortunate. Not only do we radically disagree with almost all that the book argues with regard to child custody, but we also believe that the authors have failed to support their views or to take into account the evidence available on the development of children in various home settings. They do not cite, nor do there exist, any social science data to support the proposition that a single official parent is preferable to two. They seem unaware that the family is undergoing profound changes, and that these changes cannot help but affect our attitude toward custodial care.

The new forms of family life that are coming into being are increasingly evident in intact, as well as divorced, households. As men and women move beyond sex-defined roles, parenthood and the family are being subject to reevaluation. More women are seeking careers outside the home and more men are finding that they want to, or must, share responsibility for the children. Nor do we anticipate that this trend will be reversed. If anything, our present cultural climate virtually ensures that once a marriage is severed, shared parenthood is more necessary than ever.

We do not mean to imply that there are no problems associated with joint custody. The mere logistics of the arrangement take time and energy. Nevertheless, it is fairly obvious that those who choose joint custody are willing to work out whatever difficulties arise; indeed, concerned parenthood seems to be at the root of the success that joint-custody parents report. And when parents display such concern, then surely the trade-off that joint custody often exacts—two homes in exchange for two parents together—is well worth it.

What problems do arise are endemic to marital dissolution: the child may at times prefer one household to the other. Or one parent may want to relocate and discovers that the need for geographic proximity to the ex-spouse and children makes any major move impossible, as in the case of the physicist who shared with his wife the joint custody of their young daughter. Because the parents lived at a great distance from each other, their daughter spent alternating years with each of them. The system worked well for four years, at which point the physicist decided to move to England and tried to persuade his wife to continue the same arrangement. She refused, however, and the case went to court; she won sole custody of their child. But when single-parent households experience similar conflicts, there is neither the opportunity nor, more important, the commitment, to arrive at a satisfactory solution.

Although we cannot be certain that joint custody is the answer for all those who raise children after a divorce, it appears to be the most logical and emotionally sound choice. Unlike sole (generally maternal) custody, it does not banish the father or overburden the mother, and, just as important, it does not sever ties between one parent and the children. Quite the reverse: by maintaining the family structure in reorganized form, joint custody, we believe, resolves most of the problems raised by sole custody. Nor is joint custody a negative solution; we think it offers positive advantages and opportunities for growth for each of the family members.

We also recognize that our convictions reflect only what is, so far, possible to know. Until more studies are conducted, and there are more households that adopt a joint-custody arrangement within a sympathetic society, it is well to remain somewhat cautious. With an issue as intricate and emotionally charged as the fate of children after a divorce, caution—by which we mean a respect for the complexity of human affairs—will always be desirable.

There is no reason to suppose that joint custody will soon become commonplace for postdivorce families in America. Almost everything in our society militates against its widespread adoption, which is highly ironic. Although our evidence suggests that joint custody should increasingly be the pragmatic (and hence characteristically American) choice, current attitudes and institutions indicate that its widespread adoption is no less than a revolution away.

When Fathers Have to Raise Families Alone—

A recently widowed Midwestern father, raising two children on his own, thought he was accustomed to single parenthood until his young son brought home an envelope from school.

Enclosed was a Mother's Day card—one which every child was supposed to take home. It was a painfully sharp reminder of the man's missing mate and his difficulties serving as a "double parent," forced by circumstances to be a mother figure as well as a father.

The incident is typical of the dilemmas facing a large number of American men. Because of divorce, separation or the death of their mate, many have become solitary parents, a role often held by women but rarely by men in the past.

Now more than 710,000 children under the age of 18, some 80,000 of them preschoolers and kindergartners, live with only their male parents. The 446,000 fathers involved represent a 61 per cent increase over the 277,000 who had sole custody a decade ago.

The trend, social workers say, has had profound effects on the lives of families who have had to adjust to nontraditional roles not only for the parents but also for children. In many cases, sons and daughters are called upon to become partners in raising the family, with traditional lines of authority blurred.

Growing acceptance. The development also marks a significant change in the attitudes of many segments of society—from neighbors to the courts—regarding single-male parenthood.

Sociologists say that growing acceptance of the single father is reflected by the granting of custody of more and more minor children to male parents, sometimes with the acquiescence of mothers.

Notes Elliott Diamond, Virginia representative of Men's Equality Now, a men's-rights group: "The laws seem much fairer today. There is less preference to mothers."

A nationwide study conducted by a divorced father seeking custody of his 6-year-old daughter illustrates the trend. Clint Jones of Fountain Valley, Calif., found in three years of researching 16,000 divorce cases involving minor children that fathers gained custody of both sons and daughters more often than in the past.

At the same time, Jones found in a study of more than 2,000 Orange County, Calif., cases that fathers had been granted custody of their offspring in only 33 per cent of the cases when both parents requested custody.

The Californian observes: "This shows the bias of the courts. They don't believe a father is as good a parent as a mother. It isn't fair."

In many cases, psychologists say, men seeking the custody of children have profited from the women's-liberation movement and new economic demands on female parents. The courts, in recognizing women's rights, also have been forced to pay more attention to male roles in raising their sons and daughters.

Sociologists say that virtually all members of the family are strongly and sometimes traumatically affected by the sudden absence of a female parent. One of the greatest difficulties reported involves the apportioning of duties once undertaken by the mother.

Dick Greene of Denver, Colo., first faced such problems when his 16-year-old son Don lived with him and again when his 14-year-old daughter Kelly moved in and Don moved back to his mother's. In both situations, Greene found that he did all the work. He observes: "The house isn't as clean as when I lived alone. I give Kelly chores to do, but I get impatient with the time it takes her to do them so I end up doing them myself."

A heavy-equipment operator, Greene does the shopping, the cooking and most of the cleaning, and says he spends "more time doing housework and cooking than I'd like, but I do manage to do other things, too."

Greene is a local chapter officer of Parents Without Partners International, and he and Kelly participate in the family and teen activities it sponsors.

Week-ends, father and daughter are as likely to be found in the hills sledding as at home watching their favorite team, the Denver Broncos, in a televised football game. Sometimes he even takes her on his dates.

Greene says a father sometimes offers a happier, more secure home for a child than a mother. "Kelly asked to move in with me," he notes. "I'm more inclined to stay at home than my wife was. It once seemed difficult, but I now have things under control."

Worst problem: money. Many single fathers say their worst problem is money—divorce costs, alimony payments and the expenditures necessary for providing for their family at home. Once-adequate salaries suddenly seem to shrink under the weight of multiplied expenses.

A typically financially burdened parent is Joe Jenkins, of Norwalk, Calif., who has three children too young to accept much responsibility for running the house. His day begins at 5 a.m. when the baby-sitter arrives and he leaves for his job as a supervisor in a meat-packing plant in Los Angeles.

The sitter makes breakfast and lunch for the youngsters—Melanie, 9, Joseph Robert, 6, and Alicia, 3. Jenkins makes dinner and does other household chores when he returns home.

He says alimony, rent, and pay for the baby-sitter account for a substantial part of his earnings. He also says that he has "practically zero social life."

A Mormon, Jenkins takes the children to church and is involved in a Parents Without Partners group, which he says he joined more for the children than for himself. He explains that "there are activities, such as potluck suppers, which give the children an opportunity to be with other children like themselves."

He sometimes worries about what effects the changes have had on his children. Yet despite his difficulties, Jenkins has relatively few complaints.

"I'm very happy," he explains. "My children are my whole world. I'm trying to be a mother and father to them."

Bridging a gap. Sociologists say that the greatest difficulty faced by many fathers is bridging the communication gap with their youngsters. In much of Western society, mothers usually are the primary source of information and comfort for sons and daughters, and it is often hard for parents and children to readjust these roles when the mother is gone. It is especially troublesome, in many cases, with fathers and daughters.

Rusty Oliphant, a Rockville, Md., auto mechanic, admits he had problems at first when three of his daughters moved in with him after he was divorced. The girls are 16, 14 and 12. He says he found it hard to discipline the children.

"They were used to running on their own and needed to be slowed down," he explains. "I try to give them a choice of things to do, but if they don't volunteer, I assign jobs."

Oliphant says he has had considerable difficulty persuading his daughters to discuss with him their problems about growing up. He notes: "When a girl starts to become a woman, it's hard to get her to talk about it. One of mine just won't talk about it. I can be a friend and a father, but there is quite a bit of adjusting I have to do."

He also is having problems relating to his youngest, whom he describes as a beautiful child who needs a lot of love and open affection. Nevertheless, he says, "the whole thing is working out much better than any of us thought. We'll make it O.K."

A problem common to many single fathers is a sense of loneliness and frustration in trying to raise children on their own. Normally untrained by society to cope with running a household, men often are at a loss at first in performing even the most routine chores.

"Men don't talk." Police Capt. Robert Livingston, of Kansas City, Mo., is a single father who has had to cope with such matters. He is divorced and has custody of three children, one of whom is still at home. Two are in a nearby college. The policeman says one of his main concerns is that he has no one to talk to about raising his family.

"Men don't talk as women do," he observes. "I know one other guy who has custody of his kids. We play golf together, but we don't compare notes on child rearing."

Livingston says he sometimes gets discouraged, and comments: "You get feelings of jealousy of people you know who are separated or divorced who don't have their children. You feel you aren't free. So much is a burden.

"Then you think of the choices, and you realize you're a lot happier than you'd be if they weren't with you."

Profile of Families Where Fathers Are Mothers, Too

At latest count—446,000 families with children under 18 were headed by fathers alone. Among those fathers:

MARITAL STATUS	Number	Percentage of Group
Divorced, separated	323,000	72.4%
Widowed	112,000	25.1%
Single	11,000	2.5%
AGE		
Under 25	14,000	3.1%
25 to 34	82,000	18.4%
35 to 44	152,000	34.1%
45 to 54	137,000	30.7%
55 and older	61,000	13.7%
RACE		
White	364,000	81.6%
Nonwhite	82,000	18.4%
CHILDREN		
Those in one-parent families with—		
White-male head	591,000	83.2%
Nonwhite-male head	119,000	16.8%
INCOME		
Median for families with children under 18—		
All families		$14,241 a year
Husband-wife families		$15,726 a year
Families headed by men		**$11,696 a year**
Families headed by women		$ 5,485 a year

Note: Figures as of March, 1976, latest available; details may not add to totals because of rounding.

Source: U.S. Dept. of Commerce

'Old'
is not a four-letter word

A report on those who are euphemistically called "senior citizens." The topic is especially pertinent because of the aging of the American population and because of the extension of the mandatory retirement age from 65 to 70.

Alan Anderson, Jr.

Meet Jim and Mary Johnson, Americans. Both are 65 years old, married to each other and about to embark on the perilous adventure of old age. This is a crucial year for them, and their success in getting through it—especially for Jim, who has just retired—will have a lot to do with how many more years they live, and how they feel about living. The year is crucial not because they are 65—a number more or less picked out of a hat by the Social Security Administration in the 1930s—but because the bureaucrats who set that benchmark had no idea how important it would become psychologically. Nor had they any idea how many people would be flooding past it today along the poorly marked paths of aging.

This country, with much the rest of the world soon to follow, is in the midst of a demographic upheaval unprecedented in history—a gray revolution, if you will. Today there are 21.8 million Americans 65 and older, nearly seven times as many as there were in 1900. Each day some 4,000 persons turn 65 and 3,000 in that category die, for a net gain of about 1,000 a day. By the year 2000 one out of five Americans will be over 65.

And we don't know what to do with them. They tend to be retired from work, ostracized socially, displaced from their traditional position as society's "elders." We don't yet understand them physically or psychologically, and we don't know how to make best use of their own desires and abilities to remain active. "The question of what to do with old people is a new one," says Chauncey Leake, a pharmacologist and student of aging at the University of California, San Francisco. "Over all the millennia of human existence, it could not have arisen until some 50 years ago. There simply weren't enough old people."

There are enough now, and modern America is baffled. A pension system carefully set up by Franklin Roosevelt is in trouble; within a few years, more people will be drawing from Social Security than are paying into it. We are trying (late, as usual) to stave off bankruptcy of the system. First, as everyone who works knows, Social Security taxes are zooming. Second, legislation has gone through Congress to extend the mandatory retirement age, generally 65, to 70; if the employee chooses to work until the age of 70, obviously there is no Social Security payout until that birthday. But there are more fundamental questions. How long *should* workers stay on the job—a particularly pertinent question in view of the change in mandatory retirement. What kind of job? Do they feel like working, and are they effective? Can families return to the custom of honoring the elderly? And what do Jim and Mary feel like, and how can they be most productive and happy?

The study of old people is a new pursuit—so much so that even the vocabulary is strange. Geriatrics, for example, is the study not of aging but of the aged and their diseases. The science of the processes of aging is gerontology; the first important work in this field was done as recently as the 1950s. There is also confusion between life expectancy (the expected length of a life) and life span (the theoretical limit of a lifetime). The

 From *Across the Board*, May 1978. Reprinted by permission.

average human life expectancy has stretched from about 22 years in the time of ancient Greece to 47 years in turn-of-the-century America to 71 years now. The maximum life span, about 110 to 115 years, has not increased at all.

Another new vocabulary word is ageism—like "sexism," one of the uglier terms of tin-ear wordsmiths—the prejudice against the old that Jim and Mary have begun to encounter. Old people face a painful wall of discrimination that they are often too polite or too timid to attack. Elders are not hired for new jobs, and are eased out of old ones (they are considered rigid or feebleminded); they are shunned socially (they are thought "senile" or boring); they are edged out of family life (children often regard them as sickly or ugly or parasitic); they are equated with children (common adjectives are "cute" and "adorable"). In sum, elders are treated by many as though they were no longer people. A typical study at a California nursing home showed that staff members judged the residents less interested and able to take advantage of activities than did the residents themselves. Our humor about old people implies wickedness of sex in men (old goat, dirty old man) and ugliness in women (biddy, hag, crock). Women after menopause and men after retirement lose social status rapidly. They are considered incapable of thinking clearly, learning new things, enjoying sex, contributing to the community, holding responsible jobs; in short, incapable of living.

Can this be true? How, then, was it possible for Picasso to paint masterworks until a few months before his death at 91? Michelangelo was still sculpting a few weeks before he died at 90. Verdi wrote *Falstaff* at 80; Tolstoy wrote *What Is Art* at 88. Even Freud, who was pessimistic about the minds of old people, did not begin his best work until his forties and wrote *The Ego and the Id* at 67. Titian did his finest paintings just before he died at 100, Pablo Casals was still playing the cello in his nineties, Winston Churchill was Prime Minister at 81 and Georgia O'Keefe starred in her first television special at 90.

What, then, does life have in store for Jim and Mary Johnson? Though the science of gerontology is still in its adolescence, we can at least erase some old myths and make some predictions. In general, the needs of older persons are not much different from those of younger persons: They do best when they can enjoy friendships and social contacts, keep busy with work and leisure activities and maintain reasonably good health. True, they are more vulnerable to stresses. Physically they have less resistance to shock and disease; psychologically they are prone to loneliness, dependence, the effects of family conflicts, loss of status. But there is good evidence that failure is not inevitable. Instead it seems that the health and happiness of old people decline because we expect them to—and old people believe us.

As a married couple of 65, the Johnsons are typical in some ways and unusual in others. The marriage itself is unusual and important: Married elders live on the average five years longer than unmarrieds. Most older women (69 percent) are not married, most older men (79 percent) are. This is both because women live longer than men (75 versus 68 years) and because women tend to marry older men (by an average of three years). Although more boys are born than girls, women outnumber men by 130 to 100 in the 65–74 category; by 74+ they're ahead by 169 to 100, and by 85+ by two to one. The U.S. Bureau of the Census predicts 1,000 women to 675 men by the year 2000, with widows outnumbering widowers four to one. It's not only a gray revolution; it's a gray female revolution.

The Johnsons are typical in that they live in their community. Until a decade ago, it was widely assumed that most of our elders lived in nursing homes or other institutions. In fact, only about 5 percent do, though the number is rising. And though the Johnsons have a few chronic problems (Jim has arthritis and Mary has high blood pressure), they are freely mobile (as are about 81 percent of elders in the community). Both wear eyeglasses (90 percent do); have no hearing aids (about 5 percent do); will spend $791 each on health care this year (more than three times that spent by people under 65; about two-thirds of the bill will be paid by the government); will take in $3,540 in Social Security for the two of them; completed eight years of school each; are white (fewer blacks live to this age); and have no jobs (only 22 percent of men over 65 and 8 percent of women do). Oh, and they always vote: 51 percent of our elders do, and they are becoming an ever-stronger bloc.

Physically, Jim and Mary have aged in similar fashion. Both have slowed: Their base metabolic rate has dropped about 20 percent since they were 30. This means they need slightly less to eat and the effects of drugs and alcohol last longer. (Dr. Robert Butler, director of the two-year-old National Institute on Aging, recommends no more than one-and-a-half ounces of hard liquor a day or two six-ounce glasses of wine.) Their body temperature has declined to as low as 90°F.; the aging King David tried to prolong his life by lying against the bodies of warm young virgins.

Perhaps the most significant change is that the entire circulatory machinery is less efficient. There is less elastin, the molecules responsible for the elasticity of heart and blood vessels, and more collagen, the stiff protein that makes up about one-third of the body's protein. The heart rate does not rise as well in response to stress, the heart muscle cannot contract and relax as fast and the arteries are more resistant to the flow of blood. Heart output—about five quarts a minute at age 50—has been dropping at about 1 percent a year. With the heart muscle less efficient and the vessels more resistant, heart rate and blood pressure both rise—and are both related to heart disease. Jim's blood pressure was 100/75 when he was 25; now it is 160/90. His blood carries less oxygen to the brain and lungs. If he rises too suddenly from a chair he gets dizzy. Likewise, if Mary climbs the stairs too fast she must stop to catch her breath.

4. TERMINATION OF RELATIONSHIPS

Both are slightly shorter than they used to be, and have a tendency to stoop. This is due both to muscle wastage (less skeletal muscle to hold the skeleton upright) and to loss of bone tissue. The individual vertebrae settle closer together as the discs that separate them flatten and collapse. Mary's bones began a steady loss when she was about 40; by the time she is 80 her skeleton will weigh 25 to 40 percent less. Jim's bone loss, unsuspected until two decades ago, began just a few years ago and will be less severe. Gerontologists do not understand the mechanism or cause of bone loss, though there is some evidence that a good diet (containing adequate calcium, in particular) and regular exercise can slow it.

Both Johnsons are in less direct communication with the world around them. Each is slightly nearsighted and slightly farsighted; to focus near or far the lens of the eye must flex, and their lenses are more rigid; the ciliary muscles that control the flexing are also weaker. But neither condition will get much worse and both can be corrected by bifocals. Eye pressure increases (which may lead to glaucoma) and the lens may become more opaque, leading to cataracts; the latter can now be corrected by surgery. The Johnsons cannot smell as well. Both optic and olfactory nerve fibers will eventually dwindle to about 25 percent of the number present at birth, and they are irreplaceable. Elsewhere in the body the sense of touch has begun to dull, faster in the feet than in the hands, and the pain threshold has risen, creating a greater danger from hot or sharp objects. The taste dims; the number of taste buds will have decreased by a third by age 75.

The nerve cells people worry about most are those of the central nervous system—principally the spinal cord and the brain. Studies as early as the 1920s indicated that brain cells begin to die off around age 30 and in 1958 one researcher estimated the loss rate at 100,000 a day. Unlike skin, blood, liver and other regenerative cells, neurons cannot be produced after maturity. It is now known that the brain of an aged person weighs about 7 percent less than it did at maturity. But there is no direct correlation between brain size and intelligence, and there is still no evidence that loss of brain cells means loss of intelligence.

There are, of course, other changes in the brain more worrisome—changes that seem to impair mental function. These changes are all microscopic, and involve the proliferation of abnormal blobs, tangles and intracellular "garbage." The blobs are plaques containing an abnormal protein called amyloid. By now both Jim and Mary are almost certain to have some plaques, but their role in the aging process is unknown. The tangles—called neurofibrillary—are inside nerve cells (and others) and just as poorly understood. They resemble old, snarled fishing line. The "garbage" is a mysterious brown pigment called lipofuscin, or age pigment. The accumulation of lipofuscin among cells is thought always to accompany aging, but it is not known whether the pigment is simply a by-product of cellular activity or is harmful. Pellets of lipo-

fuscin form an outer coat by the same process oil-based paints harden, and are resistant to normal "garbage-removal" enzymes.

These mysterious blobs, tangles and pigments are linked to one of the least understood and most abused terms in the lexicon of aging: senility. The word is frequently used to apply to any act or gesture by an "old" person—forgetfulness, selfishness, a desire for a nap and so on. Health care professionals now seldom use it except to indicate senile brain disease, sometimes called chronic brain syndrome. Even these terms are vague; Robert Butler calls them "wastebasket diagnoses." Their greatest weakness is that they fail to separate those who are "senile" from those who are "normal." One expert, Adrian Ostfeld of the Yale University School of Medicine, decides it this way: "If a person knows when to get out of bed, wash, dress, eat and pay his bills, he is not a case."

Nor is there any certainty about whether dementia (the commonest designation is Alzheimer's disease) is really a disease or simply a normal part of the aging process. One reason for this confusion is that the primary indicators of dementia (plaques, tangles, lipofuscin) are also present in "normal" older people like Jim and Mary. Most cases of Alzheimer's disease show no simple pattern of inheritance, and no evidence that they are contagious. What is certain is that they are rare—more so than commonly supposed. Because diagnosis is so uncertain, the true incidence is not known. But it is known that only about 5 percent of elders live in institutions, and only a very small percentage of them can truly be called senile. In one study of 3,141 low-income persons between 65 and 74, only 12 could be identified as cases of senile brain disease. Most of the institutionalized elderly are victims of stroke, injury, arthritis, chronic respiratory diseases, alcoholism and other nonsenile conditions.

Physically, then, the elders have slowed somewhat, but they are by no means incapacitated. There is no physiological watershed at age 65 that should prevent people from working if they want to. Their strength is down slightly, their wind reduced; but neither condition is crippling and certainly not serious enough to disqualify them from most activities of "normal" life. But what of behavior? Is there something different about the workings of an older mind?

I have mentioned the irony of Sigmund Freud: At the same time he mistrusted elders (he seldom took them as patients), he himself did his best work after the age of 40. Freud referred to a "rigid ego" in old age and an "inverted Oedipal complex"—an exaggerated attachment to a child figure rather than a parent figure of the opposite sex. Jung, unlike Freud, refused to lump older people in such psychic ignominy, treating each as a unique individual.

In fact, there are signs of subtle, broad psychic changes in old age, but nothing to deserve Freud's prejudice. These are tough to test because old people are slightly less motivated than the young to take tests. A University of

Why do we have to die?

By nature's rules, death is as much a part of the game as life. Shortly after puberty (in humans as in other animals), the first signs of aging begin—a steady loss of irreplaceable cells, an accumulation of "wear-and-tear" mistakes, a slowing of metabolic rate. Eventually the accumulation of these changes and mistakes becomes fatal in one way or another.

But the death that comes to us all is not really so simple as this organic falling-apart. Otherwise we might be able to stave it off through care, just as we prolong the life of a well-loved automobile by proper maintenance and garaging. The hard truth is that humans and other animals have a maximum life expectancy that is rarely, if ever, exceeded. No matter how well sheltered from predation, disease and other "natural" causes of death, the Norway rat does not live past the age of four years, the gray squirrel past 15, the black bear past 35, the Asiatic elephant past 70 or *Homo sapiens* past 110. If death were the random result of accident and rusting away, we would expect to encounter wide variations in nature—the occasional octogenarian squirrel or, at the opposite extreme, the elephant that ages quickly and dies at 14. It is clear that a program for death is written in our genes.

The location and trigger of that program constitute the most hotly debated questions in gerontology today. By one theory, championed by Leonard Hayflick of Stanford, a clock of aging lies in each of our cells, where DNA molecules bear a gene or genes for their own destruction. Hayflick bases his thinking on his discovery less than two decades ago that even cells carefully nourished outside the body in tissue culture are programmed to die. Previous to that time, cells in tissue culture were thought to be immortal. But in the chick embryo cells he uses, Hayflick has shown that cell division ceases after about 50 generations—a seemingly clear case of genetic self-destruction. Similarly, he believes that cells in a whole-body context give orders, by some mysterious timing, for a progressive disruption of protein assembly lines and eventually their own death.

A more popular, though not incompatible, theory is that death is controlled by the endocrine system through some unidentified "death hormones." W. Donner Denckla of the Roche Institute of Molecular Biology in New Jersey is a leader in testing this hormonal clock theory. "I don't care what happens to cells in tissue culture," says Denckla. "What is important is what people die of." Denckla's clock, controlled by the brain and mediated by the thyroid gland, would, like Hayflick's, have genetic gearworks. The mechanism for either is not yet clear.

Why should we die at all? That is an evolutionary question, but one which gerontologists must consider. Presumably, the reasons humans live as long as they do is that the species is well served by a hierarchy of elders who are able to think, be wise and pass on their wisdom to younger generations. Why not let old humans do this to the age of 200, getting ever wiser? The most reasonable explanation is that more frequent death—and new life—among individuals is necessary to the survival of the species. Evolution by means of natural selection is based upon the selection of "favorable" genes and their passage to successive generations. This genetic turnover must be rapid if we are to keep up with environmental changes.

Ah, you say—but that's old-fashioned! We are seizing control of our evolution now; we'll soon be able to engineer our genes to fit the environment of our choice. That may indeed be true, and if it is we'll also be able to correct the genes that bring death. We might learn how to live in good health and sound mind to the age of 200 or 500; perhaps there will be no limit. But we can only begin to guess at the social tumult that would accompany this sudden excess of new old people. Many of us would probably prefer the stance of Lewis Thomas, president of Memorial Sloan-Kettering Cancer Center in New York and author of *The Lives of a Cell.* "At a certain age," says Thomas, "it is in our nature to wear out, to come unhinged and to die, and that is that."

—A.A. Jr.

Chicago report on interviews with schoolteachers indicates a general laying back with age: "One of the things they talked about is that they had come to deal with professional interests with less intensity in middle age. A high school principal said: 'When I started out, each disciplinary problem in the school was a special problem for me. I intervened; I went all out for it. Now I withdraw a little more and let the teacher handle it until I can see what is going on.'"

Jim and Mary find that they move more slowly now, mentally as well as physically. Instead of making a quick response to a question, then tend to ponder it for a moment before answering. Their reaction time has slowed; in a simple response test requiring them to push a button as soon as a red light came on, both Jim and Mary took .212 seconds to react when they were in their fifties, .217 seconds now. In 10 years it will take them .245 seconds to push the button. To some people, this is evidence that older people should take driving tests periodically.

The breadth of their interests has narrowed a good deal; this seems to peak around the age of *nine,* when children respond to almost anything. They watch about the same amount of television they did when they were younger, though they prefer variety and talent shows to serious dramas or mysteries. They have adopted more solitary pursuits, especially reading, going to art galleries and spending evenings at home with each other. Both have less interest in driving automobiles, in sports and in exploring.

According to one psychologist, there is more concrete behavior after age 60, less conceptualizing. Jim and Mary are more likely to think there is only one answer to a question, or one meaning to a situation, than they used to. In one thinking test reported in the *Journal of Gerontology*, involving subjects aged 12 to 80, the older people tended to rely more on past experience for answers rather than on analytical thinking. Other intelligence tests indicate a decrease in short-term memory, more difficulty putting three random words in a sentence, poorer word association, less facile picture composition.

In other areas, the Johnsons have experienced no such decline. Their vocabulary, for example, has nearly doubled since their twenties. Definitions, verbal understanding, naming countries, counting pennies all stand up well with age. Worker studies have indicated that individual speed and efficiency do drop with age, but older people tend to take care of their age-associated handicaps better than young people take care of their deficiencies. "Considering total job behavior," writes Harold Geist, a clinical psychologist and professor at San Francisco State College, "the older worker is found to be more efficient than the younger—especially when considering accuracy, absenteeism and motivation." Other studies have revealed little or no truth in the myth that most jobs are too strenuous or dangerous for elders. The U.S. Department of Labor has found that only 14 percent of jobs in industry require much physical strength, and many surveys have shown that older workers have fewer accidents than younger workers.

Much of the pressure to retire, it seems, comes not from an inability to perform but from the negative attitude of younger people. The University of Maryland's Center on Aging has found that children typically view elderly people as "sick, sad, tired, dirty and ugly" and insist that they themselves would never be old. And the most damaging aspect of such attitudes is that old people themselves come to believe them. "They are being told it's all downhill financially, it's all downhill sexually, it's all downhill intellectually," says Edward Ansello of the Maryland group.

New research, however, is revealing no evidence that life has to be significantly downhill for the old. Duke University's Center for the Study of Aging and Human Development has been keeping tabs on more than 200 elders for the last 20 years, and the group's conclusion so far is that most old people remain sound of body and mind until the final weeks of life. "The characteristic they seem to suffer most from," says George Maddox, head of the Duke Center, "is the tendency of society to treat them as though they are all alike."

Take sex, for example. NIA president Robert Butler has written a book called *Sex After Sixty* in which he says that this is one area where all people over a certain age are—wrongly—thought to be alike. "Many persons—not only the young and the middle-aged but older people themselves—simply assume that [sex] is over. This is nonsense. Our own clinical and research work, the work of other gerontologists, the research of Kinsey and the clinical discoveries of Masters and Johnson all demonstrate that relatively healthy older people who enjoy sex are capable of experiencing it often until very late in life."

Butler and other gerontologists argue that the myth of the sexless old is one of the most insidious symptoms of "ageism." He condemns the "aesthetic narrowness" by which we think of only the young as beautiful, and which makes it so difficult for grown children to deal with their parents' sexuality. Indeed, single or widowed parents who live with younger relatives are often made to feel guilty or indecent for wanting to date.

The field is riddled with additional myths. One of the most anxiety-producing is the fear of many men that they will have heart attacks during intercourse. It is, of course, possible, but fewer than 1 percent of all coronary deaths occur then, and 70 percent of those are during extramarital sex, which tends to feature nonphysical stresses like guilt or lack of time.

Another myth is the fear among women that a hysterectomy means the end of sex. In fact there is no evidence that removal of the womb produces any change in sexual desire or performance.

Then there are the false aphrodisiacs tried by many older people: alcohol (especially wine), Spanish fly, Cayenne pepper, black snakeroot, bloodroot, vitamin E, marijuana. Sometimes alcohol has benefit as a social icebreaker, but there the benefits end. Any stimulant works more on the mind than the body, and the effects lessen with use. The only true aphrodisiacs are good diet and good exercise.

Menopause in women, which typically occurs between 45 and 50, is a rich source of both myth and misunderstanding. Physiologically it is fairly straightforward, characterized by the ending of menstruation and a sharp decline in the output of hormones—chiefly the estrogen group. Some women, however, use menopause as an excuse, for themselves or others, to slow or even halt their sexual activity. Actually, about two-thirds of women experience no dramatic changes or discomfort with menopause. With a positive attitude, there is no reason that sex cannot remain a source of pleasure long after menopause. It is even common for sex to improve with the freedom from anxieties about becoming pregnant.

Jim, like Mary, can look forward to years of enjoyable sex. Both his fertility (the ability to have children) and potency (the ability to have intercourse) should last one or two decades, possibly even longer. Havelock Ellis, the renowned British psychologist and sexologist, overcame a lifetime of impotence when he reached old age. Jim will not have to go through the broad hormonal changes experienced by Mary; there is no menopause in men (though some experience a similar psychological shock) but rather a gradual decline in the output of testosterone, the male hormone.

If we make the assumption that old age is not a curse—and it now seems clear it should not be—can and should we prolong it? Here we come upon a stumbling block: It is assumed that aging is an inexorable part of life, programmed somehow in our genes, yet some scientists think that the wear-and-tear disease of aging might be "cured" by clever manipulation of body machinery. It seems, in any event, that for the foreseeable future our time on earth is limited to about 71 years. (See box on A/E page 153.)

Even the conquest of common diseases would not lead us to immortality. If all cardiovascular diseases—now causing more than half of all deaths—were eliminated, the average lifetime would increase only about ten years. If cancer were no longer a killer we would gain another two years. Wipe out all infectious and parasitic diseases and we'd last another year; hold all accidents, suicides and homicides and that's two more years—still far short of immortality. In fact, despite all the medical gains documented since 1900, most of which lessened the threats of infant death and childhood diseases, Jim and Mary at 65 stand to live only about two years longer than they might have in 1900.

Despite an immense amount of research, the only known ways to extend a human lifetime (not a human life span) are to have long-lived parents, to eat properly and to get regular exercise. The first possibility, of course, is beyond our control. The last two are matters of will. Most gerontologists agree that Americans are eating themselves into early graves. We eat too much fat, too much sugar, too much protein, too much refined carbohydrate and not enough fresh vegetables, whole grains or other roughage. Take calories alone: Male Americans aged 55–64 now get about 2,422 a day, and most nutritionists believe this is too much. The world's longest-lived people thrive on far less. The same age group of men in Hunza, in West Pakistan, get about 1,925 calories a day; the men of the Caucasus in southern Russia about 1,800. Life insurance actuaries judge that being overweight subtracts from three to 10 or more years from a lifetime. So does

---

Prejudiced Shakespeare?

The sixth age shifts
Into the lean and slipper'd pantaloon,
With spectacles on nose and pouch on side,
His youthful hose, well sav'd, a world too wide
For his shrunk shank; and his big manly voice,
Turning again toward childish treble, pipes
And whistles in his sound. Last scene of all,
That ends this strange eventful history,
Is second childishness, and mere oblivion,
Sans teeth, sans eyes, sans taste, sans everything.

As You Like It, Act II

---

cigarette smoking: for one pack a day figure seven years; for two packs, 12 years. High blood pressure, high cholesterol level, a tense disposition, and a high pulse all shorten the average lifetime as well.

Exercise is increasingly acknowledged to be an effective ingredient in building a long lifetime. But it is important that it be an endurance building kind—not intermittent bursts of youthful enthusiasm followed by weeks of spectatorship—and it must be continued into old age. The point of exercise is to strengthen the heart, and the best kinds for doing that are jogging, cross-country skiing, swimming, rowing, cycling, long walks—anything that gets the heart pumping and keeps it pumping for 20 minutes or more. It has even been demonstrated that the much-maligned weekend athlete, if he or she is vigorous enough, gains some protection against heart ailments. A recent study of 17,000 Harvard alumni has shown "strenuous leisure time exercise" to be valuable even if there are other negative factors, like cigarette smoking. And, of course, those long-lived folks from Hunza and the Caucasus get plenty of outdoor exercise all their lives.

Typically, we slow-to-arouse Americans do not yet realize the urgency of the gray revolution. Before 1950 little thought was given to systems for the elderly—easier-to-use mass transit, housing situated near vital services, a health system that has the patience to diagnose and cure old people's chronic diseases. Only now, with the emergency upon us, are we beginning to think about how to live with our elders. An important first step must be an attack on "ageism" and an acceptance of the old people who will be a larger and larger component of modern society. More and more it will have to be "in" to be old.

Marital Adjustment in the Post-Retirement Years

*This paper presents a theoretical framework from which to analyze marital adjust-
ment in the post-retirement years. A lack of consistent usage, among professionals,
regarding the concept marital adjustment is noted. Furthermore, attention is drawn
to the duality nature of defining the concept. Four major dimensions of marital adjustment are discussed: (a) self-esteem, (b) interpersonal commitment, (c) availability of resources, and (d) goal consensus. An examination of marital dynamics in the
post-retirement years includes a discussion of three ideal-typical conjugal relationships: (a) The Husband-Wife, (b) The Parent-Child, and (c) The Associates. The
framework presented herein is thought to provide a foundation for developing suggestions that may subsequently enrich the marital lives of older persons.*

MORRIS L. MEDLEY

Morris L. Medley is Assistant Professor, Department of
Sociology and Social Work, Indiana State University, Terre
Haute, Indiana 47809.

Is not marriage an open question, when
it is alleged, from the beginning of the
world, that such as are in the institution
wish to get out, and such as are out
wish to get in?

Ralph Waldo Emerson
Representative Men: Montaigne

The experience of a large proportion of the
married population living together for several
years following their retirement from the labor
force is a relatively recent phenomenon. In
1974, 84.3 percent of the males and 47.6
percent of the females in the 65 to 74 age
category were married; likewise, in the 75
years and over category the percent married
was 68.0 and 24.4, males and females
respectfully (U.S. Bureau of the Census,
1975, p. 38). With slightly more than 10 percent of the nation's population in the 65 years
and over age category, it is clear that a
sizeable number of persons are both married
and retired. Prior to World War I, few married
women were employed outside the home—
while men were likely to be employed, at least
on a limited basis, until their death. At the
turn of the century, farmers and small
businessmen (who made up a larger
proportion of the labor force than today)
would commonly continue working in their
later years while gradually relinquishing more
and more responsibilities to younger men. In
this manner, many men were never actually

"retired." Moreover, death took a larger
proportion of persons prior to age 65 than
today. For example, in 1900 only 39.2 percent
of white males reached 65 years of age, compared to 67.5 percent of their 1973 counterparts (U.S. Department of Health, Education,
and Welfare, 1975, p. 5-4). Futhermore, in
1974 women comprised 37.9 percent of the
labor force — this number included 57.7 percent of the married women with a husband
present (U.S. Bureau of the Census, 1975,
p. xviii). It is apparent, therefore, that a large
number of women are both directly and indirectly afffected by retirement. The possible
effects of dual retirement upon marital adjustment, i.e., self and spouse, has yet to be
explored.

Although one may "retire" at any age, the
Social Security Act of 1935 has more or less
established "the age of retirement" at 65. In
some occupations, particularly among military personnel, policemen, and firemen —
pre-65 retirement is commonplace; however,
for most forms of employment the ages 62 to
65 are more nearly synonymous with retirement.

The Concept of Marital Adjustment

Marital adjustment, at various stages in the
family life cycle, has been the subject of
numerous research investigations; nevertheless, definitive conclusions remain elusive.
The term marital adjustment is not used by
students of the family in any consistent
technical sense. When the term is used, it is
generally operationalized and applied to a
specific research problem. Spanier, Lewis
and Cole (1975, p. 264) note that ". . . studies

assessing the quality of the marital relationship over time have used a variety of concepts to characterize the dependent variable," e.g., "satisfaction," "happiness," "success," and "adjustment." If there is any commonality running through the various attempts to assess the quality of marital relationships, it is an implication that marital adjustment denotes a relatively harmonious relationship within and between individuals, resulting in a sense of well-being. The term marital adjustment, as used in this discussion, further implies a dynamic process—as compared to a static state or condition. Perhaps the most common observation regarding marriage is that it is a dynamic relationship characterized by continuous change. Thus, any attempt to examine marital adjustment must take into account the changing nature of the marital relationship. If we accept the marital relationship as "alive" and "ongoing," we are in a more advantageous position to assess and appreciate the changes in behavior exhibited by marriage partners during the course of their relationship (Kline & Medley, 1973, p. 220). Clearly, marital adjustment, as used in a processual sense, refers to both the individual and the paired nature of the relationship.

The Dimensions of Marital Adjustment

Marital adjustment difficulties and/or accomplishments appear reducible to four major dimensions: (1) self-esteem, (2) interpersonal commitment, (3) availability of resources, and (4) goal consensus. Although in the process of marital adjustment the nature of the discord may vary considerably from time to time, the above dimensions seem likely to arise in each specific case. The four major dimensions are not, of course, of equal importance to all married couples, nor are they likely to maintain the same importance to any particular couple over the entire life cycle.

Self-Esteem

If individuals are to interact over time, on an intimate level, in such a fashion as to produce feelings of self-fulfillment and well-being, a sufficiently high level of self-esteem would seem mandatory. Without a positive sense of self-worth, individuals are likely to follow one of two roles, perhaps, alternating them on occasion. The first role might be labelled "the door-mat." Persons with a low sense of self-worth may believe themselves incapable of possessing a worthwhile idea; a sense of moral correctness, and/or the ability to behave creatively. Thus, for these people, the "safest" way of relating is to "follow" and to "obey" in an unquestioning manner. The second role follows a pattern of aggression.

The "agressor" is likely to "fear" ideas, values, and attitudes that conflict with his or her own. Therefore, lacking in positive self-esteem, the "agressor" is unable to tolerate and/or support the expression of any discordant views without the feeling of threat. To avoid the feeling of being threatened, the "agressor" attacks the spouse mentally and, perhaps, on occasion physically.

Individuals with sufficient positive self-esteem possess the confidence to permit and to encourage the expression of alternative views, and to reverse oneself when rational evidence suggests this course of action. The self-confident person realizes that there is no need to fear one's spouse. Moreover, the secure person recognizes that by making another's life more satisfying, one is likely personally to experience a greater sense of well-being and self-fulfillment.

Interpersonal Commitment

The term interpersonal commitment is used here to describe the strength of commitment by each spouse to maintaining the paired relationship. The degree to which each individual is committed to maintaining the marital union most certainly influences the couple's willingness and ability successfully to adjust to each other and to their marital roles. An individual or individuals with a low level of interpersonal commitment may retard the adjustment process as a means to dissolve the union. Moreover, if one individual has a minimum interpersonal commitment, while the spouse feels a strong commitment, the partner with low commitment may "control" the other, and subsequently the marriage by threatening to end the relationship.

On the other hand, if both partners are deeply committed to maintaining the paired-nature of their relationship, each is likely willingly to engage in accommodation, compromise, and the general avoidance of potentially troublesome areas. In fact, areas that may appear problematic for persons with low interpersonal commitment may be entirely overlooked or viewed as a welcome challenge by the deeply committed. The deeply committed may include couples experiencing a "total" or "vital" relationship (Cuber & Harroff, 1963), or they may be partners who have become disaffected with one another but perceive a lack of attractive alternatives to their existing marriage.

Availability of Resources

The availability of resources dimension carries a broad and wide-ranging interpretation. This dimension includes financial security, health, effective communication, rationality, and external socio-emotional support.

Financial security. In 1974, the age category 65 years and over comprised 15.7 percent of the total persons classified by the U.S. Bureau of the Census (1975, p. 403) as below the low income level. This same category of persons made up only about 10 percent of the total population. Moreover, in 1974, the median money income of white families with the "head" being 65 years or older was $7,807 compared to $13,271 for all white families. On the other hand, blacks are in more serious financial difficulty. For black families with a "head" 65 years or older the median money income was $4,874, compared to $7,807 for the total number of black families (U.S. Bureau of the Census, 1975, p. 397). The financial situation for "totally" retired families is probably more critical than the above figures indicate, as these figures include employed persons 65 years and older. In any event, a large proportion, perhaps a majority, of persons in the post-retirement years are experiencing financial insecurity. Not surprisingly, financial insecurity is found to be a major factor in marital discord at nearly every stage in the family life cycle. Adequate financial resources do, of course, relate to the attainment of such basic life necessities as food, shelter and health.

Health. The relationship between an individual's state of health and marital adjustment is neither based strictly upon an "objective" medical determination, nor upon the person's state of mind. Nevertheless, " . . . the people with the most serious health problems were most likely to be dissatisfied with their marriages" (Renne, 1970, p. 63). This relationship may be viewed as possessing both direct and indirect effects. If the illness, whether physical or mental, is serious enough hospitalization or similar treatment may physically separate the couple. Moreover, if the ill person remains with the spouse, the relationship may be subjected to unusual stress resulting from a variety of sources. These include the need for the "healthy" partner to assume additional responsibilities in caring for the ill spouse, the home, and financial demands. Furthermore, illness is apt to reduce sexual interest, desire for travel, ability to work, and interest in mutual friends and activities. Perhaps the most significant indirect effect involves the financial drain that illness places on the couple's economic base. For whatever reason(s) it is clear that health is an integral factor in marital adjustment.

Effective communication. The term communication refers to "The transmission of information, ideas, attitudes, or emotions from one person or group to another (or others) primarily through symbols" (Theodorson & Theodorson, 1969, p. 62). Communication can be achieved through either verbal or nonverbal forms. Marital partners must, if they are to obtain a maximum sense of self-fulfillment and well-being, not merely communicate; they must communicate effectively. "In effective communication the meaning conveyed to the recipient corresponds closely to that intended by the sender" (Theodorson & Theodorson, 1969, p. 62). the willingness and ability to communicate effectively is not, of course, a panacea for resolving all martial difficulties. Nevertheless, as Levinger and Senn (1967, p. 237) note, "Communication is a basic requirement for the development and maintenance of interpersonal relationships." Effective and open-communication are important to marital adjustment not only by the exchange of information, but most significantly via the attainment of empathic understanding.

Rationality. Rationality is a most difficult concept to operationalize; however, its inclusion as a factor in marital adjustment is vital (Eisenberg & Zingle, 1975). Rationality implies several qualities, including: the power of reasoning, the possession of reason, and the likelihood of behaving in a judicious manner. Behaving in a fashion consistent with rationality is akin to Berne's (1964) admonishment to get one's "adult" in control. Nearly everyone can recall instances of interpersonal disharmony arising from irrationality. These occasions may range from the exhibition of mild anger accompanying a minor faux pas, to constant bickering over the lack of planning for the future, to rage produced by jealousy. Although it is probably true that no one can always behave in accordance with rationality, marital harmony and personal self-fulfillment will probably be enhanced by individuals acting in conformity with reason.

External socio-emotional support. It is common to assume that a marital couple does not exist in a social vacuum. Thus, it becomes necessary to consider external forces in any examination of marital adjustment. For the purposes at hand, we shall limit our concern to select external socio-emotional supports. The external socio-emotional support indices contains a duality aspect. First, the couple is influenced by each individual's previous familization experiences (Holland, 1970). It is probably within our family of orientation that most persons receive their first, and sometimes most lasting, impressions of what are deemed appropriate husband and wife roles. Moreover, individuals are likely to engage in a more or less constant pattern of communication with such significant others as family members and friends. Thus, depending on their importance to the individual, these significant others will most assuredly influence the relationship between the marital couple. Secondly, the relationship is likely to be influenced by the social norms expressed through the legal, education, and religious institutions. Moreover, individuals may adhere to the values transmitted via such socialization settings as newspapers, magazines, films, and television. It would seem fair, therefore, to conclude that all marital relationships are affected to some degree via sources external to the married pair.

Goal Consensus

Bernard (1964, p. 679) notes " . . . that adjustment is telic, that is, goal-oriented." All marital interaction is not, of course, goal-oriented; however, our present concern is with marital adjustment behavior. A goal may be defined as "A condition or object sought by an individual to satisfy a need or want, thus motivating behavior" (Theodorson & Theodorson, 1969, p. 174). Goal consensus, as used here, refers to the unanimity shared by a marital couple regarding individually held goals. Goal-oriented marital interaction has a decidedly multifarious nature. Therefore, in order to include goal consensus as a dimension in marital adjustment, one must recognize the implied qualities of agreed importance, degree of differences, and the time frame of reference. Each individual possesses many goals, likewise, these many goals are apt to be arranged in a mental hierarchy of importance. Thus, it becomes necessary to know not only if a couple share a certain goal; but, whether or not the goal has the same importance to each person. If we should recognize a difference in priorities, it may well be important to further identify the degree of difference. The time frame in which the goal-oriented behavior occurs is also important in clarifying the goal consensus dimension. First, behavior may be directed toward a specific and immediate time, e.g., the husband wishes to visit his parents tonight. Secondly, the behavior may concern time in an ongoing fashion, e.g., the partners attempt and desire to project the image of a "happily" married couple to their neighbors. Thirdly, the goal-oriented behavior may refer to a futuristic projection, e.g., a young couple may share a vision of retirement at age 50, with a home in the mountains.

Married couples may, therefore, share or not share goals. If they share common goals they may or may not share them with the same degree of intensity. Furthermore, the goals may imply a time reference that includes specific-immediacy, constancy, and remoteness. If goal consensus exists between a married couple, the principal focus is likely to be upon determining the most efficacious means for goal achievement. On the other hand, if goal consensus is minimal or non-existent, the adjustive process is strained and becomes increasingly dynamic.

Marital Dynamics in the Post-Retirement Years

Studies of marital adjustment (or similar concepts), over the family life cycle, have become common during the past two decades. These studies do not, however, generally arrive at the same conclusions. One group of studies (Townsend, 1957; Blood & Wolfe, 1960; Pineo, 1961; Paris & Luckey, 1966; Safilious-Rothschild, 1967) suggest that following the initial year(s) of marriage there is a continual decline in marital adjustment throughout the life cycle. On the other hand, some studies (Rollins & Feldman, 1970; Rollins & Cannon, 1974) report a curvilinear trend with a decline in marital adjustment following the initial years; a leveling off, followed by an increase during the post-retirement years. The issue regarding a possible relationship between marital adjustment and stage of the life cycle has become further clouded by recent studies that do not consistently support the continual decline, nor the curvilinear hypothesis (Deutscher, 1964; Burr, 1970, Hayes & Stinnet, 1971; Spanier, Lewis, & Cole, 1975). It becomes readily evident that any assessment of the role played by aging and retirement to marital adjustment is likely to be somewhat speculative.

The onset of retirement is likely to bring a couple "face-to-face" in a manner that it has not experienced since the initial years of marriage. By the advent of retirement, most couples have passed the child-rearing phase of marriage (a condition that will become increasingly widespread with the succeeding generation); thus, with disengagement from the labor force, the couple finds their marital life laid bare before them. In the pre-retirement stages, couples may avoid the intimate nature of the marital relationship by focusing their energies upon child-rearing and occupational duties. However, during the post-retirement years, these possible "escape" mechanisms (which may be, to some extent, socially acceptable) are no longer available. Of course, not all couples avoid the intimacy of the man-woman relationship during the middle years. For these people, the post-retirement years are likely to offer increased satisfaction with the marital adjustment process.

For many persons, in the post-retirement years, their conjugal relationships and adjustive patterns are probably a continuation of adjustments made in earlier stages of the life cycle (Fried & Stern, 1948). Moreover, the adjustments that each individual makes regarding his or her marriage is likely to be less extensive than in previous years. Nevertheless, the view that marriages and marital adjustment behaviors are similar for all persons in later life is short-sighted (Deutscher, 1964). Adherents to the "elderly mystique" would have us believe that all post-retirement marriages are composed of chronically ill, physically and socially isolated, low-income, and senile persons (Rosenfeld, 1965). However, only the most naive and uninformed individuals would accept the above characterization as valid.

Marriage in the post-retirement years, like those at any stage in the life cycle, reflect wide-ranging variation. Nevertheless, certain patterns of marital behavior suggest the legitimacy of applying select ideal-typical concepts to describe the conjugal relationships. If permitted the latitude of broad interpretation, three marital ideal-types would seem to encompass most, if not all, conjugal relationships. These ideal-types are: (a) The Husband-Wife; (b) The Parent-Child; and (c) The Associates. Each of these ideal-types is intended to personify the most dominant theme, characterizing the interpersonal relationship between a married couple. All three marital ideal-types are probably found at each stage in the life cycle; however, the proportion of couples categorized in any particular type is likely to vary with the passage of time.

Marriages typified by the Husband-Wife relationship find couples stressing the intimate, and shared nature of their relationship. These persons focus their marriage around the husband and wife roles, however not necessarily to the exclusion of other roles. Moreover, couples characterized by the Husband-Wife relationship are likely to feel that the interpersonal interaction with one's spouse is the most rewarding aspect of marital life.

The Parent-Child ideal-type infers that one spouse assumes the role of parent and the other the role of child, in their marital interrelationships. The spouse assuming the parental role acts in a nurturant, protective, and dominant fashion. On the other hand, the spouse assuming the child role behaves in a dependent and submissive manner. This relationship is most likely to develop among couples in which one person becomes incapacitated or assumes the "sick role," although such conditions are not prerequisites.

The Associates, refers to couples who are likely to be more or less friends and although they may appreciate one another's company— they find their most rewarding moments outside the intimacy of the husband-wife relationship. The Associates are apt to be quite efficient at the "business" of managing marital and family life. The friendship experienced by the pair, coupled with satisfaction derived from their parental and extra-family roles, is likely to enhance the continuation of their marriage.

The ideal-types noted above are not perceived as positions in a marital cycle, nor are they thought to necessarily last a lifetime. Individuals and couples may, however, adjust to any of the ideal-types. Likewise, all three types are likely to provide some marital partners with a sense of self-fulfillment and a feeling of well-being.

Implications and Conclusions

An unstated theme running through this paper has been the potential for enhancing marital adjustment in the post-retirement years. Likewise, the continuity between the stages in the life cycle has been continually stressed. Although the notion that marital adjustment in the post-retirement years is influenced by earlier life experiences is supported, it is further suggested here that activities may be undertaken to enhance marital adjustment in later life. These activities may be categorized according to their most promising source. We may, therefore, describe the activities as stemming from either an interpersonal or societal level.

Marital adjustment is a creative process; like all creative processes it is not a fixed mechanical sequence. Therefore, no mere list of suggestions for enhancing marital adjustment will do justice to the complexity of the process. Nevertheless, it is proposed that an orchestration of activities suggested by the theoretical framework presented here will enrich marital relationships among older persons.

In reviewing the field of marital adjustment, we conclude that although an abundant literature exists, the theoretical and empirical base remains inconsistent and inconclusive. The purpose of this paper is to present, in a logical and readable manner, a comprehensive theoretical framework for analyzing marital adjustment. It is hoped that this paper will serve the pragmatic interest of older persons by serving the intellectual interests of counselors, family life educators, and persons working in the area of family services.

REFERENCES

Bernard, J. The adjustments of married mates. In H. T. Christensen (Ed.) *Handbook of marriage and the family.* Chicago: Rand McNally, 1964, 675-739.

Berne, E. *Games people play: The psychology of human relationships.* New York: Grove, 1964.

Blood, R. O., & Wolf, D. M. *Husbands and wives: The dynamics of married living.* Glencoe, Illinois: Free Press, 1960.

Burr, W. R. Satisfaction with various aspects of marriage over the life cycle. *Journal of Marriage and the Family,* 1970, 32, 29-37.

Cuber, J. F., & Harroff, P. B. The more total view: Relationships among men and women of the upper middle class. *Marriage and Family Living,* 1963, 25, 140-145.

Deutscher, I. The quality of postparental life. *Journal of Marriage and the Family,* 1964, 26, 52-60.

Eisenberg, J. M., & Zingle, H. W. Marital adjustment and irrational ideas. *Journal of Marriage and Family Counseling,* 1975, 1, 81-91.

Fried, E. G., & Stern K. The situation of the aged within the family. *American Journal of Orthopsychiatry,* 1948, 18, 31-54.

Hayes, M. P., & Stinnett N. Life satisfaction of middle-aged husbands and wives. *Journal of Home Economics,* 1971, 63, 669-674.

Holland, D. Familization, socialization, and the universe of meaning. *Journal of Marriage and the Family,* 1970, 32, 415-427.

Kline, A. F., & Medley, M. L. (Eds.) *Dating and marriage: An interactionist perspective.* Boston: Holbrook, 1973.

Levinger, G., & Senn, D. J. Disclosure of feelings in marriage. *Merrill-Palmer Quarterly,* 1967, 13, 237-249.

Paris, B. L., & Luckey, E. B. A longitudinal study of marital satisfaction. *Sociology and Social Research,* 1966, 50, 212-223.

Pineo, P. C. Disenchantment in the later years of marriage. *Marriage and Family Living,* 1961, 23, 3-11.

Renne, K. S. Correlates of dissatisfaction in marriage. *Journal of Marriage and the Family,* 1970, 32, 54-67.

Rollins, B. C., & Cannon, K. L. Marital satisfaction over the family life cycle: A reevaluation. *Journal of Marriage and the Family,* 1974, 36, 271-283.

Rollins, B. C., & Feldman, H. Marital satisfaction over the family life cycle. *Journal of Marriage and the Family,* 1970, 32, 20-28.

Rosenfelt, R. H. The elderly mystique. *The Journal of Social Issues,* 1965, 21, 37-43.

Safilios-Rothschild, C. A comparison of power structure and marital satisfaction in urban Greek and French families. *Journal of Marriage and the Family,* 1967, 29, 345-352.

Spanier, G. B., Lewis, R. A., & Cole, C. L. Marital adjustment over the family life cycle: The issue of curvilinearity. *Journal of Marriage and the Family,* 1975, 37, 263-275.

Theodorson, G. A., & Theodorson A. G. *A modern dictionary of sociology.* New York: Crowell, 1969.

Townsend, P. *The family life of old people.* London: Routledge and Kegan Paul, 1957.

U.S. Bureau of the Census. *The American almanac: The statistical abstract of the United States.* New York: Grosset and Dunlap, 1975.

U.S. Department of Health, Education, and Welfare. *Life tables: Vital statistics of the United States,* 1973 (Vol.2—Sect. 5), Rockville, Maryland: National Center for Health Statistics, 1975.

COPING WITH DEATH IN THE FAMILY

The key to minimizing the impact of death in the family, say experts on the subject, is more honesty on the part of everyone involved. The patient should be told—as much as possible—about the seriousness of the illness. And the rest of the family should openly express their own feelings.

The dramatic news today is that there are experts on death and dying and a large and growing body of knowledge about the subject. Thanks to the work of such people as Chicago psychiatrist-author Dr. Elizabeth Kubler-Ross, the burden of coping with death—from the shock of learning that a spouse or a child is terminally ill, through the death, funeral, and subsequent adjustment period—is being lightened for many families. "There's a healthier, more open attitude today toward death and how to handle it," says Dr. Austin H. Kutscher, who teaches a new course called thanatology (the study of death) at the Columbia University medical school. "People are getting help they couldn't have gotten two or three years ago."

Kubler-Ross, who has written extensively on the subject, is one of many experts who travel widely today lecturing on death at schools, hospitals, and religious institutions around the country. Dr. Mary Cerney, a psychologist at the Menninger Foundation in Topeka, says she has just finished a lecture series on death at a Kansas high school. More and more hospitals and university psychology departments offer seminars on coping with death. The Candlelighters, with 39 chapters around the country, provides counsel to the families of children stricken with cancer, and the National Foundation for Sudden Infant Death tries to help grieving parents.

Orville Kelly was a newspaper editor in Davenport, Iowa, when he was stricken with lymphatic cancer in 1973. He launched Make Today Count for other cancer patients a year later and now counts 54 chapters. "As a cancer patient, I can now share my frustrations and anger with other patients," says 45-year-old Kelly. "We talk, we have speakers, we have hope."

Perhaps the biggest change has come among those who deal with terminal patients in hospitals (where 80% of all Americans die). Dr. Stephen E. Goldston, a psychologist with the National Institute of Mental Health in Rockville, Md., finds hospital personnel increasingly aware that "the dying need to be dealt with honestly, without pretense, and safeguarded against the greatest pain of death, which is terrible loneliness."

Goldston warns the family of someone approaching death that false good cheer only serves to deepen the patient's fear and anxiety. The survivors, in turn, require a period of unrestrained grief in order to adjust to a loved one's death, and that goes for children as well as adults.

"Children," says Goldston, "need to be told the truth and not lied to about a death in the family." Sugarcoating death, say Goldston and others, can cause greater pain—and sometimes serious guilt feelings—among children. "Families have a chance to educate their growing children about death," says Edward K. Leaton, president of a New York City consulting firm, whose two sons died of muscular dystrophy. "This need not be frightening. The death of a pet or a bird gives you a chance to explain and remove fears."

The patient

Step one in coping with death is

dealing with the patient, and here the old approach of telling the patient nothing is giving way to a new realism. Patients are being told more today—often to the point of telling a person that he or she is going to die. "Ideally, the patient should be the first to know," advises Dr. Herman Feifel, professor of psychiatry at the University of Southern California medical school. "The only question is how to tell the person. Some must be told gradually."

There are practical reasons for revealing the truth to a terminal patient. The patient, if "protected" by family and friends, suffers through hours of pointless, trivial talk. Another reason for telling the truth is that the patient will then feel less guilty in demanding services or attention or openly crying and expressing grief. Grieving is vital, since it enables the patient to accept the reality of death more easily.

Admitting the likelihood of death to a terminal patient is not a step to be taken lightly. Hope alone can sometimes prolong life; denial of hope can sometimes prod a person to suicide. Obviously, the matter should be discussed thoroughly with the patient's doctor and probably with a clergyman, as well. Several important questions must be answered: Is the doctor absolutely certain that the person is going to die? Does the patient really want to know the truth? "Some people decide to tell the dying person out of a compunction to be honest or a need to absolve their own guilt," says Dr. Kenneth D. Cohen, psychiatrist and clinical director of the Philadelphia Psychiatric Center.

Some people should not be told at all. A strong, relatively independent person can handle the news far better than someone who tends to be weak and dependent. The patient who still

How to handle the five stages of dying*

*Based on the five stages of death outlined in *On Death and Dying* by Dr. Elizabeth Kubler-Ross, psychiatrist and author

PATIENT BEHAVIOR	STAGE	FAMILY RESPONSE

DENIAL

In effect, the patient says, "It cannot be true." Patients often search frantically for a favorable diagnosis.

Understand why the patient is grasping at straws. Patience and willingness to talk are important.

ANGER

The patient says, "Yes—but why me?" Deep anger follows, and the patient may bitterly envy those who are well and complain incessantly about almost everything.

Consider that the patient is angry over the coming loss of everything: family, friends, home, work, play. Treat patient with understanding and respect, not by returning the anger.

BARGAINING

The patient says, "Maybe I can bargain with God and get a time extension." Promises of good behavior are made in return for time and some freedom from physical pain.

If the patient's 'bargain' is revealed, it should be listened to, not brushed off. This stage passes in a short time.

DEPRESSION

The patient grieves, and mourns approaching death.

Attempts to cheer up or reassure the patient mean very little. The patient needs to express sorrow fully and without hindrance.

ACCEPTANCE

The patient is neither angry nor depressed, only quietly expectant.

News of the outside world means little, and few visitors are required. There will be little talk, and it is time merely for the presence of the close family.

Mario De Vincentis—BW

hopes for recovery probably should not have those hopes dashed. Rather, the matter should usually be postponed until the patient raises the question of whether he or she is going to die.

"You do not rush the person into a recognition of their condition," says Columbia's Kutscher. "You listen carefully for hints of a desire to discuss the possibility of death." Cohen agrees that "the telling must be approached delicately." A basic point to get across, he feels, is that the patient is not alone and will not be alone.

"Above everything, don't make pretenses," advises a New York City advertising executive whose wife died of cancer. "When you feel that the suffering person wants the truth—tell it. Pretense keeps two people from ever really talking. I regret that before my wife died, we never got to the stage of real frankness. It made her death harder for both of us."

HONESTY IS BEST, WITHIN REASON

Kutscher and others suggest that the wishes of the dying be heeded when it comes to deciding on desperate life-prolonging measures. "Most terminal patients at this point know they will die," says Kutscher. "I suggest that you listen to them. They will probably make their wishes felt about this last-minute fighting to stay alive."

Sometimes, the word of impending death simply can't be concealed from the patient—when there is a will or other legal or business papers to be signed, for instance. Some people are anxious to get their affairs in order, and doing it can help them face death. "But do this gently," Kutscher suggests. "Have the family lawyer present the will. He can be more casual about it than you would be."

Most experts agree on the need to tell children as much as they can handle about a parent's illness. "If a parent has a terminal illness, even a small child should be told what this means—in terms the child can understand," says Dr. Edward Rydman, a Dallas psychologist. "Families tend to shy away from dealing with this," he adds. Says Dr. David A. Switzer, a Southern Methodist University psychologist: "The children need to know

that their father or mother is going away, and not just for 15 minutes or overnight."

Most psychologists agree and point out that in explaining the terminal illness of a parent, the child should be told in such a way that he or she can fully comprehend that death is permanent, that every effort was made to save the parent's life, that the loss will be painful, that it is good to cry or get angry to express grief, and that the parent's duties will be taken care of.

"In addition," says Goldston of NIMH, "I would make it clear that the rest of the family will remain together—assuming this is true." He notes that if the terminal patient is a brother or sister, it is important to let the other children know that "any evil wishful thinking they have had about the sick child doesn't really count for anything." This, he explains, can ease often dire guilt feelings among children, who frequently do "wish" bad things on siblings—the wish that a brother or sister would disappear for ever, for example.

Don't resort to fairy tales. Telling a child that "your mother went to sleep and will forever rest peacefully" can be frightening, not reassuring. "They will be afraid to go to bed," says Sandi D. Boshak, of Dix Hills, N.Y., whose son died in infancy. Boshak, who is active in group meetings of the National Foundation for Sudden Infant Death, feels that honesty is vital in explaining death to small children, as well as to teen-agers.

Another common mistake, say both psychologists and parents, is to use a religious explanation of a death in a family that has had no religious background. "Such an explanation will mean little to the child, may create fear, and can cause the child to later react negatively to religion," Goldston explains.

A child's role

Honest explanations to children in cases of a dying parent can also have a positive effect on the parent. Some children secretly fear that they are to blame for their parent's illness. Freed of this anxiety, the child will relate more closely to the ill parent and make the parent feel better. A child should rarely be kept apart from a parent who is dying. "Even though our daughter was only three years old, we kept her in contact with her mother," says a New York businessman whose wife died of cancer several years ago. "She fed her mother cracked ice," he adds. "This made her understand that her mother was very sick, and helped both of them when death came."

When a parent or sibling dies, even children as young as seven or so can and should take part in the mourning ritual observed by the family, say psychologists. "Ask yourself if a young child is capable of participating along with the adults and older children," says Cohen, of the Philadelphia Psychiatric Center. "Most children are capable of this, but some families want to protect and keep the child away from the funeral." This is a mistake, he feels, because the child is denied the outpouring of grief that helps lead to acceptance of the death.

"Equally important," advises Cohen, "is that the remaining parent, or both parents if a sibling has died, be with the child afterward to help the youngster with his or her feelings and talk about the death if the child wants to talk. And there is no need to be a 'stout fellow' about it. It's better to cry."

A number of specialists say today that even a child should be told—very cautiously—about his or her own terminal illness. Says Kübler-Ross: "Children can deal with death sometimes much better than grownups. The worst thing you can do is lie to them."

But the news—if it is told at all—must be greatly softened. David M. Kaplan, director of clinical social work at Stanford University, feels that "you might use such statements as 'you are very sick and we hope the doctor can help.'" But children as young as five or six usually sense that they are seriously ill, he explains, and pretense and lying only loses you their trust and isolates them, making their loneliness more difficult.

"With a child," advises Kutscher, "the task is to be honest—but not frightening. A parent will want to discuss these points with the doctor, clergyman, and possibly other family members, before deciding what to tell a child." But all the warnings about how—and when—to tell a dying patient, apply doubly with a child.

The household routine should be kept as normal as possible when a child is at home with a terminal illness. "That's important to the sick child and the other children," says Spencer Smith, an Atlanta businessman whose four-year-old daughter died after an 18-month fight against cancer.

"We did our best not to change our lifestyle, and treated Margaret as normally as possible," Smith adds. "Cobalt treatment caused her hair to fall out, and we got a wig for her. For 6 of her

Putting your house in order

There are a number of practical matters that must be dealt with despite the emotional pain and distraction of a loved one dying. A terminally ill person will often feel better knowing that his or her affairs are being put in order. The details can be handled by a spouse, if able to, or by a family lawyer.

DURING ILLNESS

Will: Make necessary changes. Examples: specific financial provision for children's education and provision for personal guardianship of children. This is the time to make any changes in the choice of executor (often spouse or relative) or coexecutor (lawyer, bank). A letter apart from the will can cover nonmandatory instructions to the executor—for example, naming children's schools.

Estate tax: Consider buying "flower bonds" to pay any estate taxes. These Treasury issues can be bought at a discount and used to pay estate tax at the full face amount. Discuss with the lawyer a tax-saving trust for the children.

Bank account: Provide funds to carry the family immediately after the death by setting up (or increasing) a savings account in the surviving spouse's name. Bank funds in the patient's name will be frozen upon death. Funds in a joint account are not frozen, but since any jointly owned property becomes part of a decedent's taxable estate, any money withdrawn still would be subject to the estate tax.

Investments: Alter instructions to patient's broker where necessary—"stop orders," for example, that ought to be dropped. It may be wise to sell shares to buy flower bonds or to take the family out of speculative situations.

Gifts: Consider making gifts of the patient's property to family members. If the gift-tax exemption has been used up, there will be a tax. But the taxpayer will be entitled to a credit against estate tax; there may be a net tax saving.

Insurance: Make sure that life insurance beneficiary clauses are up to date. A gift of ownership of the policy itself (right to convert, borrow, and such) will not take benefits out of the patient's taxable estate because of the three-year contemplation-of-death rule.

Power of attorney: Consider a "durable, general" power of attorney, with the power assigned by the patient so the surviving spouse can perform all transactions. This is particularly necessary where a patient becomes incapacitated.

Benefits: Contact the employee benefits department of the patient's company to ensure that desired beneficiaries are named. If an individual is named, noncontributory benefits (mainly pension and profit-sharing) are kept out of the taxable estate.

Funeral: Consider making advance arrangements for the funeral. A funeral director will handle purchase of a cemetery plot and bill you later along with other charges (assuming death is imminent). If you deal directly with a cemetery company, it will want full payment for one grave and will finance the balance if you wish.

AFTER DEATH

Lawyer-executor: Arrange to see the family lawyer and executor or coexecutor together, preferably in the lawyer's office, within two or three days after the funeral. Speed is important because the lawyer starts probate of the will.

Papers: Send military discharge papers of deceased to the funeral director so he can file a claim with the Veterans Administration for routine $400 cash death benefit ($800 if a service-connected death). Provide Social Security number for a similar $255 benefit if the deceased was covered.

Miscellaneous: Phone life insurance companies to request claim forms. Notify insurer carrying deceased's homeowner's and auto insurance policies, employee benefits department, banks used by decedent (thus freezing accounts), and stockbrokers (automatically nullifying any brokerage instructions and freezing accounts). Notify credit card companies, and destroy or surrender the cards.

last 10 months, things were pretty normal and Margaret was a happy child." Smith speaks of his other small children: "We had fully explained her illness to the others, ages 5 and 8, telling them about the cancer and that there was a good chance she would not survive. When Margaret died, they understood and were not shocked. They accepted it."

Facing yourself

Your own personal adjustment to a death or terminal illness in the family is made easier to the extent that you can open up to others. "People who share the struggle, who are open rather than secretive, seem to do better," says James Gibbons, director of chaplaincy at University of Chicago hospitals. But "talking it out" may not be easy.

"The well person may have a deep fear of death," notes Menninger Foundation psychologist Cerney. "If a husband has a terminal illness, the wife may freeze and deny the coming death, pretending that it won't happen." The wife might then remain aloof from the husband and cause more pain for both.

Cerney suggests that the spouse of a terminal patient who is concerned about his or her own inability to cope should first try to come to grips with the fear of death.

"The books of Kübler-Ross [such as *On Death and Dying*] offer real help," she advises. "Or phone your local university and ask someone in the psychology department about one-day seminars on thanatology. There are more and more of these—and they aren't morbid."

Hearing a good talk and being a part of a question-and-answer session can help lift some of the unreal fears of death and send a seminar participant home with a clearer idea of how to relate to the terminal patient.

"I dreaded the death seminar idea," confesses a Columbus (Ohio) businessman whose wife had terminal cancer. "But it seemed I was the one pulling us down, while she was the one having the chemotherapy. I went to the sessions at the hospital and came away feeling tolerably better about those difficult talks with my wife."

In Tiburon, Calif., near San Francisco, Nora E. Grove, a lawyer's wife, tells how attending Candlelighters Society meetings helped her family adjust to having a child at home with terminal cancer. "You meet once a month in a church hall for about two hours with 30 to 40 other parents of cancer children," she explains. "You have coffee and then listen to a speaker and have group discussions. Personally, I got some sanity. I felt I would cave un-

der, but meeting with the other parents helped me to know about physically caring for the boy and got me through the sadness."

Most people are psychologically unprepared for their own reaction to the death of a spouse or child, or in some cases, a parent. "The death of a parent usually is manageable," says Goldston, "but losing your wife or child is a different story." And a sudden, unexpected death is the most difficult to face.

There are many psychosomatic side effects from grief, from an inability to concentrate at work to trouble in making even routine decisions. There may be headaches or insomnia, and psychologists note that some people even take on the symptoms of the deceased—stomach pains, where the death was from stomach cancer, or chest pains following a heart attack death.

HOSTILITY IS ALSO A STAGE OF GRIEF

Anger and hostility, a stage of dying, are also a stage of grief and mourning, and awareness of this is especially important when a child dies. "Some men suffer more than their wives when a child dies," says Sandi Boshak whose son died in infancy. "From formal meetings with other parents of deceased children, I've seen that the husband has a harder time with his grief. He tends to bottle it up, while his wife cries openly." She explains that feelings of guilt can bog a parent down, particularly following the death of a first child. It is then that meetings of such groups as the National Foundation for Sudden Infant Death, with chapters in 40 cities, can help most.

An excessive grief reaction may justify psychotherapy if daily life has become impaired, at home or the office, and you realize your own conduct is hurting others. But avoid rushing into therapy. "See a therapist only if the level of grief is getting beyond you," says Dr. Harold Visotsky, chief of psychiatry at Northwestern University medical school.

If deep grief lasts more than two months or so, it may be wise to seek help, preferably using a psychologist, psychiatrist, or social worker who has had experience with similar problems. "Just any 'qualified' person won't do," says a Washington (D. C.) psychologist. "You must have somebody who knows thanatology." Most major hospitals will provide such a lead.

Be careful in using drug sedation to cope with excessive grief. "The risk of sedation is that you will lose the impact

of the personal loss suffered, and your grief will only be delayed or prolonged," advises Cohen.

Adjusting after a death

Managing a household as a lone surviving parent, and "dating" to start new relationships, is the last phase of adjustment to the death of a spouse.

A formula for handling the children, including teen-agers to age 15, is suggested by an executive who is a widower: "First, if you are a working widow or widower, get a good housekeeper, if possible. She must be kindly and concerned about the kids, but still firm. And she must have the authority she needs to run things. If this is unrealistic, then make contacts with close married friends who have children the same age. Ask for their advice and help. At the least, you'll need some after-school-to-suppertime supervision for the kids."

And there is this cardinal rule: Maintain a spirit of discipline among the children. "The death of a parent should be no excuse for drifting into excessive permissiveness," says the executive.

A structured daily home life should be continued for the children's sake as well as your own. The older children should be given greater responsibilities to help make the household operate smoothly. But it is unwise to treat a teen-ager as a peer. This instant-adult treatment is a common mistake, say the specialists.

Dating again, after a spouse has died, can cause problems. "First of all, don't date to get over your grief," warns USC's Feifel. "Once you start dating," he explains, "it should be a signal that you have worked the mourning through." Catching a new person "on the rebound"—to override your grief—is a common mistake usually leading to new relationships that are shaky, at best.

Conversely, if you experienced a long period of grief before your spouse died and mourning has been fulfilled, then a new successful relationship can be approached fairly soon. "Some people are ready even to remarry after two months," says Kübler-Ross.

The children's reaction to a dating parent, however, poses a difficult problem. Cohen notes that "it is very difficult for the kids to accept another woman or man." Keep family communications open and try to talk matters through with the children.

One point is certain: A parent who waits for the children's approval of a proposed new marriage partner runs a good risk of staying single.

5 Alternative and Future Relationships

The cultural norms of many societies put limits on the life-styles of its members. Our society has always been one that stressed autonomy and independence, and in the last decades seems to have allowed more options in marriage, sex, and family life as well.

In early America, the roles of males and females were planned in advance. Urbanization, industrialization, and mechanization, however, have led to greater variety in male and female roles. Today education is required for many jobs, so marriage is often delayed. Women with college degrees marry 2.3 years later on the average than do high school graduates. Because women have more options available to them regarding life-style, they must no longer be totally dependent on males for support. The "pill" and other forms of effective contraception allow women control over their own bodies and give them the choice of having sex for reproduction, pleasure, or not at all. On the whole, our society has made the single life more palatable for women and men.

The hallmark of the 1980s may be flexibility—more opportunity to try alternative life-styles with relatively minor risks and sanctions from the broader society. Even so, it is predicted that in the year 2,000 over 90% of college age students will marry and have children. These marriages, however, may not only be less traditional than the marriages of the past but may be preceeded more frequently by experimentation in cohabitation and communal living. And more often than not these marriages will probably find both husband and wife employed outside the home.

This section briefly explores several alternative life-styles both before and after marriage. One such trend is that although money is the main reason that many women work, there has been an increase in the number of women planning a career instead of just accepting a job. Some of these women will remain childless by choice, others will have children and remain in the labor force as men do, and others still will leave the labor force after the first child is born to reenter it when the last child is in school.

The future of more egalitarian sex role relationships in marriage offers exciting possibilities for marriages of the future. However, most persons presently entering a marriage relationship were influenced by traditional role models. The change to a more egalitarian division of labor and power within the marriage will be accompanied in many cases by trial and error, confusion, and outside interference from more traditional parents and peers.

The advantages and disadvantages of both dual worker and dual career marriages are discussed in this section as well as the problems of displaced homemakers—women who after many years as wife and mother exclusively, must enter the labor force because of death of a spouse or divorce.

Looking Ahead: Challenge Questions

What is the explicit contract, if any, when people get married? What is the implicit contract?

Is it possible to raise children today as little persons instead of little boys or little girls? What are the advantages and disadvantages for the parents? for the children?

Does our system of marriage narrowly define female identity?

How can one judge whether the traditional or nontraditional patterns of marriage are best for a particular couple?

Can individual couples or families maintain nontraditional life-styles in a traditional society?

ALTERNATIVE LIFE-STYLES

Robert N. Whitehurst

Are they a threat to conventional family life?

Most of the social forces that we presume made past marriages and family life solid, if not happy, seem to be evaporating in front of our eyes. At the same time, a great variety of alternatives to conventional marriage and family have suddenly loomed on the horizon. Recent changes seem to favor more divorce and family disorganization; dissatisfactions with marriage tend to create an atmosphere of distrust of this basic institution.

It may be that marriage and family forms will become even more diverse in the future; but this will probably be contingent upon economic and political conditions. In any case, it is unlikely that the nuclear family will fade out as a dominant form, unless the whole human race goes with it—a distinct possibility as human behavior is now going! In the exploration that follows, it will be suggested that marriage is not a healthy institution for many people today, but it is not about to die; further, the future of alternatives is simply not predictable, given the status of current political winds and economic uncertainties. Given certain conditions, however, some probable options might come to fruition. In the following pages, these options will be speculated upon.

Making Marriage Work

One of the first items in the discussion of the functioning of future family life is inevitably the Western institution known as marriage. Traditionally, marriage as we know it has emerged from a particular ethos. When people have experienced a strong sense of community, a strong set of principles adhered to rigidly as life guidelines, complete with strong sanctions and a tight supportive group, a customarily rigid family form has emerged. Since we have in this century weakened the basis of most of the previously effective social controllers, such as religion, the community, and the family, we should not be surprised that marriages fail more frequently. During the present period, no one knows if marriage is better, worse, or simply more of the same in qualitative terms. We only know with some degree of certainty that as a culture we are "hooked" on the notion of finding happiness in marriage but that it doesn't really seem to happen that way very often. It seems likely that the key differences between marriage in the past and contemporary marriage are attributable to our leisure, affluence, higher expectations, and mobility, coupled with an inordinately high opportunity level to meet potential mates. We are probably no more nor less neurotic as a people than those before, but we distinctly have fewer solidifying forces compelling us to obey the still-dominant conventional community norms. *Social structure, not personality, is what must be understood if we want to know why divorce is rampant and why families are not "happy."*

As a society, we have cut loose more people (the young, with their own rooms, TV sets, cars, booze, drugs, money, free time, and, most of all, freedom from responsibility), with more tragic results, than any people in history. Most of our older people are stashed in retirement villas or "nursing" homes and, as Jules Henry and others have shown, are simply the unwanted surplus of a rapidly moving technological society. The high social cost of over-specializing the family and creating children who flounder, oldsters who despair, and the rest of us who are uncertain, doubtful, or anxious can be seen not only in divorce rates but in simmering family problems that prevent real living and meaningful relating among people. The rise of alternative forms can be seen in part as a response to conventional family failure to satisfy many of the needs that have been developed recently in a freer kind of society. In contemporary life, custom, religion, and community have come to mean less. The needs for family and marriage, however, have come to mean more. We have reached a hiatus involving a large potential for those who either seek or promote alternatives to traditional marriage.

"The search for alternatives grew out of conventional family failures created by a changing and unstable society. Alternatives can thus be perceived less as a threat to the family than as a means of reconstituting it in different forms."

In a society changing as rapidly as ours, it is impossible to maintain stable marriage forms not aligned with people's real needs. If we free women to go into the marketplace, give people leisure, money, and opportunity to meet others, and take them away from home for long periods, solidarity in the old-fashioned sense cannot be the result. The need for intimacy is probably a constant in humans, but our sense of legitimizing multiple ways of searching for it is subject to radical changes over time. We have expected more intimacy from relationships today, and we have provided more means of searching for it than in former times. It is doubtful that people have ever been able to find much intimacy, but the fact that we *expect* it today and have *expanded means of seeking* it makes the search for alternatives an understandable imperative.

One of the salient factors in understanding the rise of alternatives may lie in comprehending the nature of the need for intimacy, both physical and emotional. Christianity has traditionally placed heavy emphasis on fidelity and monogamy. No one has yet made the case, however, that rigid insistence in such matters is mainly a reflection of a religious institution's need to control people in terms of the biases of its later apostles. The conditions that prompted these demands on humankind may have since vanished. We now have a markedly different situation. In short, as people are freed to live closer to themselves as natural, not churchly, beings, we may expect forms to emerge that reflect the true diversity of human desires and needs instead of a narrow monolithic institutional imperative. This seems to be a part of what is happening now.

It need not be feared that there is an immediate danger of masses of people dropping their marriages and joining communes, swinging clubs, or other such activities. The institutional forces still alive in the culture have enough sanctioning power to prevent total chaos from enveloping families; the institutions that prevail, however, do not have enough power to keep families and marriages on an even keel, as was more true in the past. Thus, the dilemma we now face involves having more freedom than in the past to live as many of us would wish, but not enough to live as many would see fit if we had a truly pluralistic and open society. It is in this cultural limbo, this no-man's-land of vague and shadowy family supports that are more apparent than real, that we find ourselves today. Bereft of old supports to make them operate well, families limp their way along. Alternative-searching goes on in this limbo, in which we are neither enslaved to a past nor freed to a positive future, but caught in an uncomfortable place between. In such a situation, it would be difficult to conclude that family life is endangered by the existence of alternatives to marriage; marriage and family life, if they are threatened at all, are in jeopardy because the entire social structure and set of institutional underpinnings is in jeopardy. It is as rational to see alternative-seekers as trying to save the family as trying to destroy it. In some sense, however, old forms are always dying, so it is probably true that alternative-seekers may in some ways be hastening the demise of the family—at least as it is presently known. It is patently false to assume that the existence of alternatives has created the problem of the family today. The quest for alternatives is only one of many reactions to family strains and problems.

Given a situation as described above, it would be a false conclusion to claim that the family is in trouble today because people are seeking alternative routes to sexual satisfaction and family life; rather, it would be more correct to suggest that the search for alternatives grew out of conventional family failures created by a changing and unstable society that made some new forms both possible and seemingly desirable in a changing social context. Alternatives can thus be perceived less as a threat to the family than as a means of reconstituting it in different forms.

Alternatives Are Not a Threat

In the following descriptions of alternatives, it will be suggested that *none of these will replace conventional monogamous marriage as a modal form in the foreseeable future*. There is no sign of divorce rates lowering, but this does not necessarily pose a threat to family life as long as we are so enamored of marriage as the only way to live. Indeed, divorce hurts and disrupts both children and adults, but it does not appear to materially affect cultural stability. The same can probably be said for extant alternatives today. This is especially so since most of them occupy so few people in terms of statistical significance. Be this as it may, we are likely to see changing and even expanding rates of alternate life-styles, dependent on future economic and political changes, especially inflation, recession, and depression. Among the rationales for the formation of alternate life-styles are ecological and economic arguments, as well as stressing the needs for intimacy in groups larger than the conventional nuclear-family group. It is assumed that the forms enumerated below will predominate as alternatives, roughly in decreasing order of importance as they are described. These involve modified open marriage, post-marital singlehood, triads, a variety of cooperatives, urban collectives and urban communes, extended intimate networks, rural communes, and finally swinging, cohabitation, and part-time marriage. Rationales will be discussed of why each of these will be more or less successful and why some will persevere into the future.

Modified Open Marriage

With changing sex-role socialization, with people's liberation (including men's groups as well as women's), with increasing legal equality for children and women, and with a likely increase in women workers at all levels, it will be imperative that more marriages extend the benefits of greater freedoms to both sexes. This will eventuate in a form of marriage that will not likely be fully open in terms of free sexuality, but will be vastly different from the average marriage of today. It is probable that there will be more sexuality practiced outside of marriage because of these new freedoms for women, but the forms are not distinguishable at this time.

The basic revolution before us lies in sex roles, not in sexuality—at least the equalizing of sex roles should be the first order of business. The middle seventies have brought only the barest beginning of equality for husband and wife in work, household tasks, and child care. Whether this will in its turn bring the incidence of female sexual activity up to or beyond that of the average male is unknown. Given what we know now about female sexuality, it is likely that many females will surpass many of their brothers in this sphere; the impact of this upon marriage and family forms is simply unknown.

Post-Marital Singlehood

Given the high divorce rates and the uncertainties of remarriage, larger numbers of people will probably opt for longer periods of singlehood in the future. In a world where there are more singles than ever before, we are likely to develop some norms that will put them into the "normal" range, which is not generally the case at present. Although pressures are still tremendous for people to marry and remarry, this may change so that a more benign atmosphere will enable people to tolerate singlehood more easily. Many young people today are either wary of marriage or are extremely cautious about getting into second marriages; given the continuance of this trend, social acceptance of this form as a more or less permanent adaptation to adult life will become a reality. Support for nonmarriage is developing in many avant-garde quarters. Although making predictions is risky, it is safe to suggest growing numbers in this category. Since it is likely that freer sexuality will be practiced among nonmarrieds and that our norm of valuing privacy will continue, it is probable that more people will be able to make it without marriage, supported by the apparent success of those already in the group. This will, of course, still constitute a small proportion of most of the adult population; we are still reared to think that marriage is the only right way to live. There are simply not, as yet, that many deviants in this culture, and nonmarriage is surely a form of deviancy from conventional norms. An increase in singlehood of all kinds may be predicted, but it will not become a modal form.

Triads

With present urban sex ratios favoring men in the marketplace of sex and partner selection, triads will likely become a more important form of living arrangement as an alternative to conventional marriage. Not only will more people be willing to share a spouse, but as the benefits of this form come to be known, more people are likely to be willing to try this adaptation. Among the more obvious advantages: greater flexibility in child care, more adult models in the family, better and more equitable distribution of household chores, better economic foundation for the family, less social isolation for some now living alone, and the greater ease of three people making accommodative rules and adaptations to each other than in other alternative forms.

To form a triad, there must be three people who like each other and have some tolerance for being alone at times, as well as being left out at times. There have been numerous cases of triads working for long periods of time, and they stand to become more numerous, given present conditions. If we add to this the relative ease with which the extra family member can be explained away to conventional society, we can see how this form might become more prevalent. Although the triad has its drawbacks and is definitely not a panacea, it is more likely to occur than many other forms of living arrangements now being tried.

Cooperatives, Collectives, Urban Communes, and Extended Intimates

A panoply of cooperatives, communes, and other sharing arrangements is currently being developed with varying results. Churches of moderately liberal suasion are even attempting to establish forms of community, sharing patterns, and extended intimacy networks. Although such forms at times develop into sexual sharing, this is not a dominant mode as yet and tends to be associated with problems, if not divorces and remarriages, because supports for sexuality outside marriage in the usual urban cooperative or collective have not worked smoothly. Short of large-scale renovation of marital and sexual norms, this will apparently not happen. It is also for this reason that alternatives might best be seen as an adjunct to marriage and not as a replacement for it—at least for a large number of people now participating in so-called alternate life-styles. There is, however, some evidence that people unavoidably get into sexual problems outside their marital relationships once alternatives are entered. The rate of successful integration of extramarital sexuality into the average marriage is apparently low. For all this, there are many attempts to try to extend family conceptions by enlarging the number of people included in economic sharing, social rituals, and a variety of other quasi-family experiences, sometimes even including sexuality. Given economic hard times, these groupings stand to proliferate. In the less likely event of increased leisure and affluence, such arrangements still may expand on some kind of experimental basis as a way to salvage the goodness of family life and the ethic of sharing. These styles will be juxtaposed against what is perceived as the relatively isolated and encapsulated existence currently being experienced by most nuclear families.

Swinging and Group Marriage

Although the research of Larry and Joan Constantine has shown that there are some stable and lasting forms of group marriage, the complexities and problems of four or more people being married to each other loom so large that this form is impractical for large numbers. Hitherto privatized, nuclear-family cultures do not lend themselves easily to such an adaptation; our sense of possessiveness with spouses and jealousy still bulk in the way of such solutions. Perhaps another generation, reared without sexism and jealousy, will adapt better to such a form, but the numbers are few who can make it work well today. Swinging, although declining as a family sport, can be said to arise basically as a variation of the older clandestine adultery pattern. In no way does most swinging tend to alter family behavior. Most couples do not indoctrinate their young into swinging. With the exception of valuing the variety in swinging, no value changes are apparent in the lives of the swinging population. Although large numbers (but small percentages of the total populace) still continue this pattern, there is no indication that swinging will replace clandestine adultery as the model pattern of extramarital sexual practice. Among the principle ways swinging affects marriage is the creation of tension between partners with unequal commitment to the activity. Divorce,

then remarriage to someone with more consonant values, often follows. Swinging does not seem to constitute a genuine alternative; rather, it involves a sorting mechanism to insure value-similar partners for the swingers' activities.

Cohabitation

Increasing interest in the living-together, patterns of the unmarried over the past several years has eventuated in some good research on the topic. We still do not know if the practice, in fact, makes for better marriages; it may do so in the short run, but probably has little overall effect on marriage in the long run. Cohabitation does not appear to substantially affect marriage rates or marriage stability, at least as far as we know.

Cohabitation cannot seriously be considered as an alternative to marriage for many people; it is rather a *preliminary* for most who practice it and an occasional habit of people not yet ready to settle down into a second marriage; it is seldom an alternative to marriage. No doubt a more sensible mate-selection device than methods previously used, cohabitation does not seem to deter large numbers from the goal of formal marriage.

Part-Time Marriage

An increasing number of married partners are engaging in what might be called part-time marriages. These are usually professionals who for career reasons must separate on occasion and for varying periods of time. Some marriages survive these periods of separation and some do not. Some remain as monogamous in absence as in presence, but some do not. There seems to be a wide variation in the patterns possible in part-time marriages. Although the habit is still quite new and obviously a function of high-mobility and dual-career marriages, it may increase as people tend to find separateness an advantage for a period of time. This adaptation does not affect great numbers of people now and probably will not, unless current trends regarding women's employment and liberation proceed at a faster pace than at present.

Other Possibilities

If we engage in the mental exercise of extending current behavior patterns into the future and extrapolating from them, we may find some interesting potential for alternate life-styles of the future. For example, if the clandestine-adultery pattern becomes a more ubiquitous phenomenon, it seems unlikely that nearly everyone could go on playing the hiding game forever; at some point, it is possible that a consensus will emerge that casual adultery is "okay"—given certain contexts and sets of rules by which the players must abide. Already, there is a set of informal and well-understood rules by which clandestine adultery is played. Firm consensus and more players is probably all that is necessary to create an informally institutionalized code of sexual behavior for large numbers of people. This would not necessarily constitute an alternative to marriage; rather, it would be one more addition to the already complex set of roles that spouses must play today.

For those who want something more than the "game" described above, there may be such a concept as informally sanctioned *binogamy*. Although this term bastardizes two standard terms used in family sociology (*monogamy* and *bigamy*), it seems apropos—although contemporary binogamists cannot be *married* to two wives, they very often, in fact, render loyalty and fealty to two persons, one of whom is the legal spouse. This pattern, a bit unlike triads, does not necessarily involve a common living arrangement. It is rather an extension of the long-lasting affair, which even when it becomes known is still not dropped in favor of monogamy. Caring, some sharing, and continued sexual relations may all be a part of this pattern. This pattern is already practiced by an unknown number of people and, by all signs, the number is increasing. Whether binogamy can be considered a true alternative is moot, since it is distinctly nonmonogamous and in some ways considerably alters nuclear-family interactions. It is, however, functional, in that it appears to ease social isolation, sexual frustration, and, perhaps, economic problems of some who maintain social and sexual needs and are not married.

Summary and Conclusion

A key characteristic of the times is the tendency to open up marriages and to provide more opportunites for expression of life-styles at variance with older patterns. It is true that conventional marriages are floundering because of the failure of supportive institutions and groupings that once worked to keep people on track. At the same time, so-called alternatives—most of which are neither true alternatives to marriage nor threatening to it—are emerging and being practiced in a normative vacuum, which makes most of them problematic in terms of their longevity. What seems to be emerging is an era of pluralism, unlike anything ever before witnessed in the Western world. Homosexuals are "coming out," many people are less prone to keep their sex lives secret, and varieties of living forms, with some exception, are becoming at least tolerated, if not more understood. In an era of economic hardship, however, people are still careful not to jeopardize their jobs by blatantly flouting sexual mores. It is fairly clear by now that neither the supporters of conventional norms nor alternative-seekers have an easy time of adapting in the seventies; relationships are simply difficult, no matter what the variety.

If the economy and the political situation both tighten up and create a repressive environment, alternatives will change form; although there will be less blatant sexuality, there will be more sharing, cooperative ventures, and perhaps a developing sense of community, as people are no longer able to use the wheeled escape. If the economic situation becomes more optimistic, there will probably be more sexual deviation surrounding marriage, more experimentation, and, perhaps, more forms yet to emerge as yet unknown. Both inflation and depression give birth to their own styles of conservation, but perhaps the days of easy affluence, which spawned much of the enhanced interest in sexuality, are gone. We have known the flower child. The earlier modes of a more constrained existence are not likely to return.

Pluralism seems to be the key word of the near future; we have not as yet learned to live easily with it. A democratic-humanistic approach can be more positive than the monolithic and repressive experience of the past. We have only made a beginning at developing enlightened cultural supports for sensuousness, pleasure, and a broader-based sexual practice that does not press all people, regardless of taste and desires, into a common behavioral mold. It is now a moral imperative to develop norms of acceptance for differences. Perhaps the rest of this century will correspond with the last one in the respect that our new laissez-faire policy will extend into our conception of other people's sexuality.

The Sexual Bond: Alternative Life-styles

James W. Ramey

James W. Ramey is senior research associate at the Center for Policy Research, founder and director of the Center for the Study of Innovative Life Styles, and consultant to the University of Southern California Medical School and Bowman Gray School of Medicine. Formerly he served as executive director of the Institute for the Advancement of Medical Communication. He is the author of three books, most recently Intimate Friendships.

We are aware of the various life-styles that have been sensationalized in the press in recent years, but few of us realize the great diversity in life-styles that has always been a part of the American tradition. It was not until after the Civil War that we began to idealize and espouse the monogamous nuclear family, consisting of a breadwinner-father, housewife-mother, and children. After years of pressuring for this ideal, most people began to assume that the average person actually lived in such a family, and bureaucratic agencies began to deliver services based on this assumption.

Nontraditional Family Structures

Few adults actually live in such a home. Most of us have spent some part of our lives in several different family forms. According to the Bureau of Labor Statistics, adult Americans are distributed in a variety of households (see Table 1). Even the 13 percent figure for adults living in single-breadwinner nuclear families is not the bottom line, however, for both the law and the "ideal" demand that these should be *monogamous* nuclear families. The evidence suggests strongly that they are not.

TABLE 1

TABLE 1
**Distribution of Adult Americans
by Types of Household
(percent)**

Heading single-parent families	16
Other single, separated, divorced, or widowed	21
Living in child-free or post-child-rearing marriages	23
Living in extended families	6
Living in experimental families or cohabiting	4
Living in dual-breadwinner nuclear families	16
Living in no wage-earner nuclear families	1
Living in single-breadwinner nuclear families	13

Source: News release, Bureau of Labor Statistics, 8 March 1977.

In 1948 Alfred Kinsey estimated that 50 percent of husbands and 28 percent of wives engaged in extramarital sex by age 45. In 1968 Paul Gebhart updated those figures, estimating that 60 percent of husbands and 40 percent of wives engaged in extramarital sex by age 35. In the Research Guild Study, conducted in 1968, it was also found that among first-married couples under age 25 as much extramarital sex occurred in the first two years of marriage as was experienced by all married individuals in other age groups in their entire married lives. Thus it is reasonable to assume that today, nine years later, probably not more than half of all marriages are monogamous. Since nuclear families are most likely to involve couples in the 21–45 age group, it is also likely that at least half of these nuclear families are not monogamous nuclear families.

Current interest in sexual behavior seems to be focused on those in nonmonogamous primary relationships, whether married or unmarried. Such interest can be further narrowed to consensual nonmonogamy. There cannot be adultery without monogamy, since the concepts are interdependent. It follows that when extramarital sex becomes the majority practice, attention shifts to those who not only do not pretend that human beings are by nature monogamous, but who base their relationship on the premise that intimate relationships outside the primary relationship are acceptable, or even desirible, attributes of the primary relationship.

Building Relationships

What happens to people who build their primary relationship on such a premise? What is the survival potential of such a relationship? Are there couples that have successfully negotiated such relationships for a reasonable length of time?

Masters and Johnson have strongly suggested that such a relationship is dysfunctional, extremely rare, and doomed to failure. John Cuber and Peggy Harroff, however, found that the most mature, well-adjusted couples in their study were those who practiced sexually open relating as a matter of principle. In this article the focus is on research findings from the two studies to date that have dealt specifically with sexually open relating, mine and Jacquelyn Knapp's, and on how these practices appear to relate to other changes occurring in our society.

A sexually open relationship, in which partners agree to retain sexual freedom on an individual basis, can occur in a marriage or in any other type of primary relationship, such as a living-together arrangement involving two singles. Such an agreement is most often encountered in situations in which the couple is striving toward mutual personal growth and self-actualization within an egalitarian relationship. Such a relationship has been characterized as a "peer bond." The outside or secondary relationships are expected to involve lesser degrees of social, emotional, intellectual, family, career, and sexual intimacy than the primary relationship, but the mixture of these various types of intimacy will vary between secondary relationships. This situation is in marked contrast to "swinging," in which married couples practice mate swapping but only in situations in which both mates are present and usually with distinct prohibitions against any kind of nonsexual intimacy.

Most of the difference between the Knapp respondents and mine relates to the length of their outside relationships. I was concerned with the long-term impact on the primary relationship, and therefore focused on those who had been involved in sexually open relating for at least ten years. Knapp, who was concerned with the transition from monogamy to nonmonogamy, focused on those who had been involved for less than ten years.

The average age of my 334 respondents was 42, as compared to 30 for Knapp's 34 respondents. Each of her respondents was married to someone else in the sample, whereas only two-thirds of my respondents were married—not necessarily to each other—and 80 percent of my sample were in primary relationships. Knapp found 79 percent in a first marriage and 21 percent in a remarriage, as compared with 78 percent first married and 22 percent remarried in my study. However, three-fifths of Knapp's group had been married less than six years, whereas 95 percent of the marrieds in my study had been married at least six years and the average had been married twenty-three years.

Knapp found 53 percent first borns in her sample, as compared to 57 percent in my study. This is an unusually high proportion of first borns. My group included one-third with college degrees, another 18 percent with M.A., LL.B., or M.D., and another 8 percent with a Ph.D. Knapp found 21 percent with a college degree, another 26 percent with a masters degree, and 12 percent with a Ph.D. However, 26 percent of her sample were graduate students at the time of the study, so that ultimately her respondents will have achieved considerably higher educational status. Their occupational status is middle class, but currently lower in status that my respondents, most of whom are in professional, academic, managerial, or creative arts careers (both men and women). Knapp respondents enjoyed an annual household income of $15,000, while household income was twice that figure in my sample, even though a number of my respondents were retired.

Intimate Friendship: Participant Profile

Intimate friendship—an otherwise traditional friendship in which sexual intimacy is considered appropriate behavior—is another term for sexually open relating. Over time people seem to gravitate toward friends who share a similar philosophy. When that basic philosophy involves sexually open relating, it is common for primary partners to get to know each other's intimate friends and their primary partners and friends. Eventually a network of individuals who espouse sexually open relating develops—a network in which social, sexual, intellectual, emotional, family, and career intimacy is shared.

Thus intimate friendship might be alternately defined as a person-to-person relationship that may, but does not necessarily, include genital-to-genital relating. In my study 14 percent of the respondents had had *no* sexual involvement with other members of the group (6 percent for the Knapp group), and 58 percent had shared sexual intimacy with only one other member of the group or network aside from their mate—if their primary partner were also in the network (24 percent for the Knapp respondents). In other words, as the participants themselves see it, intimate friendship rests on the premise of open acceptance of *potential* sexual intimacy rather than on sexual involvement. It should be noted that my study responses refer only to contacts within the intimate group or network, whereas Knapp counted all contacts since only seven of her respondents were involved in groups or networks as yet (because the establishment of such networks takes considerable time).

Individuals involved in such intimate friendships do not appear to be promiscuous pleasure seekers. The vast majority have known and valued primary relationships both before and after marriage. They do appear to differ from other national samples in their sexual preparation for such friendships in that they were likely to have masturbated at a somewhat earlier age and were slightly more likely to have engaged in premarital intercourse. On the other hand, although 82 percent of my sample reported at least one experience with premarital intercourse, two-fifths were over 20 when it occurred and 54 percent of the reported premarital partners were friends, steady dates, or fiancees. This pattern suggests that the majority of my sample followed Reiss's "permissiveness with affection" sexual code: they approved of sexual intercourse before marriage so long as it was with persons who had an affectionate relationship. This assessment is confirmed by their *attitude* toward premarital sex; 85 percent felt that it was okay when the partners were in love or were affectionate.

Half of the Knapp respondents and 85 percent of my respondents received little or no sex education from their parents, in keeping with the traditional approach to this sensitive area. In view of the age differences there was a clear trend toward more liberal views on sex education by the Knapp group's parents. In both samples respondents strove to rectify this state of affairs. Only 8 percent of my group reported that they had failed to educate their own children in sexual matters, and 95 percent consider their children's masturbation to be a healthy activity. Furthermore, 77 percent expect their children to have experienced sexual intercourse by the age of 18. Knapp's respondents were even more liberal with respect to the sexual growth of their children, being almost unanimous in both their actions and their expectations with respect to their children's sexuality. Only 59 percent of the Knapp respondents were parents, and a very low percentage of the Ramey respondents (31 percent) were parents.

Intimate Friendship: Sexual Activities

The sexual activities of both Knapp's and my respondents were varied and uninhibited in keeping with findings from other studies of the sexual behavior of professionals, but differing somewhat from the less varied experience of general population samples. Sex is a pleasurable activity for these individuals, who generally rate their sex lives as very satisfactory and who engage in sexual activity somewhat more frequently than the average. The majority indicate that most of their sexual activity occurs with their primary partner. Major involvement with outside contacts was found to be nonsexual in nature, involving intellectual, social, and emotional rather than sexual intimacy. More contact had to do with business and career than with sex, and family involvement was only slightly less frequent than sexual involvement.

The four most frequently cited reasons for Knapp respondents becoming involved in sexually open relating were close friends, pressure from spouse, own feeling of unmet needs, and books. My study respondents cited more personal freedom, the acceptance of sex as normal between friends, adding depth to social relationships, and allowing sexual exploration in a nonjudgmental setting. Bearing in mind that we are comparing 334 responses with 34, the differences are probably not significant—except for "pressure from spouse," and this finding may reflect the fact that my *average* respondent had been involved in sexually open marriage for over fifteen years, whereas only half of the Knapp respondents appear to have been involved for more than one year. It is entirely possible that there was initial pressure from a spouse in the Ramey sample which has long since been forgotten. In this context it is interesting to note that in both studies it was more often the man who first suggested opening the marriage sexually, but in the vast majority of instances it was the woman who first became sexually intimate outside the primary relationship.

These intimate friendships not only seem pleasurable and satisfactory, but in most instances are felt to bolster the primary relationship. Almost 10 percent of my respondents began relationships with others in their networks before becoming married to their spouse, and 4 percent of them married one of those network partners. This pattern is in marked contrast to the assertions of Masters and Johnson; it also contrasts with those clinical studies which find that the majority of Americans are dissatisfied or unhappy with their marriages. Over 95 percent of my sample and 93 percent of the Knapp respondents were satisfied with their primary relationship, and the vast majority of this group expressed increased satisfaction as a result of having become involved in sexually open relating—despite the fact that over 70 percent of their partners also had intimate friends. Almost one-third reported an actual increase in the quantity of contact with their primary partner, and almost two-thirds reported an increase in quality.

Further evidence supporting the notion that the primary relationships of these respondents involved in intimate friendships were exceptional is the great importance they placed on communication and the value they attached to that experience. Over 70 percent felt that the primary relationship was "never threatened" or "strengthened more than it was threatened" by the intimate friendships. The majority contended, moreover, that either they had never experienced jealousy or that it had greatly diminished since their partners became involved in intimate friendships. These sentiments were echoed by the Knapp respondents.

On the whole, these respondents seemed to be very comfortable with their life-style. Many volunteered the conviction that they would never return to monogamy, yet most were guarded about revealing their life-style to in-laws, parents, or associates. Over 80 percent were sure that neither parents nor other relatives were aware of their life-style, and over 50 percent felt that their work associates were in the dark. About two out of three reported that their friends knew what they were doing, however, and an even greater percentage reported that their friends were also in sexually open relationships.

Disadvantages and Problems

The most often cited problems or disadvantages with intimate friendships were lack of time, scheduling, different expectations about the importance of outside partners, situational complexities, and interruptions, but almost one out of four respondents reported no disadvantages. How important are these disadvantages?

Only if one were able to talk to all individuals who had tried a sexually open relationship, including those who found that it was not for them, would it be possible to fully answer the question as to which disadvantages were the most important and why. Since both Knapp's study and mine dealt only with those who were still involved in intimate friendships, the best we could do was to ask respondents to rank order the disadvantages, resulting in the rank order cited above. On a very ad hoc basis, it has been possible to talk to several people who have actually broken up a marriage or cohabiting relationship because the partners disagreed over the issue of sexually open relating.

In five of these eight couples it was the woman who insisted on maintaining intimate friendships even at the expense of the primary relationship. The relationship ranged from one of slightly less than two years to one of over twenty years, and the duration of sexual openness from six months to eight years. In each instance there was a clear difference of opinion about monogamy versus nonmonogamy, and in six cases both partners indicated that they would have stayed together except for this issue. In those six cases one ex-partner is now functioning in monogamous fashion and the other in a sexually open fashion. In the other two cases other matters were also at issue, and none of the ex-mates have resolved things.

Trend Setters

The kind of people who are now involved in sexual

openness are the type that have traditionally been opinion leaders—those who were willing to tread new ground which the rest of us followed at some later date. Let us not forget that it was this sort of "pioneering" that slowly shifted our view of marriage from the traditional mechanism for transferring name and property to future generations to a primary relationship that should involve companionship with one's spouse. More recently there has been a further shift in the nature of this relationship, which is now expected to involve equality as well as companionship, again following the lead of those who advocated self-actualization and freedom to grow within the partnership.

Some of these couples have gone one step further, reasoning that if trust and openness have produced such freedom to grow and happiness in their primary relationship, it might have the same salutory effect between friends. Evidence from my study and that of Cuber and Harroff suggests that the testing of such relationships has been going on for some time. Will this practice spread, or is it an isolated phenomenon?

A structural approach to this question may be enlightening. This article began with a comment about the current breakdown of adults in the United States according to the type of household they live in. The figures reported are for 1975, and they reflect some interesting shifts since 1970. The trend has definitely been away from households including children except in the dramatic instance of the single-parent family, which increased 45 percent in those five years. The largest single group is now those adults who live in child-free or post-child-rearing marriages, a group that has doubled in size in five years.

My study, even more clearly than the Knapp study, indicates that sexually open couples tend to be dual-career couples, the majority of whom are either child free or post-child rearing, or child-free cohabiting adults. Twenty percent of my respondents were singles who were not currently in a primary relationship. Almost all of these individuals were living alone, although a small minority had children. Because these family forms are more amenable to sexually open relating than child-centered family forms, it is conceivable that the practice could spread.

To the degree that the traditional barrier between the married and the unmarried erodes, to be replaced by an adult-centered versus child-centered orientation, the growth of intimate friendships in the adult-centered portion of the population is more likely simply on the basis of the growing disproportion between these two groups and the differential difficulty of managing the logistics when one does or does not have children. Aiding and abetting this possibility is the already reported increase in extramarital sexual activity on the part of women working outside the home, and the number of working wives is increasing every year.

The question of whether consensual nonmonogamy is outside the mainstream of marital relationships in the United States or is an extension of our ongoing manipulation of the framework of marriage to suit current ideas about the nature of people and what is "ideal" behavior must be viewed in the context of the demographic, economic, biological, and technological changes that have occurred in the past few years. As previously mentioned, unless the environment is receptive, upper-middle-class preferences will not trickle down, nor will they be built into our laws and social customs.

Social and Sexual Transition

It would appear that we are in the midst of the most significant transition period in Western civilization since the Industrial Revolution—one that will have profound and far-reaching results because it involves the superimposition of several revolutionary effects one upon the other. We live in a new age, one in which for the first time the family is no longer the basic unit of society, having been replaced by the individual. Today the individual, male or female, can perform all the functions once reserved to the family unit. This situation is possible because we live in a country in which a single male or female can be self-supporting, and in which the female finally has control over her own biology, so that it is no longer possible to keep half the population in subjugation by keeping it "barefoot and pregnant."

Already the pill, which only became generally available in 1962, has been superseded by contraceptive sterilization as the primary means of birth control, both in the United States and in the world at large. Women who lived an average of 47 years, 18 of them childbearing years, in 1900, now live an average of 76 years, only 10 of them childbearing years—a demographic revolution. Add to these three revolutions the technological revolution in communication, which has cut down to weeks or months the transmission of information that used to take decades or generations, and we are faced with such an escalation of change that it is now literally impossible to predict what will happen in the next twenty years.

Women's liberation has been trying to happen ever since women began to lose their freedom with the decreasing need for their labor. It could not happen without the aforementioned changes that for the first time made it possible for women to bargain from a position of strength rather than one of weakness. We are only beginning to see the results of that liberation in the sexual area. Today more women than men college students have sexual experience, and among young first marrieds the women now have as much extramarital experience as their husbands. It is not surprising that among those practicing open sexual relating, it is women who initiate the first and have the most sexual contacts.

What will the cumulative effects of these changes in our society be over the next decade? Perhaps one will be that the practice of sexually open relating, now confined largely to upper-middle-class individuals, will be much more widely practiced as but one of many acceptable forms of sexual relating in a society that will be more willing to accept the fact that a plurality of life-styles exists, and that such pluralism is actually a sign of strength and not of weakness.

In the 1960s and 1970s we have seen a proliferation of attempts to achieve "instant intimacy" ranging from communes to swinging to encounter groups. Just as there are a multiplicity of primary relationship patterns, ranging from "male dominant/handmaiden-to-God" couples through various stages of greater sex role equality to androgynous couples, there is a similar range in sexual patterns from strict monogamy to sexually open relating. The correlation between sexual pattern and sex-role structure in the primary relationship is less than perfect, however. Some very traditional couples have open marriages, while some who relate on a peer basis are monogamous. Yet in a general way the less traditional the role relationship, the more likely the couple is to practice sexually open relating. Lessening of sex-role typing appears first to extend to the woman more sexual freedom within the primary relationship, and then to provide her with equality of sexual freedom with the male outside the primary relationship.

Degree of Involvement

At least a portion of the extramarital sex occurring in this country is consensual intimacy among friends over long periods of time. It is almost invariably characterized by participants as a kind of supportive kinship network in which the partners are chosen and in which the possibility that intimacy might become sexual is accepted by both participants and their primary partners or mates. The degree of family and career—as well as social, emotional, and intellectual—intimacy observed, and the long-term trend toward ever greater involvement in ways usually associated with kinship groups among these practitioners of intimate friendship, appear to support their claims. Apparently it is possible for some couples, as well as some singles, to maintain both primary and ancillary long-term intimate relationships that may include sexual intimacy, and not only tolerate but thrive on such a complex pattern of relating.

While it is true that the demographic grouping within which we can observe such couples is growing, it does not follow that this pattern of relating is likewise growing. Only time and national probability sample research will tell us how many people are involved now or provide trend information in the future. Such research has been proposed and is now under consideration for federal funding.

READINGS SUGGESTED BY THE AUTHOR:

Knapp, Jacquelyn. "An Exploratory Study of Seventeen Sexually Open Marriages." *Journal of Sex Research* 12 (August 1976): 206–19.

Murstein, Bernard I. *Current and Future Intimate Lifestyles.* New York: Springer Publishing, 1977.

Ramey, James W. *Intimate Friendships.* Englewood Cliffs, N.J.: Prentice-Hall, 1976.

Smith, James R., and Smith, Lynn G. *Beyond Monogamy: Recent Studies of Sexual Alternatives in Marriage.* Baltimore: Johns Hopkins University Press, 1974.

Sussman, Marvin B., ed. *Variant Family Forms and Life Styles.* Minneapolis: National Council on Family Relations, 1976.

Cohabitation: Does It Make For A Better Marriage?

This paper attempts to answer the question: "What are the effects of cohabitation on preparation for marriage?" More specifically, the purpose of the paper is to: (a) identify the major types of cohabiting relationships; (b) specify the personal characteristics (e.g., interpersonal skill level) and relationship characteristics (e.g., egalitarian relationship) of each cohabiting relationship type; and (c) outline the potential benefits and costs to the individual in each type of cohabiting relationship. Guidelines for counseling potentially cohabiting couples are also provided.

CARL A. RIDLEY,

DAN J. PETERMAN,

AND ARTHUR W. AVERY

Carl A. Ridley is Chairman, Department of Child Development and Family Relations, University of Arizona, Tucson, 85721; Dan J. Peterman is a Clinical Psychologist at the Mid-Coast Mental Health Center, Rockland, Maine 04841; Arthur W. Avery is Associate Chairperson and Professor in Charge of the Graduate Program, Department of Home and Family Life, Texas Tech University, Lubbock, Texas 79409.

In the classroom and in counseling, individuals persist in their desire to know if living with their boyfriend or girlfriend will prepare them better for a satisfying marital relationship in the future. In addition, a common question in counseling is: "My girlfriend/boyfriend and I have been dating for a while and . . . ah, well, we were wondering what, ah, . . . you think about people living together before marriage?" As counselors and educators, our initial response to such an inquiry is to clarify the nature of the question and the feelings that underly it. Beyond that, however, we often find ourselves saying, "Well, . . . sometimes living together before marriage can provide positive experiences that will better prepare you for marriage, whereas

other times living together is simply a matter of convenience for the individuals involved and is not likely to provide a better foundation for marriage."

No doubt all of us have witnessed cohabiting relationships which have proven particularly valuable for the individuals involved. The partners have learned to be more aware of their needs, more open and honest in their communication, more accepting of their own strengths and weaknesses and those of their partner, and perhaps more aware of the reciprocity necessary for maintaining satisfactory heterosexual relationships. Unfortunately, we have also seen situations where cohabiting relationships, not unlike some marital relationships, have been sources of constant misunderstanding, frustration, and resentment for the persons involved. Interactions of this type where one or both partners leave the relationship with a loss of self-esteem and a lack of self-confidence in their ability to maintain relationships with the opposite sex are not likely to encourage successful heterosexual relationships in the future.

Based on an understanding of our students and clients, then, we need to determine the likely benefits and costs of a cohabiting relationship. Unfortunately, as Blaine (1975) so aptly pointed out, "no scientifically valid survey has yet been made which shows the effect of living together beforehand upon marriage" (p. 32). As is frequently the problem, we are forced as counselors and teachers to advise individuals without having sufficient information on the issue at hand.

This research was supported in part by NIMH, Mental Health Research Grant MH 22477-01. The authors thank Judy Lyness and Graham Spanier for their constructive comments on an earlier draft of this paper.

5. ALTERNATIVE AND FUTURE RELATIONSHIPS

Despite the general lack of careful empirical study on the effects of living together before marriage on later marital success, it seems reasonable to conclude from the available evidence that not all cohabiting relationships have the same impact on individuals. In an initial attempt to describe the differential impact of cohabitation on the individuals involved, the authors focused their attention on a recent study by Peterman, Ridley, and Anderson (1974) that describes the background, personal, and interpersonal characteristics of cohabiting college students. It was apparent from a review of these findings that there is not a single type of cohabitation relationship, but rather several different types. In one type, both partners perceive themselves as well-adjusted and see the relationship as a positive learning experience. In another type, however, one or both partners see themselves as not well-adjusted and perceive the relationship as a source of dissatisfaction.

A basic assumption of this paper is that cohabiting relationships are not inherently good or bad for the persons involved, but rather they have the potential to be both depending on the goals, expectations, and skills of the cohabiting individuals. In the following section, several types of cohabiting relationships are discussed in the hope that by recognizing individual and relationship characteristics associated with positive cohabiting experiences and comparing those to characteristics associated with negative cohabiting experiences, we will be better able to assess the likely impact of a cohabiting experience on those who seek our counsel.

Types of Cohabiting Relationships

Four commonly observed types of cohabiting relationships are described in terms of their potential value as marriage preparation experiences for the individuals involved. The major objective of this typology is to identify and explain some of the general discernable themes of cohabiting relationships, not to describe numerous individual relationship variations. The typology is based on an integration of information from existing research on cohabitation (e.g., Henze & Hudson, 1974; Lyness, Note 1; Macklin, Note 2; Peterman, et al., 1974) as well as on clinical observations.

Each type of cohabiting relationship described ("Linus Blanket," "Emancipation," "Convenience," and "Testing") has outcomes that can be evaluated as providing positive and negative marriage preparation experience. In all types of cohabiting relationships, some learning takes place (e.g., increased knowledge base, increased self-awareness), but in some the potential loss of self-esteem mitigates many of the gains.

"Linus Blanket." The first type of cohabiting relationship described here, "Linus Blanket," is characterized by what appears to be an overwhelming need for one member of the pair to have a relationship with *someone,* with little apparent regard for whom, or under what conditions. To have someone to be with, even though he or she may treat you badly, is better than not having anyone at all. It seems that the need to feel secure through a relationship makes it virtually unimportant to evaluate the circumstances of relationship formation, the motivations of the partner, or the conditions surrounding relationship continuation. Thus, the primary goal of this relationship is one of emotional security. For example, the insecure partner (male or female) in this situation comes across as a clinging vine. When interacting with others, this individual typically stays physically close to the partner, depends on him/her to carry the conversation, and when the individual speaks, comments revolve primarily around the partner. So long as the more secure partner does not feel trapped in this situation and their behavior remains predictable, the insecure partner's basic needs are likely to be met. The fragility of this relationship seldom leads to the type of interaction between partners that increases the development of interpersonal skills important for maintaining heterosexual relationships. The insecure person attempts to elicit interaction with the secure partner which can be interpreted as self-confirming. Negative statements made to the insecure person (frequently in the form of criticisms) are often interpreted as a severe questioning of his or her self-worth. The result is that the more secure person perceives and/or acts as if the partner is fragile ("can't take criticism") and that they cannot "rock the boat" without hurting their partner and the relationship.

Since it is through the constructive handling of disagreements that internal relationship changes take place (e.g., Raush, Barry, Hertel, & Swain, 1974), the more secure partner is often forced into accepting the relationship as it is or leaving it. If the relationship is maintained, open communication and successful problem solving do not take place and thus the experience does not serve as "practice" for improving the skills of the partners. Continued interaction is likely to be ritualized following traditional lines of male-female role behavior. In this case, the "Linus Blanket" relationship provides an opportunity to learn sex role stereotyped behaviors. When a "Linus Blanket" type relationship terminates, the insecure individual typically suffers a loss of self-esteem which neutralizes much of the

178

potential gain of having lived with someone in an intimate relationship.

"Emancipation." Peterman, et al. (1974), found that more than 75 percent of the "repeating" cohabiting males and females (those with more than one cohabiting experience) reported that their longest cohabiting experience lasted less than six months. Two relatively distinct types of cohabiting relationships appeared typical of this group—"Emancipation" and "Convenience." Although the "Emancipation" type of cohabiting relationship was apparent for both males and females, perhaps the clearest example of this pattern was found among Catholic females who started cohabiting early in their college years and maintained a pattern of short duration but frequent cohabiting relationships (Peterman, et al., 1974). It was concluded that these females must be experiencing pulls, pushes, and resistances to becoming involved in cohabiting relationships. Such resistances may reside primarily in socialization to strict sexual standards from family and church which deny guilt-free participation in sexualized heterosexual relationships. The restrictions seem to be countered by internal pushes to loosen external controls and to demonstrate increased freedom by becoming sexually active. Peer pressures which typically support a liberalized set of sexual norms place the Catholic females in a potentially double binding situation. The double bind develops something like this: peer pressure and the desire for more self control result in her becoming involved in a cohabiting situation. The subtle guilt feeling of "doing something wrong," however, makes it difficult for her to become actively involved in the cohabiting situation and ultimately forces her exit. Once out of the relationship, the pulls and pushes reassert themselves and the cycle repeats itself. In an attempt to determine the effect of this type of cohabiting situation on the female, a general principle originating in Gestalt therapy provides an interesting perspective. Namely, when someone is carrying around extensive "unfinished business," it is difficult to function adequately in the here and now. The "unfinished business" in the "Emancipation" type of cohabiting relationship continues to encourage cohabiting relationships while a value system does not support it. Tenuous involvement in the cohabiting relationship does not allow for the type of practice necessary to improve interaction skills. When the pattern is left unchecked, reasons for exit from the relationship are rarely understood and result in confusion and self-doubt on the part of both partners. Should the cohabiting experiences serve the purpose of helping the person work through the value-behavior discrepancy, then the increased self-knowledge would be reflected in better preparation for future heterosexual relating.

"Convenience." A third type of cohabiting relationship, "Convenience," is perhaps best exemplified in the short duration cohabiting relationship of freshmen or sophomore males. This cohabiting situation allows the male to have regularized sexual contact and the luxuries of domestic living without the responsibilities of a committed relationship. The performance of many of the domestic tasks falls to the female simply because she is thought to be more skilled and/or has been socialized to perform them. His major task is to keep the female interested in the relationship when it appears that she is putting more into the relationship than he is. If he can maintain this type of relationship, and most do not, he is probably exhibiting a fairly high interpersonal skill level even though the inequity of the relationship may seem somewhat unjust. This type of cohabiting situation provides a rich opportunity for both the male and the female to learn the idea of reciprocity—mutual giving and getting in a relationship. She can learn that unconditional giving can have limited long-range payoff and that assessments of what one is giving and getting are important in certain contexts. At times it appears that the female is trying to make the male so dependent on her that he would not think of leaving the relationship. At other times, it appears she is simply fitting into the culturally prescribed role for women. It appears that the male is getting much practice at strategic interaction by trying to maintain his freedom to interact with others (keeping his options open), but at the same time presenting to his partner a high level of involvement in the cohabiting relationship. Generally, he seems to learn a great deal about the day-to-day aspects of domestic life (role behavior) and at least some exchange skills. His guarded openness serves the purpose of preventing the type of involvement that escalates the relationship toward a premature commitment.

Although it may appear from the above description that the male is getting the better end of the deal, it should be noted that both the male and female are learning important aspects of "survival" within intimate relationships—even though this learning may be painful for one or both of them. Although the authors have found from their experience that this situation is most typical with the male in the convenience role, the situation is sometimes reversed with a more assertive female forming and maintaining the relationship primarily for its convenience qualities. Future research will be needed to determine if this type of heterosexual interaction early in the college years makes it more difficult to make permanent commitments later in life.

"*Testing.*" Individuals who are in the "Testing" type of cohabiting relationship are typically well-adjusted people (lacking extensive past grievances or major individual problems) who exhibit a higher than average interpersonal skill level upon entrance into a cohabiting relationship. Macklin (1974) suggests that one of the most difficult tasks in a cohabiting relationship is to form a good intimate relationship while at the same time maintaining individuality and autonomy. The mutuality-autonomy issue seems to surface primarily when the individuals involved have met their security needs and are motivated to try out a quasi-committed relationship with the intent being to learn more about themselves and complex intimate relationships. When their basic needs have been met, they are then able to move outside their own skin and become interested in the well-being of their partner. This willingness to get to know one's partner facilitates deeper reciprocal levels of self-disclosure. In a sense, the partners seem to use the relationship to get to know more about themselves—their likes and dislikes, and to learn more about how intimate relationships of this type apparently lead to a deeper level of self-understanding for both individuals. However, when the relationship solidifies too quickly—prior to the development of individual interests and preferences—the partners feel overinvolved and dependent on the relationship with the accompanying sense of loss of identity (Macklin, Note 2).

The combination of perceived loss of identity and high relationship cohesiveness *without* commitment increases the probability that many "Testing" relationships will terminate at this juncture. If the mutuality-autonomy issue is handled successfully, the relationship may develop in one of three directions:

1. The relationship can terminate because the primary objectives for its formation (of which they may or may not have been aware) have been accomplished (increased self-understanding within a relationship context and increased knowledge of day-to-day intimate living).

2. The relationship can become an enduring cohabiting relationship similar to a marriage relationship, but without formal commitment and the ever-present possibility of terminating the relationship. The effects on the relationship of a lack of formal commitment and the availability of alternative sources of gratification is as yet unclear. It might be suggested that the persons involved would have to possess sufficient interpersonal skills to maintain this type of relationship without experiencing continuous crises through attempts to establish relationship predictability.

3. Another direction the relationship could take is for the goal to be extended from increasing self-understanding within the relationship context to developing a marital relationship which would involve further testing of compatibility and the ability to work together. If the cohabiting experience demonstrated to the couple that they could not work together, the relationship would likely terminate. If compatability testing were positive, escalation toward marriage would be likely.

The authors have taken a special interest in the termination of those "Testing" relationships which are less traumatic for the participants with the idea that much can be learned about the acquisition of interpersonal skills and marriage preparation under these conditions. Although it is unclear why some terminations are as easy as they are, some information is available that may help to explain it:

1. Most of the individuals in "Testing" relationships have had a rich dating history in which the outcome was a confirmation of their desirability to the opposite sex and a developed repertoire of interpersonal skills.

2. Cohabitation was a small step from their previous experiences in terms of the degree of involvement and complexity of the heterosexual relationship. Although frequently not at a conscious level, participants had ordered their experiences with increased complexity so that cohabitation was only different from previous involvements in degree, not type. Thus, they were largely prepared for what would be required of them in a complex cohabiting situation. It has been hypothesized that heterosexual relationship termination (including cohabitation termination) will be traumatic when the involvement that is being terminated is very different from the previous level of involvement. It is when this gap exists that the relationship is most "potent" in terms of its positive or negative impact on the participants. For example, termination of a cohabiting relationship would be more traumatic when the highest level of previous involvement had been "casual dating" than when the previous involvement had been "going steady."

3. Another factor which cushions the impact of termination is that "Testing" cohabitors typically have a fairly extensive network of like and opposite sex relationships (Peterman, et al., 1974) that provide friends at termination and a pool of possible eligibles for future involvement. Rather than being alone in their loss, they have friends to talk to and to become involved with and the known ability to start new heterosexual involvements when desired.

4. Lastly, they exhibit a high interpersonal skill level at termination by "closing the door" to the relationship. When termination was the result of unresolved problems, each partner knew what went wrong and how they contributed to the problem.

In short, the major potential advantage of a cohabiting relationship is its structural complexity. The potential extensive demands of a cohabiting relationship, in particular a "Testing" type of relationship, more closely approximate marital demands than any other courtship pattern. Thus, if individuals have experience in which gradual increments of interpersonal skills were learned, cohabitation can be an ideal situation for "trial marriage" and for learning the complexity of intimate relationship functioning. However, if preparatory experiences have not occurred, cohabitation tends to result in: (a) social isolation, and (b) solidification of non-adaptive interactional patterns within the cohabiting relationship.

Implications

It should be apparent at this point that a specific answer to the question of whether cohabitation makes for a better marriage is as yet unavailable. With a knowledge of the cohabitation typology presented here *and* an accurate understanding of the persons involved, however, it should be easier to assess the potential effects of cohabitation on the individuals. In order to do this effectively, several important factors must be considered, including: (a) partners' motivations for cohabiting, (b) partners' expectations for the cohabiting experience, (c) partners' personal and interpersonal needs and goals, (d) partners' interpersonal skill levels, (e) the present status of the relationship (e.g., level of commitment), (f) the effects of the partners' previous heterosexual experiences, and (g) the support structure of the partners' interpersonal networks.

Fortunately, much of this information can be obtained either through personal interaction or observation of the individuals involved. Although it is obvious that there are wide individual differences in these areas, as a general rule it appears that cohabiting relationships are likely to provide positive learning experiences and better preparation for marriage when the participants: (a) have as cohabitation goals, greater self-understanding within a heterosexual context and increased knowledge of day-to-day aspects of intimate living, (b) have realistic and mutually agreed upon expectations for the cohabiting experience, (c) do not have strong "deficiency" needs for emotional security (e.g.,

"Linus Blanket") or a residue of past grievances and/or unfinished business (e.g., "Emancipation"), (d) have higher interpersonal skill levels (e.g., the ability to openly and honestly express their feelings, the ability to understand and accept their partner, and the ability to mutually solve problems), (e) have had a relationship where the present degree of involvement closely approximates that of a cohabiting relationship (e.g., steady dating rather than casual dating), (f) have a rich dating history resulting in positive self-perceptions in terms of their desirability to the opposite sex, and (g) have a fairly extensive network of like and opposite sex relationships where important needs are being met.

Although the above guidelines outlining conditions under which cohabitation is likely to provide positive learning experiences and better preparation for marriage are critical, an equally important factor is how the counselor will obtain sufficient information from the couple to assess these relationship dimensions. One effective way is through a series of open questions, both indirect and direct, that will likely give the counselor and the couple enough information to make the above assessments about the cohabiting experience. A list of questions which the authors have found particularly useful in their counseling experience is presented in Table 1. Questions posed by the counselor to the couple are noted in the first column, while several "good signs" (i.e., general indicators that the couple has at least adequately attended to the issues posed in the question) or "concern signs" (i.e., general indicators that additional attention needs to be devoted to the issues or that the couple's response calls into question the value of cohabitation for the couple) are shown in the second column. The questions are designed to help the counselor obtain information from couples on several important issues identified earlier as important for cohabiting couples (e.g., partners' motivations and expectations for cohabiting). These sample questions are not intended to be definitive or inclusive of all possible questions nor are they presented in any sequential order. A given counselor will of course want to select particular questions aapropriate to his/her goals as well as the unique characteristics of the individuals involved. These questions, however, should give the counselor a general idea of one approach to assessing the effects of cohabitation as a marriage preparation experience.

Summary and Conclusions

The degree to which cohabiting experiences prepare individuals for marriage de-

5. ALTERNATIVE AND FUTURE RELATIONSHIPS

Table 1.
Sample Counselor Questions for Couples Contemplating Living Together

Counselor Questions	"Good" signs and "Concern" signs
1. Could you talk a little bit about how each of you came to the decision to live together?	*Good signs:* Each partner has given considerable thought to the decision, including the advantages and disadvantages of living together. *Concern signs:* One or both partners have given little thought to the advantages and disadvantages of living together.
2. Perhaps each of you could discuss for a minute what you think you will get out of living together?	*Good signs:* Each individual is concerned about learning more about self and partner through intimate daily living. Both wish to obtain further information about each other's commitment to the relationship. *Concern signs:* One or both partners desire to live together for convenience only. They want to live together to show independence from parents or peers.
3. Could each of you discuss what you see as your role and your partner's role in the relationship (*e.g.,* responsibilities, expectations)?	*Good signs:* Each individual's expectations of self and partner are compatible with those of partner. *Concern signs:* One or both individuals have given little thought to the roles or expectations of self and/or partner. Individuals disagree in terms of their expectations.
4. Could each of you identify your partner's primary physical and emotional needs and the degree to which you believe that you are able to fulfill them?	*Good signs:* Each individual has a clear understanding of partner's needs and is motivated and able to meet most of them. *Concern signs:* One or both individuals are not fully aware of partner's needs. Individuals are not motivated or able to meet needs of partner.
5. Would each of you identify your primary physical and emotional needs in your relationship with your partner? To what degree have these needs been met in the past? To what extent are these needs likely to be met if the two of you were to live together?	*Good signs:* Each partner clearly understands his or her needs. Most of these needs are presently being met and are likely to continue to be met in a cohabiting relationship. *Concern signs:* One or both partners are not fully aware of their needs. Needs are not being met in the present relationship and/or are not likely to be met if the individuals live together.
6. Could each of you discuss what makes this relationship important to you? What are your feelings toward your partner?	*Good signs:* Partners care deeply for each other and view the relationship as a highly significant one. *Concern signs:* One or both individuals do not care deeply for their partner or do not view the relationship as a highly significant one. Partners have an emotional imbalance with one partner more involved in the relationship than the other.
7. Could each of you explore briefly your previous dating experiences and what you have learned from them?	*Good signs:* Both individuals have had a rich dating history. Individuals have positive perceptions of self and opposite sex and are aware of what they learned from previous relationships. *Concern signs:* One or both partners have had minimal dating experience. Individuals have negative perceptions of self and/or of the opposite sex and do not seem aware of having learned from their prior relationships.
8. Perhaps each of you could talk for a minute about how your family and friends might react to the two of you living together?	*Good signs:* Each individual is aware of the potential repercussions of family and friends should they learn of the cohabiting relationship. Family and friends are supportive of the cohabiting relationship, or couple has considered how they will deal with opposition. *Concern signs:* One or both individuals are not fully aware of possible family and friends' reaction to their living together. Family and friends are not supportive of the cohabiting relationship.
9. Could each of you discuss your ability to openly and honestly share your feelings with your partner?	*Good signs:* Each individual is usually able to express feelings to partner without difficulty. *Concern signs:* One or both individuals have difficulty expressing feelings to partner or do not believe expressing feelings is important.
10. Could each of you discuss your partner's strengths and weaknesses? To what extent would you like to change your partner, relative to their strengths or weaknesses?	*Good signs:* Each individual is usually able to accept feelings of partner. Individuals are able to accept partner's strengths and weaknesses. *Concern signs:* One or both individuals are not able to understand and accept partner. Individuals have difficulty in accepting partner's strengths and weaknesses.
11. How do each of you handle relationship problems when they occur? Can you give some examples of difficult problems you have had and how you have dealt with them?	*Good signs:* Both individuals express feelings openly and are able to understand and accept partner's point of view. Individuals are able to mutually solve problems. *Concern signs:* One or both partners have difficulty expressing feelings openly or in accepting partner's point of view. Couple frequently avoids problems or fails to solve them mutually.

182

pends in part on the needs, goals, motivations, and competence of the persons involved. It would seem unfortunate to conclude that cohabitation is inherently good or bad preparation for marriage, but rather it should be viewed as having the potential for both, with the characteristics of the individuals and the relationship being of critical importance in determining the long-range effects of cohabitation.

Educators and counselors can discuss the concept of living together before marriage with the openness and objectivity with which they discuss other premarital heterosexual experiences. They can outline the personal skills and abilities which individuals typically require in order to function effectively in marriage as well as how certain types of cohabiting arrangements can facilitate growth in these areas. One such area where a cohabiting experience can prepare individuals for marriage involves sex roles and sex role expectations. With changing socialization patterns, sex role structures and expectations of husbands and wives are no longer as clearly defined as they once were. As Peterman (1975) noted.:

> Partners must now work out a role differentiation to suit their own unique personal and pair characteristics rather than simply following models handed down by tradition. To do so requires replacing romantic myth by a capacity to be more aware of one's own needs, learning habits of openness, practicing becoming accurately empathic, acquiring information and technique in human sexuality, ridding oneself of sexist attitudes, and so forth. (p. 40-41)

Lee (1975) expressed another potential positive outcome of cohabitation: "The essence of marriage is commitment, the contract and the concern shared by the couple. If they express these mutual responsibilities as living together without formal marriage, it is likely that when the formal promises are made the marriage will have greater endurance" (p. 41). The authors have argued that living together before marriage may also result in unpredictable or clearly negative consequences:

"If living together is undertaken as a trail of compatibility motivated by curiosity rather than by commitment, the results are likely to be as whimsical and unpredictable as the curiosity of the participants" (p. 41).

In summary, the guidelines presented in the previous section—linked to the cohabitation typology outlined earlier—hopefully will serve as a first step toward increasing our understanding of how cohabitation affects preparation for marriage. Future research is sorely needed, however, to further clarify the types of cohabiting relationships, the degree to which couples might move from one type to another, and to identify the person and relationship characteristics that play an important role in determining the long-range effects of living together before marriage.

REFERENCE NOTES

1. Lyness, J. F. Open marriage among former cohabitants: "We have met the enemy: Is it us?" Manuscript submitted for publication, 1976.
2. Macklin, E. D. *Unmarried Heterosexual Cohabitation on the University Campus*. Unpublished manuscript, Cornell University, 1974.

REFERENCES

Blaine, G. B. Does living together before marriage make for a better marriage? *Medical Aspects of Human Sexuality*, 1975, **9**, 32-39.

Henze, L. F., & Hudson, J. W. Personal and family characteristics of cohabiting and noncohabiting college students. *Journal of Marriage and the Family*, 1974, **36**, 722-727.

Lee, R. V. Does living together before marriage make for a better marriage? *Medical Aspects of Human Sexuality*, 1975, **9**, 41-44.

Peterman, D. J. Does living together before marriage make for a better marriage? *Medical Aspects of Human Sexuality*, 1975, **9**, 39-41.

Peterman, D. J., Ridley, C. A. & Anderson, S. M. A comparison of cohabiting and noncohabiting college students. *Journal of Marriage and the Family*, 1974, **36**, 344-354.

Raush, H. L. Barry, W. A., Hertel, R. K., & Swain, M. A. *Communication, conflict and marriage*. New York: Jossey-Bass, 1974.

LIVING

The Ménage à Deux

Sketches by Ed Koren

"The whole concept of having a family scares me right now," says Stephen Fenichell, 21. "I wouldn't even want to have a dog. All the possessions I have in the world fit in the back of a station wagon." Still, for the past four years, Steve has been living with Mary Jane Reilly, 22, in dormitories at Harvard College. "Sometimes I would like a symbolic statement that says this is my legitimate boyfriend," says Mary. "It might turn out to be more convenient later on to be married. At least if I went to visit my relatives with Steve, they wouldn't make us sleep in separate rooms."

"Sometimes I look at Maureen and feel like I've only known her for two weeks," says Ed Myers, 27. "Being married would destroy that feeling. It's very irresponsible in a way, but I like that." Last spring, after living together for five years, Ed and Maureen O'Leary, 27, put a down-payment on a modest house in Atlanta and moved in. Maureen's Irish Catholic family press constantly for a wedding, Ed says, and "I'm not sure Maureen can hold out. It'll make me retch, but I'll do it just to make them happy."

"It's cool with our friends, it's cool with our neighbors—our biggest inconvenience is that we don't know what to call each other." For fully ten years, Ron Nagle, 39, has been living with Cindy Ehrlich, 31, his 13-year-old son, Thatcher, and their two dogs. Ron and Cindy own a house together in San Francisco and celebrate anniversaries the same way married couples do. "We used to talk about marriage a lot more than we do now," says Cindy, "though we might consider it if we decided to have a child—or if we get inspired by a Cary Grant movie where he ran off and got married."

It used to be called "living in sin"—and Jimmy Carter and millions of other Americans still think of it that way. Last winter, the President even asked a group of government workers to cut it out and get married. And it used to be done mostly by the very rich, who could afford to flout society's rules, and the very poor, who had nothing to lose by ignoring them. But now it's a way of life that takes in college students, divorcees, pensioners and thousands of young adults in transition from swingledom to suburbia.

Since 1970, Census Bureau figures show, the number of unmarried people of the opposite sex sharing a household has doubled, from 654,000 to 1.3 million—and that almost surely understates the total. "Of all the revolutions that began in the 1960s, this is the only one that took hold among young people," says theologian and social critic Martin Marty. "It is not a momentary phenomenon, but a symbolic shift in attitudes that has great social significance."

And as social shifts go, this one went with blinding speed. It was only nine years ago that a Barnard College sophomore named Linda LeClair created an instant scandal by admitting that she had been living, unmarried, with a man. The news made the front page of The New York Times and LeClair was nearly booted out of college. Today, few major colleges retain parietal rules and many have coed dormitories. If Doris Day and Rock Hudson were models of uptight virtue in the movies of their day, modern film protagonists, such as Sylvester Stallone and Talia Shire in "Rocky" and Woody Allen and Diane Keaton in "Annie Hall," casually shack up. And if celebrities themselves see nothing new in having live-in lovers, they haven't always flaunted them so openly. People magazine makes a staple of happily unmarried couples, and one recent cover subject, 18-year-old actress Linda Blair, burbled about the 19-year-old musician she lives with—in her parents' house in Westport, Conn. "Mom says nothing stands in the way of love," Linda explains.

Linda Blair's parents are still the exception, however. Most surveys show that the great majority of parents think that cohabitation is immoral, emotionally unhealthy and unwise. And for the millions of Americans who retain strong and formal religious ties, what used to be called "living in sin" remains just that. "It is unmitigated adultery, which is clearly forbidden in the Bible, seriously injurious to the well-being of families and a sin against God," says Foy Valentine, executive secretary of the Christian Life Commission of the Southern Baptist Convention.

Social scientists believe the trend toward living together indicates an alarming loss of faith in institutions. "The real issue is not cohabitation but the meaning of marriage," says sociologist Richard Sennett. "Something about making a lifetime commitment of marriage doesn't work any more—that's what cohabiting shows. The idea of a permanent commitment to another human being has lost its meaning." Psychologist Urie Bronfenbrenner believes that cohabitation is seriously weakening the family and undermining the sense

The Introduction

TOGETHER

of obligation in all love and work relationships. "Society needs some kind of custom or institution in which people are committed to each other, no matter what," he says. "In sleeping together you don't develop those commitments."

People choose to live together for many reasons—but wariness about the troubled prospects of modern marriage may be the key one. One out of three marriages of couples between 25 and 35 years old will end in divorce and it is partly because of such bleak statistics that, for better or for worse, many people are moving so cautiously toward making lifelong commitments. The women's movement has encouraged its followers to demand the same rights and privileges as men, and many women argue that cohabitation offers the best of both worlds—intimate relationships on the one hand, and freedom from the traditional roles they might adopt in marriage, including economic dependence, on the other. At the same time, with premarital sex widely tolerated and contraception and abortion readily available, couples can openly enjoy intimate relationships without getting married.

Some people cohabit because they are philosophically opposed to marriage, and others see cohabitation as a practical short-term option when the lease is up or a roommate moves out. But for most couples, living together is a positive trial period or prelude to marriage. "I discovered a lot I never could in a marriage," says 20-year-old student Pamela Brown, who has been living with her boyfriend for the past year in Portland, Maine. "When we lived apart we ate every meal together. Now we don't eat together all the time. If I had been married I would have felt the pressure of filling the wife-and-cook role. I believe in marriage but I'm not ready for it yet. I want a career first." Most couples who live together do marry sooner or later, especially when they want to have children.

Cohabitation may be delaying marriage. Since 1960, the incidence of never-married women 20-24 years old has jumped from 28 per cent to 40 per cent; among men aged 23, the never-marrieds jumped from 42 per cent to 52 per cent just since 1970. But conclusive views on its effects are difficult to come by, partly because research in the area is so spotty. While cohabitation has rapidly become a favorite dissertation subject for Ph.D. students and a Cohabitation Newsletter is published for those in the field, the research has focused almost exclusively on college students, the sampling techniques have been notably unscientific and studies aimed at long-term comparisons of couples are almost nonexistent. Most important, the research is frustratingly inconclusive both as to whether cohabitation is generally more or less satisfying than marriage, and whether it helps set the groundwork for better and more enduring relationships.

This uncertainty is reflected—sometimes ludicrously—in the difficulty couples have trying to find labels for each other and their arrangements. "That is no accident," says San Francisco psychotherapist Lillian Rubin. "Language and

custom tend to interact." The absence of such a terminology here, she says, implies that "there is not yet agreement that this is really a legitimate form of coupling." Elizabeth L. Post, author of "The New Emily Post's Etiquette," suggests "covivant" as the most appropriate way to refer to one's roommate. Others have suggested such exotica as attaché, companẽra, unlywed, paramour, apartmate, checkmate and swain. Some try coy double entendres such as 'spose (" 'spose they'll get married?") and sin-law. Parents, suggests Washington D.C., writer Jane Otten, may finally have to settle for "my daughter's er and my son's um." Most people talk about their "friends," with or without special stress, or just use unadorned first names.

Cohabitation creates considerable problems of protocol, especially in Washington, some of which journalist Sally Quinn wryly described in a recent Washington Post article. According to Quinn—who shares a house with her executive editor, Ben Bradlee—social secretaries are "having nervous breakdowns" over addressing invitations, making introductions and seating guests according to the rank of their roommates. For invitations, both names can be listed on the envelope, alphabetically and on separate lines. When it comes to inviting one partner and not the other, there are no easy answers. The same is true of introductions, although Elizabeth Post suggests an interesting compromise—use "friend" for elders and "the person I live with" for peers. As for seating arrangements, says Quinn, "for now, the protocol demands that the spouse assume the rank of the spouse and an unranked roommate is simply not counted."

At the White House, where the President's views on living together are well known, protocol problems

5. ALTERNATIVE AND FUTURE RELATIONSHIPS

have been obviated by a rash of marriages since January. Although staffers insist that Carter does not interfere with their personal lives, the fact is that a number of his aides have belatedly tied the knot—including Jack Watson, Greg Schneiders, Tim Kraft and Rex Granum, Federal Trade Commission head Mike Pertschuk and State Department official Richard Holbrooke. "It does seem to defy the laws of probability," admits one White House insider.

At most other houses, the stickiest protocol problems arise when children show up for visits with their mates. Many parents remain adamantly opposed to letting them sleep together. "I'd never let any of my children shack up in my house on a weekend," says a Westchester, N.Y., mother of four. "I insist on my standards being respected." Columnist Ann Landers, who unstintingly opposes cohabitation, agrees that parents have the right to set the rules in their own household, but cautions them not to be "judgmental" about their children's arrangements.

More and more parents, however, are trying to adapt to the new morality—no matter how difficult it may prove. Peggy Scott, a New York City mother of four, first confronted the situation six years ago. "We arrived for a weekend at our Vermont house, only to find that my 19-year-old son had been living there with his girlfriend for about ten days. My husband and I felt very shaken up and incredulous and there was this terrible moment where we didn't know what to do. They were not trying to conceal it, though, so we welcomed the girl

and have sexual relations, is against the law in twenty states, with penalties for conviction ranging as high as a three-year jail sentence in Massachusetts and Arizona. Fornication—sexual intercourse between a man and a woman who are unmarried—is a crime in sixteen states. But such laws are rarely enforced.

For the most part, childless couples living together face only minor hassles—mostly economic. While cohabitors usually get the same rates as married people for life insurance and face no greater problems in obtaining mortgages than do married couples, disadvantages often include higher auto- and home-insurance rates, exclusion from family medical plans, scattered difficulty in renting apartments and traveling in foreign countries, and perhaps most important, a lack of legal standing for their children. Income-tax rates give the best break to the married couple in which only one member works. For moderate-income couples in which both partners work, the tax bite is worse in many cases for those who are married, since they are entitled to a single standard deduction compared with two for singles living together. For example, a married couple earning a joint income of $20,000 may pay nearly $400 more in taxes than a comparable cohabiting couple.

Old people complain that, for them, the social-security system invites living in sin. Louis Marathon, 80, and Madeline Clarke, 81, met in a Miami nursing home last year and lived together for several months, between his hospital stays. A former schoolteacher, Madeline received $285 a month from her husband's social-security benefits. Lou gets a World War I veteran's pension of $425 a month (he received no social security since he had been self-employed). Last June, they got married and Madeline may now lose her benefits. "If they cut her off, I'll go to the VA and get an increase as a married man," says Louis, a double amputee. Even if their money is reduced, however, the Marathons are glad they married. "There's more respect," says Madeline, who is almost blind. "If we live together, it's just common-law, and with that anyone could get disgusted and walk out."

Social Security

Ed Koren

and just hoped everything would come out all right." It has, at least to parental eyes: they eventually got married. Today, when the Scotts' other sons come home for weekends, they are permitted to stay in the same room with their mates. "It was a very hard decision," says Mrs. Scott, "but I knew they were living together during the week, so what difference did the weekend make?"

But if societal sanctions against cohabitation are easing, there are still certain legal barriers that remain. Cohabitation, where two unmarried people share a residence

Is living together any different from marriage? Research indicates that people who live together are less likely than others to be involved with formal religions, and that they see themselves as more liberated from traditional sex roles but just as monogamous as their married counterparts. But beyond that it is almost impossible to generalize. On the one hand, cohabitation can be a sensible way to explore a loving relationship. On the other, it tends to rule out experiments outside one rigid structure. The one conclusion from all the evidence is that the degree of commitment among people living together is considerably less than that of married couples.

For Rich, 31, and Ilene, 25, both recently graduated from Boston College, living together was anything but a romantic adventure in young love. "It is much cheaper," says Rich. "We share the costs on rent and food." Both anticipate marriage eventually, though not necessarily to each other, and they don't even agree on how and where they'd like to live. Rich wants to look for work in a rural setting; Ilene would prefer an urban one. "We're trying to work on it but I'm not sure a compromise can be reached," says Ilene. Whatever happens, both Rich and Ilene say that their experience has been a good one.

According to author Gail Sheehy, whose book "Passages" explores the stages of adult life, Rich and Ilene's attitude may be appropriate for them. "Establishing what you want to do and who you are is necessary before you can truly believe that commitment to another person does not threaten your own individuality," she says. "The whole stage in which one is trying to gain a footing in the adult world requires that one put hope and effort into trials. Like early friendships, they may dissolve, but how are you going to learn without trying?"

What troubles some social critics about the notion of trial intimacy is that it undermines the concept of enduring loyalty that is integral to marriage. "Intimate bonding should be based on deep concepts of fidelity," says Martin Marty. "A lot that is convenient and exploratory undercuts that. There is no society when everything is based on ad hoc, and if we can't trust each other, we have no lives." Notre Dame campus chaplain William Toohey sees living together as part of the problem of making open-end promises. "I think it is a weakness in society that we have a feverish desire not to be hurt," he says. "Dammit, life is vulnerability. You've got to give of yourself and it does make you vulnerable."

Couples who have married after living together confirm the fact that the institution deepens their sense of commitment. Lenny, 29, and Inger, 33, married last May after living together for four years in Washington, D.C. "One thing it has done is make me realize I am going to drop dead someday," says Lenny, an attorney. "The job has become more serious. I need to get the career going and I'm feeling more responsible." "Until you get married you aren't aware of being part of something that's bigger than yourself," says Inger.

For Katie Charles, who is getting married in August after five years of cohabitation, the very things she once feared might encroach on her independence now are welcome. "It's a real step, standing up before your friends and saying I'm going to make my life with this person," says the 30-year-old Chicago mental-health counselor. "Before it was somewhat temporary. Now I'm turned on to the idea of being a family. I'm becoming more traditional than I thought I was. It's a return to the values I learned as I was growing up."

But the values many young people bring to marriage these days are changing, too. Married couples are just as likely to pursue separate careers and intermingle roles as those who live together. And the problems of married couples and those living together are remarkably similar. "Most of the problems unmarried couples have—sex, money, power, the need for

Jose Azel

Clarke and Marathon: Marriage means losing money

space—are the same ones married couples mention," says Dr. Frederick G. Humphrey, president of the American Association of Marriage and Family Counselors. "Unmarried couples may want the pseudointellectual belief that they are free to leave, but when they split up, the emotional pain and trauma is often virtually identical to married couples getting a divorce." In fact, so many unmarried couples are seeking counseling these days that the AAMFC is seriously considering retitling its members "relationship counselors."

Unlike cohabitation, however, marriage is reinforced by its traditions and religious associations. "Marriage is a form of intimate coercion," says Sennett. "That's why it is ritualized so strongly. It's a legal way of saying you can trust someone to be there." Los Angeles actress Elizabeth Allensworth, for instance, believes that the relationship she had with her former boyfriend might have survived had they been married. As her career got under way, problems developed over independence and money. "All the hostilities, I think, would have been dealt with in a different way if we'd been married," she says. "That's a much more long-range ball game, not just a here-and-now situation. For a couple that's living together, it's so easy to say the hell with you, I'm leaving."

Some believe, however, that the very fragility of living together makes cohabitors less likely than married folk to take each other for granted. "Married people are more apt to put up with a problem rather than divorce, but couples living together are more likely to try and work out the differences between them," says New York psychiatrist Avodah Offit. "There is the fear of losing each other." But there is also, for many couples, the unspoken issue of "if you really loved me, you would marry me." During almost a year of living together, Jenny and Mark Bluestein had spats over staying out late and small jealousies. "It was the tensions and feelings of wanting to possess without being possessed," says Mark, 25, who works for a beauty shop in St. Louis. "We were both suffering through different insecurities about each other so we both said, 'OK, I'll show you I do too love you.' We got married to solidify the commitment, to reassure each other."

Many people—especially mothers—believe that the insecurities of living together harm women more than men. "I'm bitterly opposed to living together," says Mrs. Dorothy Grossman, a Nashville mother of four grown daughters, some of whom have tried cohabiting. "A woman is more subservient to a man if she enters this type of arrangement. The woman goes and sets up house, gives more than 50 per cent of the effort, and when it breaks up she always gets the bad deal. It's almost always the man who walks out."

Some research indicates that the level of commitment among women who live together with men is indeed consistently higher than that of their partners. Ohio State sociologist Nancy Moore Clatworthy interviewed 100 young couples in Columbus, Ohio, and concluded that most of the women consented to living with men only because they felt their partners wanted to. "The women had feelings of guilt," she says. "Living-together couples often haven't proved what they wanted to prove—that marriage is the same as cohabitation."

But in one way, that may be changing. Last December, the California Supreme Court ruled that singer Michelle Triola had the right to pursue her claim for both support payments and property rights from actor Lee Marvin, the man she had lived with for seven years. The ruling said that in the absence of a legal marriage contract—or even a verbal agreement—the court can infer a contract from the conduct of the parties. As a result, Triola—and others in her situation—may have the right at least to communal property if not support after a relationship breaks up.

Since he represented Triola, Los Angeles lawyer Marvin M. Mitchelson has already taken on four more celebrity cases. "A

5. ALTERNATIVE AND FUTURE RELATIONSHIPS

problem with the Marvin-Triola decision," says Mitchelson, "is that it states that the court can examine the relationship of the parties to determine who contributed what. So you get back to a fault system"—just what the no-fault divorce law was designed to eliminate. It also means the courts may have to decide the value of services and the equity of imposing the economic obligations of lawful spouses on people who have rejected matrimony to avoid such obligations. Mitchelson foresees that the California finding may encourage couples to sign what he calls "non-nuptial agreements" spelling out what obligations they are and are not taking on.

Although non-nuptial contracts have been advocated over the years, perhaps no one has taken the concept quite as far as Edmund Van Deusen, a 53-year-old California writer. Himself the product of a failed marriage, Van Deusen advertised in a newspaper for a partner. He offered to pay her $500 a month to live with him, provide companionship but not necessarily sex or love, and perform light household duties. That was five years ago. Since then he has been sharing his Laguna Beach home with the woman he chose—under a contract that includes a 30-day cancellation clause on either side. Neither one has exercised it. "A marriage contract is 24 hours a day," Van Deusen says. "We only commit a bargained amount of our time. It allows people who live together to follow familiar rules that also guarantee independence."

At the moment, the overwhelming majority of Americans still strongly disapprove of living together "without benefit of clergy," and even the people involved in those relationships find them not wholly comfortable. If the divorce rate continues to climb, widespread cohabitation may one day peacefully coexist with marriage, either as an interim option or as a practical alternative. But if it is to be the trend of the future, couples will discover that it is no magic solution: the problems of living together take as much time and effort to work out as the problems of modern marriage.

—TONY SCHWARTZ with MARY LORD in Washington, DEWEY GRAM in Los Angeles, PAMELA ELLIS SIMONS in Chicago, LISA WHITMAN in New York and bureau reports

What Happens When a Homemaker Loses Her Job

*Lorraine Poole must find work.
After twenty years of marriage her husband
walked out, leaving her to raise
six children and create a new life for herself.*

Rollie Hochstein

Just a few years ago, Lorraine Poole was the kind of woman that many of us, less sure of our roles, regard with wonder and envy. At almost forty, Lorraine was the happy housewife, together inside and out, in love with her handsome and successful husband, content to keep his house, help him in his work and bring up the six delightfully outgoing children they had adopted.

Lucky Lorraine had everything under control. Her twelve-room house, which she had decorated herself and kept without hired help, looked like a magazine ad. The kids, whose ages now range from eight to fifteen, were all active, attractive, favorites among their friends, achievers at school, wholesomely involved in after-school sports and church and community service. Her husband, John, a dedicated and dynamic minister, rejoiced in his family and appreciated a wife who was always there when he needed her, a gracious hostess always ready for surprise dinner guests, a perceptive counselor, a ready traveling companion and a competent keeper of the home front when he traveled without her. Despite the press of duties, Lorraine, who is blonde, slim and always handsomely dressed, managed to have lots of fun with her family. There were brithday parties galore, packs of kids in her station wagon, picnics, beach and skiing trips. Sometimes the whole family, including John's mother who lived with them, jumped on their nine bicycles and rode off for a jaunt.

"Lorraine was always very quiet in the presence of her husband," one old friend recalls. "A lot was expected of her and she was a perfectionist." That was the way Lorraine liked it. She told me recently, over a cup of brewed coffee in her bright, spotless, plant-filled kitchen, that she had seen herself as part of an ideal couple. "We went to church together, had fun with the kids, went out a lot. I loved my life and I thought it would never change."

But change has come. About three years ago, Lorraine noticed a difference. John was home less, working more. There were disagreements, a feeling of distance. Formerly, John had included Lorraine in everything, even his church work. He had wanted her company on out-of-state missions; sometimes he would call her to join him for lunch with a troubled parishioner; he confided in her. Then he became different—as if, Lorraine says, he were carrying on his life without her. "I'd hear his plans from other people. If I complained, I knew I wasn't the cheerful, supportive wife I was expected to be."

Lorraine told herself that things would work out. As an ultradependent wife, who cleared every purchase with her husband and relied on his decision for any choice that faced her, she couldn't imagine surviving without him. A year ago, however, John packed his bags and left home. "He told me he felt he couldn't make me happy," Lorraine said. "I feel that perhaps the pressures of his life, of his work and family may have been too much." And after twenty years of marriage, Lorraine was alone, a supporting player with no leading man, a provider of background for an empty stage. How does such a woman feel? Deflated. Defeated. Lost. Scared. Overwhelmed by a rush of responsibilities to cope with on her own. Assaulted by a sense of failure.

"At the time," Lorraine told me, "I thought I was doing the best job I could. What hurts is that there was no communication about his feelings—that he didn't give me a chance to discuss it." Many women whose husbands' accumulated resentments explode suddenly and too late share Lorraine's shock and dismay. *If he had only told me. If we could have talked about it.* "If he doesn't complain, you think everything is fine," Lorraine said.

The shock sent her spinning, but Lorraine has come out of it right side up. Good friends, loving children and reserves of inner strength have helped to sustain her. Today, with growing confidence, Lorraine is working as a substitute teacher, looking for a permanent job and going to school to qualify for a good one. She runs her house on seventy dollars a week, supplemented by her own teaching earnings when possible, and tries to keep up a "business-as-usual" atmosphere for her children's morale as well as her own. At forty-two, this engaging, outgoing, hard working woman who expected to be her husband's wife all her life is facing single responsibility, financial uncertainty, totally unfamiliar business and legal problems, unanticipated loneliness and the necessity of making her own plans for her own life. Married less than two weeks after her graduation from college, Lorraine would have celebrated her twenty-first wedding anniversary in June. Instead, she marked her first year of do-it-yourself living. It was a rough one—a year of self-doubt, flagging courage, disillusionment and the confrontation of painful truths. But it was also a year of discovery and development.

"I didn't go to bed and pull up the covers and have a depression," Lorraine told me as we had a salad lunch in a pleasant restaurant near her home in Cherry Hill, New Jersey. "I got through each day, functioning as usual, on the hope that maybe he'd walk through the doorway that night. It took me a long time to face the idea that he really might not come back."

Facing facts was a call to action. There were problems to work on—problems with money, self-esteem, friends, the children. Gradually, Lorraine made her moves. She is a gentle and sunny woman, brought up strictly and lovingly by her own churchly parents, but she had never learned to live on her own. In her marriage, John had made the decisions—Lorraine would even ask him if she could buy a dress or a sweater. She didn't know his income, how much insurance he held or where his papers were kept. Lorraine could write checks on their joint account, but she never knew what the balance was. Learning to handle money was to be one of her major challenges.

She says she felt the weight of responsibility "almost literally falling on my shoulders." For not only did she have to learn to budget, but to manage on much less than she was used to. No more ski trips or winter breaks in the tropics. No more silver-service restaurant feasts. Last August John was asked to give up his position with the church, whose conservative members don't approve of separation and divorce. He has been trying since then to establish an insurance business. Money is short. While he has so far managed to keep up maintenance payments on the mortgage, car insurance and utility bills, he gives Lorraine only $10 a week for herself and each child, a total of $70, to cover day-to-day expenses.

Dollar-stretching is new for her, but she's learning to serve lots of soup, to make her popular Spanish rice with one pound of hamburger instead of three. She has a new sense of the difference between convenience and necessity. Always creative in home decoration—making her own flower arrangements, macramé holders for baskets, needlework accessories—she's now also creative at economizing. Last Christmas she climbed to the attic, collected armfuls of old clothes—hers and the children's—and sold them to a second-hand shop for $150. With careful shopping and ingenious wrapping, this helped to make a bountiful holiday for the kids.

Managing the present, though, doesn't insure the future. Lorraine looks ahead to a big question mark. What she needs, she knows, is a job. She needs it not only for the money, but also for company and social identity. "When John was home," she explains, "I had a reason to be there, to have his meals ready, to keep the house looking nice for him. Now, with the kids in school, there's no reason for me to be home. It's a terrible feeling to be home without a reason."

Job hunting has been no picnic. Twenty years ago, fresh from college with a B.S. in chemistry and biology, Lorraine had her choice of attractive jobs and worked productively in a medical research lab for more than five years, until her first son was adopted. Last year, with the added poise, presence and experience of maturity, she was consistently ignored in her applications for a job. She was shocked to find herself (so useful as a wife) so unemployable in business.

She did all the right things: sent out fifty resumes, answered all likely want ads, called all possible contacts. She even visited every lab, hospital and manufacturing company within a twenty-mile range of her house. She knows what skills she has to offer. Her former boss, one of her advisers on job-seeking, was sure it would take no more than two weeks of on-the-spot training to bring her up to date.

Results were a disappointment. Only three of her letters were answered, and those said "No thanks." Many companies refused to take applications. One receptionist slipped an application to her through the slot under the window.

"Couldn't I talk to someone?" Lorraine asked.

"No," said the receptionist.

Lorraine filled out the application and slipped it back.

In all, she was granted a handful of interviews, offered one job piling oil drums outside the lab she wanted to work in and another managing a fast-food eatery at night, a time when she wants to be home with her children. Apparently her single status, the reason she needs the job, is what keeps her from getting one. "Who'll take care of your kids?" the would-be employer asks. (Actually, this is a discriminatory question in violation of the Fair Employment Practices law, but Lorraine wants a job too much to protest.) Lorraine explains that she doesn't foresee missing any time because of the kids: they're competent, she's responsible, she'll make proper arrangements. Still, she has been consistently rejected for jobs in her chosen field, usually in favor of women fresh out of college.

In stopgap work, however, she has proved, to herself and to the world, that she can meet demanding professional standards. At a friend's suggestion, she telephoned the local Board of Education one day last October, had an interview the following day and was substitute-teaching the next. Since then she has been called to come in for all but six teaching days and has missed none of them. Twenty-five dollars a day is low pay and it's not available in vacation time, but it helps. What's more, Lorraine has turned out to be a gifted teacher, popular with her students and in high demand by regular teachers because she excels at getting their lessons taught.

Donald Savitz, chairman of the physical science department of Cherry Hill High School East (over three thousand students), is enthusiastic about her work. "The kids know when Lorraine walks in that there's a job to be done. I know that she'll be there, not just on time, but early, and that she's ready to do anything extra we ask of her. She's not just putting in hours."

Gratified by her success in the classroom, Lorraine is keeping teaching as an iron in her career fire. She may return to college this summer for regular certification. Meanwhile, she is taking courses in new laboratory techniques and, at this writing, has begun working toward a realtor's license. "I'm not waiting for a job to fall in my lap." Lorraine is after the most rewarding work she can get, in terms of money and future satisfaction. Though she'd like to have her husband in the house again, she never again wants to be so vulnerably dependent.

While the need for money is immediate, it's not necessarily the most painful or pressing problem. The newly husbandless woman finds herself without an emotional prop. Suddenly she needs from other people what she is used to providing: love, reassurance, morale-boosting, even physical help. The Poole household has always been run with great efficiency, with chores for each child and general pitching in on yardwork and meal preparation. But now, with Lorraine working days and tired at night, the kids have even more responsibility. Jennifer, fourteen, does most of the cooking on school days. Jeffrey, fifteen, joins her in being especially solicitous of their mother. When Lorraine had friends in recently for a little dessert party, both Jeff and Jennifer called from their baby-sitting jobs to see how she was doing.

Two children, Jodi, eleven, and Jared, eight, are sister and brother and were born in Korea. Joel and Jonathan are eleven and twelve. John and Lorraine Poole had always planned to adopt children, even before learning that they couldn't have their own, so as Lorraine says, "These children weren't second best." Go to the Poole house and you'll see community action. Kids playing chess, kids setting up for dinner. They do things together and their friends come in and do them too.

As a minister's children, the kids have been brought up to get along with adults as well as with their peers. They've always paid attention in school, been active in athletics and cheerfully committed to volunteer service work. Lately, though, some of them have begun to show signs of stress. In particular, their school marks have slipped, some of them drastically. Teachers have called Lorraine to find out why a formerly outgoing and enthusiastic student has become diffident and withdrawn. And though Lorraine is careful not to speak negatively about their father, she knows that the children can't help being aware of the tensions of the situation. John continues to be attentive to his family, sometimes cooks dinner for the kids in his nearby one-bedroom apartment, and takes them out regularly. But there is no easy way to protect kids from the effects of a parental breakup.

To Lorraine, the children have been loving and steadfast. Her parents, too, have come through for her. They visit often and are unfailingly sympathetic, ready to repair a leak, help with homework, take everybody out for a treat. Not all of Lorraine's friends, though, turned out to be so dependable. Some found it hard to deal with a split couple and spared themselves by bowing out of Lorraine's life. Others she thought her friends were really her husband's friends only.

"It was a jolt when the phone stopped ringing," Lorraine admitted. "People who'd been here for dinner and who'd gone out with us just disappeared. I think I stayed in the background so much that I wasn't a real person to many of John's friends." She spoke softly and directly, without self-pity, but she admitted having suffered from loneliness and still feeling hurt at times. However, she has made new friends and kept close to the old ones who stuck by her. She feels she has gained by knowing who her true friends are. "I may not get as many invitations," she says, "but the friends I have are loyal and accept me for myself."

Two kinds of friends have helped through the roughest days. One couple, friends from church with grown children, simply showed up one day soon after John had left and, without asking what they could do, just started helping. They kept up regular visits, bringing food, gifts for the children and even biscuits for Liza, the Pooles' fluffy Wheaton terrier. This couple gave comfort and con-solation—offering shoulders to cry one, arms to lean on. "Today is one day closer to the day when things will be better," they told Lorraine to buck her up.

Another old friend, a neighbor, talked hard, solid sense. Playing down the sympathy, he treated Lorraine not as a victim, but as a strong person meeting a challenge. Lorraine might have preferred, in the beginning, to pretend that things would right themselves. Her friend told her to face facts. "He kind of shook the dreamdust out of my head," Lorraine recalls with a frank smile. "He urged me to stand on my own feet, be rational, go to school, get a job, see a lawyer. I guess you need both kinds of friends—comforters and straight-talkers. They really helped me."

In hesitating to get legal advice, Lorraine was like many women in her position. "It makes things so final," she said. "You can't fool yourself any longer." It took her until January to make the move, but she feels the move she then made was the right one. Lorraine didn't want to fight with her husband or to rush a divorce. She wanted two specific things: a regular weekly allowance (so she wouldn't have to hold her hand out for money) and regular visiting arrangements (so she could plan ahead for the times when John would take the children out). These arrangements made Lorraine's life easier and gave her the dignity of solid rights to stand on.

Lorraine's lawyer was understanding, informed on cases like hers and no hawk about dealing with her

WHEN THE UNTRAINED WOMAN MUST FIND A JOB

Untrained women can become displaced homemakers.
Here is advice from experts on what you can do if it happens to you.

■ Lorraine Poole is a displaced homemaker, one of an estimated 3,500,000 in this country. A displaced homemaker is usually a woman (some men qualify too) over the age of forty who, because she has lost her husband through divorce, separation or death, is forced to support herself—perhaps for the first time in her life. Often she has dependent children to support as well.

These women have little or no money. A divorced or separated woman may find alimony and/or child support payments small, sporadic or nonexistent; sometimes the partner walks out with everything, including savings, insurance and other assets. If she is widowed, her husband's terminal illness may have drained all the family funds.

A displaced homemaker is too young to receive social security payments. She may be eligible for welfare, but will have to meet certain requirements; for example, her housing costs must not exceed a certain amount and she will have to prove that she has no other source of income.

Centers for Displaced Homemakers are one answer to the many needs of these women, places where they can find practical help on getting a job and emotional support in starting a new life. The centers provide free counseling as well as job training and placement; often there is a staff member who gives special inspiration—she was probably once displaced herself. In April 1978, the office of Rep. Yvonne Braithewaite Burke (D-Calif.) reported that twenty-eight states had either passed legislation or had bills pending to help the displaced homemaker. To date however, only eight states have provided the funds to open centers. Those now functioning are in Oakland, California; Eugene, Oregon; Omaha, Nebraska; St. Paul, Minnesota; Cleveland, Ohio; Arlington, Texas; Orlando, Florida; and Baltimore, Maryland. Additional centers are in the process of being opened in Buffalo, New York; Fayetteville, North Carolina and Los Angeles.

In May committees in both houses of Congress approved the Displaced Homemaker Assistance Act, which is one of the proposed amendments to the new version of the Comprehensive Employment and Training Act of 1973 (CETA) that expires September 30.

This amendment would provide money to set up programs across the country for displaced homemakers. At this writing, the House and Senate were expected to vote on this bill in early summer, with CETA scheduled to be ready for the President's signature by September. If you would like more information about this bill, or about the center nearest you, write to The National Alliance for Displaced Homemakers, 3800 Harrison St., Oakland, Calif. 94611. Please include a self-addressed stamped envelope.

If You Are a Displaced Homemaker

Whether or not you live near a displaced homemakers' center, there are things you can do to help yourself. This is what the experts advise:

● If you are separated, or about to be divorced, find a lawyer. Even if you are not planning to file suit yourself, a lawyer will give you advice to help you protect what is yours. Dr. Dolores Ferrell, executive director of the Women's Law Centers in Dallas, emphasizes the importance of a lawyer's help. "If you don't have a lawyer, or if you are not satisfied with the one you have, check with a woman's organization such as NOW, which keeps a list of attorneys who are sympathetic to women," Dr. Ferrell advises. Lawyers registered with NOW usually negotiate fees, but if you haven't any money at all, call your local Bar Association for the nearest branch of the Legal Aid Society or the Legal Services Corp. If you meet their requirements (which are usually very strict, Dr. Ferrell warns), you will be able to obtain a lawyer at no charge.

● Don't try to go it alone. Find a counselor. "You do need someone to talk to—someone to help you decide what your needs are, help you assess your skills, help you decide where you are going," says Liz Boyington, assistant director of the displaced homemaker center in Eugene, Oregon. You should be able to find a counselor through the YWCA, a family service agency, even a local hospital.

● Joining a group can give you new friends, support and comfort. It might be a widows' club, an organization for single parents or a more specialized one, such as the Divorced Catholic Groups.

● Take advantage of available help.

There are training opportunities and career counseling that you can get for a small fee or even free. Check local community colleges, continuing education programs and women's centers, such as the YWCA or NOW, to see what is offered. Ask a school counselor if there are any scholarships, apprenticeships or other financial assistance available. Some programs do require substantial fees, but loans can sometimes be obtained. The National Alliance for Displaced Homemakers publishes a job tip sheet that you can get free by sending your request and a self-addressed stamped envelope to the address given in the adjacent column.

● Believe in your strengths. "To convince an employer that you can do the job, you must first convince yourself," says Cynthia Marano, director of the Center for Displaced Homemakers in Baltimore. "Homemaking and volunteer work do provide experience, but many people just don't know it."

What Every Woman Should Know

No matter how secure you may feel right now, you, too, could become a displaced homemaker. Many of the displaced homemakers we talked to said that they never expected it to happen to *them*. Here are three things you can do *now* that will help you—just in case you are suddenly left on your own.

● Develop a working skill and use it before you are forced to. Do volunteer or temporary work so your skills won't get rusty.

● Find out about your financial situation. How much money does your family have? Where is it spent? What and where are your savings and investments? Do you know your husband's social security number? Does your family have medical and life insurance; if so, how much? Have you established a credit rating by taking out charge accounts and a loan in your own name? Remember, according to the Federal Credit Opportunity Act, discrimination against women in granting credit is illegal.

● Keep in touch with the outside world. Become self-sufficient. Learn how to drive, to make minor adjustments on the car, to repair things around the house. Be sure to have your own friends so that you will always have them.   *The End*

husband. He told her not to sign anything and to call if she had a problem. John was cautioned by the lawyer to pay his weekly stipend and to give four days' notice before fetching the kids. Nothing else has changed except that Lorraine has become a different woman—in many ways much more of a person than she used to be. Life is not the lyrical bowl of cherries, yet it holds enormous satisfactions. As she puts it: "When John first left, I was down all the time because he wasn't here. Now I'm up most of the time because I'm learning to live with myself."

A great benefit has been Lorraine's growing self-confidence. Success as a teacher, the building of her own friendships and the management of family affairs have helped her see herself as a competent and accomplishing woman—not her husband's "shadow" or the "financial idiot" she once thought she was. Furthermore, she has developed a new, more relaxed way of looking at things. Learning to live one day at a time and not let anxiety overtake her is a big dividend for this former worrier. Because she is less anxious, she finds herself more easygoing with the children. "I'm not so taken up with my minister's-wife image," Lorraine claims. "The kids get more TV time these days, and there's more pop music in the house. And though I have less time, I think we have more fun."

Bobbi Harrison, a friend and neighbor, told me she's surprised at how well Lorraine is doing. "I didn't know she had it in her," Bobbi marvels. "I didn't think she was this strong an individual."

Lorraine didn't know it either. But as she gets through every day, meeting its responsibilities and opportunities, she recognizes her power. I asked her if she was still eager to have her husband back and she was not quick to reply. At last she said, with characteristic honesty, that she would like him to return, but not on the old Big Man—Little Woman terms. And not right away. Someday, maybe. But not until she's done some more growing and learning about living her own life.

"IT'S MY TURN NOW"

Iris Sangiuliano, Ph.D.

In her search to trace the pattern of women's adult development, the author, a psychotherapist, interviewed dozens of middle-class women, all married or formerly married, most of them college-educated, and ranging in age from their 20s to their 50s. The result of her four-year study is a forth-coming book In Her Time *(William Morrow and Company, Inc.), from which the following article is adapted.*

How often have you heard "Aren't you Bill's wife?," or "Johnnie's mother," or "the daughter of so-and-so"? Our life course has been narrowed by our gender identification as women. We have been defined as daughters by our parents; as wives by our spouses; and as mothers by our offspring. And for many of us that has meant that we're forever and only daughters, wives and mothers.

But the yearning for a personal identity exists in us all. Some of us are only too aware of its absence. Others drown ourselves in daily routines. More and more women, however, are discovering that their lives cannot be reduced to making this or that choice unto perpetuity. Relationships change as we change. Marriages can and do dissolve through divorce, death, shattered illusions and emotional distances. Children grow and leave us, as they should.

Divorced at the age of 45, her daughter away at college, one woman explained that ever since childhood her dream had been to be a wife and the *best* mother ever. Wistfully, she continued, "Now I wish I'd latched my dreams elsewhere, to something that has a bit more mileage."

And more mileage is precisely our concern here as we follow the paths that three women have taken toward a second birth—journeys strewn with their share of byways and dead ends—and explore what's given them the impetus to move from that sheltered *us* to seek the *I* within it.

Since our concern is with mileage or, technically, with life-span development, let's turn for a moment to theories about how adults develop.

The currently popular theory of adulthood as a series of developmental tasks or crises that the adult must resolve at various stages of his life underlies the notable works of Erik Erikson, Robert Havighurst, Daniel Levinson and Freud. Like most theories, however, it has its shortcomings. One of them is in the area of predictability.

The view of adulthood as a series of orderly, predictable age-related progressions makes little room for the impact of those "unexpected" critical events that so often change the focus and direction of our lives. If an event is predictable, it's unlikely to be experienced as a crisis, and if it isn't experienced as a crisis, it's unlikely to "shock" women into growing.

By the unpredictable, I mean the unique and personal response each woman has to such central common events as leaving home, getting married or taking a job, as well as her unique response to those "unexpected" but also critical events that disrupt her innocence and shake her dependency.

Women, paradoxically, are groomed to be docile and dependent, and in a sudden moment are confronted with the realization that they're required to be resolute and independent. When we learn to meet those contradictions not only as losses but also as potential gains, not just as obstacles but as challenges, we grow.

Let's say you're skirting 40 or 50 and those expectations of marriage and babies didn't come through. Or they did—but there's still a black pit centered in your gut.

You got your house in the suburbs. And you've built that extra wing. And you've supported him on his way. You've raised your children. You even took that Caribbean cruise. You got most of what you'd wanted. And some of what you expected. And lots that you hadn't. So what now?

Now most women tell themselves it's their turn. Remember, they had said *after* the children are in school, *after* the children are away at college, *then* I can start thinking about myself. Maybe go back to school. Maybe get a job.

Well, now it's *after* and we're forced to face change. We feel we're running out of time, running out of projects, and even running out of dreams.

After is no specific age. It is being 36, or 46, or 56. *After* is a state of mind when we begin to question: What's it been all about? In social psychologist Bernice Neugarten's words, it is a time when our lives become "time-left-to-live" rather than "time-since-birth."

After is the beginning realization, for one reason or another, that we may have to stand alone. It is a time when our meanings and priorities must change, if we're to change. A time when the urgency of generating our own meanings is heightened.

Let's consider one woman who faced the challenge: Katherine Butler. (The names and identifying details of the women interviewed have been changed to protect their privacy.)

I phoned Kate because I'd learned that her fabric designs were being featured in a fashion show and that her career had begun a slim ten years before. Just 50, she has been married 27 years to George Butler.

Kate had been raised by a demanding mother who alternated between an all-encompassing love and histrionic fits of temper. Kate became a barometer of others' moods, an expert at pleasing. She described herself as a "joy" to her parents, teachers and classmates. In fact, she was voted the most popular, the best natured and the sweetheart of the class—in retrospect, dubious honors.

At the age of 22, she met George Butler and it was love at first sight. He'd returned from military service and was going back to college to complete his degree in physics. He seemed lost, vulnerable, and she thought she could heal him. The transition from her parents' house to that of her husband was turbulent. Her mother disapproved of George, and Kate's effort to separate from her family plunged her into another bind. No longer pleasing her mother, she now set out to please her young husband.

They moved to Connecticut, where he taught at a small college and continued his studies. The next ten years of her life went by unexamined as she tried hard to please, fulfilling the image of the best wife and mother.

The tone of the marriage was soon set. Each morning George would leave her with a list of things to do—taking his suit to the cleaners, phoning the garage man about the muffler, phoning the insurance man about renewing the fire coverage. Each evening she'd face a glacial evaluation of her performance. Her own identity was submerged, and she desperately relied on George's approval as a sign of her worth.

The first "shock" in their union occurred with the birth of their baby. A buoyant

 From *McCall's*, July 1978. Adapted from IN HER TIME by Iris Sangiuliano, Ph.D. (William Morrow and Company, Inc.)

redhead with sparkling eyes, Kate seemed to wilt as she spoke of that time. "When I came home with the baby, I discovered that my husband had the worst temper I've ever seen. I don't remember what about, but he got very angry with me, picked up a bud vase and smashed it against the wall. For years after, he was the sensitive one, and I learned to do circles around his temper! Every frustration he had at work he took out at home by breaking dishes, pencils, chairs, and once he even threatened me."

That first fissuring in their relationship, however, only prodded her to try harder. A year and a half later another baby was born, and Kate's center shifted from being the perfect wife to being the perfect mother. Since George was disinterested and possibly even resentful of the children, she became their constant companion, taking them to swimming lessons, ice skating, fishing. "All the things a father should do. I got so involved with the children that I became even more dependent on my husband. I couldn't go anywhere socially without him. I couldn't even carry on a conversation except about the babies and the house.

"I seemed to lose all interest in myself. I gained weight and even though I liked being well-dressed, we got so used to living on a budget, even when we didn't have to any more, that I saved all our money. I got caught up in an image of what I thought a wife should be, a Mrs. Goodwife, and what I thought he wanted. I played out my role to the extreme, I guess."

Before she knew it, Kate was 34 and faced with what she called Shock Number Two: "I developed a persistent cough. I went to our family doctor, and he said it was nothing. But the cough didn't go away. Finally he X-rayed, and I had to face cancer." Alive and energetic one day, she was faced with dying the next.

If that was Shock Number Two, in Kate's words, it also turned out to be Miracle Number Two because it changed the direction of her life. (Miracle Number One was her survival in the battle with cancer.)

"For a while after the operation I wasn't sure how it would turn out," she said. "Then, gradually, as I grew stronger, I suddenly became conscious of time. Not so much my-whole-life kind of time, but everyday time—the way I was spending my time . . . . Life suddenly became very sweet. The air smelled sweeter. People's faces looked different. Color became more intense. My children looked more beautiful. It was as if I'd been pointed in a new direction! And you know, that was sixteen years ago, and I still haven't gotten over it.

"I was given the gift of life," she said, barely audibly. Indeed, she discovered the gift of *her* life—a life that slowly was to disentangle itself from being exclusively a wife-and-mother. She learned that our lives are lived, not in great sweeps of cosmic time, but in small, graspable, everyday time.

Without conscious intent concerning long-term goals or a career, she set out on a small palpable goal—to change the direction of her everyday living.

"Here in Westport," Kate explained, "there is a community of ladies who go to the beach and spend the day with their children, gossiping, playing duplicate bridge, knitting—that sort of thing. Well, life became too precious suddenly. So I told myself, I don't want to be one of those women. In order to have a little privacy and be with my children—they were preteens—I needed to find something to do. So I went into town and bought some artist's supplies. I thought: Why not? I can be on the beach with my children and also paint. That would isolate me from the women and their talk. And very important, I'd changed. I didn't care any more that they'd say, 'Isn't she peculiar? She's painting.'

"Then I showed my work to an art-gallery owner nearby, and that started me off to what eventually became my fabric designs. But I didn't take it seriously at first. Of course, George laughed. That wasn't his idea of a housewife, but it hadn't been mine either."

But the more involved Kate became with her painting, the more her husband's anger flared. Yet, despite their chaotic relationship, Kate considered his rages evidence of his involvement, and they kept her very much concerned with his life.

Only when Kate suffered a severe blow to her self-esteem—what she describes as Shock Number Three and Miracle Number Three—did she overcome her masochism. She changed in fundamental ways, not because she was 46, but because those unexpected events—social, biological and psychological—propelled her changing. "I was shocked, really shocked," she said. "when I discovered George had been having an affair. One evening I picked up his briefcase to take it into the den. It's funny now; I was still being the perfect wife. The briefcase was open and I dropped it. Drafts of his love letters spilled out, and I read them. I was devastated; I thought it was the end of my world.

"I realized how much we'd grown apart. I confronted him and, he said, 'I'm never going to discuss it with you.' I offered him a divorce, but that's not what he wanted.

"It was his Saturday affair. Every Saturday he'd say that he was going shopping . . . . He'd leave at one and get back home at six.

"Those letters were so beautiful. So romantic. The thought that he could express himself to another woman tormented me."

Every morning for three months she vomited. She felt sick in body and spirit. She'd been betrayed.

That image of the other woman sliced through her and became a nagging obsession. What did she look like? Was she tall? Slender? Young? She imagined her as someone he worked with at the college—someone intelligent, informed and involved in the world.

She tried to picture them together—how they made love. What were the things they talked about? Science? World affairs? Were they *still* together? What really were his plans for the future?

She summoned a leaden resolve to face up to George and, more important, to face herself. Slowly she began shedding the sackcloth and ashes of the perennial victim. Slowly, what she'd thought of as her competition—that "other" woman—became a beacon to the other woman in her that she'd hidden away.

"I know this must sound funny," Kate observed, "but the woman my husband was involved with changed my image of myself—of what a woman should be. I went out and bought a completely new wardrobe. Don't misunderstand—I don't mean that as a surface thing. I suddenly really *cared enough about myself* to want to take care of myself. I'd lost fifteen pounds because I'd been upset, but it was becoming. I didn't want to be a gray-haired lady any more either. So I went red!

"I got shocked out of my complaceny in many ways. She did me a service. I wanted to be the woman I imagined him with. An involved independent woman. Maybe it was the kind of woman I wanted to be all along but never dared be. But now I knew that I might be standing alone. It motivated me. I became more serious about my work—which led to my being picked up by a fashion designer, and to the fashion show of my fabrics. And craziest of all, now George really wants me. But I've become so used to the feeling of freedom that it doesn't matter. I'm not sure where our marriage is headed. But that isn't important any more, either. Not now that I've got me."

As I was getting ready to leave, Kate reached for my hand. "I think it's so important," she began hesitantly, "for women to be let into other women's lives. What I'd like to share with others is that fifty is a great age to be. Despite all my downs and ups, my life has been joyous. I've been able to put things in their right slot. Age has helped me. I see that the problems I've had aren't *all* of who I am. I've reached the point in my life where everything is finally coming together. From forty-nine to your mid-fifties can be a glorious time for a woman. It's a time for reaping." . . .

Just as the "other" woman freed the other woman in Kate, her adolescent children's bolt for freedom freed Maureen Cleary.

I met Maureen at a NOW meeting for the older woman—older being 35 and over. She was one of four speakers. "I'm a forty-four-year-old woman going on twenty-one," she said, laughing. She'd been married for 22 years and had five children—the three oldest now in their own apartments and self-supporting, one away and one readying to leave.

One morning, she explained, on her knees scrubbing the kitchen floor, she heard herself asking: "What's a nice girl like you doing in a place like this?" Armed with a 15-year-old summa cum laude B.A., she went looking for a job. At the time her teenage daughter was hospitalized for a drug-induced breakdown; her husband, angry, refused to pay the $17,000 for the hospital care. Maureen took a job and paid for her daughter's treatment. Shortly after, she discovered her husband was having an affair with a 20-year-old. At this point in her story, Maureen pointed to the *Exit* door with a grand gesture and swept off the stage to thunderous applause.

That night I phoned Maureen to ask for a meeting. She'd recently moved into her own apartment, which she shared with another woman. Maureen was a runaway of sorts. As she sat opposite me, her long legs crossed, she said the word that best characterized her life at the moment was "rocky."

"Rocky" characterized her past as well. Maureen came from working-class parents who had separated when she was ten. She'd worked hard to put herself through college. She had married Douglas Cleary, a magazine editor, immediately after graduation to get away from her mother, who'd become controlling and resentful.

Her marriage, however, proved a poor escape. Maureen became a cliché of the nagging, harried housewife; Douglas began to drink. For the first 15 years of their marriage, she spent all her time with the children—the first four babies came in as many years; the fifth came along because she saw herself as "Superwoman." As a family, they were set in a familiar pattern. Maureen explained: "Even though they outnumbered me, and they had more hands than I did, and were stronger, I did all the work. And my husband was fond of making big speeches like: 'Mother is the disciple of the gospel of work. She thinks cleanliness is next to godliness.'" Motherhood and homemaking were both venerated and denigrated.

Maureen was starving to death both intellectually and emotionally. As the economic pressures of supporting a large family mounted, her husband became increasingly distant and more and more found comfort in alcohol. A meticulous homemaker, she buried herself in the house and in the children.

With the birth of her last child, she became seriously depressed. Moreover, she felt guilty about being depressed. Her head spun in a familiar female litany: She had a handsome professional husband. Yes, her house was falling apart, but it was on a beautiful tree-lined street in the suburbs. And she had five beautiful children. Why wasn't she happy?

Why was she getting up every morning in a paroxysm of fear? Sit up, she'd tell herself. Put your feet on the floor. Stand up. Robotlike, she gave herself orders. "I couldn't take it out on the children," she explained. "It wasn't their fault. So I'd wait until they were asleep and then I would fall on the kitchen floor and cry."

The next six years were a waking nightmare: "Douglas tried to help but he wasn't used to taking responsibility and he was unhappy at work. I drove him out.

"I was thirty-seven, the youngest child was three, and the other four were in their teens. Can you imagine four teenagers under one roof, acting up?

"Well," she continued, "my husband found himself a twenty-year-old vine-ripened tomato who looked at him with adoring eyes. He rented an apartment, and they began living together. I was annihilated. When I confronted him, he told me he wanted a divorce. I said, 'Fine. Go get it!' But I couldn't stand on my anger. I felt abandoned. With no self-esteem and little dignity, I coaxed him back. I was determined to carry on my home and hold the kids together."

Once again, Maureen postponed herself, ostensibly for the "children's sake."

"Things just went downhill," she was saying. "That's when a friend asked me to join him in a psychodrama group where people reenact their problems.

"My children thought it was really far out that their mother was doing psychodrama. And one by one they asked if they could come along. So I let them, all but the youngest.

"My kids tore into me. They said I should have done something about my marriage. After all, I was the sober one and he was the sick one. Because I couldn't get along with their father, they said, I deprived *them* of a father. They said I was super-responsible, compulsive, overprotective, and took up too much space! They went on and on, blaming and accusing. I'd been trying to keep the kids from going under, and they told me I really was keeping them from their father.

"But later I realized it was the most beneficent thing that could have happened to me! I was unglued, devasted. I went home that night and lay awake: *What had all the blood, sweat, and tears been for?* All those sacrifices? I wasn't happy. My husband wasn't happy. And the kids weren't happy. What was it all about?

"I kept looking at the door with such longing. I thought I'd just like to walk out and keep going. But I was trapped in the fear that my husband wouldn't be responsible for the children. It was the worst night of my life. And then I had a dream—that's what pushed me out the door."

"The dream was so vivid I'll never forget it. I was in an apartment, and it was a dingy, dingy place. The living room was furnished in early mother-in-law hand-me-down furniture. So the only thing you could do was throw it out or burn it, because there was dirt in the very molecules of the fibers. I was working and working and making no progress, when I was called into an equally dingy kitchen.

"There I saw two of my children. I started to clean up—first on top of the refrigerator—when I saw what I took to be a family pet, a little monkey. He had a collar on. He was chained to the door. He was shriveled, mummified.

"I looked at the monkey and felt awful. Oh, my God, I had forgotten he was there. I hadn't fed him. I didn't remember the last time I'd even given him water. I said to my daughter, 'I didn't feed the monkey!' She had a little gerbil she was feeding, and she said, '*I'll help you.*' The poor animal just fell on the food.

"When I awoke I realized that I was that mummified monkey, and that I was starving, and that it had been going on for twenty years!"

Tears streamed down her cheeks. I felt touched, but she seemed unconcerned with me or the effect she was having. Maureen had changed, even before my very eyes.

At 37 Maureen had thought of herself as old. She felt her youth fading, her childbearing years coming to an end, her children separating and her husband indifferent. It wasn't the empty womb, the emptying nest or even the empty bed that escalated Maureen's panic, but the emptying image of herself. She found it more and more difficult to continue identifying herself through the reflected image of her professional husband or through her children, who were seeking their own independence. Eventually she made the decision to leave her family in her husband's care, but she also saw to it that she was available when her children needed her.

It is noteworthy that in Maureen's dream it is her teenage daughter who helps her. Paradoxically, a number of women have admitted that they've looked to their daughters as their role models. As Maureen struck out for her own autonomy, her daughter illuminated the way.

I asked Maureen what it was she'd want most, if she could be granted any wish in the world. She replied: "I'm slowly working myself out of my chains. What I really and truly would like, as long as I'm reaching for the moon, is to achieve autonomy in intimacy. To have a loving relationship without giving myself up."

Elaine Cole is yet another woman who has labored with a "second birth." A frail, petite woman of 41, in a chic pantsuit, Elaine was soft-spoken and somewhat hesitant. Although her parents advised her not to marry young, that was really all they'd groomed her for. She graduated from Radcliffe in June with a job waiting for her in September on a national magazine. That summer she became pregnant, and shortly thereafter she married the young man, who'd merely been a "summer romance." Marriage, she thought, was better than facing what would have been, for her, the ordeal of the threatening, competitive world of journalism.

Six years later she found herself with three children, a marriage that was splintering, a large house in the suburbs and blinding headaches. Her young husband, meanwhile, had begun his ambitious climb to success, and Elaine was alone a lot. Her thoughts began to twist and knot inside her. She was sure she'd developed a brain tumor.

The internist studied her quietly, and after a silence that seemed endless he asked, "What do you do besides take care of your children?" She couldn't think what to reply, but his question had fallen like a beacon squarely on its target.

Alone that night, she lay in bed thinking. Her husband was on a trip and she had to face it: She was relieved. She was relieved and resentful and lonely. She also had to face the fact that she'd made a questionable choice that fateful summer. She'd thrown a dozen veils over her mind, and now they'd started to peel away. It took a year before the decision formed itself. Just as he was about to leave on another trip, she asked him for a divorce.

She returned to her parents' house and "waited" out the next seven years. She'd gone from her parents to her husband and back to her disapproving parents, always cushioned financially and still very much the child.

Looking back on her life, she was quick to admit that those seven years were ones of hibernation. She couldn't fathom why she hadn't gotten her master's degree and a job, especially since all the children were in school. Except that it hadn't occurred to her. She was waiting, after all, for what every girl is supposed to have—a man who would cause her to hear bells. She met him in the shape of Matt Cole, a confirmed bachelor.

Elaine remarried and took up her life where she'd left off. Eleven years after her divorce, she had five children—two daughters with Matt—a home in the suburbs, a herb garden, a station wagon, a sports car, and a marriage suffering from weighty expectations. The babies,

the home and hearth were what she felt she had to give. They also were a way of cementing the bonds, staking her claim and distancing herself from the world out there.

Her youngest child was born shortly before her 40th birthday. "Something happened," she explained, "when I realized I wasn't going to have any more children. I started thinking about my life differently. I knew I had to find something that was all my own—something other than keeping house. I had to become someone besides Matt's wife."

Uncertain where to begin, she consulted an institute for vocational and career planning, and there she was given a battery of tests. That, she explained, was the beginning of an entirely new attitude toward life, a turning point.

The day she was to return for her test results was also her baby daughter's birthday. She felt torn, guilty about leaving her. To make matters more difficult, her housekeeper phoned that she was ill. Realizing what the meeting meant to her, Matt offered to stay home from the office. He'd become as interested as she in her new image. Reassured of her abilities by the encouraging report, she went back to school and took up journalism, an abandoned dream. After a time she began free-lancing, and sold several articles to magazines.

Elaine's efforts to carve out a personal identity, however, have been hampered by a past in which her sense of worth leaned heavily on being Matt Cole's wife. Still, Elaine's conflict cannot be flatly characterized as a struggle between marriage and homemaking. Hers is a conflict common to a great many women who are overloaded in their roles, straddling the old and the new. Women are quick to point to their guilt as the great wall barring them from doing something for themselves. They are slower to acknowledge, however, the greater barrier, those entrapping feelings of wanting to be taken care of. It was Elaine's immobilizing fear of failing, and perhaps even of succeeding that plunged her into a precipitous pregnancy and marriage.

At the time I first spoke with Elaine, she was in the beginning heady flush of learning and working at a new craft. She had taken her heart in hand, ignored her guilts regarding the family, and overcome the reentry anxiety. The making of a professional, however, requires still another labor: that of facing the "givens," of most work—the competition; the rejections; the need to fight for what we want; the anxieties about failing and—equally as defeating—those about succeeding.

Primarily, we battle our own dependency and only secondarily that of our spouse and children.

Woman, any woman, almost always leads a serial life—with times of hibernation and times of renewal, with times of postponement and times of actualization. By and large we are late bloomers; we postpone ourselves.

Unlike men, we haven't been expected to think about what to do with our lives. While boys spend their adolescence establishing an identity, dreaming dreams of achievement, girls use their youth laying the groundwork for an "us," dreaming dreams of rescue. In men's development, identity precedes intimacy; in women's, intimacy precedes and postpones a separate identity.

To be a good wife and mother, we've been taught, is the center of a woman's life and the source of all her meaning. Only later do we discover that there are many meanings. We're "shocked" to discover that every merger bears the seeds of its own distancing; every enchantment, of disenchantment. Those are the female "shocks" of change. Those are the jolts that disrupt the dream of rescue—the shocks that trigger self-knowledge.

How we perceive those shocks and what we do with them determines our development.

At first, the shaping of a personal identity is so labyrinthine as to defy detection. It begins with a subtle turn of events, a broken promise, a feeling of betrayal. We merge to "settle"; life, we find, is not for settling. Still, the female "I" remains riveted in the "us." Fearful of loss, we often grip those we love in the stranglehold of the drowning. To cement bonds, we have houses, gardens, station wagons and children. The "us" unravels and reshapes itself around another center, the family, and once more the separate "I" is postponed.

Then, sometime in our late 40s or early 50s, we begin to listen to our own voices. Perhaps, freed from the imperatives of union and motherhood, the "I" turns inward and takes stock of itself. Abruptly, seemingly out of nowhere, we become concerned with our personal identity and often even unearth a buried dream.

Thus, today's "new" woman is not necessarily in her 20s, but is often in her 40s, 50s and even 60s—a mutation and a new female experience. She is the woman who has learned that her existence on this earth is not only as a companion to man but also as a person in her own right.

How to Write Your Own Marriage Contract

Susan Edmiston

Susan Edmiston is a writer, editor, columnist and contributor to many national magazines.

First we thought marriage was when Prince Charming came and took you away with him. Then we thought that marriage was orange blossoms and Alençon lace and silver patterns. Then we thought that marriage—at least—was when you couldn't face signing the lease on the new apartment in two different names.

But most of us never even suspected the truth. Nobody ever so much as mentioned that what marriage is, at its very heart and essence, is a contract. When you say "I do," what you are doing is not, as you thought, vowing your eternal love, but rather subscribing to a whole system of rights, obligations and responsibilities that may very well be anathema to your most cherished beliefs.

Worst of all, you never even get to read the contract—to say nothing of the fine print. If you did, you probably wouldn't agree to it. Marriage, as it exists today, is a peculiarly vague, and yet inflexible, arrangement of institutionalized inequality which goes only one step beyond the English common-law concept of husband and wife as one, and, as the saying goes, "that 'one' is the husband." We have progressed from the notion of wife as legal nonentity to the notion of wife as dependent and inferior.

In recent years, many people have taken to writing their own marriage ceremonies in a desperate attempt to make the institution more relevant to their own lives. But ceremonies, they are finding, do not reach the heart of the matter. So some couples are now taking the logical next step of drawing up their own contracts. These agreements may delineate any of the financial or personal aspects of the marriage relationship—from who pays which bills to who uses what birth control. Though many of their provisions may not be legally binding, at the very least they can help us to examine the often inchoate assumptions underlying our relationships, help us come to honest and equitable terms with one another, and provide guidelines for making our marriages what we truly want them to be.

Before their first child was born, Alix Cates Shulman and her husband had an egalitarian, partnership marriage. Alix worked full time as an editor in New York, and both shared the chores involved in maintaining their small household. After two children, however, the couple found that they had automatically fallen into the traditional sex roles: he went out and worked all day to support his family; she stayed home and worked from 6 a.m. to 9 p.m. taking care of children and housework. Unthinkingly, they had agreed not only to the legalities of marriage but to the social contract as well.

After six years at home—six years of chronic dissatisfaction—Alix became involved in the Women's Liberation movement and realized that it might be possible to change the contract under which she and her husband lived. The arrangement they worked out (see page 72), basically a division of household duties and child care, rejected "the notion that the work which brings in more money is more valuable. The ability to earn . . . money is a privilege which must not be compounded by enabling the larger earner to buy out of his/her duties."

Sitting down and writing out a contract may seem a cold and formal way of working out an intimate relationship, but often it is the only way of coping with the ghosts of 2,000 years of tradition lurking in our definitions of marriage. Now, after three years, Alix has written six books, and both Shulmans find that their agreement is a new way of life rather than a document to be followed legalistically.

No less an antagonist than Norman Mailer has attacked the Shulmans' contract. After describing it in *The Prisoner of Sex*, he writes (in his characteristic third person): "No, he would not be married to such a woman. If he were obliged to have a roommate he would pick a man. . . . He could love a woman and she might even sprain her back before a hundred sinks of dishes in a month, but he would not be happy to help her if his work should suffer, no, not unless her work were as valuable as his own." Mailer's comment makes the issues clear: under the old contract the work of child-rearing and housekeeping is assumed to be less important than the work a man does—specifically, here, the career of self-aggrandizement Mailer has cut out for himself—and a wife, unless she is able to prove otherwise, is the one who must do the housework.

The Shulmans' contract renegotiates husband's and wife's roles as far as the care of children and home are concerned. Psychologists Barbara and Myron Koltuv took their agreement one step further.

"We agreed in the beginning that since I didn't care a bit about the house, he would do a lot of cleaning and I would do a lot of cooking," says Barbara. "He does a lot of the shopping, too, because he likes to buy things and I don't. Whenever either of us feels 'I'm doing all the drudge work and you're not doing anything,' we switch jobs. Gradually we've eliminated a lot of stuff neither of us wanted to do. In the early days, we'd cook dinner for people because we didn't feel it was hospitable to ask them to go out, but now we often go out instead.

"In the beginning we literally opened up separate bank accounts. We split our savings and checking accounts. At the time he made a third more money than I did. I deferred to him all the time, even though it was only a third. I felt that if he didn't spend so much money on the eight dozen book clubs he belongs to, I would only have to work about two hours a day. He would claim I wasn't being realistic, that I didn't know how much we had and was being tight.

"Each of us paid the bills alternate months. I thought this was the only way to prove to him I could handle money. After six months, when I figured out how much I was spending and how much of his money I was using, I decided to take on more patients to expand my practice. I found I was spending as much on cabs as he was on book clubs. Since that time we haven't had a single argument about money."

When the Koltuvs' child was born, they reopened negotiations. "We decided to split the care of our daughter between us equally. We knew there were certain hours we'd both be working so we found a woman to take care of her during these hours. Then I had the mornings and he had the evenings. The person whose time it was had to make all the decisions—whether or not she could have Pepsi-Cola, whether she could go to a friend's house, and so forth.

"The hardest thing was being willing to give up control. What we call responsibility is often control, power, being the boss. When I was really able to recognize that my husband's relationship with Hannah is his and mine is mine, everything was all right. He's going to do it differently but he's going to do it all right. We've been teaching her all along that different people are different."

Agreements to disagree with the common marriage mores are nothing new. They have their roots in a fine old tradition that probably began with Mary Wollstonecraft, that first feminist of us all, who in 1792 wrote *A Vindication of the Rights of Women*. Though Mary and her husband, English essayist and political theorist William Godwin, submitted to marriage, it was on their own terms. Godwin took an apartment about twenty doors from the couple's house to which he "repaired" every morning. A letter of the time describes this arrangement: "In order to give the connection as little as possible the appearance of such a vulgar and debasing tie as matrimony, the parties have established separate establishments, and the husband only visits his mistress like a lover when each is dressed, rooms in order, etc." The couple agreed that it was wrong for husband and wife to have to be together whenever they went out into "mixed society" and therefore, as Godwin writes, "rather sought occasions of deviating from, than of complying with, this rule."

The principle of separate quarters, which recently cropped up again in reports of a contract between Jacqueline Kennedy and Aristotle Onassis (see page 69), also appears in the agreement birth-control pioneer Margaret Sanger signed with her husband, J. Noah H. Slee. Their contract stated that they would have separate homes and, later, separate quarters within the same house. Neither was to have the slightest influence over the business affairs of the other, and, when both were busy, communications were to be exchanged through their secretaries. They also agreed that Margaret Sanger would continue to use her own name. (Sanger, in fact, was the name of her first husband, but she had already made it a famous one.)

The ultimate feminist contract, however, was the one Lucy Stone and Henry Blackwell wrote when they married in 1855. Their agreement is a concise catalogue of the legal inequities of marriage in America at that time:

"While we acknowledge our mutual affection by publicly assuming the relationship of husband and wife," they wrote, "we deem it a duty to declare that this act on our part implies no sanction of, nor promise of voluntary obedience to, such of the present laws of marriage as refuse to recognize the wife as an independent, rational being, while they confer upon the husband an injurious and unnatural superiority." The contract went on to protest especially against the laws which gave the husband custody of the wife's person, the sole ownership of

> **"We have progressed from the notion of wife as legal nonentity to the notion of wife as dependent and inferior"**

her personal property and the use of her real estate, the absolute right to the product of her industry and the exclusive control and guardianship of the couple's children. Finally, they protested against "the whole system by which 'the legal existence of the wife is suspended during marriage' so that, in most States, she neither has a legal part in the choice of her residence, nor can she make a will, nor sue or be sued in her own name, nor inherit property."

While it is obvious that we have made some progress since Lucy Stone's day, in many ways we are still living under the heritage of the kind of laws she deplored. The American institution of marriage derives from English common law, which developed a peculiar concept, unknown on the Continent, called the "unity of spouses." As Blackstone put it, "By marriage, the husband and wife are one person in law; that is, the very being or legal existence of the woman is suspended during marriage, or at least is incorporated or consolidated into that of the husband."

Beginning in 1839, one version or another of what was called the Married Women's Property Act was passed in each state of the Union, correcting some of the gross injustices of marriage. Most of these laws granted married women the right to contract, to sue and be sued without joining their husbands, to manage and control the property they brought with them to marriage, to engage in gainful employment and retain the earnings derived from it. Like a case of bad genes, however, the fiction of the unity of the spouses has never quite gone away. Husband and wife today are like Siamese twins: although largely separate persons under the law, they are still joined together in one spot or another. In one state, the wife's ability to contract may still be impaired; in another, she may not have full freedom to use her maiden name; in a third, she may not be considered capable of conspiracy with her husband.

These vestiges of the unity of spouses, however, are not the only ways in which marriage treats man and woman unequally, for we have evolved a different—but still unequal—concept of marriage. Today we regard husband as head of household and wife as housewife; husband as supporter and wife as dependent; husband as authority and wife as faithful helpmeet. This concept of marriage has not been *created* by the law but is an expression of culturally shared values which are *reflected* in the law. It is the conventional notion of marriage consciously embraced or unthinkingly accepted by many, if not most, Americans today.

What's wrong with it? The responsibility of support is commonly thought to favor women at the expense of men; I leave it for men to

document how this notion injures them and will only deal here with the disabilities from a woman's point of view. Like all commonly held notions, the idea of marriage as a relationship between supporter and dependent is so much a part of our very atmosphere that it is hard to see it objectively. (To counter this difficulty, many women's groups are suggesting that people wishing to get a marriage license should have to take a test on the laws, as they do to get a driver's license.) Basically, the bargain in today's unwritten marriage contract is that the husband gets the right to the wife's services in return for supporting her. Whereas under common law the husband had "the absolute right to the product of the wife's industry," today the husband has only the absolute right to the product of the wife's industry *within the home*. "The wife's services and society are so essential a part of what the law considers the husband entitled to as part of the marriage," says Harriet Pilpel in *Your Marriage and the Law*, "that it will not recognize any agreement between the spouses which provides that the husband is to pay for such services or society."

The concept of the husband as supporter and wife as dependent underlies all the current legal inequalities of married women. To cite some specific examples:

Property. In common-law property states— like New York—husband and wife each exercise full control of what they own before, or acquire during, the marriage. But the woman who works only inside the home never has a chance to acquire property of her own, and therefore may never have any legitimate interest in, or control of, the family assets. (The only way she can acquire property is by gift, which makes her subject to her husband's patronage.) As John Gay said in *The Beggar's Opera*, "The comfortable estate of widowhood is the only hope that keeps up a wife's spirits." Her situation is improved by her husband's death; in every common-law property state, each spouse has a non-barrable interest in the estate of the other. However, this sometimes adds up to very little. For instance, in New Jersey, a wife only has "dower rights"; if her husband dies, she is entitled to one-third of the income from his real property. If the couple lived in an apartment and didn't own any real estate, the law guarantees her nothing.

Even in six of the eight community-property states where the spouses share equally in the property acquired during the marriage, the husband is given management control. Thus a woman may earn as much as her husband and have no say in how her money is spent. In the two exceptions, Washington and Texas, husband and wife have separate control of the property each acquires. Even this arrangement

"The higher up the ladder her husband is, the better a woman is supported and the fewer services she gives in return" leaves the non-earning spouse without any control of the purse strings.

Name. In many states the law deprives the wife of full freedom to use her own name: in Illinois in 1965 when a woman sought the right to vote although she had not registered under her married name, the Appellate Court said she couldn't. In a recent case, a three-judge Federal court upheld the Alabama law requiring a woman to assume her husband's surname upon marriage by ruling that a married woman does not have a right to have her driver's license issued in her maiden name. In Michigan, if a man changes his last name his wife must also change hers; she may not contest the change, although the couple's minor children over the age of sixteen may do so.

Domicile. Domicile is a technical term sometimes defined as a "place where a person has a settled connection for certain legal purposes." (You can live in one place and be domiciled in another.) Domicile affects various legal rights and obligations, including where a person may vote, hold public office, serve on juries, receive welfare, qualify for tuition advantages at state educational institutions, be liable for taxes, have his or her estate administered, and file for divorce. In general, a wife's domicile automatically follows that of her husband and she has no choice in the matter. (NOW members are currently challenging this law in North Carolina.)

The husband, generally, also has had the right to decide where he and his wife live, although recently he has been required to make a reasonable decision taking her wishes into account. The burden of proving she is reasonable, however, still rests with the wife.

To some women the loss of these rights may seem a small price to pay for support. In fact, the arrangement works out differently depending on economic class. The higher up the ladder her husband is, the better a woman is supported and the fewer services she gives in return. For the many millions of women who work outside the home, on the other hand, the bargain is not a terribly good one: in reality all they earn for the services they give their husbands is the responsibility of working outside the home as well as in it to help their families survive. These women learn another price they pay for the illusion of support—the low salaries they receive compared with men's are ironically justified by the argument that the "men have families to feed." This is not the fault of husbands but of a society that has structured its economy on the unpaid services of women.

But the heaviest price those women who accept the role of dependent pay is a psychological one. Economic dependency is in itself corrupting, as can be seen in rawest form in country-and-Western songs of the "I-know-he's-being-untrue-but-I-never-confront-him-with-it-because-if-he-left-me-who-would-support-the-children" variety. And economic dependency breeds other kinds of dependency. The woman who has no established legal right in the family income fares better or worse depending on how well she pleases the head of the household. In the attempt to please she may surrender her own tastes, her own opinions, her own thoughts. If she habitually defers to or depends on her husband's decisions she will eventually find herself incapable of making her own.

The solution is not that wives should never work in the home or that husbands should not share their incomes with them. The solution is that we must begin to recognize that the work wives do belongs to them, not their husbands, and should be accorded a legitimate value. If wives make the contribution of full partners in their marriages, they should receive the rights of partners—not only, like slaves, the right to be housed, clothed and fed, or in other words, supported. This is hardly a new idea: in 1963 the Report of the President's Commission on the Status of Women recommended that "during marriage each spouse should have a legally defined right in the earnings of the other, in the real and personal property acquired through these earnings, and in their management."

There is, however, hope of progress. Although the Uniform Marriage and Divorce Act drafted by the National Conference of Commissioners on Uniform State Laws has not yet been adopted anywhere (Colorado has adopted the divorce portion of the law), it embraces some of the principles of marriage as partnership. It would make irremediable breakdown of the marriage the only ground for divorce, institute a division of property based on the assumption that husband and wife have contributed equally to the marriage, and determine custody according to the best interests of the child without the traditional bias in favor of the mother.

Should the Equal Rights Amendment be passed, it may require that most of the inequalities in the marriage relationship be abolished. According to an analysis published recently in *The Yale Law Journal*, the amendment should give women the freedom to use any name they wish, give them the same independent choice of domicile that married men have now, invalidate laws vesting management of community property in the husband alone, and prohibit enforcement of sex-based definitions of conjugal function. "Courts would not be able to assume for any purpose that women had a legal obligation to do housework, or provide affection and companionship, or to be available for sexual relations, unless men owed their wives exactly

"Women often assume, erroneously, that everything their husbands own belongs to them"

the same duties. Similarly, men could not be assigned the duty to provide financial support simply because of their sex." Even should the amendment pass, however, it will take years of action in the courts to implement it. Meanwhile, perhaps the best we can do is to say with Lucy Stone and Henry Blackwell that while we wish to acknowledge our mutual affection by publicly assuming the relationship of husband and wife, we do not promise obedience to those laws that discriminate against us. And, perhaps, by writing our own contracts we can modify the effect of the laws upon us.

The problem with a husband and wife sitting down together and drafting a legal contract incorporating their beliefs concerning marriage is that the state immediately horns its way into the act. Marriage, contrary to popular belief, is more *ménage à trois* than *folie à deux*. It is a contract to which the state is a third party, and though you and your spouse may be in perfect accord, there are certain things the state will not tolerate. Most of these things are against what is known as public policy. Under public policy, according to Harriet Pilpel, "the courts, in many states, will not enforce any agreement which attempts to free the husband from the duty of support to the wife. . . . Nor will the courts uphold any agreement which attempts to limit or eliminate the personal or conjugal rights of marriage as distinguished from property rights. An agreement that the parties will not live together after marriage is void. So is an agreement not to engage in sexual intercourse or not to have children. One court has even held that it is against public policy for an engaged couple to agree that they will live in whatever place the wife chooses. Under the law, said the court, that is the "husband's prerogative and he cannot relinquish it." Public policy also forbids contracts which anticipate divorce in any way. Agreements defining what will happen if a couple divorces or the conditions under which they will divorce are seen as facilitating the dissolution of marriages.

There are certain contracts, called antenuptial agreements, that the state clearly permits us to make. These contracts, according to Judith Boies, a matrimonial and estates lawyer with the New York law firm Paul, Weiss, Rifkind, Wharton & Garrison, may concern property owned before marriage, property acquired after marriage by gift or inheritance, and property rights in each other's estates. A wife cannot waive support, but she can waive interest in her husband's estate.

Some lawyers believe that people should be able to make whatever marriage contracts they like with one another. "Why should marriage be any different from any other contract?" asks

---

THE UTOPIAN MARRIAGE CONTRACT

1. The wife's right to use her maiden name or any other name she chooses.

2. What surname the children will have: husband's, wife's, a hyphenated combination, a neutral name or the name the children choose when they reach a certain age.

3. Birth control: Whether or not, what kind and who uses it. (One couple—the wife can't use the Pill—splits the responsibility 50-50. Half the time she uses a diaphragm, the other half he uses a condom.)

4. Whether or not to have children, or to adopt them, and if so how many.

5. How the children will be brought up.

6. Where the couple will live: Will the husband be willing to move if the wife gets a job offer she wants to take? Separate bedrooms? Separate apartments?

7. How child care and housework will be divided: The spouse who earns less should not be penalized for the inequities of the economic world by having to do a larger share.

8. What financial arrangement will the couple embrace? If husband and wife are both wage-earners, there are three basic possibilities:

a) Husband and wife pool their income, pay expenses and divide any surplus. (This was Leonard and Virginia Woolf's arrangement. At the end of the year, after payment of expenses, they divided the surplus between them equally so each had what they called a personal "hoard.")

b) Husband and wife pay shares of expenses proportional to their incomes. Each keeps whatever he or she has left.

c) Husband and wife each pay 50 per cent of expenses. Each keeps what he or she has left.

If husband earns significantly more than wife, the couple might consider a) that the disparity is a result of sexist discrimination in employment and there should perhaps be some kind of "home reparations program" to offset this inequity, and b) whether the couple really has an equal partnership if one has greater economic strength, and therefore possibly greater power psychologically, in the relationship.

9. Sexual rights and freedoms. Although any arrangement other than monogamy would clearly be against public policy, in practice some people make arrangements such as having Tuesdays off from one another.

10. The husband might give his consent to abortion in advance. —S. E.

---

constitutional lawyer Kristin Booth Glen, who teaches a course in women's rights at New York University Law School. She believes that the state's intervention in people's marriages may be in violation of Article I, Section 10, of the United States Constitution, which says that the states are forbidden to pass laws "impairing the obligation of contracts." Other lawyers feel that

"A utopian contract might include division of housework and child care, finances, sexual rights and freedoms, birth control, and whether or not to have children"

we don't really know which of the contracts we might wish to make concerning marriage would be enforceable. "There will have to be some litigation first," says Kathleen Carlsson, a lawyer for the Lucy Stone League. "In the light of the new feminist atmosphere, the decisions rendered today might not be the same as those rendered twenty years ago."

Judith Boies concurs with this view and feels that couples should begin right now to make whatever contracts suit their needs. If both spouses are wage-earners, they should contract how money and expenses will be divided. If they decide to have any joint bank accounts, they should sign a written agreement defining in what proportions the money in the account belongs to them. Then if one party cleans out the account—a frequent if unfortunate prelude to divorce—the contract would establish how they had intended to share the property.

Wives often assume—erroneously—that everything their husbands own belongs to them. In the common-law property states, property belongs to the person whose name it is in. When property is jointly owned, half presumably belongs to each spouse. However, this presumption is rebuttable. The husband can claim, for instance, that he and his wife only have a joint account so she can buy groceries.

The second kind of agreement couples might make is one in which the husband agrees to pay the wife a certain amount for domestic services. If there is no money to pay her, the debt accrues from year to year. When money becomes available, the wife would be a creditor and have first claim on it.

A third kind of financial contract could be made between husband and wife when one spouse puts the other through medical school or any other kind of education or training. The wife could agree to provide the husband with so much money per year to be paid back at a certain rate in subsequent years. This contract has a good chance of being enforceable, since even the tax laws recognize that husbands and wives make loans to one another.

"All these financial contracts have a reasonably good chance of standing up in court," says Judith Boies. The one with the least chance is the one providing payment for household services, although passage of the Equal Rights Amendment might strengthen its position. Since the financial contracts are more likely to be valid than those affecting personal aspects of the marriage, they should be made separately.

Judith Boies believes that, ideally, the personal contracts should also be valid. "The state shouldn't even marry people; it should just favor every contract that makes adequate provision for wife and children." The areas that might be covered in a comprehensive, total, utopian contract might include the wife's right to use the name she chooses, the children's names, division of housework and child care, finances, birth control, whether or not to have children and how many, the upbringing of the children, living arrangements, sexual rights and freedoms, and anything else of importance to the individual couple. (See box at left.)

Since the marriage relationship is not a static one, any contract should permit the couple to solve their problems on a continuing basis. It should be amendable, revisable or renewable. One possibility is to draw up the first contract for a relatively short period of time, and renegotiate it when it expires.

Although current policy clearly makes any agreement concerning it invalid, our utopian contract might also cover divorce. After all, the court in California's Contra Costa County now permits couples to write their own divorce agreements and receive their decrees by mail.

At this point, many readers are probably thinking, "Why get married at all, why not just draw up a contract that covers all contingencies?" Again, the state got there first. Such an agreement would be considered a contract for the purpose of "meretricious relations," or in other words an illicit sexual relationship, and therefore would be invalid.

Other readers are probably thinking, "But we love each other, so why should we have a contract?" As Barbara Koltuv says, "Part of the reason for thinking out a contract is to find out what your problems are; it forces you to take charge of your life. Once you have the contract, you don't have to refer back to it. The process is what's important."

Whether these contracts are legally enforceable or not, just drawing them up may be of great service to many couples. What we are really doing in thrashing out a contract is finding out where we stand on issues, clearing up all the murky, unexamined areas of conflict, and unflinchingly facing up to our differences.

" 'Part of the reason for thinking out a contract is to find out what your problems are; it forces you to take charge of your life. Once you have the contract, you don't have to refer back to it. The process is what's important' "

X: A FABULOUS CHILD'S STORY

BY LOIS GOULD

Once upon a time, a baby named X was born. This baby was named X so that nobody could tell whether it was a boy or a girl. Its parents could tell, of course, but they couldn't tell anybody else. They couldn't even tell Baby X, at first.

You see, it was all part of a very important Secret Scientific Xperiment, known officially as Project Baby X. The smartest scientists had set up this Xperiment at a cost of Xactly 23 billion dollars and 72 cents, which might seem like a lot for just one baby, even a very important Xperimental baby. But when you remember the prices of things like strained carrots and stuffed bunnies, and popcorn for the movies and booster shots for camp, let alone 28 shiny quarters from the tooth fairy, you begin to see how it adds up.

Also, long before Baby X was born, all those scientists had to be paid to work out the details of the Xperiment, and to write the *Official Instruction Manual* for Baby X's parents and, most important of all, to find the right set of parents to bring up Baby X. These parents had to be selected very carefully. Thousands of volunteers had to take thousands of tests and answer thousands of tricky questions. Almost everybody failed because, it turned out, almost everybody really wanted either a baby boy or a baby girl, and not Baby X at all. Also, almost everybody was afraid that a Baby X would be a lot

more trouble than a boy or a girl. (They were probably right, the scientists admitted, but Baby X needed parents who wouldn't *mind* the Xtra trouble.)

There were families with grandparents named Milton and Agatha, who didn't see why the baby couldn't be named Milton or Agatha instead of X, even if it *was* an X. There were families with aunts who insisted on knitting tiny dresses and uncles who insisted on sending tiny baseball mitts. Worst of all, there were families that already had other children who couldn't be trusted to keep the secret. Certainly not if they knew the secret was worth 23 billion dollars and 72 cents—and all you had to do was take one little peek at Baby X in the bathtub to know if it was a boy or a girl.

But, finally, the scientists found the Joneses, who really wanted to raise an X more than any other kind of baby—no matter how much trouble it would be. Ms. and Mr. Jones had to promise they would take equal turns caring for X, and feeding it, and singing it lullabies. And they had to promise never to hire any baby-sitters. The government scientists knew perfectly well that a baby-sitter would probably peek at X in the bathtub, too.

The day the Joneses brought their baby home, lots of friends and relatives came over to see it. None of them knew about the secret Xperiment, though. So the first thing they asked was what kind of a baby X was. When the Joneses smiled and said, "It's an X!" nobody knew what to say. They couldn't say, "Look at her cute little dimples!" And they couldn't say, "Look at his husky

little biceps!" And they couldn't even say just plain "kitchy-coo." In fact, they all thought the Joneses were playing some kind of rude joke.

But, of course, the Joneses were not joking. "It's an X" was absolutely all they would say. And that made the friends and relatives very angry. The relatives all felt embarrassed about having an X in the family. "People will think there's something wrong with it!" some of them whispered. "There *is* something wrong with it!" others whispered back.

"Nonsense!" the Joneses told them all cheerfully. "What could possibly be wrong with this perfectly adorable X?"

Nobody could answer that, except Baby X, who had just finished its bottle. Baby X's answer was a loud, satisfied burp.

Clearly, nothing at all was wrong. Nevertheless, none of the relatives felt comfortable about buying a present for a Baby X. The cousins who sent the baby a tiny football helmet would not come and visit any more. And the neighbors who sent a pink-flowered romper suit pulled their shades down when the Joneses passed their house.

The *Official Instruction Manual* had warned the new parents that this would happen, so they didn't fret about it. Besides, they were too busy with Baby X and the hundreds of different Xercises for treating it properly.

Ms. and Mr. Jones had to be Xtra careful about how they played with little X. They knew that if they kept bouncing it up in the air and saying how *strong* and *active* it was, they'd be treating it more like a boy than an X.

 From MS. Magazine, December 1972. Copyright © 1972 by Lois Gould. Reprinted by permission.

But if all they did was cuddle it and kiss it and tell it how *sweet* and *dainty* it was, they'd be treating it more like a girl than an X.

On page 1,654 of the *Official Instruction Manual,* the scientists prescribed: "plenty of bouncing and plenty of cuddling, *both.* X ought to be strong and sweet and active. Forget about *dainty* altogether."

Meanwhile, the Joneses were worrying about other problems. Toys, for instance. And clothes. On his first shopping trip, Mr. Jones told the store clerk, "I need some clothes and toys for my new baby." The clerk smiled and said, "Well, now, is it a boy or a girl?" "It's an X," Mr. Jones said, smiling back. But the clerk got all red in the face and said huffily, "In *that* case, I'm afraid I can't help you, sir." So Mr. Jones wandered helplessly up and down the aisles trying to find what X needed. But everything in the store was piled up in sections marked "Boys" or "Girls." There were "Boys' Pajamas" and "Girls' Underwear" and "Boys' Fire Engines" and "Girls' Housekeeping Sets." Mr. Jones went home without buying anything for X. That night he and Ms. Jones consulted page 2,326 of the *Official Instruction Manual.* "Buy plenty of everything!" it said firmly.

So they bought plenty of sturdy blue pajamas in the Boys' Department and cheerful flowered underwear in the Girls' Department. And they bought all kinds of toys. A boy doll that made pee-pee and cried, "Pa-pa." And a girl doll that talked in three languages and said, "I am the Pres-i-dent of Gen-er-al Mo-tors." They also bought a storybook about a brave princess who rescued a handsome prince from his ivory tower, and another one about a sister and brother who grew up to be a baseball star and a ballet star, and you had to guess which was which.

The head scientists of Project Baby X checked all their purchases and told them to keep up the good work. They also reminded the Joneses to see page 4,629 of the *Manual,* where it said, "Never make Baby X feel *embarrassed* or *ashamed* about what it wants to play with. And if X gets dirty climbing rocks, never say 'Nice little Xes don't get dirty climbing rocks.' "

Likewise, it said, "If X falls down and cries, never say ' Brave little Xes don't cry.' Because, of course, nice little Xes *do* get dirty, and brave little Xes *do* cry. No matter how dirty X gets, or how hard it cries, don't worry. It's all part of the Xperiment."

Whenever the Joneses pushed Baby X's stroller in the park, smiling strangers would come over and coo: "Is that a boy or a girl?" The Joneses would smile back and say, "It's an X." The strangers would stop smiling then, and often snarl something nasty—as if the Joneses had snarled at *them.*

By the time X grew big enough to play with other children, the Joneses' troubles had grown bigger, too. Once a little girl grabbed X's shovel in the sandbox, and zonked X on the head with it. "Now, now, Tracy," the little girl's mother began to scold, "little girls mustn't hit little—" and she turned to ask X, "Are you a little boy or a little girl, dear?"

Mr. Jones, who was sitting near the sandbox, held his breath and crossed his fingers.

X smiled politely at the lady, even though X's head had never been zonked so hard in its life. "I'm a little X," X replied.

"You're a *what?*" the lady exclaimed angrily. "You're a little b-r-a-t, you mean!"

"But little girls mustn't hit little Xes, either!" said X, retrieving the shovel with another polite smile. "What good does hitting do, anyway?"

X's father, who was still holding his breath, finally let it out, uncrossed his fingers, and grinned back at X.

And at their next secret Project Baby X meeting, the scientists grinned, too. Baby X was doing fine.

But then it was time for X to start school. The Joneses were really worried about this, because school was even more full of rules for boys and girls, and there were no rules for Xes. The teacher would tell boys to form one line, and girls to form another line. There would be boys' games and girls' games, and boys' secrets and girls' secrets. The school library would have a list of recommended books for girls, and a different list of recommended books for boys. There would even be a bathroom marked BOYS and another one marked GIRLS. Pretty soon boys and girls would hardly talk to each other. What would happen to poor little X?

The Joneses spent weeks consulting their *Instruction Manual* (there were 249½ pages of advice under "First Day of School"), and attending urgent special conferences with the smart scientists of Project Baby X.

The scientists had to make sure that X's mother had taught X how to throw and catch a ball properly, and that X's father had been sure to teach X what to serve at a doll's tea party. X had to know how to shoot marbles and how to jump rope and, most of all, what to say when the Other Children asked whether X was a Boy or a Girl.

Finally, X was ready. The Joneses helped X button on a nice new pair of red-and-white checked overalls, and sharpened six pencils for X's nice new pencilbox, and marked X's name clearly on all the books in its nice new bookbag. X brushed its teeth and combed its hair, which just about covered its ears, and remembered to put a napkin in its lunchbox.

The Joneses had asked X's teacher if the class could line up alphabetically, instead of forming separate lines for boys and girls. And they had asked if X could use the principal's bathroom, because it wasn't marked anything except BATHROOM. X's teacher promised to take care of all those problems. But nobody could help X with the biggest problem of all—Other Children.

Nobody in X's class had ever known

an X before. What would they think? How would X make friends?

You couldn't tell what X was by studying its clothes—overalls don't even button right-to-left, like girls' clothes, or left-to-right, like boys' clothes. And you couldn't guess whether X had a girl's short haircut or a boy's long haircut. And it was very hard to tell by the games X liked to play. Either X played ball very well for a girl, or else X played house very well for a boy.

Some of the children tried to find out by asking X tricky questions, like "Who's your favorite sports star?" That was easy. X had two favorite sports stars: a girl jockey named Robyn Smith and a boy archery champion named Robin Hood. Then they asked, "What's your favorite TV program?" And that was even easier. X's favorite TV program was "Lassie," which stars a girl dog played by a boy dog.

When X said that its favorite toy was a doll, everyone decided that X must be a girl. But then X said that the doll was really a robot, and that X had computerized it, and that it was programmed to bake fudge brownies and then clean up the kitchen. After X told them that, the other children gave up guessing what X was. All they knew was they'd sure like to see X's doll.

After school, X wanted to play with the other children. "How about shooting some baskets in the gym?" X asked the girls. But all they did was make faces and giggle behind X's back.

"How about weaving some baskets in the arts and crafts room?" X asked the boys. But they all made faces and giggled behind X's back, too.

That night, Ms. and Mr. Jones asked X how things had gone at school. X told them sadly that the lessons were okay, but otherwise school was a terrible place for an X. It seemed as if Other Children would never want an X for a friend.

Once more, the Joneses reached for their *Instruction Manual.* Under "Oth-

er Children," they found the following message: "What did you Xpect? *Other Children* have to obey all the silly boy-girl rules, because their parents taught them to. Lucky X—you don't have to stick to the rules at all! All you have to do is be yourself. P.S. We're not saying it'll be easy."

X liked being itself. But X cried a lot that night, partly because it felt afraid. So X's father held X tight, and cuddled it, and couldn't help crying a little, too. And X's mother cheered them both up by reading an Xciting story about an enchanted prince called Sleeping Handsome, who woke up when Princess Charming kissed him.

The next morning, they all felt much better, and little X went back to school with a brave smile and a clean pair of red-and-white checked overalls.

There was a seven-letter-word spelling bee in class that day. And a seven-lap boys' relay race in the gym. And a seven-layer-cake baking contest in the girls' kitchen corner. X won the spelling bee. X also won the relay race. And X almost won the baking contest, except it forgot to light the oven. Which only proves that nobody's perfect. One of the Other Children noticed something else, too. He said: "Winning or losing doesn't seem to count to X. X seems to have fun being good at boys' skills *and* girls' skills."

"Come to think of it," said another one of the Other Children, "maybe X is having twice as much fun as we are!"

So after school that day, the girl who beat X at the baking contest gave X a big slice of her prizewinning cake. And the boy X beat in the relay race asked X to race him home.

From then on, some really funny things began to happen. Susie, who sat next to X in class, suddenly refused to wear pink dresses to school any more. She insisted on wearing red-and-white checked overalls—just like X's. Overalls, she told her parents, were much better for climbing monkey bars.

Then Jim, the class football nut,

started wheeling his little sister's doll carriage around the football field. He'd put on his entire football uniform, except for the helmet. Then he'd put the helmet *in* the carriage, lovingly tucked under an old set of shoulder pads. Then he'd start jogging around the field, pushing the carriage and singing "Rock-abye Baby" to his football helmet. He told his family that X did the same thing, so it must be okay. After all, X was now the team's star quarterback.

Susie's parents were horrified by her behavior, and Jim's parents were worried sick about his. But the worst came when the twins, Joe and Peggy, decided to share everything with each other. Peggy used Joe's hockey skates, and his microscope, and took half his newspaper route. Joe used Peggy's needlepoint kit, and her cookbooks, and took two of her three baby-sitting jobs. Peggy started running the lawn mower, and Joe started running the vacuum cleaner.

Their parents weren't one bit pleased with Peggy's wonderful biology experiments, or with Joe's terrific needlepoint pillows. They didn't care that Peggy mowed the lawn better, and that Joe vacuumed the carpet better. In fact, they were furious. It's all that little X's fault, they agreed. Just because X doesn't know what it is, or what it's supposed to be, it wants to get everybody *else* mixed up, too!

Peggy and Joe were forbidden to play with X any more. So was Susie, and then Jim, and then *all* the Other Children. But it was too late; the Other Children stayed mixed up and happy and free, and refused to go back to the way they'd been before X.

Finally, Joe and Peggy's parents decided to call an emergency meeting of the school's Parents' Association, to discuss "The X Problem." They sent a report to the principal stating that X was a "disruptive influence." They demanded immediate action. The Joneses, they said, should be *forced* to tell whether X was a boy or a girl. And then X should be *forced* to behave like whichever it was. If the Joneses refused to tell, the Parents' Association said, then X must take an Xamination. The school psychiatrist must Xamine it physically and mentally, and issue a full report. If X's test showed it was a boy, it would have to obey all the boys' rules. If it proved to be a girl, X would have to obey all the girls' rules.

And if X turned out to be some kind of mixed-up misfit, then X should be Xpelled from the school. Immediately!

The principal was very upset. Disruptive influence? Mixed-up misfit? But X was an Xcellent student. All the teachers said it was a delight to have X in their classes. X was president of the student council. X had won first prize in the talent show, and second prize in the art show, and honorable mention in the science fair, and six athletic events on field day, including the potato race.

Nevertheless, insisted the Parents' Association, X is a Problem Child. X is the Biggest Problem Child we have ever seen!

So the principal reluctantly notified X's parents that numerous complaints about X's behavior had come to the school's attention. And that after the psychiatrist's Xamination, the school would decide what to do about X.

The Joneses reported this at once to the scientists, who referred them to page 85,759 of the *Instruction Manual.* "Sooner or later," it said, "X will have to be Xamined by a psychiatrist. This may be the only way any of us will know for sure whether X is mixed up—or whether everyone else is."

The night before X was to be Xamined, the Joneses tried not to let X see how worried they were. "What if—?" Mr. Jones would say. And Ms. Jones would reply, "No use worrying." Then a few minutes later, Ms. Jones would say, "What if—?" and Mr. Jones would reply, "No use worrying."

X just smiled at them both, and hugged them hard and didn't say much of anything. X was thinking, What

if—? And then X thought: No use worrying.

At Xactly 9 o'clock the next day, X reported to the school psychiatrist's office. The principal, along with a committee from the Parents' Association, X's teacher, X's classmates, and Ms. and Mr. Jones, waited in the hall outside. Nobody knew the details of the tests X was to be given, but everybody knew they'd be *very* hard, and that they'd reveal Xactly what everyone wanted to know about X, but were afraid to ask.

It was terribly quiet in the hall. Almost spooky. Once in a while, they would hear a strange noise inside the room. There were buzzes. And a beep or two. And several bells. An occasional light would flash under the door. The Joneses thought it was a white light, but the principal thought it was blue. Two or three children swore it was either yellow or green. And the Parents' Committee missed it completely.

Through it all, you could hear the psychiatrist's low voice, asking hundreds of questions, and X's higher voice, answering hundreds of answers.

The whole thing took so long that everyone knew it must be the most complete Xamination anyone had ever had to take. Poor X, the Joneses thought. Serves X right, the Parents' Committee thought. I wouldn't like to be in X's overalls right now, the children thought.

At last, the door opened. Everyone crowded around to hear the results. X didn't look any different; in fact, X was smiling. But the psychiatrist looked terrible. He looked as if he was crying! "What happened?" everyone began shouting. Had X done something disgraceful? "I wouldn't be a bit surprised!" muttered Peggy and Joe's parents. "Did X flunk the *whole* test?" cried Susie's parents. "Or just the most important part?" yelled Jim's parents.

"Oh, dear," sighed Mr. Jones.

"Oh, dear," sighed Ms. Jones.

"*Sssh,*" ssshed the principal. "The

psychiatrist is trying to speak."

Wiping his eyes and clearing his throat, the psychiatrist began, in a hoarse whisper. "In my opinion," he whispered—you could tell he must be very upset—"in my opinion, young X here—"

"Yes? Yes?" shouted a parent impatiently.

"*Sssh!*" ssshed the principal.

"Young *Sssh* here, I mean young X," said the doctor, frowning, "is just about—"

"Just about *what?* Let's have it!" shouted another parent.

". . . just about the *least* mixed-up child I've ever Xamined!" said the psychiatrist.

"Yay for X!" yelled one of the children. And then the others began yelling, too. Clapping and cheering and jumping up and down.

"*SSSH!*" SSShed the principal, but nobody did.

The Parents' Committee was angry and bewildered. How *could* X have passed the whole Xamination? Didn't X have an *identity* problem? Wasn't X mixed up at *all?* Wasn't X *any* kind of a misfit? How could it *not* be, when it didn't even *know* what it was? And why was the psychiatrist crying?

Actually, he had stopped crying and was smiling politely through his tears. "Don't you see?" he said. "I'm crying because it's wonderful! X has absolutely no identity problem! X isn't one bit mixed up! As for being a misfit— ridiculous! X knows perfectly well what it is! Don't you, X?" The doctor winked. X winked back.

"But what *is* X?" shrieked Peggy and Joe's parents. "*We* still want to know what it is!"

"Ah, yes," said the doctor, winking again. "Well, don't worry. You'll all know one of these days. And you won't need me to tell you."

"What? What does he mean?" some of the parents grumbled suspiciously.

Susie and Peggy and Joe all answered at once. "He means that by the time X's sex matters, it won't be a secret any more!"

With that, the doctor began to push through the crowd toward X's parents. "How do you do," he said, somewhat stiffly. And then he reached out to hug them both. "If I ever have an X of my own," he whispered, "I sure hope you'll lend me your instruction manual."

Needless to say, the Joneses were very happy. The Project Baby X scientists were rather pleased, too. So were Susie, Jim, Peggy, Joe, and all the Other Children. The Parents' Association wasn't, but they had promised to accept the psychiatrist's report, and not make any more trouble. They even invited Ms. and Mr. Jones to become honorary members, which they did.

Later that day, all X's friends put on their red-and-white checked overalls and went over to see X. They found X in the back yard, playing with a very tiny baby that none of them had ever seen before. The baby was wearing very tiny red-and-white checked overalls.

"How do you like our new baby?" X asked the Other Children proudly.

"It's got cute dimples," said Jim.

"It's got husky biceps, too," said Susie.

"What kind of baby is it?" asked Joe and Peggy.

X frowned at them. "Can't you tell?" Then X broke into a big, mischievous grin. "It's a Y!"

INDEX

adoption: American system of, 118; vs. restoration to natural parents, 116-119

adoptive parents, vs. natural parents, 116-119

adulthood, theories of, 194

aged: and Alzheimer's disease, 152; changes in brain of, 152; changes in physical features of, 151, 152; changes in thinking of, 152, 153; marital adjustment after retirement, 159-161; myths about, 154, 155; number of in U.S., 150; prejudice against, 151; and senility, 152; social attitudes about, 151, 154; stereotyping of, 155; theories of cause of aging, 153

ageism, 150 (def.)

aging: Clock of, 153; "death hormone" theory of, 153; theories of, 153; *see also* aged

All Our Children, 58

alternative life-styles: cohabitation, 170; communes, 170; modified open marriage as, 169; part-time marriage, 170; post-marital singlehood, 169; reasons for, 168-169; swinging and group marriage, 170; triads, 169-170

Alzheimer's disease, as brain disorder in aged, 152

American Association of Sex Educators and Counsellors (AASEC), 83

American family, *see* family

American Psychiatric Association (APA), on "narcissistic personality disorder," 7, 9

assertion, 16

Associates relationship, as type of marriage, 160

autonomy, 16

Avery, Arthur W., on cohabitation, 177-183

baby boom: more aged as result of, 96; end of, 95; next coming, 101-105

baby bust, 95, 101

Baby X, Project, 204-208

Balswick, Jack O., on inexpressive male, 68-70

Bane, Mary Jo, on American family, 41-43

Bernstein, Dr. Mark H., 78

binogamy, 170-171

birth rate: declining, 95, 100, 101; from 1910 to 1976, 102

Borden, Lizzie, 125

Borderline Conditions and Pathological Narcissism (Kernberg), 7

brain, effects of aging on, 152

Brazelton, T. Berry, on day care, 108

Brodsky, Archie, 25

Bronfenbrenner, Urie, 18, 47

Cadwallader, Mervyn, on marriage, 61-64

Carnegie Council on Children, 109

catharsis myth, of violence, 129, 130

childrearing: and day care, 106-109; differences between fathers and mothers, 120-121; factory-sponsored aids to, 114; by fathers, 111; by grandmothers, 109-111; guidelines in choosing programs, 114-115; and moral maturity, 17-20; and narcissism 8; problems in nuclear family, 54-56; options available, 112-113; schools aid to, 113-114; by older siblings, 111-112

children: adopted vs. restored, 116-119; success in adulthood, 38; as asset to marriage, 87; use of corporal punishment on, 125; effect of day care on, 106-109, 122; and death in family, 162-164; delinquency in, 47; effects of divorce on, 142; fewer per family, 95-96; joint custody of, 143-147; as a liability, 100; impact of nuclear family on socialization of, 50, 54-56; effects of single-male parenthood on, 148, 149; effect of working mothers on, 39, 122-124

Clanton, Gordon, 11

class myth, of violence, 127

Clock of aging, as theory on aging, 153

cohabitation: 170; and commitment, 187-188; contractual, 45-46, 188; need for counseling on, 177-178, 182-183; legal barriers to, 186; vs. marriage 186-187; President's views on, 184, 185; protocol problems with, 185, 186; reasons for, 185; study on types of relationships, 178-181; *see also,* coupling, living together

Cohen, David, on adoption, 116-119

cohort theory, 101-103

Coleman Report, 57

Constantian, Carol A., 15

contracts, marriage, 198-203

contractual cohabitation, 45-46

"Convenience" relationship, 179-180

corporal punishment, by parents, 125

corporate mobility, vs. family, 40

coupling: 29-31; case studies on, 30-31; vs. marriage, 31; *see also,* cohabitation, living together

courts, attitude on joint custody, 145, 146

cowboy type, 68-69

cross-sex empathy, 51

day care: after school, 113-114; government funded, 112; guidelines for choosing, 114-115; nonprofit private, 113; other options for, 113; proprietary, 112-113; pros and cons of, 106-109

death: adjustment of family after death of member, 165; and children, 162, 163, 164; coping with in family, 162-165; development of research on, 152; and excessive grief reaction to, 165; and legal matters after, 164; *see also,* dying

"death hormone" theory, of aging, 153

Defining Issues Test, 16

Denckla, Donner W., and theory of aging, 153

Devereux, Edward, 18

Diagnostic and Statistical Manual of Mental Disorders (APA), 9

displaced homemaker: advice to, 192; case study of a, 189-193

Displaced Homemakers Act, 93

divorce: argument for, 138, 139; case study of effect on homemaker, 189-193; contagious principle of, 138; cooling-off period, 48; economics disincentives for, 93; effect of personality of women on, 136, 137; effect of social set on, 139; emotional adjustment to, 141, 142; how to prevent needless, 139, 140; and joint custody, 143-147; "measles pattern," of, 138; poor parents after, 142;

Credits/Acknowledgments

Cover design by Charles Vitelli
Color insert: FAMILY OF SALTIMBANQUES (1905) Picasso, National Gallery of Art, Washington, D.C.
1. Formation of Interpersonal Relationships
Facing overview—Freelance Photographer's Guild/R. Duane Cooke and Sue C. Cooke.
25—Reprinted by permission of *Psychology Today* Magazine. Copyright ©1974 Ziff-Davis Publishing Company.
2. Maintenance of Relationships
Facing overview—David Attie ©1978.
95—Sandy Hoffman.

3. Change as a Function of Relationships
Facing overview—Freelance Photographer's Guild/Carole Graham.
102 & 104—Tom Lulevitch.
4. Termination of Relationships
Facing overview—Freelance Photographer's Guild.
5. Alternative and Future Relationships
Facing overview—Freelance Photographer's Guild.